DEMOCRACY DETAINED

DEMOCRACY DETAINED

Secret, Unconstitutional Practices in the U.S. War on Terror

Barbara J. Olshansky

Foreword by Nat Hentoff

SEVEN STORIES PRESS

New York I Toronto I London I Melbourne

Parts of chapter 9 of this book were originally published as a pamphlet entitled *Secret Trials and Executions: Military Tribunals and the Threat to Democracy* (Open Media Pamphlet Series / Seven Stories Press, 2002).

Seven Stories Press
140 Watts Street
New York, NY 10013
http://www.sevenstories.com

In Canada: Publishers Group Canada, 559 College Street, Toronto, ON M6G 1A9

In the UK: Turnaround Publisher Services Ltd., Unit 3, Olympia Trading Estate, Coburg Road, Wood Green, London N22 6TZ

In Australia: Palgrave Macmillan, 627 Chapel Street, South Yarra VIC 3141

Library of Congress Cataloging-in-Publication Data
Olshansky, Barbara.
Democracy detained : secret, unconstitutional practices in the U.S. war on terror / Barbara J. Olshansky.— A Seven Stories Press 1st ed.
    p. cm.
    Includes index.
    ISBN-13: 978-1-58322-634-6 (pbk. : alk. paper)
    ISBN-10: 1-58322-634-6 (pbk. : alk. paper)
    1. Military courts—United States. 2. Due process of law—United States. 3. Detention of persons—United States. 4. Terrorists—Legal status, laws, etc.—United States. 5. War on Terrorism, 2001- I. Olshansky, Barbara. Secret trials and executions. II. Title.
KF7661.O44 2006
343.73'0143—dc22
2005017606

College professors may order examination copies of Seven Stories Press titles for a free six-month trial period. To order, visit www.sevenstories.com/textbook
or fax on school letterhead to (212) 226-1411.

Book design by Jon Gilbert
Printed in the USA.
9 8 7 6 5 4 3 2 1

To my mother, Phyllis Franco Hennisch,
who continues to teach me about compassion,
truth, and justice.

Contents

Foreword

by Nat Hentoff

A vital contribution of this book to understanding how deeply the Bush administration has eroded the Bill of Rights and other parts of the Constitution is Barbara Olshansky's puncturing of the euphemism that many critics of the USA PATRIOT Act and its progeny—including this critic—have been promulgating.

This attack on our fundamental liberties is not being perpetrated by Bush's "parallel legal system," as I have written. Actually, as Barbara Olshansky documents, this is a *lawless* administration.

Lincoln Caplan, editor of *Legal Affairs*, a magazine affiliated with Yale University Law Scholars, puts the danger we are in plainly: "The outlook of Richard Nixon was that he was above the law. Watergate disabused him of the notion. The position of George W. Bush is that he is a law unto himself. . . . The President's lawyers are resolutely seeking to make this the country's view."

Consider, to begin with, the administration's "war" on terrorism. In the *Cardozo Law Review* (April 2003), Michael O'Connor and Celia Rumann cited the key fact that the Joint Resolution from Congress authorizing the use of force (passed on September 18, 1991) "*was not a declaration of war.*"

Section 8, Article I of the Constitution: "The Congress shall have Power To . . . declare War." This was *not* such a declaration.

In *Democracy Detained*, Barbara Olshansky demonstrates how the law is simply being made up by the president—as commander in chief in this "war"—along with his equally lawless associates in the Justice Department, the Department of Defense, the FBI, the CIA, and other government agencies."

Barbara Olshansky illuminates the CIA's practice of "extraordinary renditions" by which suspected terrorists are kidnapped and transferred to countries known for torturing prisoners and by which the results of these extractions are conveyed to the CIA.

As reported by the *New York Times* on March 6, 2005, this clear violation of both international law and American statutes was authorized by the commander in chief in a unilateral classified directive he signed a few days after September 11, 2001. But on June 26, 2004, George W. Bush—marking United Nations International Day in Support of Victims of Torture—solemnly declared, not for the first time: "America stands against and will not tolerate torture."

The resistance to this rampant lawlessness has created a coalition of not only the American Civil Liberties Union and the grassroots Bill of Rights Defense Committee in nearly 400 towns and cities across the country but also the American Conservative Union and the Free Congress Foundation, whose chairman, Paul Weyrich, a staunch conservative, wrote on August 2, 2005: "Because of the War on Terrorism, America may be on the verge of becoming a national security state, which in the past used to be called a 'garrison state.' That means citizens will allow the state to do almost anything it wants so long as it justifies its actions in terms of 'national security.' In effect, the Constitution and the rule of law itself go out the window, along with our liberties. . . . Can there be any doubt that we [conservatives] will someday become the targets of the surveillance that we enable?"

What makes Barbara Olshansky so deeply knowledgeable about the continual subversion of our liberties by this government is that not only does she call insistent attention to our losses of liberties in her writings, but she also is one of the leading litigators in active defense of our purportedly "guaranteed" constitutional rights.

As director counsel of the Global Justice Initiative of the Center for Constitutional Rights, she is a forceful presence in the courts for an organization that is on the cutting edge of wielding the *actual* rule of law against the most lawless administration in American history.

I say "most lawless" not in indignant hyperbole but because no previous administration has had the continually advancing surveillance technology that—through databasing and other forms of secret surveillance of us—is indeed making us "a national security state."

In her introduction to this book, Olshansky warns—and then goes on to prove in unassailable detail—that this war on the Bill of Rights could permanently transform our "constitutional landscape." I would substitute "transmogrify" for "transform."

Even without another 9/11—though a variation of it is surely possible—as this "war on terror" goes on and on, a new generation of Americans will become accustomed to—as she puts it—these "wartime" national security measures becoming our institutional norms. The Bill of Rights will become an anachronism—a relic, like even the illusion of privacy—of a lost age.

Further examples include the imprisonment without charges, without even elemental due process, of suspected terrorists in American custody, that the commander in chief has ordained is justified as being necessary until "the end of hostilities."

But, as columnist Eugene Robinson underlines in the June 21, 2005, *Washington Post*: "'Until the end of hostilities' is not an acceptable answer. It would make sense in a conventional war, but not in this bizarre, asymmetrical conflict that's more a battle of ideas and religion . . . than a war between two clear, definable sides. It could last decades. . . . And when will we even know it's over? How will we ever be certain that terrorism—which is a tactic not a sovereign nation—has been finally vanquished."

What makes this book essential in exemplifying, like a slogan of the Bill of Rights Defense Committee, that "dissent is patriotic" is its underscoring of the increasingly dangerous lack of accountability of those in government responsible for building these walls of lawlessness and secrecy around us.

Army Reserve Brigadier General Janis Karpinski was the commander of

Abu Ghraib in Iraq when the torture photographs exploded around the world. Her demotion to colonel makes her the highest-ranking officer punished for the repugnant abuse of prisoners. But Janis Karpinski is refusing to be the sacrificial general in the cover-up of the war crimes that reach all the way to the top of the chain of command.

In an August 24, 2005 Truthout/Report (www.truthout.org/docs), Karpinski tells law professor Marjorie Cohn, who is also executive vice president of the National Lawyers Guild: "We're never going to know the truth until they do an independent commission or look into this independently. This is about instructions delivered with full authority and knowledge of the Secretary of Defense and probably Cheney. I don't know if the President was involved or not. I don't care. All I know is, those instructions were communicated from the Secretary of Defense's office, from the Pentagon . . . to Abu Ghraib."

I care if the president was involved. So does Barbara Olshansky, and a persistently rising number of Americans—liberals, conservatives, libertarians, and dissenters beyond categories. As commander in chief, how could George W. Bush not be responsible for what has been done under his command—not only at Abu Ghraib but in all the other proofs of this government's contempt for law? This is the question that resounds throughout *Democracy Detained.*

If all those accountable—including the government lawyers in the Justice and Defense Departments responsible for degrading the Constitution, some of whom have been promoted to prestigious law professorships and even the federal bench—are not put on trial, with the due process they deny to their victims, this "war" on us will expand and deepen.

This book is written in self-defense of our rights and liberties under the Constitution of the United States.

In Anticipation of History's Judgment

I believe that we are living in a time that history will judge thoroughly and harshly. The terrorist activities of recent years will be much discussed for decades to come, but I wager that the years following the September 11 attacks will be viewed largely within the context of the United States' use of unprovoked military force to promote its ambitions for empire.

And why not? The hallmark of post September 11 America is a country governed by politicians who seek unchecked power to pursue their global "war on terror" and who express a chilling disregard for human rights and the rule of law in that pursuit. It is a government that ignores the concerns expressed by many nations about this use of power and that resists the scrutiny of United Nations human rights experts. Our government undermines its own moral credibility, casts aside its role of advancing human rights in the world, and makes us all much less safe by committing humanitarian and human rights law violations in the name of national security. Through our unprovoked aggression, our indefinite executive detention of prisoners without due process, and our torture and abuse of them, we model and legitimize repressive conduct for nations around the world. When, the world wants to know, will our actions match the vision and rhetoric of the Founders of this country?

Meanwhile, here at home, we are also forsaking our democratic principles. A fair, open, and just society is no longer the national aspiration. Officials

1

seem only to express the need to protect the country from outside forces bent on doing us harm. In the name of subduing this fear, we have given the executive branch free reign to adopt secret policies that disregard the separation-of-powers principle and weaken our system of checks and balances. In its pursuit of unfettered executive power, the Bush administration runs roughshod over the constitutional foundation of our democracy. No longer should we expect our government to be open or responsive to the people: transparency is incompatible, they say, with fighting a "war on terror" against those who would hide in caves or among us. With dishearteningly few exceptions, even Congress no longer appears to have the will or the power to demand accountability from executive branch officials. The administration refuses to report to the legislative branch on its use of the laws or its newly self-appointed powers, and no one commands such an accounting.

We, *the People*, have been too willing to cede not only our privacy rights but also our responsibility to demand compliance with all of our civil rights and liberties. We stand by while Congress, at the White House's demand, enacts a law that permits "sneak and peek" warrants and roving wiretaps, turning the Fourth Amendment's protection against unreasonable searches and seizures into a malleable tool of law enforcement. We watch while the administration maintains its brutal military prisons at Guantánamo and Abu Ghraib and secret prisons scattered around the world, part of a new military structure that is devoid of the due process safeguards built into our civil and military justice systems. And we remain mostly silent about the other components of this shadowy system: the CIA's extraordinary rendition program, under which the United States seizes suspects and transports them to other countries for unlawful detention, interrogation, and torture; the "enemy combatant" designation, under which the executive branch orders indefinite detention for investigative or preventative purposes; the use of interrogation techniques that constitute torture or cruel, inhuman, or degrading treatment; and investigatory immigration detention and expedited expulsion to one's country of origin regardless of the likely result.

National security is ill-served by a system that never tests the allegations against suspects in a court of law. Without a mechanism that assists us in divining the truth, we will never know what has occurred or why. Our democracy fails if we divest ourselves of our responsibility to safeguard the moral principles that are embedded in our Constitution. And our country will fail us—and fail the world—if we permit our leaders to abandon the commitment to human dignity embodied in our domestic and international obligations.

If we do not look, we cannot know what is being done in our name. History will not—indeed, it should not—absolve us for that failure. And so we must investigate and learn, and then speak and act.

A CALL TO ACTION IN THE NAME OF HUMANITY

The September 11 terrorist attacks on the United States created fertile conditions for the adoption of laws and implementation of policies and practices that had been on the Far Right's wish list for many years.[1] Many of the policies discussed here were not newly developed in the post–September 11 era but were laid out in the 1990s in "white papers" that advocated a bold new U.S. agenda for the Middle East and, ultimately, the world.[2] But when these ideas were first publicly expressed, they garnered little media attention. Then, as many are fond of saying, everything changed.

The USA PATRIOT Act (the Act)[3] was rushed through Congress within six weeks of the September 11 attacks, cobbled together from bills that had previously been introduced and rejected by many Congresses over the years.[4] Comprising hundreds of pages—amending dozens of laws on the books—the Act was adopted virtually without debate and without the vast majority of our federal legislators understanding the ramifications of many of the different sections of the bill they were voting for. But, at that time, for any congressman to call for a calm and thorough analysis of the serious changes proposed to our historic commitment to civil liberties meant risking being labeled a traitor and sentenced to political death. History bears witness to the fact that this is no exaggeration.[5] One example of the Bush administration's invocation of war-time specters of treasonous neighbors stands out above the rest: in December 2001, John Ashcroft, attorney general at the time, stated before the Senate Judiciary Committee that any person who expresses concern about the erosion of constitutional protections "aids terrorists" and "scares peace-loving people with phantoms of lost liberty."[6]

Well, I, for one, am a peace-loving person, I don't support terrorism, and I'm not afraid of ghosts. But, as this book shows, the threat our executive branch poses to our civil liberties and human rights is not ephemeral, it is all too real—and all the more so because the administration seeks to cloak a wide range of its activities in secrecy. It may be generations before we know the whole truth about what has been done in the name of national security. But it is critical that we attempt to find out if we—*the People*—want to take back the reins and save our democratic institutions; if we want to ensure the vitality of the moral and legal principles that are not only embedded in our Constitution but in our common understanding of what our country stands for: freedom, fairness, justice, and democracy.

The September 11 terrorist attacks had a devastating effect. Many, if not most, Americans had the understandable response that any security measures that could be taken should be taken. But now that we have seen nearly the full measure of the administration's unconstitutional and immoral responses, there are doubtless few people left who feel that a blank check is in any way appropriate, even if they might have thought so five years ago. Instead, we now have the words of Supreme Court justices firmly stating that no such license has been given to the president, and that none can ever be given:

> [W]e necessarily reject the Government's assertion that separation of powers principles mandate a heavily circumscribed role for the courts in such circumstances. . . . [T]his approach serves only to *condense* power into a single branch of government. *We have long since made clear that a state of war is not a blank check for the President when it comes to the rights of the Nation's citizens.* Whatever power the United States Constitution envisions for the Executive in its exchanges with other nations or with enemy organizations in times of conflict, it most assuredly envisions a role for all three branches when individual liberties are at stake.[7]

Despite the Supreme Court's rulings, the administration has stubbornly and purposefully refused to deviate from its itinerary of operating outside the rule of law. And because the government now cloaks these most egregious actions outside the law from public view, we, *the People,* must insist on pulling back the mantle to expose the truth and to hold those in charge responsible for what they have done in our name. We must understand the consequences that arise when an administration views itself as completely unfettered by our country's core democratic principles, by the strictures of our Constitution, by binding international law, or by modern civilization's most basic moral tenets preserving human dignity.

Of course, we could, alternatively, simply choose to ride along in the back-seat and let the few at the top who feel comfortable using malleable definitions of integrity, justice, and human dignity and the most constricted view of our democratic principles, determine our country's path. But if we take that easy way out, we will have empowered the Bush administration—and perhaps succeeding administrations—to eliminate our country's core principles of an open government of limited, enumerated, and delicately balanced powers, and of leaders accountable and responsive to the people; a government that reserves for the people the widest array of individual freedoms. We then will have fully acquiesced to an executive branch that has promoted a climate of fear in order to justify the many troubling acts we examine in this book. Clearly, the Bush administration believes that it can use the "war on terror" as leverage to permanently uproot the cornerstone upon which the Founders of this country built our constitutional democracy.

The political and ethical souls of the American people are under siege, but the enemy is not *at* the gate—the attack is coming from those whom we have chosen to guard it. Within days of the September 11 attacks, our hard-won civil freedoms—paid for with the blood and tears of those who were the backbone and forward ranks of the civil rights movement—were being sacrificed on the altar of national security with no public discourse about what our response should be. And within a very short period—again, it took only *six weeks* for Congress to pass the USA PATRIOT Act—many of the rights enshrined in the Constitution and woven into the fabric of this country were deliberately rent in an effort to exploit the country's grief and channel its rage. But this was not the only objective of the USA PATRIOT Act; it was also a part of a much larger agenda incubated by right-wing organizations like Project for the New American Century (Project).

This nonprofit group states that its goal is to promote American global leadership, but that seemingly benign mission of Project for the New American Century masks its true agenda.[8] Writings by Project's members and supporters—who include Vice President Dick Cheney, Secretary of Defense Donald Rumsfeld, and former deputy secretary of defense Paul Wolfowitz—expound its positions promoting U.S. global domination.[9] For example, Gary Schmitt of Project writes that the "awesome military power of the United States . . . [is] on exhibit for the whole world to see" in the war against Iraq and states that "a unipolar world" in which the exercise of American power is preeminent is the only realistic alternative to a United Nations that "can only operate by majority consensus."[10] Postulating that without the United States, no country "would be left to hunt down Islamic terrorists increasingly interested in getting hands on weapons of mass destruction" or could have "defeated a tyrant like Hussein [thereby] preventing him from becoming the dominant power in the Middle East," Schmitt offers us the false dichotomy of *willfully transforming regimes through military might* or of *doing nothing*. In Schmitt's calculus, "the danger in doing nothing—of pretending that the volatile Middle East mix of failing regimes, rogue states, weapons of mass destruction and terrorism can be contained safely if we only let it alone—is far greater."[11] Of course, he does not even mention the many real options available, such as working toward greater understanding through diplomacy, assisting indigenous groups with their efforts to strengthen the institutions of civil society, or providing increased strategic aid to countries and societies in need. None of that is considered: instead, fear-driven power should be the currency of American influence employed around the world.

While groups with views like that of Project become stronger and more numerous, we have also witnessed a revival of measures designed to infiltrate, monitor, and undermine groups whose sole purpose is to express progressive views. Beyond even the surveillance and infiltration of such groups, local law enforcement officers, frequently acting as part of a joint terrorism task force with their federal counterparts, now regularly interrogate progressive activists arrested for civil disobedience about their political associations and the planned political activities of their organizations. Civil rights groups that battle to maintain the vitality of the Bill of Rights are simply unable to take on the full breadth of this attack on democracy, and voices of dissent are squelched every day.

Nor do our government's lawless activities stop at our borders. In our efforts to roust Al Qaeda and the Taliban from Afghanistan, we have contradicted so many of our established principles that the United States has lost its credibility as the world's leader of democracy, freedom, and justice. Though plainly the world's strongest and longest-lived democracy, the United States no longer sets an example that we can point to with pride when speaking about the balance of powers in our government, the delineation between military and civil society, the sanctity of personal freedoms, or our commitment to the moral principles embodied in our governing document. To much of the world, the United States now symbolizes lawless power and even brutality, and being a U.S. citizen abroad can be an embarrassment, if not a danger.

The Bush administration's global "war on terror" was not authorized by Congress as part of its September 18, 2001, decision to permit the use of military force in Afghanistan against those responsible for the terrorist attacks nor as part of its October 16, 2002, Joint Resolution to authorize the use of force against Iraq.[12] More important though, at least for our purposes here, is the fact that there has yet to be an open, frank, and in-depth discussion in this country over either the domestic or international human rights implications of this new type of war. The executive branch's acknowledgement that the global "war on terror" is a war that defies definition and has no beginning, middle, or end, implies that all of the policies, rules, regulations, and laws that have been adopted as part of our "wartime" national security measures will become our institutional norms, permanently transforming our nation's constitutional landscape along with its place in the community of nations.

Is this the legacy that we want to leave for the generations to come? Democracy is being held hostage by the forces of greed and lust for power, and restrained by fear and ignorance. But the light of truth and reason can be a very powerful force. I hope that you will join me in investigating our country's actions and demanding that our democracy be set free.

CHAPTER ONE

America's Secret Prisoners

Democracy dies behind closed doors.
—*Judge Damon Keith, U.S. Court of Appeals for the Sixth Circuit*

It sounds like a movie about the dark doings of a fascist South American country or a Cold War Soviet bloc regime: "enemies" of the state disappearing into military custody, no notification to the families of the disappeared, no public accounting of their whereabouts or treatment, and perhaps worse yet, no acknowledgment that these people are even being held. But this nightmare became reality for the thousands of people swept up in the Bush administration's program of secret executive detention. And the administration has wielded this terrifying power in such a way that it has largely succeeded in seizing people both here and abroad and holding them indefinitely without charge or trial.

While the law is clear that the president has the authority, when acting in his wartime role as commander in chief of the armed forces, to capture and detain people who are participating in military activities in a battlefield zone, *until now* this authority has never been used—or even asserted—as a basis to arrest people all over the world, far from any battlefield, and regardless of whether they have participated in any war. Nor has such power been wielded to arrest and hold American citizens without charge or trial since that shameful period during World War II when the country imposed curfews and then confined Japanese Americans in internment camps. Yet, during the last five years, the Bush administration has exercised this unlawful power to:

➤ arrest and detain hundreds—perhaps thousands—of immigrants and foreign visitors staying in this country and hold them for months *even after* immigration judges decided that they should be allowed to return home to their resident countries;

➤ arrest an unarmed U.S. citizen while he was on his way to visit his son in Chicago and hold him for years in solitary confinement without charge or trial or access to any court;

➤ arrest a Canadian citizen passing through the United States on his way home to Ottawa, place him in solitary confinement, deprive him of meaningful access to counsel, and send him to Syria for interrogation under torture against his strenuous protests;

➤ arrest numerous individuals living or working in countries like Bosnia, Zambia, and The Gambia who were never near Afghanistan, Iraq, or any other zone of military hostilities, and transport them to military confinement in the U.S. Naval Base at Guantánamo Bay, Cuba;

➤ arrest dozens of individuals and hold them off of the books in the Guantánamo and Iraqi detention facilities so that the International Committee of the Red Cross (ICRC) could not review the conditions of their detention as required under international treaties and covenants; and

➤ arrest untold numbers of people from many different countries and transfer them to secret CIA detention facilities around the world far from all public scrutiny and judicial review.

Although the names of a few of the thousands of people who have been seized and held incommunicado by the government are now well-known—Jose Padilla and Yaser Hamdi, for example—many of those taken and held in secrecy remain faceless and nameless. A few—Americans citizens like Padilla and Hamdi—have been arrested and held in U.S. military brigs based solely on the bare executive allegation that they are "enemy combatants"; many hundreds—foreign nationals also alleged to be "enemy combatants" seized as part of the "war on terror"—have been sent to the U.S. Naval Base at Guantánamo Bay, Cuba, for indefinite detention without trial; and perhaps thousands of others—known only as "ghost detainees"—have been snatched off the streets of their towns and cities and sent to secret CIA detention centers around the world. In fact, the term "ghost detainee" was only recently coined to refer to people who are held, unregistered and far from public scrutiny, in these U.S. detention facilities—prisons like those in Guantánamo, the Bagram Air Base in Afghanistan, the Abu Ghraib Prison in Iraq, and other detention camps—the locations of which, with few exceptions, have never been revealed.[1]

The following chapters examine in detail the circumstances under which people have disappeared or been placed in executive detention and raise serious questions regarding the government's broad use of secret policies and practices. While these strategies have been used previously in the United States, their use has been accelerated and expanded by the Bush administration. We should be greatly concerned about the effect of this trend on the future of our rights and the rights of people everywhere to live in free, open, and just societies. The trend toward secrecy in government should also lead us to question how we will be able to hold our elected representatives accountable for their misdeeds or errors and how we will be able to correct those mistakes to ensure our country's continued commitment to democratic principles.

We must demand to know what is being done in our names, by whom, and on what authority. Then we must decide whether we agree with those actions. These are not just academic questions; they are deeply personal, moral, and political questions. Do we as Americans want to be identified with our government's unconscionable acts—disappearances, human rights violations, disregard for our constitutional principles, and contempt for the rule of law? Is this how we want history to record our era? I know that this is *not* how I want to be remembered—as a citizen of a country that contracts out for torture services. To avoid the harsh judgment of history and the legacy of a terrible example for the nations of the world to follow, we must, as concerned citizens, make our voices heard, call for independent investigations of the executive branch's actions, and demand a return to the moral principles upon which this country was founded.

CHAPTER TWO

The Vanishing of Visitors and Immigrants

Imagine that you are from a Middle Eastern country and have come to this country seeking political asylum. You are now a legal permanent resident of the United States living with your American wife and American-born children in New York City. Imagine next that you are stopped by the police because you have a broken taillight on your car and that when the officer enters your name into the computer accessible from his car, the readout shows that you have failed to register your recent change of address with the federal immigration authorities. You are immediately arrested and placed in immigration detention in a federal correctional facility. What happens next? Even though you are here legally, and even though you have a family living here, and even though you have sought political asylum to escape the problems in your country, chances are that after spending many months in detention here you will be deported back to face your persecutors yet again.

For people all over the world this country still remains the embodiment of a dream—a land of liberty and opportunity where they hope and pray they will be able to live a life free from racial, religious, or political persecution. For the many thousands who come here for a better life, the idea of America as a country of refuge has not wavered. The harsh reality of the erosion of our welcoming shores, in the wake of restrictive legislation and policies implemented after the September 11 attacks, must come as a terrible shock to those who have not tempered their dreams before their arrival.

There has been a drastic change in this country's identity. For more than two hundred years, the United States has openly welcomed people from all over the world fleeing persecution and seeking a better life; and it was, for the most part, a land that valued the traditions of immigrants and the contributions of refugees. But we have recently undergone a complete metamorphosis; we are now a nation that willingly sacrifices fairness and compassion in the name of security. The change is evident in many areas, but is perhaps harshest in the area of access; we have very nearly closed the famous doors to the "land of opportunity." The due process safeguards previously offered in our immigration proceedings—the legal embodiment of our commitment to fairness—have been replaced by an "expedited removal" process under which asylum seekers face immediate mandatory detention[1] as soon as they arrive in the United States.[2]

For immigrants and visitors who were living in this country at the time of the September 11 attacks, the immigration system that since 1996 had already been steadily closing off their avenues to a life in the United States became part of a nightmarish machine. The changes in federal law, policies, and practices made in the name of national security have affected—and continue to affect—many, many people, including those seeking political asylum, visitors, those here on work or student visas, and even legal permanent residents. In the vast majority of cases, only achieving citizenship can provide protection from the harsh new rules. Among the many changes initiated after 2001 in the name of national security were

> ➤ a new nationality-, ethnicity-, and religion-based immigration detention policy targeting people from Middle Eastern and South Asian countries and those of the Muslim faith for special enforcement efforts in order to "rule out any terrorism connections";

> ➤ a new policy and practice of arresting and detaining immigrants from the specifically identified countries who were guilty of only minor civil immigration violations that previously were not treated as a basis for arrest;

> ➤ the expansion of the government's detention authority by means of an interim regulation, permitting indefinite immigration detention without charge or hearing;

> ➤ the sealing of immigration court records and schedules, and the issuance of gag orders to attorneys, in order to prevent access by the public and the press to any facts about the court proceedings; and

> ➤ the transfer of decisions regarding the continued detention of asylum seekers to the Department of Homeland Security, thereby eliminating all appeals on asylum issues that previously were heard by independent judges.

THE ARREST, DETENTION, AND DEPORTATION OF MIDDLE EASTERN, SOUTH ASIAN, AND MUSLIM IMMIGRANTS AND VISITORS

The Bush administration draped a dark—and nearly impenetrable—cloak of secrecy over its actions from the very outset of its response to the September 11 attacks. Within a day of the attacks, more than a thousand immigrants and foreign visitors were swept up in a nationwide dragnet and placed in federal detention in immigration and prison facilities around the country. This first wave of arrests terrified immigrant families and greatly unnerved civil rights and faith groups around the country. Husbands, fathers, brothers, and sons were seized from their homes in the middle of the night or from their jobs in the middle of the day, without explanation. Families and friends were denied access to information about how to locate or help their loved ones. Calls from distraught family members seeking assistance began flooding into community centers, schools, mosques, synagogues, churches, and civil rights organizations. News of the arrests rippled like shockwaves in the cities and neighborhoods across the country with large Middle Eastern populations, like the greater metropolitan New York City area, Detroit, and Los Angeles. In the end, our best estimate of the full scope of the immigration detention program is that as of January 2004, more than five thousand foreign nationals had been seized and detained through the government's antiterrorism preventive detention efforts.[3]

The government arrested mostly Middle Eastern, Muslim, and South Asian men, relying on one of two justifications: the commission of minor, non-criminal immigration violations or the government's need for the individual under the federal material witness statute. Many men were arrested and detained merely for overstaying a lawfully obtained visa, even though our immigration laws do not provide criminal penalties for this offense. Other immigration arrests were also for minor violations, such as working while here on a tourist visa or failing to register for a sufficient number of courses to fulfill the minimum credit-hour requirements of a foreign student visa.[4]

Others were held under the federal material witness statute. Historically, this law has been used by prosecutors to detain witnesses to crimes to ensure that the witnesses do not flee before they appear in front of the grand jury.[5] The government abused the traditional purpose of material witness warrants when it continued to hold some witnesses *despite* their willingness to stay in the jurisdiction and testify before the grand jury. Worse yet, none of those held as material witnesses have ever been brought to testify before a grand jury. In short, the material witness law was merely a pretext for preventive and investigative detention—a means by which people were imprisoned for interrogation purposes until the government decided what it wanted to do with them.[6] Seemingly overnight, the immigration system had been converted into a mechanism for sanctioned vigilante activities and unrestrained invasive and abusive interrogations.

THE ANATOMY OF A DISAPPEARANCE

The experience of one immigration detainee, Ibrahim Turkmen, provides an example of what happened to the men who were seized in the first wave of the terrorism investigation arrests. In early October 2000, Ibrahim Turkmen came to New York City on a tourist visa to visit an old friend from Turkey who was living on Long Island in New York. In late October, Turkmen, at his friend's suggestion, found work at a service station in Bellport, Long Island. He worked there several days a week until the middle of January 2001, when he took a job at another service station in the same village. Turkmen worked at this service station several days a week for three months until April 2001, when he began working part-time for a locally based Turkish construction company.

From his arrival in the United States until he was taken into Immigration and Naturalization Service's (INS) custody, Turkmen frequently called his wife and four daughters back in Turkey. While dearly missing them, he decided to remain in the United States to earn money in order to better provide for their support. Each week, Turkmen sent most of his meager earnings home to his family.

At about 2:30 p.m. on October 13, 2001, slightly more than a month after the September 11 attacks, two Federal Bureau of Investigation (FBI) agents visited Turkmen at the apartment where he was staying with several Turkish friends in West Babylon, New York. Without advising him of his right to counsel, they asked Turkmen whether he had any involvement in the September 11 terrorist attacks and whether he had any association with terrorists. They also asked him about his immigration status.

Turkmen had great difficulty understanding the FBI agents' questions, given his limited knowledge of English and the lack of an interpreter. All the same, he did his best to answer truthfully. He denied any involvement with terrorists, terrorist organizations, or terrorist activity. The FBI agents, nonetheless, charged Turkmen with being an associate of Osama bin Laden, placed him under arrest, confiscated personal items (passport, identification, and credit cards) and money, and searched his home without his consent.

Turkmen was taken to an INS facility in Nassau County, New York, fingerprinted, and interrogated again, this time by an INS official. Once again, he was not advised of his right to counsel. Due to the lack of an interpreter, Turkmen again had great difficulty understanding the questions. That evening, at approximately 11:30 p.m., Turkmen was brought to another INS facility in Manhattan, where INS officials asked him still more questions in English. For the third time, he denied any involvement with terrorists, terrorist organizations, or terrorist activity.

Early the next morning, October 14, 2001, Turkmen was taken to the Passaic County Jail in Paterson, New Jersey, where he remained confined—except for a single trip to the Immigration Court in Newark, New Jersey—until February 25, 2002, a period of nearly four and one-half months.

Shortly after arriving at the Passaic County Jail, Turkmen received a Notice to Appear document from the INS, charging him with overstaying his tourist visa and scheduling a hearing for him at the Immigration Court in Newark, New Jersey, on October 31, 2001.

On October 29, 2001, two FBI agents visited Turkmen at the Passaic County Jail. They asked him still more questions about his immigration status, his reasons for entering the United States, his work experience, his religious beliefs, and other personal matters. Another Turkish post September 11 detainee fluent in English translated the questions for Turkmen, who answered them all truthfully. For the fourth time, he denied any involvement with terrorists, terrorist organizations, or terrorist activities.

Two days later, on October 31, 2001, Turkmen was taken to the Immigration Court in Newark, New Jersey, where he appeared without counsel before an immigration judge. While this time Turkmen was provided with an interpreter, that interpreter (who was not of Turkish descent) was fluent in neither Turkish nor English. After conceding that he had overstayed his tourist visa, Turkmen accepted a voluntary departure order requiring him to leave the United States by November 30, 2001. He declined to request release on bond solely because the judge assured him that he would be allowed to return to Turkey *within a matter of days.* The INS never appealed the voluntary departure order issued to Turkmen.

When he returned to the Passaic County Jail later that day, Turkmen called a friend to ask him to purchase a plane ticket so he could return to Turkey. Two days later, on November 2, 2001, Turkmen's friend brought the ticket to the INS's offices in Newark, New Jersey. Turkmen remained, nonetheless, in the Passaic County Jail until February 25, 2002.

Turkmen was detained for nearly four more months longer than necessary to effectuate his voluntary departure from the United States, solely on the remote possibility that law enforcement authorities might someday connect him to terrorist activity. He was never, however, brought before a neutral judicial officer to determine whether there was probable cause to believe that Turkmen engaged in terrorist activity. Nor was an indictment against Turkmen ever filed with a court citing criminal charges on which his continued detention was based.

While confined in the Passaic County Jail, Turkmen was not allowed to call his wife and four daughters back home in Turkey. He learned through a friend, however, that his wife had been hospitalized for a month with an undisclosed ailment so serious that she lost most of her hair and teeth.

On January 17, 2002, more than three months after he was taken into custody and more than two and one-half months after he received a voluntary departure order, Turkmen was visited again by an INS agent. The agent informed Turkmen that he had been "cleared" by the FBI but still needed to be "cleared" by the INS. When Turkmen asked how long the latter clearance might take, the agent replied that he did not know.

One month later, on February 17, 2002, Turkmen was visited by another INS agent, who told Turkmen that he had received INS "clearance" and would be allowed to depart the United States within the next two weeks. Eight days later, on February 25, 2002, INS agents took Turkmen in handcuffs from the Passaic County Jail to Newark Liberty International Airport, where they put him on a plane to Istanbul, Turkey—without a single penny or lira in his pocket. Although Turkmen requested the return of fifty-two dollars confiscated from him at the time of his arrest—money that he needed to pay for, among other things, the eight-hour bus trip from Istanbul Atatürk International Airport to his home in the city of Konya—that request was denied.

As soon as Turkmen disembarked from the plane at Istanbul Airport, he was met by a Turkish police officer who escorted him to a nearby police station, where he was interrogated for about an hour concerning his four-and-one-half month detention in the United States. Once again, Turkmen denied any involvement with terrorists, terrorist organizations, or terrorist activity. After the interrogation concluded, he was allowed to leave for his hometown, though he still had no money to buy the bus ticket. But for the kindness of a complete stranger who lent him the necessary funds, Turkmen might still be stranded in Istanbul.

Turkmen was again interrogated at length about his detention in the United States, this time by Konya's Security Intelligence Division (KSID). At the close of the interrogation, KSID's superintendent told him to "be careful." Approximately ten days later, the head of gendarmerie in Konya's

Karapinar District, Turkmen's birthplace, contacted Turkmen's father to ascertain Turkmen's current address, ostensibly in order to give it to human rights organizations trying to reach him. Several days later, the head of gendarmerie in the Cumra District asked Turkmen's former employer for his personnel file. After reviewing the file, that gendarme took with him all the documents relating to Turkmen's sixteen years of public service.

The presumption of guilt follows Turkmen long after his deportation from the United States, despite the fact that he has never been involved in any criminal or terrorist activity and despite the complete absence of any evidence of his involvement in such activity. Because of this cultural and political presumption, Turkmen is deemed a "security risk" and is unable to return to his prior government position. In fact, securing gainful employment now seems to be an unattainable goal for Turkmen. His family will likely long shoulder the burden created by Turkmen's unlawful detention in the United States.[7]

Unfortunately, Turkmen's story is not unique. For the many hundreds—and likely thousands—of people caught in the net of overzealous and admittedly biased law enforcement efforts, their circumstances would not be much different. As far as civil and human rights groups have been able to learn, the immigration detainees eventually deported by the United States after "being cleared" suffer from a stigma that seemingly cannot be washed away, no matter how much the international community condemns the United States for these practices and for the suffering of those subjected to them. The secrecy surrounding the transfer of the immigration detainees back to their home countries coupled with the lack of open reporting laws in many of the receiving governments has meant that information about the treatment of the detainees after they were released has been very difficult to come by. However, human rights groups are still continuing their efforts to follow those who suffered these indignities to find out how they are faring back home in their communities.[8]

A CHALLENGE TO ASHCROFT'S INFORMATION BLACKOUT

In an attempt to help find people whose families were desperately searching for them and to ascertain the extent of the sweeps, a coalition of civil rights groups demanded answers about the seizures from the attorney general, John Ashcroft, under the federal law guaranteeing public access to the records of federal government agency actions, the Freedom of Information Act (FOIA).[9] The coalition sought information regarding how many people had been seized and detained, where they were being held, their nationality and/or ethnicity, the basis upon which they had been seized and detained,[10] the length of time that material witnesses would be held before being called to testify, the basis for the government's request to hold secret proceedings and to place attorneys under gag orders, the facts regarding access to counsel for the detainees, and the number of cases in which the government was or would be relying on secret evidence.[11]

The attorney general denied the FOIA request, refusing to provide any information beyond a changing estimate of the numbers of people seized, and the coalition filed a lawsuit seeking to compel the government to release the information.[12] The Justice Department claimed that the release of the information requested could have "catastrophic" consequences for its investigation of the terrorist attacks. It argued that there would be "dire consequences" "from even one unnecessary disclosure,"[13] of the identity of a possible terrorist. Remarkably, the government also argued that the release of the names of the detainees would violate the detainees' privacy interests in not being associated with the terrorist attacks.

The flaws in the government's arguments are obvious. First, it made no effort to explain how a catastrophe would result from disclosing the identity of a detained terrorist when, after so many months, terrorist organizations would undoubtedly be aware of the detentions. Second, the government's position was belied by its own release of information about people it had captured and publicly identified as important members of Al Qaeda. For example, the government announced that it would question the operations director for Al Qaeda, Abu Zaydah, and would then make public the information gleaned from that interrogation.[14] The government's selective disclosures flatly contradict its position that its investigation would be seriously jeopardized if it identified "even one" of the many thousands of people arrested on immigration charges after September 11. Third, by the time the government raised this issue, it had already admitted that many of the immigration detainees arrested had been "cleared" of any terrorist connections. Thus, none of these arguments supported the government's position that release of the requested information would have threatened national security in any way.

Even the government's "privacy" argument purportedly raised on behalf of the immigration detainees—that they should not be portrayed as terrorists because they had not even been accused of having any connections to terrorism—was highly suspect given that the administration had already openly claimed that it could not "rule out" links to terrorism for any of those arrested. Had the Bush administration truly been concerned about protecting these detainees from the stigma attached to such allegations, it would publicly have announced that none of them had been linked to terrorism when it reached that conclusion.[15] Given that the government had already associated its immigration arrests with the September 11 attacks, the damage had already been done.

The power of the government to detain people is potentially its most dangerous power, and the consequences of mistakes or abuse of that power are dire. In this area, then, the need for public scrutiny to ensure accountability is greatest. Without information about the exercise of this power, we cannot know how to direct our government, and democracy is thwarted.

The Ashcroft Justice Department could cite no authority or logic to justify its policy of secretly detaining hundreds of people without charge or trial when it had no information of any kind linking those individuals to terrorism. Under FOIA, the government's burden in justifying nondisclosure is very high.[16] In fact, because the public interest in the disclosure of the detainees' identities was so great, the government should have acceded to the public's demand for the information.

Although the FOIA plaintiffs won in the lower court,[17] that decision was reversed on appeal.[18] In a strong dissenting opinion, U.S. Circuit Court of Appeals Judge David S. Tatel wrote that his colleagues' "uncritical deference to the government's vague, poorly defined arguments for withholding broad categories of information about the detainees . . . eviscerates both FOIA itself and the principle of openness in government that FOIA embodies."[19] While acknowledging the "uniquely compelling" government interests in the investigation of September 11, Judge Tatel noted that the decision failed to consider the interest of America's citizens in knowing whether the Bush administration "is violating the constitutional rights of hundreds of persons whom it has detained in connection with its terrorism investigation."[20] Judge Tatel concluded that "[j]ust as the government has a compelling interest in ensuring citizens' safety, so do citizens have a compelling interest in ensuring that their government does not, in discharging its duties, abuse one of its most awesome powers, the power to arrest and jail."[21]

Despite the public outcry at the reversal, the United States Supreme Court declined to review the decision, and the government's refusal to disclose the information was upheld. However, as a result of significant public pressure brought to bear while the cases were being argued in the courts, the Justice Department announced that 1,182 people had been arrested in conjunction with its initial September 11 investigation. The Justice Department subsequently indicated that 548 individuals were being held for alleged immigration violations, that 93 individuals were being charged with crimes, and that none of those being detained had any links to the attacks. The disparity in these sets of figures has never been explained.[22]

Neither the names of those detained nor the places of their detention were ever given in the case of the immigration detainees.[23] As a result, we may never know how many people were taken, how long they were held, or on what grounds. We may never find out what happened to them. The roundup of immigrants and visitors that commenced on September 12, 2001, marks the beginning of our government's policy of disappearing people.

SECRET ARRESTS, SECRET DETENTIONS, AND DELIBERATE MISDIRECTION

Eventually, many of the people caught in the immigration dragnet that took place in the fall and winter of 2001 and the spring of 2002 were spirited out of the country after they had been held in jails and prisons without charge or trial for months or years. At least in part, this dreadful situation lasted as long as it did because the government shrouded the entire operation in secrecy.

From seizure to deportation, so little information was made available to family members, community activists, faith groups, lawyers, and consulates, that very little of the assistance offered by dozens of organizations could be used.

From the beginning of the dragnet, people were taken from their homes in the middle of the night. A loud knock on the door was the only warning provided before armed agents entered the house and demanded to see one or more family members. No useful information was provided amid the shouting of the agents; family members were told only that "Agent Mike" or "Agent Jane" was arresting the person being seized; no documents, no agency identification, no detention locations, no badge numbers, no last names were provided. Without the name of the agency involved or even the full name of the arresting officers, family members were without any clues about how to locate their missing family loved ones. What law authorized the Ashcroft Justice Department to cloak the identities and affiliations of their agents and permit the seizure and detention of people living in the United States without charge or trial? None. Indeed, the Fourth, Fifth, and Sixth Amendments to the Constitution clearly prohibit it.

Decisions not to record immigration case proceedings on court dockets impeded attorneys' efforts to find out whether missing family members had appeared before any court. Attempts to ascertain the location of the immigration detainees in federal, state, and county jail facilities were obstructed by the Justice Department's communications blackout policy. Under this policy, the immigration detainees were barred from receiving telephone calls, visitors, and mail. Because they were barred from placing telephone calls,[24] they were unable to make any contact with attorneys or with their own families.[25] Further blocking outside assistance was the government's classification of many of the immigration detainees as "of interest" to the FBI's September 11 investigation, which led the people in charge of the detention facilities to turn away lawyers and family members who went to the facilities to ask in person to see detainees by falsely stating that those people were not being held inside.[26] Finally, the frequent transfers of the immigration detainees to different county jails, federal prisons, and immigration facilities around the country also served to perpetuate the secrecy surrounding their detentions and undermine their ability to seek and receive assistance from their families and lawyers.[27] In short, the government made a large and very comprehensive effort to keep these detainees incommunicado and unreachable by all those who wished to help them.

Civil rights attorneys began their efforts to locate missing family members and friends in local police precinct houses, moved on to regional FBI and INS offices, and finally began knocking on the doors of county, state, and federal prisons. But for the two-month period after the arrests began, lawyers trying to locate their clients' family members and friends faced virtually insurmountable hurdles. Detention facilities' staff told lawyers that the people they were looking for were "not in the system," even though they were in fact being held in detention there.[28] At the courthouses, lawyers found that there were no lists of cases or clients as would normally be the situation. It was much later on that advocates would learn of the September 21, 2001, memorandum issued by Chief Immigration Judge Michael Creppy (the Creppy Policy Directive) to immigration judges and court administrators (written at the instruction of the Justice Department), which required that formerly open and public immigration hearings be closed to family members, the public, and the press in all cases involving anyone designated by the attorney general to be "of interest" to the terrorism investigation. In addition, all information regarding those cases was to be excluded from all court papers and schedules.[29]

The Creppy Policy Directive also instructed court personnel to neither confirm nor deny whether any case was scheduled for a hearing—creating an entirely secret hearing for the immigration detainees "of interest." With this policy change, this country began to move incrementally closer to codifying the antidemocratic practices used to inspire fear and suppress dissent in those countries—like North Korea and the former Soviet Union—whose human rights records we have decried for years.

Advocates filed legal challenges to the secret hearing policy in two federal circuits, the Third and the Sixth, and the two courts split on the question of whether the policy violated the public trial requirements of the First Amendment. The Sixth Circuit Court of Appeals ruled in August 2002 that the press had a First Amendment right of access to the immigration hearings covered by the Creppy Policy Directive unless the judge assigned to the case made a specific determination that secrecy was required *in that particular case* in order to protect national security.[30] Judge Damon Keith, the author of the opinion for the Sixth Circuit Court of Appeals, explained the court's position this way: "Democracies die behind closed doors. . . . When government begins closing doors, it selectively controls information rightfully belonging to the people. Selective information is misinformation."[31]

The second lawsuit, filed in New Jersey, involved similar claims, also alleging that the media had a First Amendment interest in attending these immigration hearings. The federal district court ruled in favor of the media and issued an order preventing the government from barring the public and the press from detention and deportation hearings without undertaking a case-by-case assessment.[32] The Third Circuit Court of Appeals, however, disagreed with the lower court's ruling, upheld the Creppy Policy Directive, and permitted the closure of immigration hearings.[33] Despite the fact that this split between the circuit courts would mean that there would be different rules regarding access to hearings depending upon where a person's case was being heard, the Supreme Court decided not to resolve the dispute in May 2003, leaving the disparity in place.[34] Solicitor General Theodore B. Olson, arguing for the government, urged the Supreme Court not to review the *North Jersey Media Group* decision (the decision granting the public and the press access to the hearings), noting that the Creppy policy may change and that, in fact, most of the hearings had already been held. The government's brief indicated that, at the time, 766 detainees had been designated as being of "special interest," 611 closed hearings had already been held, and 505 noncitizens had been deported as a result.

THE BUSH ADMINISTRATION'S PRETEXTUAL IMMIGRATION JUSTIFICATION

The ostensible "authorization" for holding the detainees in jails before any immigration charges were filed was a new interim immigration regulation put into effect after September 11. Prior to that date, the immigration regulation on the books required that the INS make a decision about what violation to charge a person with and whether to hold him within twenty-four hours of his warrantless arrest. That regulation properly reflected our understanding that immigration arrest and detention constitute serious deprivations of liberty and so must be subject to immediate review and justification by the government. We all understood that due process principles demanded no less.

Within seven days of the attacks, however, the old immigration regulation was changed in order to expand the initial holding period to forty-eight hours and to provide that, in the event of "an emergency or other extraordinary circumstance," the deadline for the government's statement of its justification and judicial review of the case would be extended so as to require a determination only within "an additional reasonable period of time."[35] Because the new regulation included no definition for the phrase "reasonable period of time," the INS immediately began using it to provide cover for its decision to hold immigration detainees for many weeks without filing any immigration charges at all.

Even when the legally required immigration proceedings were belatedly held for the immigration detainees, these, too, were deeply flawed in terms of respecting the detainees' constitutional rights. When detainees' attorneys sought their clients' release on bond until the hearing date, they were told that such efforts would be futile.

The Immigration and Nationality Act, as amended, gives the U.S. attorney general the power to decide whether to hold an immigration detainee in custody or release him on bond while proceedings are pending. A noncriminal immigration detainee, however, is not ordinarily held unless he is found to pose "a threat to the national security . . . or . . . is a poor bail risk."[36] Furthermore, even after a request for release on bond has been denied, an immigration detainee always has a right to apply to an immigration judge for a redetermination of his custody status.[37] Unfortunately, during these types of rehearings the government has sometimes sought to use, and in fact, has successfully used, undisclosed, classified information to prevent detainees' release on bond.[38]

After September 11, the Attorney General's office adopted a policy of *automatically* denying bond to any noncitizen deemed "of interest" to its terrorism investigation until they had been cleared by the FBI, even when no government agency had evidence that the person was dangerous, a flight risk, or in any way connected to terrorism.[39] This infamous "hold until cleared policy" turned presumption of innocence on its head. When the FBI was uncertain about whether a particular detainee was actually "of interest," it simply declared him to be so and detained him until he was "cleared."[40] Then attorney general, John Ashcroft made the government's commitment to this new practice abundantly clear in his immigration detention policy announcement at a conference of U.S. mayors: "Let the terrorists among us be warned. If you overstay your visa even by one day, we will arrest you. If you violate a local law we will . . . work to make sure that you are put in jail and . . . kept in custody as long as possible."[41]

In stark contrast to the changes made to the prehearing regulations after September 11, the law governing the treatment of immigration detainees *after* they have had an immigration hearing and received a final removal order *did not change* after the attacks. That law still provides that an immigration detainee must be sent home within ninety days of the judge's final decision. Given that this law remains on the books, there is no doubt that the lengthy detentions ordered by Ashcroft—several of which lasted nearly three and one-half years—were illegal.[42] Further confirming the unconstitutionality of these unlawfully extended detentions is a Supreme Court decision handed down just weeks before the September 11 attacks holding that our constitutional notion of liberty places strict limits on lengthy immigration detention, noting that "[f]reedom from imprisonment . . . lies at the heart of the liberty that [the Due Process] Clause protects."[43] In short, despite the clarity of the law on this issue, the immigration detainees swept up in the profiling dragnet were kept months, and frequently years, in post-decision illegal detention. The "clearance" process took an average of eighty days and as long as fourteen hundred days to complete.[44] Despite the fact that they are bound by strict time limitations under which they must accomplish the deportation or voluntary departure of immigration detainees, federal immigration officials flatly disregarded these laws so that the immigration detainees could be held until they were "cleared" by the FBI, whenever that might occur.[45]

The use of secret evidence in these (and other) immigration cases also raises serious constitutional concerns. Individuals confronted with only vague hints of disparaging or incriminating information certainly were unable to help with the preparation of their defense. For those who have done nothing wrong at all, their hearings must have seemed truly Kafkaesque. All of these people faced the same perplexing circumstances: there had been no charges issued against them beyond the immigration violations that had been ruled upon by a judge, their departure was authorized by a court, and yet they continued to be jailed without explanation or trial.

Under the FBI's "hold until cleared policy," the noncitizens arrested were plainly detained *not* for any legitimate immigration-law enforcement purpose, but rather simply to hold them while federal law enforcement authorities supposedly sought to investigate and determine whether the detainees had any ties to terrorism. Individuals were deemed "of interest" to the terrorism investigation on the basis of their immigration status, national origin, or ethnicity, or even the location where they were picked up. Even when the government had no evidence of a person's connection to terrorist organizations or acts of terrorism, he would be held so long as the FBI could not immediately rule out any connection.[46]

Though the government was plainly keeping the immigration detainees in custody *solely* for the purpose of this broad scale criminal investigation, it did not honor the constitutional rights to which all criminal suspects are entitled. The detainees had no hearing before a neutral judicial officer to determine whether there was "probable cause" to believe that they had engaged in any criminal activity as required by the Supreme Court decisions interpreting the Fourth Amendment.[47] They were not given criminal indictments or any other document reciting any criminal charges against them, nor were they given counsel or a speedy trial. These constitutional rights were denied despite the fact that the Supreme Court has made clear that "[i]t is not the function of the police to arrest, as it were, at large and to use an interrogating process at police headquarters in order to determine whom they should charge before a committing magistrate on 'probable cause.'"[48] Under the Fourth Amendment, law enforcement authorities can claim "no legitimate interest in detaining for extended periods individuals who have been arrested without probable cause."[49] Moreover, just as the Fourth Amendment prohibits law enforcement authorities from *arresting* individuals based on a mere suspicion that they have engaged in criminal activity, it also prohibits law enforcement authorities from *continuing to detain* individuals (even those already in lawful custody for some other matter) merely on suspicion of criminal activity. As the Supreme Court has repeatedly stressed: "To continue [the defendants'] custody without presentment [before a judicial officer] for the purpose of trying to connect them with other crimes [than the ones for which they were lawfully arrested] is *to hold in custody for investigation only, and that is illegal*; its operative effect is essentially the same as a new arrest and, if not supported by probable cause, it is an illegal detention."[50]

Put differently, since the Fourth Amendment bars law enforcement authorities from delaying an *unlawfully* arrested defendant's release in order to "gather additional evidence to justify the arrest,"[51] it also bars them from prolonging a lawfully arrested defendant's custody in order to "build a separate case against him" on other crimes.[52] Instead of being afforded any of these fundamental protections, however, the Justice Department under Ashcroft's direction, held the immigration detainees in jails and prisons indefinitely pending the outcome of FBI and INS "clearances." Instead of being presumed innocent until proven guilty, *the immigration detainees were presumed guilty of terrorism until proven innocent* to the satisfaction of law enforcement authorities.

THE CHALLENGE TO THE GOVERNMENT'S SECRET IMMIGRATION DETENTIONS

Eventually—many weeks after the arrests began—lawyers located several immigration detainees who were being held in federal detention facilities in New York and New Jersey. Based on interviews with these people, the Center for Constitutional Rights (CCR), a national not-for-profit legal and educational organization for whom I work, filed a lawsuit in April 2002 entitled *Turkmen v. Ashcroft*,[53] challenging the unlawful detention of immigrants and visitors after September 11. Subsequently, a report was released by the Justice

Department's inspector general on June 2, 2003, entitled "The September 11 Detainees: A Review of the Treatment of Aliens Held on Immigration Charges in Connection with the Investigation of the September 11 Attacks" (the OIG Report). The OIG Report provides a wealth of detail regarding the government's mistreatment of Arab and Muslim nationals from South Asian and Middle Eastern countries. It shows how people were wrongfully arrested, detained, and designated as "persons of interest" to the government's investigation and then subjected to an array of unconstitutional practices. We know now that the stories of the people interviewed by civil rights groups mirror those of many other people seized after the attacks.

Examples of how the government mistreated people abound. In one example, the *Turkmen* lawsuit alleges that on September 30, 2001, shortly before Pakistani-French citizen Asif-Ur-Rehman Saffi's U.S. tourist visa expired, the INS detained him for working in the United States without authorization. Saffi had come to United States to visit family and friends and while in the country earned a modest sum fixing computers and doing data processing for small businesses. Despite the INS's authority to return Saffi to France for a violation of the conditions of his visa, within days of his arrest, and despite Saffi's immediate acceptance of a voluntary departure order permitting him to leave the country and return home, he was held in custody for nearly five months after all immigration proceedings had concluded. During that time he was repeatedly interrogated, denied medical care, shackled, and prevented from observing mandatory religious practices. Saffi was held in the Metropolitan Detention Center (MDC) in Brooklyn, New York, in the Special Housing Unit, commonly known as the "Hole," where convicted criminals who present special disciplinary problems are placed. He was confined to his cell for up to twenty-three hours a day and suffered severe beatings at the hands of prison guards, one time to the point of being rendered unconscious. A dangerous terrorist? No, Saffi was *never charged with a crime* and was *found to have no links to terrorism*. In fact, he has no criminal record in this or any other country.[54]

The *Turkman* lawsuit describes how many other immigrants arrested by the government were also held on minor violations and subjected to the FBI's blanket "hold until cleared policy."[55] The government subjected detainees to a protracted series of unconstitutional practices. Once placed in detention, detainees were not served with a notice of the charges on which they were being held and therefore could not understand the reason for their detention, obtain legal counsel, or request release by posting a bond.[56] They were classified as being "of high interest" to the government's terrorism investigation, though there were no standards for making such a determination, nor any evidence that they were involved in terrorism. Then, on the basis of this specious classification, they were placed in solitary confinement and subjected to a communications blackout that interfered with their access to counsel and prevented them from seeking redress in the courts.[57] Finally, after receiving final removal orders or grants of voluntary departure, detainees were held in immigration custody far beyond the ninety day period provided to the government to deport an individual and the 120 day period provided to facilitate voluntary departure from the United States.[58]

On June 14, 2006, Federal District Court Judge John Gleeson dismissed the challenges to the racial profiling and prolonged detention of the *Turkmen* plaintiffs, but allowed the conditions of confinement and religious discrimination challenges to proceed. The ruling rejected attempts by senior administration officials, including FBI director Robert Mueller and former attorney general John Ashcroft, to avoid answering the accusations that they had personal involvement in ordering the extremely harsh conditions of confinement. The ruling unfortunately also states that it is permissible for the government to create two tiers of rights, one for citizens and one for noncitizens, and that prolonged detention for criminal investigative purposes for noncitizens who are "out of status" is not unconstitutional. The judge's decision is deeply troubling because it appears to condone the racial and religious profiling used by the Bush administration to seize immigrants and justify their differential treatment. The Center for Constitutional Rights plans to appeal this aspect of the decision.

Much of the information relied upon by the FBI-led task force when it made arrests and deemed immigrant detainees "of interest" was wholly uncorroborated and, in many instances, plainly unreliable. In fact, many arrests were made on the basis of anonymous tips called in by members of the public sus-picious of their Arab, South Asian, and Muslim neighbors.[59] In one illustrative example noted in the OIG Report, a person was arrested and detained on immigration charges and treated as a terrorist-related detainee because someone called the FBI to report that a grocery store in which the person worked was "operated by numerous Middle Eastern men, 24 hrs-7 days a week" and that there were "too many people to run a small store."[60] Supervisors told joint ter-rorism task force agents that when in the course of looking for a particular person they should arrest all individuals encountered at the scene who were out of immigration status.[61] According to the Justice Department's inspector gen-eral, "no distinction generally was made between the subjects of the lead and any other individuals encountered at the scene 'incidentally,' because the FBI wanted to be certain that no terrorist was inadvertently set free."[62] The failure to distinguish between noncitizens who were the subject of a specific investiga-tion and those people who were encountered coincidentally by task force agents led to the arrest and unlawful detention of many hundreds of people.

The OIG Report denounced the Justice Department's process for classify-ing immigration detainees at varying levels "of interest" as seriously flawed, "indiscriminate and haphazard."[63] The report concluded that the "hold until cleared policy" resulted in the imprisonment of immigrants, often in harsh conditions, who "had no connection to terrorism."[64] The Justice Department's failure to identify and correct "this disconnect" in categorization and treat-ment was inconceivable to the Inspector General.[65] The report further admonished that when it became clear that the FBI could not complete its "clearance investigations" in a matter of days, the Justice Department "should have reviewed all cases and kept on the list only those detainees for whom it had some valid basis to suspect a connection to terrorism."[66]

THE MISTREATMENT OF THE IMMIGRATION DETAINEES

Under the lock and key of our own government officials, the immigration detainees were subjected to horrendous treatment. What were the conditions like? Many, if not all, of the people detained for these minor immigration violations were held in overcrowded and unsanitary federal prison and county jail facilities and were placed in solitary confinement. In New York and New Jersey, people were held in the specially designed segregated confinement ward, where they were placed in tiny cells for more than twenty-three hours a day, and were strip-searched, manacled, and shackled whenever they were taken out of their cells.

The assignment of the immigration detainees to the Special Housing Unit in MDC unquestionably violated all legal standards governing the treatment of prisoners. Special Housing Units are used for disciplinary segregation, and Federal Bureau of Prisons regulations require that prison officials use specific uniform criteria to determine who is subject to this punitive measure, that they hold weekly reviews of each inmate's status while he or she is housed in these units, and that they conduct formal hearings every thirty days to assess the inmate's status to see if release is warranted. These strict limitations on the use of administrative and disciplinary segregation are necessary because of the severe psychological effects of this form of social isolation.[67] Nevertheless, MDC officials were told that until the FBI had cleared a particular detainee, the detainee was to remain in the Special Housing Unit with no administrative hearing whatsoever and therefore no way out.[68] In fact, a new type of unit, the Administrative Maximum Special Housing Unit, a unit even more restrictive than that found in most Federal Bureau of Prisons facilities, was established after September 11. In these units, guards use four-man hold restraints (four guards apply handcuffs, leg irons, waist chains, and shackles before moving the detainees outside their cell), place cameras in each cell to monitor detainees, and use handheld cameras to record all detainee movements.

Virtually every aspect of how the government treated the detainees was unlawful. During their confinement, the government subjected detainees to coercive and involuntary interrogations. They were not told of their right to counsel before or during the interrogations, and detainees who asked to adjourn interrogations so that they could consult with an attorney were denied permission.[69] Some detainees found their access to counsel blocked during their immigration hearings as well and were compelled to participate in the hearings without any assistance. Indeed, when civil rights and immigrant advocacy groups sought to provide free legal services to the detainees, MDC staff refused to disclose detainees' names, the facilities in which they were being held, or any information about their cases. Government and facility officials flatly refused requests by the groups to visit jails to screen detainees in order to determine who was in need of assistance.[70] This communications blackout even extended to the detainees' access to their consular officials. Under Article 36 of the Vienna Convention on Consular Relations,[71] noncitizen detainees must be advised of their right to seek assistance from their consulates. When detainees sought to make contact, the guards either coerced them into waiving their rights by signing forms they did not understand or simply denied their requests outright.

Guards physically and verbally abused many detainees, beating some very badly.[72] The Office of the Inspector General found that the physical abuse included slamming detainees' heads into walls; twisting their arms, hands, wrists, and fingers; lifting them off the ground by their handcuffs; stepping on their leg-restraint chains; and leaving them in physical restraints for extended periods of time as a form of punishment.[73] Guards used strip searches to punish the detainees and then videotaped the searches to humiliate them.[74] All of these actions are against federal prison policy, and the inspector general concluded that in each instance of abuse, the officers' conduct violated those policies.[75] All of these facts were substantiated by the Office of the Inspector General of the U.S. Department of Justice through interviews with MDC staff and detainees' attorneys and through the observation of videotapes made at the facility.[76]

When FBI and INS officials finally made the decision to release people from detention, their process was also hidden from view. Indeed, the government has steadfastly maintained the position it took in the FOIA lawsuit: that it *never* has to disclose detainees' identities or their whereabouts.[77] Although no official data has ever been made available on how many people arrested in the immigration sweeps were subsequently deported, or where they were returned to, investigative media reports during the period from October 2001 through December 2002 indicated that mass deportations were being carried out by the government.[78] The deportations were conducted in secret, many appearing to have been accomplished from small airports like the one in a town called Waterproof, Louisiana.[79] The government did not provide any information about the flights to either the detainees or their families, and the immigration detainees were sent back to their countries of origin along with hundreds of other people who had been arrested under the government's "Absconder Apprehension Initiative" for ignoring existing deportation orders.[80]

Some of the expulsions were so abrupt that family members did not know for days after their loved one had been deported. In the case of Ali Mounnes Yaghi, his American wife and three young sons were never told that he had been deported to Jordan and spent months worried, concerned that Ali had been arrested by Jordan's security services upon his arrival in that country.[81] Yaghi had left Jordan and had come to the United States when he was sixteen and had sought residency here on the grounds of political asylum.[82] He was taken into custody on October 3, 2001, when someone reported that he had made unsettling remarks about the terrorist attacks, and he was arrested.[83] After spending nine months in jail, federal authorities determined that he had no terrorism connections and turned him over to the INS because he had overstayed his visa. He was deported on June 24, 2002, despite the fact that by that date, according to his family, his green card had finally been approved.[84]

The lack of information about the detainees' departure and about the circumstances they faced when they were returned to their countries of origin makes it impossible to tell how many people have been subjected to human rights abuses. However, human rights organizations have documented numerous instances in which claims for political asylum were flatly disregarded during the mass deportation process.[85] No one should have been forcibly removed from the country without having had their need for protection assessed and a full hearing on their political asylum claim. Yet, this occurred despite the fact that both our domestic immigration law and the international humanitarian law principle of *nonrefoulement* (non-return) provide that no person should be returned to a country where he or she would be at risk of serious human rights abuses.[86]

Disturbingly, criticisms leveled at the government for its use of these unconstitutional and inhumane practices were met with official scorn. Even though the Justice Department's own OIG Report contained measured criticism and some suggestions for reform, the Justice Department itself forcefully announced that it would make "no apologies" for its exercise of these powers.[87] This presumption of guilt has followed those eventually released back home to their countries and to their former lives. It haunts them. Because of the high regard in which the American justice system is held, the mere fact of detention in a U.S. prison is perceived as a criminal conviction in many countries around the world. And this taint has proven to be inescapable for many.

The terrible fact that the U.S. government indefinitely imprisons people who are not guilty of any offense, never charged with any offense nor even accused of one remains unaddressed. How do we now remedy this terrible wrong? What can be done to assist those people who, after visiting this country, must now live with this terrible taint? No lawsuit can change a society's response to one of its citizens who has been imprisoned in a U.S. jail.

In the end, we will likely never know the full scope of the government's investigative immigration detention program. What we do know, however, is that it was patently unlawful and carried out in total disregard of both U.S. and international law. We know also that it has not succeeded in identifying anyone who might be held accountable for the September 11 attacks.[88] It succeeded only in alienating a large segment of the immigrant community in this country, making future collaborative law enforcement efforts extremely difficult to undertake, and placing at risk all legal permanent residents living here who now fear arrest and detention for the most minor immigration infraction. Fear is replacing faith and hope as the basis for the life decisions that must be made by those who have come to this country as immigrants.

THE "VOLUNTARY" QUESTIONING OF MIDDLE EASTERN YOUNG MEN

In November 2001, the government began a program of questioning five thousand young men who had entered the country during the previous two years "on student, tourist or business visas from countries with suspected terrorist links."[89] Although none of these men were actually suspected of criminal activity, they were interrogated by the FBI, and if found "out of immigration status," they were transferred to the INS for expedited removal. With the approval of John Ashcroft, then attorney general, the INS used the most minor technical violations as a basis for deportation. How minor, you might ask? Abdel-Jaber, a thirty-year-old father of five and a legal immigrant from the West Bank, was the subject of a deportation effort when he was stopped for driving four miles per hour over the speed limit. The supposed basis for deportation was his failure to file a change of address form with the INS. Fortunately, in this one instance, the judge refused to order his deportation for so flimsy a reason.[90]

The Justice Department quickly followed the "voluntary questioning" program by implementing new regulations governing persons from certain countries who held nonimmigrant visas.[91] On August 12, 2002, Ashcroft announced the commencement of the first phase of the National Security Entry-Exit Registration System (NSEERS).[92] Under the program, all "nonimmigrant aliens whom the State Department [or INS inspectors at the port of entry] determines to present an elevated national security risk, based on criteria reflecting current intelligence,"[93] were required to register, be fingerprinted, and report periodically on where they were living, what they were doing, and when they leave the country.[94] In fact, however, the "criteria" were little more than decisions that individuals with particular backgrounds would be called in to register. The government systematically registered and created dossiers on nearly every male over the age of sixteen with origins in a list of designated (mostly Muslim) countries, who were visiting the United States or traveling through the country.[95] Many stories of harassment and rough treatment were told by the more than eighty-thousand people registered by the government.[96] Arabs and Muslims felt unjustly targeted and responded with indignation. In the end, through the NSEERS program more than thirteen-thousand people were deported from the United States and many thousands more fled the country in fear.[97]

For many people then, their cooperation with the "voluntary questioning" program and compliance with the NSEERS program led to immediate detention and deportation, often without notice to family members or loved ones. On December 16, 2002—the first deadline for men who did not have permanent resident status in the United States—the INS jailed hundreds of men who had come forward to register, be fingerprinted, have their photographs taken, and be questioned.[98] In Los Angeles alone, implementation of the new program meant that between five hundred and one thousand men were handcuffed, detained, and held completely incommunicado.[99] No access to their families or to any legal counsel was permitted. According to press reports, many of those arrested were in fact legal residents or had applied to adjust their immigration status.[100] And while the INS had insisted that the registration program would eventually include immigrants from countries other than the Arab and Muslim nations selected for this "first round," that did not happen. The NSEERS program was discontinued abruptly in December 2003 after the initial wave of enforcement.[101]

Civil liberties groups and immigration experts have called December 16, 2002 the "largest one-day incident of racial or ethnic profiling in American history."[102] While the NSEERS program undermined all of their trust in the government, people in these communities were further punished for their sincere efforts to comply with the law.[103] The message of discrimination and injustice could not have been lost on anyone. Complying with the NSEERS program and reporting for questioning led to immediate detention and ultimately to secret deportation when possible. In this way, too, then, the U.S. government "disappeared" many immigrants.

WHAT THE LAW SAYS ABOUT THE BUSH ADMINISTRATION'S PROFILING POLICIES

In addition to the many other ways these new executive policies violate the Constitution, the Bush administration's programs unquestionably violate victims' right to equal protection of the law.

Since 1896, our federal courts have consistently held that the constitutional protections provided to criminal suspects under the Fourth, Fifth, and Sixth Amendments to the Constitution apply to noncitizens present in this country as well as to U.S. citizens.[104] This means that the Fifth Amendment's restriction on the federal government's ability to make decisions using race, ethnicity, national origin, or gender as the defining factor when it restricts a person's liberty applies to the new government policies. Specifically, the Fifth Amendment requires that the government provide a "compelling" justification for its action and show that the policy is "narrowly tailored" so that it does not reach either too broadly—and thereby include people who were likely uninvolved in the problem—or too narrowly and thereby miss catching those who likely were involved.[105]

In this instance, while the government could no doubt show that its interest in national security is compelling, its solution—rounding up everyone with a background similar to the terrorists'—was neither fair nor effective. Even a superficial look at these policies shows that the government engaged in racial, religious, and ethnic profiling. The "voluntary questioning" of five thousand men was based on the age, gender, date of entry into the country, and the country of origin for those requested to report for interrogation.[106] So, too, the roundup and detention of immigrants and visitors focused on men of Middle Eastern, South Asian, or Arab ancestry and those of Muslim faith.[107] However, the net used to sweep up "suspects" was both too broad—sweeping in many people who had no connection to any criminal or terrorist activities—and too poorly focused, overlooking people such as the "shoe bomber," who posed actual threats.[108]

Similarly, the government's profiling policies violate many tenets of international human rights law, including the principle of nondiscrimination, a cornerstone of the law as it has developed in the last fifty years. This principle is expressly articulated as one of the purposes of the U.N. Charter[109] and is included in the International Convention on the Elimination of All Forms of Racial Discrimination, which was adopted by the United Nations in 1965 and finally ratified by the Senate in 1994.[110] The convention requires parties to refrain from racially discriminatory[111] actions and to take active steps to eliminate existing discrimination.[112]

The Universal Declaration of Human Rights (UDHR) also states that all persons are entitled to enumerated rights and freedoms without "regard to race, colour, sex, language, religion, political or other opinion, national or social origin, property, birth or other status"[113] and provides that all persons are to be "equal before the law and are entitled without any discrimination to equal protection of the law."[114] While the UDHR is a nonbinding resolution, the International Covenant on Civil and Political Rights (ICCPR), signed by the United States in 1976 and ratified by the Senate in 1992, is a binding international agreement that includes similar language and expressly states that "any advocacy of national, racial or religious hatred that constitutes incitement to discrimination, hostility or violence shall be prohibited by law."[115] Any way you look at it, the government's policy was a wrongheaded failure: unfair, unlawful, and ultimately, ineffective.

Unfortunately, the government's unlawful identification of large groups of people based solely on race or national origin and its indefinite detention of them based on its claim of national security are not unique to the post September 11 era. While there are examples from other eras,[116] the most recent is not too far from anyone's recollection: the internment of Japanese Americans during World War II. In 1943 and 1944, the Supreme Court, in a decision now looked back on with shame and regret, upheld the government's decision to indefinitely imprison one hundred twenty thousand people of Japanese descent—seventy percent of whom were U.S. citizens—on the basis of its unsupported claim of "military necessity."[117] At the same time as the domestic internment system was being put into place, the U.S. government was also unlawfully *abducting* more than two thousand people of Japanese descent from thirteen Latin American countries, bringing them to the United States, and imprisoning them in concentration camps, once again without charge or trial.[118] According to historians, this program was intended to create a reserve of hostages to be used in trades for Americans held by the Japanese army, but such prisoner exchanges never took place.[119] Legal challenges to these abductions and detentions were unsuccessful, and the people who were taken from their homes in Latin America received only one-quarter of the symbolic compensation awards allocated by Congress for the domestic internees.[120]

WHAT DO THESE IMMIGRATION POLICIES AND PRACTICES MEAN?

The Bush administration's policies regarding foreign nationals raise several important issues. The first, discussed above, concerns the executive branch's willingness—and perhaps eagerness—to disregard established constitutional constraints, existing laws and regulations, and international law in order to allay what it perceives as the fears of the people and to implement the broadest-scale law enforcement initiative in order to do so. In the administration's furious rush to accomplish this end, the most fundamental guarantees against arbitrary executive action (like the well-established constitutional requirement of probable cause and the right to counsel in a criminal proceeding) fly out the window.

The government's steadily increasing trend toward unconstitutional action should be of great concern to us all. The ease with which the Justice Department—the FBI and the INS—dispensed with the constitutional requirement of due process when noncitizens' physical freedom was at stake is chilling. If the officials involved are not called to account for these deliberate constitutional and human rights violations, then we have truly become a country that disappears and imprisons people indefinitely without cause or justification.

Second, the fact that the government so easily chose to sacrifice the liberty of thousands of Arab, South Asian, and Muslim foreign nationals—particularly vulnerable minorities in this country—for the purported security of the rest of the country[121] reveals a bias based on ignorance that pervades at the highest levels of government, as well as this country's deep ambivalence regarding the proper constitutional treatment of noncitizens. The category of Arab and Muslim countries whose citizens were selected for interrogation, registration, detention, and deportation made little sense given that several of those countries whose citizens were discriminatorily targeted, like Pakistan and Egypt, are now allies working with the United States in the "war on terror."

The executive branch's ambivalence about who should be afforded the protection of the Constitution is well illustrated by our Supreme Court's decisions. On the one hand, the Supreme Court has held that the cardinal guarantee of the equal protection clause is "universal in its application, to all persons within the territorial jurisdiction, without regard to differences of . . . nationality"[122] and that of the due process clause "applies to all 'persons' within the United States, including aliens, whether their presence here is lawful, unlawful, temporary, or permanent."[123] The Court has further held that when noncitizens are accused of crimes, they are entitled to all of the constitutional rights attaching to criminal trials: the right to a public trial, a trial by jury, the assistance of counsel, and the right to confront adverse witnesses.[124] Constitutional scholars have noted that this view, which holds that foreign nationals are "persons" within the meaning of the Constitution, is premised in part on the notion that the Constitution itself only expressly reserves two rights for citizens, the right to vote and the right to run for federal elective office.[125] This fact indicates that the Framers did not intend for the other constitutional rights to be exclusive to citizens.[126]

On the other hand, at various points in its history, the Supreme Court has upheld the government's decisions to exclude and expel foreign nationals from the country because of their race;[127] to bar them from owning land, even when the law provided only a thin veil for racism;[128] to deport them for their political associations, even though those associations were not unlawful at the time;[129] and to permit states to bar qualified foreign nationals from serving as public school teachers and police officers because of their immigration status.[130]

Of these two polar positions, the extension of rights to noncitizens makes sense from several important perspectives. The system of legally enforceable constitutional rights balances the scales of liberty—the government's assertion of sovereignty over individuals has as its counterweight certain limitations on the exercise of governmental power.[131] James Madison emphasized this compensating and counterbalancing function in his report condemning the Alien and Sedition Acts: "It does not follow, because aliens are not parties to the Constitution, as citizens are parties to it, that whilst they actually conform to it, they have no right to its protection. Aliens are no more parties to the laws than they are parties to the Constitution; yet it will not be disputed that, as they owe, on the one hand, a temporary obedience, they are entitled, in return, to their protection and advantage."[132] The view espoused by James

Madison that endures today is that those persons subject to the obligations of our laws ought to be able to invoke its protections as well.[133]

Furthermore, the Madisonian view fully agrees with the contemporary human rights movement's understanding that there are equal and inalienable rights to which all persons are entitled, regardless of nationality, ethnicity, religion, immigration status, or political affiliation simply by virtue of their humanity. The Universal Declaration of Human Rights, the foundational document of international human rights discourse and practice, is based on the premise of "the inherent dignity and . . . the equal and inalienable rights of all members of the human family."[134] The Universal Declaration guarantees the rights of due process, political expression and association, and equal protection[135] and extends these rights to nationals and nonnationals alike.[136] Other human rights covenants and treaties follow suit.[137]

This country's "experiments" with diverting from the founding principle that fundamental rights are owed to all persons as a matter of human dignity provide a strong argument for acting in keeping with that legal and moral principle.[138] The most frequently cited example is that of the decision in *Dred Scott v. Sandford*,[139] in which the Court held that even African Americans freed from slavery could not avail themselves of the federal courts because they were "persons who are the descendants of Africans who were imported into this country, and sold as slaves"; they were "considered as a subordinate and inferior class of beings"; they were not protected by the Constitution when it was adopted, and therefore had no rights unless the government expressly chose to grant them. Congress expressly overruled this reasoning in the Civil Rights Act of 1866,[140] and the Fourteenth Amendment made clear that all persons born or naturalized in the United States are citizens and that all persons present in the United States are entitled to due process of law and equal protection.

Finally, constitutional scholars have raised the obvious question in this area and provided the most unassailable answer.[141] Why should a country be able to take a noncitizen's life, liberty, or property without due process of law, when it cannot do the same to a citizen? People's interests in life and liberty do not vary depending on their nationality. Nor does the government's interest vary depending on citizenship status. The test used by the courts in determining how much process or constitutional protection is due to a person involves balancing the individual's interest with the government's interest, and the citizenship issue should not play any role in that assessment.

Unfortunately, neither our views as citizens nor the views of members of Congress were heard in this post September 11 debate. We were all not only locked out of the discussion about the immigration detention, registration, and deportation policies but were denied all information about its implementation. From the initial pronouncement by Ashcroft that the Freedom of Information Act was suspended during the "war on terror,"[142] to the broad and unchecked dragnet cast over the Middle Eastern, South Asian, and Muslim immigrant communities—whose only identifiable connection to terrorism appeared to be the color of their skin, their religious affiliation, or the origin of their ancestors—to the hidden imprisonment of immigrants and the shameful "hold until cleared policy," to the secret deportation of people who seized, *the people of this country have been kept in the dark.*

Under the banner of combating terrorism, Ashcroft authorized a pernicious assault on the protections guaranteed by the Fourth, Fifth, and Sixth Amendments to the Constitution. It was the Justice Department itself that impeded some of these most important rights and freedoms, including the right to personal liberty, the right to be free from unreasonable searches and seizures, the right to a speedy and public trial, and the right to individual privacy. Looking back on these actions now, who can say what we, *the People*, would have or could have done had we known of these wholesale constitutional and human rights violations?

The Unprecedented Presidential Policy of Military Indefinite Investigative Detention

The creation of crimes after the commission of the fact, or, in other words, the subjecting of men to punishment for things which, when they were done, were breaches of no law, and the practice of arbitrary imprisonments, have been, in all ages, the favorite and most formidable instruments of tyranny. The observations of the judicious Blackstone, in reference to the latter, are well worthy of recital: "To bereave a man of life, [says he,] or by violence to confiscate his estate, without accusation or trial, would be so gross and notorious an act of despotism, as must at once convey the alarm of tyranny throughout the whole nation; but confinement of the person, by secretly hurrying him to jail, where his sufferings are unknown or forgotten, is a less public, a less striking, and therefore a more dangerous engine of arbitrary government.

—*Alexander Hamilton, The Federalist No. 84 (quoting Blackstone, Commentaries, vol. 1, p. 136) (Clinton Rossiter ed., 1961) (emphasis added).*

THE NEWEST CATEGORY OF U.S. DETAINEES: "ENEMY COMBATANTS"

Declaring an "extraordinary emergency" on November 13, 2001, President Bush coined the term "enemy combatant" in an unprecedented order authorizing the creation of special military tribunals to try noncitizens suspected of terrorism, to be used at the U.S. Naval Base, Guantánamo Bay, Cuba.[1] The Military Order entitled "Detention, Treatment, and Trial of Certain Noncitizens in the War Against Terrorism" (Military Order) provides no definition for an "enemy combatant," and because the term is not recognized in international law, experts and ordinary citizens alike were confounded by the president's use of it. People understandably wanted to know who could be charged with being an "enemy combatant." Would it be limited to noncitizens held for trial before the newly created military commissions or would citizens be included? What offenses or misconduct would lead to such a charge? And what process would be used to determine who would be declared an "enemy combatant"? While these questions were raised by a few human rights organizations, the fact that no answers were forthcoming did not immediately raise a general alarm because the scope of this president's claim to new powers had not yet been fully revealed.

What has become eminently clear in the five years since the president's order is that there is no fixed definition for the term "enemy combatant." For example, although a person reading the executive order creating the military commissions might quite reasonably conclude that only a noncitizen could be declared an "enemy combatant," the president's designation of Jose Padilla, an American citizen, as an "enemy combatant" demonstrated that citizens are not immune from such treatment. Furthermore, the Jose Padilla case demonstrates that a person need not be armed, or participating in any military activities, or even be near a battlefield in order to be seized and declared an "enemy combatant" and placed in indefinite investigatory detention.

There is no U.S. or international law on the books defining the term "enemy combatant." Nor is there a law that grants the president the power to declare someone an "enemy combatant" and then lock that person away without charge or trial. Yet, President Bush continues to exercise this power. Justice Department attorneys argue that this power is part of the president's commander-in-chief power, even though that authority is a constitutionally limited power to prosecute a war.

Under the administration's policy, many of the individuals designated as "enemy combatants," unlike the post September 11 immigration detainees, are not being treated as civilians, but rather as members of a military force—either the Taliban army, affiliated forces of that army, or one of the ranks of Al Qaeda. In practice, they are considered to be participating in an ongoing armed conflict with the United States.

The Bush administration's creation of an "enemy combatant" category that includes alleged Al Qaeda fighters in Afghanistan, Taliban soldiers or affiliated troops captured on or near the battlefield there,[2] as well as terrorism suspects arrested in countries far from any battlefield, was carefully calculated. In fact, it is one of the linchpins in the administration's disturbing new legal framework that aggressively advances the notion that this is an armed conflict in which the traditional laws of war—including the Geneva Conventions, the treaties that govern such conflicts, and our own Uniform Code of Military Justice, the law that governs the actions of all of the members of our armed forces—do not apply.

International humanitarian law—also known as "the laws of war"—are the obligations of governments to individuals subject to their power during wartime. These rules are intended to be observed not only by governments and their armed forces, but also by armed opposition groups and other parties participating in the conflict.[3] International humanitarian law has been codified in a number of international treaties, with the four Geneva Conventions[4] on the Protection of War Victims and the two Additional Protocols as the principal instruments. In addition, many of these rules have been incorporated into domestic laws around the world, and many of the principles are also recognized as customary international law, binding on all nations, whether or not they are a party to specific international agreements.

In general, the laws of war outlaw specific forms of mistreatment of enemy soldiers, the wounded, prisoners of war (POWs), and civilians. The Geneva Conventions were created expressly to ensure that mankind would never again resort to the barbarous acts committed during the Second World War.[5] The conventions were therefore written "first and foremost to protect individuals, and not to serve state interests."[6] All persons captured within the context of an armed conflict are entitled to certain protections under the conventions.

Both the Third Geneva Convention,[7] which addresses the rights of prisoners of war, and the Fourth Geneva Convention, which addresses the rights of civilians, define the protections due persons captured amidst military hostilities. Under the Third Geneva Convention, members of the armed forces of a state party to an international armed conflict or members of affiliated militias are entitled to POW status upon capture. One of the convention's central protections is a detainee's right to be treated as a POW until his status or innocence can be determined by a "competent tribunal."[8] The convention further guarantees other basic dignities and fundamental procedural rights. For example, it provides: the right to humane treatment including protection from violence, intimidation, insults, public curiosity, and coercive interrogation tactics; due process rights if a detainee is subject to disciplinary or punitive sanctions; the right to communication with protective agencies; the opportunity for physical exercise; the right to proper and regular medical attention as a detainee's state of health requires; and the right to repatriation at the conclusion of active hostilities. The Third Geneva Convention expressly guarantees POWs charged with crimes fair trial rights, as well as the right to be tried by the same courts, under the same procedures, as in cases against military personnel of the detaining power.[9]

The Fourth Geneva Convention provides similar, and even more protective guarantees, as well as similar fair trial protections to "protected persons," who may be sentenced only by "competent courts" after a "regular trial." "Protected persons" under the Fourth Geneva Convention include all those "in the hands of a Party to the conflict" who are not prisoners of war, wounded, or sick. This includes not only civilian bystanders to the conflict, but even those individuals who may be "definitely suspected of or engaged in activities hostile to the security of the State."[10]

Freed from the binding constraints that the laws of war place on military conduct, the president, proclaiming that he is acting in his role as commander in chief, has granted himself the authority to write an *entirely new set of rules* for the "war on terror" and to do so without congressional approval, far from any public accountability. Remarkably, the Bush administration actually claims that within this new kind of war *there is no role for our elected represen-*

tatives in Congress or for the courts. Under this new regime, the executive branch holds all constitutional power in what it defines as the "war on terror" arena. According to the Bush administration, this arena includes not only battlefields but countries not involved in active military conflict with the U.S., as well as our own internal civilian affairs. The entire world has now become the battlefield in the global "war on terror." Any person in any country in the world is now potentially subject to the military jurisdiction of the United States if he or she is designated an "enemy combatant" and therefore is also potentially subject to indefinite investigative detention without charge or trial. Make no mistake about the Bush administration's seriousness on this issue; this is the very position that Justice Department lawyers have argued in the nation's federal courts. Now, with the recent passage of the Military Commissions Act of 2006 (MCA), discussed further in chapter 5, the administration relies on this new law to support in retrospect its creation of vast unprecedented executive powers since September 11.

THE NEW CATEGORY APPLIED TO AMERICAN CITIZENS

The Bush administration's use of the term "enemy combatant" does not fit within any existing category in international humanitarian law defining the status of participants in military hostilities.[11] Under international humanitarian law the term "enemy combatant," although very infrequently used by those knowledgeable in the field, has generically referred to any person who is authorized to fight for the opposite side in military hostilities.[12] "Combatants" are soldiers, "members of the armed forces of a Party to a conflict" who fight openly for one side in the conflict.[13] "Combatants" may not be prosecuted for the actions they take lawfully against members of the military forces of the opposing party; in a sense, they are deemed "privileged" to engage in combat activities by virtue of their membership in the armed forces of a party to the conflict. "Combatants" thus have the legal right to participate directly in hostilities. In the traditional and logical sense then, an "enemy combatant" is simply a combatant, an enemy belligerent or an authorized soldier, who is fighting for the other side. But that is *not* how the Bush administration uses this term.[14]

The term closest to that which the administration is using is that of "unlawful combatant." As understood within the law of war framework, the terms draw a distinction between civilians, who cannot participate in hostilities, and legitimate "combatants"—or recognized soldiers—in the armed conflict. The category of "unlawful combatants" includes two sets of people: (1) members of the regular armed forces of a nation who lose their privileged combatant status by disobeying certain rules or undertaking certain types of subterfuge; and (2) civilians who unlawfully participate directly in the battle.[15]

Under international humanitarian law, both lawful and unlawful combatants are entitled to well-established, but different, substantive and procedural rights. According to the Geneva Conventions, captured enemy soldiers must be provided with the specific safeguards and protections due POWs. Because the Taliban government was the effective government of Afghanistan at the time the war was started, and because both Afghanistan and the United States are parties to the Geneva Conventions, the armed attacks by the United States and other nations against the Taliban constitute an international armed conflict to which the Geneva Conventions and customary international humanitarian law apply. This means that individuals fighting for the Taliban regime in Afghanistan must be treated as prisoners of war until a neutral tribunal is held to make a proper determination as to their status. In contrast, because Al Qaeda is a clandestine network comprising people and groups from many countries and because it holds no sovereign territory, it lacks international legal power. Because it is not a nation-state, Al Qaeda cannot be a party to the Geneva Conventions, its members are not entitled to be considered combatants under international law, and members who engage in terrorist activities are properly subject to trial and punishment under each nation's criminal laws. Those persons who take up arms and are not members of the Taliban's armed forces or of Al Qaeda are civilians, and as such, they are not privileged by law to take part in hostilities.[16] Therefore, they can be tried as criminals in civilian courts.

By disavowing this long-established and internationally agreed-upon scheme, the Defense Department declared itself free from all requirements of due process and justice. While the plain meaning of the term "enemy combatant" implies, and has been traditionally interpreted as requiring, that the individual has certain delineated rights under the laws of war, President Bush's new use of the term means precisely the opposite. Within the new "war on terror" paradigm, no rules apply except those specifically designed and created by the Bush administration.

During this new kind of war, people whom the president declares to be "enemy combatants"—from U.S. citizens like Jose Padilla and Yaser Hamdi to the foreign nationals detained in Guantánamo—may be held indefinitely without charge or trial or access to any court, in short, without any process at all.[17] Thus, while the government itself invokes the laws of war and refers to "the settled wartime authority of the Commander-in-Chief to capture and detain enemy combatants" as the source and justification for the executive's power to detain people indefinitely without trial, it at the same time paradoxically refuses to comply with the requirements of the Geneva Conventions that constitute the core of these laws of war.[18]

THE EXECUTIVE DETENTIONS OF ALLEGED "ENEMY COMBATANT" CITIZENS: JOSE PADILLA AND YASER HAMDI

In the first full year of its "war on terror," the Bush administration claimed, for the first time in American history, the extraordinary executive power to arrest U.S. citizens and detain them indefinitely without charges or trial by jury.

In order to understand how such a power could even be claimed by the executive branch—let alone be taken seriously by the courts in this country— we have to look at the constitutional framework that apportions powers to the three branches of government. Article I of the Constitution gives Congress the powers "to provide for the common Defence" of the nation,[19] "to raise and support Armies," "to provide and maintain a Navy,"[20] "to make Rules for the Government and Regulation of the land and naval Forces,"[21] "to define and punish . . . Offenses against the Law of Nations,"[22] "to declare War . . . and make Rules concerning Captures on Land and Water,"[23] and to raise, support, and regulate the armed forces.[24] Article I also includes the cardinal guarantee against arbitrary executive action; it reserves only to Congress the power to suspend "the Privilege of the Writ of Habeas Corpus," the means by which people may challenge government detentions. Article II gives the president the position of commander in chief of the nation's armed forces, and provides him with the power to direct foreign affairs.[25] Under Article III, the judicial power is given to the Supreme Court and to "such inferior Courts as the Congress may from time to time . . . establish."[26] Under this three-branch system, it is the third branch—the courts—that enforce our understanding of the fundamental social compact that binds the people of this nation together in their common understanding of this country's values. The system is designed so that each branch has the power to "check and balance" the other two in order to prevent one from becoming more powerful than the others. In principle, each branch defers to the others in their area of expertise, presuming mutual respect for such deference.

In the context of our civil society, Congress has the constitutional authority to make the laws, and the courts fulfill the crucial role of deciding whether the government's actions are consistent with the Constitution and laws of, and treaties ratified by, the country. The Bush administration, however, has unilaterally changed this dynamic. By using the language of "war" in its effort to combat terrorism—in a manner much more literal from this country's "war on drugs" and "war on poverty"—it has invoked the executive branch's commander-in-chief power in order to exercise it both abroad and at home. This paradigm shift has had a cataclysmic effect upon the balance of powers among the three branches. The Bush administration has used the commander-in-chief power, which is intended to give the president the power to prosecute wars abroad, to expand his power to implement laws in the domestic sphere. For example, he has unilaterally implemented measures such as preventive and investigative detention and secret immigration hearings, and has dispensed with Bill of Rights guarantees for American citizens. Furthermore, the executive branch has taken the unprecedented position that Congress has no constitutional authority to oversee its exercise of these military-derived powers. Because the courts have largely accepted the Bush administration's justification for its deliberate erosion of the boundaries of civil society and the suppression of our civil institutions, judicial review of these new and awesome powers now takes place within extremely cramped confines. Rather than evaluating executive action for its consistency with constitutional rights and guarantees, the courts now view themselves as constrained to assess whether such action tips the balance—even if it significantly undermines individual and collective liberties—when it is weighed against the war-making power and the need to ensure national security. In short, once the president says that he is exercising power within the "war on terror," neither Congress nor the courts have been willing to even try to rein him in.

It is from within this highly restrictive constitutional box that the courts have been called upon to rule on the president's newly asserted power to imprison Americans as "enemy combatants" and place them in military custody without notifying them of the charges against them, without allowing them access to counsel or to the outside world, and without providing them with a trial before they begin serving their "sentences."

THE CASE OF JOSE PADILLA

Jose Padilla is a U.S. citizen who was born in Brooklyn, New York, in 1971. He converted to Islam in an effort to find a spiritual anchor in his life after serving time in prison. On May 8, 2002, returning home from a trip to Pakistan, Padilla flew to Chicago to visit his son. Because he was returning from a trip overseas, upon disembarking at O'Hare International Airport, Padilla proceeded to U.S. Customs along with the other passengers from his flight. However, unlike the other Americans on the same plane, he was asked to step aside by law enforcement officers and was immediately arrested.

Padilla was arrested on the authority of a material witness warrant issued by a federal court in New York in response to a request from the Justice Department. The warrant was issued ostensibly to ensure that Padilla would be available as a witness to testify before a federal grand jury that had been convened in New York to investigate federal crimes. Padilla was flown to New York late in the evening of May 14, 2002, and was taken from the airport to the high-security floor of the Metropolitan Correction Center in Manhattan. The next day, Padilla was brought before the federal district court in leg irons, shackles, and handcuffs. In court, Padilla and his court-appointed lawyer were permitted to review the affidavit that the government had filed in support of the material witness warrant.

For the next several weeks, Padilla's lawyer met with him and filed papers on his behalf, seeking his release on the ground that a material witness could not be lawfully imprisoned. Padilla's attorney anticipated receiving the court's decision on this request at a court conference scheduled for June 11, 2002. That conference never took place. Instead, on Sunday, June 9, 2002, President Bush filed a Presidential Declaration with the court that stated that Padilla is an "enemy combatant" and ordered the secretary of defense to take Padilla into military custody. Padilla's appointed counsel was not notified of this unusual Sunday court conference, and in her absence Padilla was flown to the Consolidated Naval Brig in Charleston, South Carolina.[27] For three years he was held incommunicado and in solitary confinement without being charged with any crime and without being allowed access to family, friends, or the court. Although the courts eventually ordered the government to permit Padilla to meet with his appointed counsel, those meetings were monitored by the government, and his attorneys have been under court order not to raise certain matters with him. Under these circumstances, Padilla could not speak freely with his attorneys and was unable to assist them in any way in mounting his defense. The government has never explained why Padilla, who was *already* being held in a secure facility by order of a civilian court when he was declared an "enemy combatant," needed to be held in military custody rather than in the criminal justice system.

The Presidential Declaration of Padilla's "enemy combatant" status was supported only by a single sworn statement. Michael H. Mobbs, a special adviser to the undersecretary of defense for policy, submitted a declaration in support of the Presidential Declaration and the military custody order. According to his declaration, Mobbs had no personal knowledge of any facts concerning Jose Padilla. All of his statements were based on hearsay—on Mobbs's recounting of what he apparently considered to be the relevant records and reports about Padilla. Furthermore, Mobbs openly acknowledged in his declaration that the two confidential sources he relied upon for his conclusions were two people held by the government who "have been involved with Al Qaeda for several years, . . . have not been completely candid about their association with Al Qaeda and their terrorist activities," have provided uncorroborated information, and may have been "part of an effort to mislead or confuse U.S. officials."[28] In addition, the Mobbs Declaration states that one of these two sources subsequently recanted some of the information provided, and the other source was "being treated with various types of drugs" during his interrogation.[29] In any other legal context, at any other time in history, no court would have permitted a declaration like that to be relied upon as evidence to hold Padilla.

Based upon the secondhand, uncorroborated, and unreliable information he reviewed, all that Mobbs could include in his declaration was that Padilla moved to Egypt in 1998, traveled to Pakistan "in 1999 or 2000," and "also traveled to Saudi Arabia and Afghanistan."[30] The Mobbs Declaration makes clear that the government had no basis to allege that Padilla is a member of Al Qaeda or that he took any steps in furtherance of any planned criminal activity. No allegations were made that Padilla participated in the September 11 attacks or in any other terrorist or criminal act against the United States or that he took up arms against the United States on behalf of any foreign army or terrorist organization. The Mobbs Declaration is silent as to the definition of "enemy combatant" status and as to what level of "association" or affiliation with Al Qaeda is necessary to warrant treatment by the government as an "enemy combatant."

In fact, for more than three years, Padilla was not charged with any criminal or military offense, and the secretary of defense stated during this time that the government had no intention of *ever* charging him with any crime.[31] Indeed, the government repeatedly made clear that it was keeping him in military custody solely for interrogation purposes. A declaration submitted to the district court on January 9, 2003, by Vice Admiral Lowell E. Jacoby, director of the Defense Intelligence Agency, reveals the fact that Padilla was not being held as an "enemy combatant" because of any offenses that he has committed or any plans that he has made, but rather because "[his] potential intelligence value [is] very high."[32] Admiral Jacoby makes clear that Padilla was being held in indefinite detention without any due process *solely* because he *may* have had information that the government *might* be interested in at some point in the future. Admiral Jacoby indicates that the government fully intended to detain Padilla indefinitely because the "intelligence cycle is continuous," and "[t]here is a constant need to ask detainees new lines of questions as additional detainees are taken into custody."[33]

The detention was blatantly illegal. Neither the Constitution, nor Congress, nor any court in this country has ever approved such an abuse of executive authority. Detention for investigatory purposes has never been a constitutionally sanctioned practice in the United States. That the detention of American citizens and their labeling as "enemy combatants" has occurred without so much as a nod in the direction of due process makes President Bush's radical departure from the rule of law all the more startling.

Even more chilling was the government's justification for Padilla's detention in solitary confinement:[34] that providing him with access to family or counsel may "threaten the perceived dependency and trust between [Padilla] and [the] interrogator." Elaborating on this justification, Admiral Jacoby states that "Only after such time as Padilla has perceived that help is not on the way can the United States reasonably expect to obtain all possible intelligence information from [him]. . . . Providing him access to counsel now would create expectations by Padilla that his ultimate release may be obtained through an adversarial civil litigation process."[35] Not only did the government intend to make Padilla feel hopeless, then, but it was determined to do so, according to Admiral Jacoby, no matter how long it took.[36] Perhaps one day, the government's theory holds, Padilla would feel hopeless enough to tell the military what it wanted to hear.

Rather than accusing saboteurs of crimes defined by Congress, as the executive branch did in the *Quirin* case decided during World War II, President Bush now claims a bare power to detain individuals indefinitely without any charge—without identifying any crime that was allegedly violated—and without trial. The difference is profound. An individual charged with a crime established by the legislature has notice that certain acts may be unlawful and then, when accused of these acts, has the opportunity to prove his or her innocence. An individual detained without charge or trial has no notice of the prohibited conduct, no chance to contest the allegations against him or her, and thus no hope of exoneration.

Whatever the scope of the executive's power to detain individuals may be on the battlefield, off the battlefield it is constitutionally limited to those actions necessary to the faithful execution of congressional statutes.[37] Were it otherwise, the executive's military power to detain without charge would swallow up much of criminal law. The executive could evade our constitutional criminal procedures established merely by declaring an individual an "enemy combatant"; any accused terrorist could be transferred on the president's say-so from the criminal system to indefinite detention without charge or trial.

By imprisoning Padilla *without a hearing of any sort* and *without producing any evidence against him,* the executive branch has taken one of the most drastic steps in our nation's history—it has ordered the arbitrary and indefinite detention of an American citizen, subjected him to drastic conditions of imprisonment, and thrown away the keys. Not only does this violate the Constitution, it speaks directly to the Bush administration's disregard for the moral values embodied in that document. It fundamentally weakens the backbone of democratic civilization: the rule of law. The government's unprecedented action poses a grave threat to the constitutional rights of all American citizens.

On September 17, 2004, the Justice Department announced that it had filed terrorism charges against two men it had accused of recruiting Jose Padilla to train as a terrorist agent. Padilla was not named as a defendant in that indictment.[38] However, on November 20, 2005, while Padilla's petition for review of his case by the Supreme Court was pending, President Bush directed the secretary of defense to release Padilla from military custody and transfer him to the custody of Attorney General Alberto Gonzales for the purpose of his criminal prosecution.[39]

THE CASE OF YASER HAMDI

Like Jose Padilla, Yaser Esam Hamdi is a U.S. citizen; he was born on September 26, 1980, in Baton Rouge, Louisiana, and was raised in Saudi Arabia.

The unclassified information concerning Hamdi indicates that he had traveled to Afghanistan from Pakistan on July 15, 2001, to do volunteer humanitarian relief work. He was arrested in September 2001 and held by U.S. forces in Afghanistan until January 11, 2002, when he was transported with 384 other captives to Camp X-Ray in Guantánamo.[40] In April 2002, based on records supporting Hamdi's claim of American citizenship, the government transferred him to a military jail in Norfolk, Virginia.[41]

Hamdi was never been charged with any offense and was for most of his detention denied access to an attorney and the courts. Like its position in the *Padilla* case, the government maintained that it had the authority to detain Hamdi indefinitely, incommunicado, without ever subjecting him to prosecution—civilian or military—solely because it had declared him an "enemy combatant."

According to the government, Hamdi went to Afghanistan at some point before September 2001. He remained in Afghanistan after the United States and coalition forces began military operations in that country. The Northern Alliance captured him and turned him over to U.S. forces. The government maintains that Hamdi was "affiliated" with Taliban forces and that, at the time of his capture, he was carrying a firearm that he turned over to Northern Alliance forces.[42]

In Afghanistan, the Northern Alliance held Hamdi in two different prisons. At the second prison, a U.S. interrogation team interviewed him. Thereafter, a U.S. military officer ordered his transfer to a U.S. detention facility in Kandahar, Afghanistan. After another "military screening" in January 2002, Hamdi was sent to Guantánamo.

Hamdi's designation as an "enemy combatant" was, like Padilla's, supported by a declaration submitted by Michael Mobbs, Special Advisor to the Undersecretary of Defense.[43] Again, Mobbs does not indicate that he had any personal knowledge of any facts concerning Hamdi's capture or detention, and all of his knowledge was based on his review of what he considered to be relevant records and reports.[44] Although Mobbs maintained in his declaration that he has been substantially involved with detainee operations since mid-February 2002, the *Federal Register* indicates that the position he occupied was not created until April 24, 2002.[45] Hamdi had already been detained and transferred to Norfolk by that time.

The Mobbs Declaration states that Hamdi traveled to Afghanistan in July or August 2001 and that he became "affiliated" with a Taliban military unit prior to the September 11 attacks.[46] The declaration further states that Hamdi received weapons training prior to September 11 but does not say from *whom* the training was received, *where* it was received, or of *what* the training consisted. According to Mobbs, Hamdi remained with the Taliban after September 11 and after October 7, 2001, when the United States began military operations against the Taliban. The Mobbs Declaration does not identify the Taliban unit that Hamdi was allegedly affiliated with, nor does it state whether this unit wore uniforms or what functions the unit served. No further details are provided.

The Mobbs Declaration reports that on an unspecified date in late 2001, Northern Alliance forces engaged the Taliban in battle. Mobbs does not say that the Taliban unit with which Hamdi was "affiliated" was engaged in battle with the Northern Alliance. While Mobbs says that Hamdi's unit surrendered to Northern Alliance forces, he does not say where or when this occurred, or what activity Hamdi was engaged in at this time.[47] While he was in the custody of Northern Alliance forces, Hamdi was interviewed by a U.S. interrogation team. According to Mobbs, Hamdi identified himself to the U.S. interrogation team as "a Saudi citizen who had been born in the United States and who entered Afghanistan the previous summer to train with and, *if necessary*, fight for the Taliban." The Mobbs Declaration does not elaborate on what Hamdi allegedly meant by "if necessary."

Nowhere in his declaration does Mobbs assert or even suggest that Hamdi was a member of Al Qaeda. The only definition of the term "enemy combatant" in the Mobbs Declaration is circular: "individuals associated with Al Qaeda or Taliban who were and continue to be enemy combatants."[48] The Mobbs Declaration states that based upon others' interviews of Hamdi, he was considered to be an "enemy combatant" by a U.S. military screening team that determined that he met the criteria for "enemy combatants" over whom the United States was taking control and that he also met the criteria for transfer to Guantánamo. These screening criteria, and the reasons why Hamdi purportedly met them, are not set forth in the Mobbs Declaration. They are secret. The declaration merely asserts that a "subsequent interview of Hamdi confirmed that he surrendered and gave his firearm to Northern Alliance Forces, which supports his classification as an enemy combatant."[49]

The Mobbs Declaration does not offer any factual support or explanation for Hamdi's detention in solitary confinement in the Naval Brig in Norfolk. It is silent on why he was separated from all other detainees at Guantánamo and then moved to Norfolk. Further, the Mobbs Declaration does not set forth facts or determinations made by others that would support treating Hamdi as an unlawful combatant rather than an "enemy combatant."[50] Finally, the Mobbs Declaration does not provide any factual basis for the notion that granting Hamdi's counsel access to him would have posed any threat to national security or would interfere with United States intelligence-gathering efforts in any way. No reason is given for placing Hamdi in military custody. Simply put, as was the case with Padilla, the Mobbs Declaration is *not* the kind of document that courts have *ever* determined to be sufficient to justify holding a U.S. citizen.

THE LEGAL CHALLENGES TO THE MILITARY PREVENTIVE/INVESTIGATIVE DETENTIONS OF U.S. CITIZENS

Lawyers for Padilla and Hamdi each filed challenges to President Bush's exercise of his newly asserted preventive and investigative detention power. The government's opposition to these challenges made clear that the Bush administration does not consider the fight against terrorism to be a law enforcement endeavor but rather an executive war initiative under which people—including American citizens—can be detained in the name of prevention and subjected to investigatory detention outside of all constitutional protections.[51] Secretary of Defense Donald Rumsfeld confirmed the administration's position on these issues, stating that that "we are not interested in trying [Padilla] at the moment; we are not interested in punishing him at the moment. We are interested in finding out what he knows."[52] Ashcroft echoed this position in his testimony before Congress.[53]

The Bush administration's position runs roughshod over the Bill of Rights. In the domestic law enforcement context, decisions interpreting the Fourth Amendment hold that it does not permit the seizure of a person without "probable cause" (a reasonable basis) to believe that he or she has committed a crime or is about to commit a crime. It does not permit the detention of a person beyond forty-eight hours without bringing him or her before a neutral magistrate who will examine the charges. In the law enforcement context, the Fifth Amendment prohibits the deprivation of a person's liberty without due process, and both the Fifth and the Sixth Amendments prohibit holding a person incommunicado to facilitate interrogation. Investigative detention is simply impermissible under the Constitution. The executive branch, however, has not even *attempted* to square its creation of the "enemy combatant" category with the Bill of Rights. Rather, it baldly claims that these unprecedented powers are inherent in the commander-in-chief power, and argues that they trump *all* of our constitutional and international law protections.

The administration's position appears to be based—so far as it can be divined, since the criteria used for Bush administration's original "enemy combatant" designation has remained secret from its coinage to the present[54]—solely on the *Quirin* case[55] decided more than sixty years ago, under far different circumstances, based on far different facts, and under an entirely different legal structure. It is this 1942 case, coupled with the administration's broad interpretation of Congress's Authorization of the Use of Military Force in Afghanistan (AUMF),[56] upon which the government relies.

The *Quirin* case arose during World War II, when eight trained saboteurs who were members of the German armed forces landed on the shores of Florida and Long Island, New York, on a mission to destroy war industry facilities within the United States.[57] After their arrest, President Franklin D. Roosevelt issued a proclamation and military order stating that the eight men should be tried before a military tribunal for crimes against the law of war and violations of the Articles of War. One of the eight men to be tried, Herman Hans Haupt, was a naturalized American citizen.

During the military tribunal, counsel for the German soldiers challenged the power of the military tribunal to hear their case, claiming that they were entitled to a jury trial in a civilian court. Noting first that the soldiers, after consultation with counsel, had admitted that they had been fighting for the enemy and had used subterfuge (discarding their uniforms) to enter the United States, and were therefore unlawful combatants, the Supreme Court proceeded to address the boundaries of the authority of the military tribunal.[58] As Chief Justice Stone stated, the "question for decision" is "whether it is in the power of the National Government to place petitioners upon trial before a military commission for the offenses with which they are charged."[59] Confronted with this question, the Court reached three conclusions: (1) that the charges against the saboteurs included offenses that could be tried before a military commission; (2) that the military commission was "lawfully constituted"—i.e., that President Roosevelt was authorized to create the commission in the form that he had chosen; and (3) that the saboteurs were being held "in lawful custody" for trial before the commission—i.e., that the commission had constitutional authority to try the saboteurs even though civilian courts were open at the time.[60]

Undoubtedly, the *Quirin* decision focused on the constitutionality of relegating admitted unlawful combatants to a military tribunal rather than permitting them to bring their cases before a civilian court. That ruling does not, however, authorize the indefinite detention of unlawful combatants without charge, counsel, or trial. In fact, the Supreme Court expressly rejected the exact argument being made by the Bush administration now—that so-called "enemy combatants" must be denied access to the courts because they are enemy aliens who have entered our territory.[61] As a consequence of the Court's ruling, in the *Quirin* case, each soldier was permitted to file his own petition for a writ of habeas corpus to challenge his detention. In reviewing these petitions, the Supreme Court looked carefully at the soldiers' admissions that they were unlawful combatants in order to ensure that each soldier's conduct properly placed him within the jurisdiction of the military tribunal.[62]

Although the *Quirin* decision is touted as historical precedent for the Bush administration's treatment of "enemy combatants," it, in fact, provides no support whatsoever for the proposition that the executive can hold an alleged but unproven terrorist, without charging him or her with any recognized offenses, and without providing a full opportunity to show innocence.[63] *Quirin* approved of executive action that respected Congress's enactments and allowed individuals a hearing to permit them to establish their innocence. Plainly, the Court's ruling in *Quirin* does not authorize the president to indefinitely detain American citizens without due process.

Persons who are not members of the armed forces of a party to a conflict and who are not on the actual field of battle wielding weapons have not traditionally been treated as combatants, whether lawful or unlawful. Instead, to the extent that individuals have participated in violent acts, they have historically been treated and tried as criminals under the domestic law of the captor. Contrary to the government's position in the post September 11 cases, the *Quirin* decision in fact confirmed these principles; people who aided the plot of the saboteurs in the United States, but who were not members of the German army, were not held as "enemy combatants," but were held as criminal detainees and tried in ordinary civilian courts for crimes such as treason.[64]

In short, the Bush administration merely lifted the phrase "enemy combatant" from a single inartful reference in the *Quirin* case and used it to create a new, completely fabricated category with a new set of rules completely untethered from the recognized laws of war—rules that permit indefinite detention without notice, charge, hearing, conviction, sentencing, or appeal.

The most basic principles of due process hold that executive branch officials cannot impose detention without first demonstrating the propriety of the detention at an adversarial proceeding at which the government bears a heavy burden of proof to justify the restraint upon individual liberty. The Supreme Court has consistently held that, even in times of war, constitutional principles respecting the rule of law warrant judicial review of executive action and further demand that the executive branch respect constitutional norms.[65]

Another difference between the invocation of the criminal process and the power claimed by the president in the *Padilla* case is one of accountability. The criminal justice system requires that defendants be afforded access to counsel, imposes judicial supervision over government action, and places congressionally imposed limits upon incarceration. Under the Bush administration's "justice system," none of these guarantees of accountability are present. We cannot and should not accept this greatly flawed alternative to a justice system that has been admired and respected the world over. Such a position, were it to be adopted by our courts, would totally eviscerate the limits placed on presidential authority that are meant to protect people's individual liberties.

Beyond the Bush administration's misguided reliance on the facts of the *Quirin* decision to support its plan for the indefinite detention of citizens, significant changes in the law have undermined the foundation of the *Quirin* decision. Even at the time of that decision, the Supreme Court recognized that the president's power as commander in chief is defined and limited by international law or the "law of nations": "[F]rom the very beginning of its history this Court has recognized and applied the law of war as including that part of the law of nations which prescribes, for the conduct of war, the status, rights and duties of enemy nations as well as of enemy nationals."[66] The Court's decision that unlawful combatants may be subject to capture and trial by military commissions was based on its understanding of the laws of war as they stood in 1942. But international law evolves over time to reflect the practices of nations, and our courts are bound to apply international law "as it has evolved and exists among the nations of the world today."[67] The laws of war have changed considerably in the last sixty years, such that the basis for the Court's decision in *Quirin* no longer exists.

The adoption of the Geneva Conventions in 1949 significantly changed the law of war.[68] Neither the conventions, nor the two additional protocols, nor the commentaries of the International Committee for the Red Cross refer to "unlawful" or "unprivileged" or "enemy" combatant status. According to the ICRC, the international organization charged with the responsibility of interpreting the conventions, there is *no status* under international law that permits a government to hold a person wholly outside of the law. As the ICRC states in its commentaries to the Fourth Geneva Convention: "Every person in enemy hands must have some status under international law: he is either a prisoner of war and, as such, covered by the Third Convention, a civilian covered by the Fourth Convention, or again, a member of the medical personnel of the armed forces who is covered by the First Convention. *There is no intermediate status*; nobody in enemy hands can be outside the law."[69]

The International Criminal Tribunal for the Former Yugoslavia in the late 1990s affirmed this principle, stating that "there is no gap between the Third and Fourth Geneva Conventions. If an individual is not entitled to the protection of the Third Geneva Convention as a prisoner of war . . . he or she necessarily falls within the ambit of [the Fourth Convention], provided that its Article 4 requirements [defining a protected person] are satisfied."[70] What the Bush administration has done here, then, is explicitly against the law.

THE SUPREME COURT DECISIONS

In the Supreme Court's decision in *Rumsfeld v. Padilla*,[71] Chief Justice Rehnquist, writing the majority opinion for five justices of the Court (with Justices Scalia, O'Connor, Kennedy, and Thomas), declined to address the constitutional issues raised by Padilla's case. Instead, the Court focused on the technical issue of which person should have been named as the defendant in his habeas petition. According to the majority, the papers filed on Padilla's behalf should have named Commander Melanie Marr, the commander of the South Carolina naval brig where Padilla was being held, as the defendant or respondent, rather than secretary of defense Donald Rumsfeld, because Commander Marr was "the jailer." The Court held that the wrong person had been sued and that the case had been filed in the wrong federal district; Padilla's petition should have been filed in the federal district in which he was confined, not where Secretary Rumsfeld "does business." By focusing on this issue, the majority was able to delay its consideration of the real issues in the case: the legality of the president's use of the new "enemy combatant" power to hold Padilla without charge or trial or access to counsel.

The dissenting Justices, Stevens, Souter, Ginsburg, and Breyer, were not content with this delay. They disagreed with the majority's characterization of the "bright-line" rule regarding naming the warden and filing in the district where the petitioner is being held, and noted that this rule has been "riddled" with exceptions. The more functional approach, Justice Stevens noted, was to focus on the person who had the power to release the prisoner—here, the secretary of defense. Dispensing with the technical grounds for the majority's decision, the dissenters turned to the merits of Padilla's claims, addressing the central issue of whether Padilla "is entitled to a hearing on the justification for his detention." Justice Stevens concluded that Congress's 2001 Authorization for Use of Military Force in Afghanistan did not authorize the indefinite, incommunicado detention of American citizens in the United States. In an impassioned statement, he summed up the outrage of the dissenters:

> At stake in this case is nothing less than the essence of a free society. Even more important than the method of selecting the people's rulers and their successors is the character of the constraints imposed on the Executive by the rule of law. Unconstrained Executive detention for the purpose of investigating and preventing subversive activity is the hallmark of the Star Chamber. Access to counsel for the purpose of protecting the citizen from official mistakes and mistreatment is the hallmark of due process. Executive detention of subversive citizens, like detention of enemy soldiers to keep them off the battlefield, may sometimes be justified to prevent persons from launching or becoming missiles of destruction. It may not, however, be justified by the naked interest in using unlawful procedures to extract information. Incommunicado detention for months on end is such a procedure. Whether the information procured is more or less reliable than that acquired by more extreme forms of torture is of no consequence. For if this Nation is to remain true to the ideals symbolized by its flag, it must not wield the tools of tyrants even to resist an assault by the forces of tyranny.[72]

The dismissal of Padilla's case forced him to begin his challenge all over again in South Carolina. Beyond achieving a delay in the resolution of the case, the government also succeeded in establishing the principle that it can choose the court in which it litigates by choosing the facility in which to imprison detainees.

At first it was unclear whether this tactical advantage would aid the administration in its unlawful effort. On February 28, 2005, the United States

District Court for the District of South Carolina granted Padilla's motion for summary judgment and his petition for a writ of habeas corpus, directing the government to release Padilla within forty-five days of the court's order unless it intended to hold him as a criminal defendant or a material witness.[73] The decision was then appealed by the government. In September 2005, the Fourth Circuit Court of Appeals reversed the lower court preventing Padilla's release. Rather than focusing on the issue of the whether the president's use of this new "enemy combatant" power was constitutional, the court stated the issue quite differently: "The exceedingly important question before us is whether the President of the United States possesses the authority to detain militarily a citizen of this country who is closely associated with Al Qaeda, an entity with which the United States is at war."[74] The court answered "yes."

By phrasing the issue this way, the Fourth Circuit Court of Appeals made several findings that the law does not support. First, it seemingly concluded that Padilla was associated with Al Qaeda when this factual issue was never reached by any court, and the law states that the habeas petitioner is entitled to the presumption of truth of his or her allegations. Second, the court apparently determined that the United States is at "war" with Al Qaeda, despite the fact that international humanitarian law states that this cannot be the case because Al Qaeda is a terrorist organization and not a state. On October 25, 2005, Padilla filed a petition for a writ of certiorari in the Supreme Court seeking review of the Fourth Circuit's decision.

In *Hamdi v. Rumsfeld*,[75] Justice Sandra Day O'Connor wrote an opinion in which only three other justices joined (Chief Justice Rehnquist, and Justices Kennedy and Breyer), making the decision a "plurality" decision of the · Court. The remaining justices had differing responses to that decision.[76]

Addressing the issue discussed by Justice Stevens in his dissent in Padilla, Justice O'Connor first concludes that Congress, by enacting its Authorization for Use of Military Force in Afghanistan,[77] had in fact authorized Hamdi's detention. The authorization, the Court held, trumps the existing federal law that expressly states that no "citizen shall be imprisoned or otherwise detained by the United States except pursuant to an Act of Congress."[78] According to Justice O'Connor, when Congress gave the president the authority to pursue those responsible for the September 11 attacks, that authority implicitly included the power to detain enemy forces captured in battle. This power, she noted, is consistent with the international humanitarian law rule that permits a nation to detain enemy forces captured in battle until the end of the hostilities.[79]

More importantly, Justice O'Connor narrowly defined the category of those who may be detained as "enemy combatants" under this regime: the "enemy combatant" category includes only those people who are "part of or supporting forces hostile to the United States or coalition partners in Afghanistan and who engaged in an armed conflict against the United States there."[80] Because the detention is for the purpose of "prevent[ing] a combatant's return to the battlefield," which is "a fundamental incident of waging war," this type of detention is only authorized, Justice O'Connor notes, "for the duration of the particular conflict in which they were captured."[81] In the *Hamdi* case, the plurality holds, Hamdi *could not* be held until the end of the "war on terror"—which the Court acknowledges may not have come in Hamdi's lifetime—but *only* until the end of "active combat operations in Afghanistan."[82] Finally, expressly rejecting the Bush administration's articulated justification for Hamdi's detention (as well as that for Padilla's detention), the opinion states, "Certainly, we agree that indefinite detention for the purpose of interrogation is not authorized."[83] The importance of this specific ruling cannot be overstated. The sole justification offered for the treatment of alleged "enemy combatants" such as Padilla and Hamdi was that indefinite detention was necessary in order to plumb the depths of their knowledge through endless interrogation sessions under conditions which made that despair of ever leaving their solitary confinement. This treatment the Supreme Court absolutely refused to sanction.

Justice O'Connor characterizes the real question before the Court not as whether Congress has authorized the president to detain "enemy combatants" but as whether the president's detention of American citizens without serious judicial review violates the Fifth Amendment's guarantee that no person may be deprived of his or her liberty without "due process of law." Devising a test that seeks to balance the harm of erroneous, indefinite imprisonment against the burden on the military of defending challenges brought by those seeking judicial review of their detentions, Justice O'Connor stated that "a citizen-detainee seeking to challenge his classification as an enemy-combatant must receive notice of the factual basis of his classification, and a fair opportunity to rebut the Government's factual assertions before a neutral decision maker."[84] She noted that Hamdi "unquestionably has the right to access to counsel in connection" with these proceedings. As Professor Ronald Dworkin noted in his article "What the Court Really Said,"[85] the plurality's balancing test is an effort to walk a tightrope between the district court's opinion that holds that detainees like Hamdi are entitled to all of the constitutional protections afforded criminal defendants—a ruling that the Supreme Court plurality considered too costly in terms of security risks—and the court of appeals' opinion that holds that the Presidential Declaration of "enemy combatant" status cannot be challenged at all—a ruling that the plurality thought gave too little protection to the individual being held.

THE RELEASE OF YASER HAMDI AND THE CHARGING OF JOSE PADILLA

On September 27, 2004, the government announced that a deal had been struck for the release of Yaser Hamdi from U.S. military custody without prosecution of any sort. Under the terms of the agreement, Hamdi was permitted to return to live with his family in Saudi Arabia provided that he renounce his U.S. citizenship, agree not to travel to Afghanistan or Israel or a number of other countries, agree not to seek to return to the United States for ten years, and agree to renounce any commitment to the principle of violent jihad. For his part, Hamdi has remained constant in his position that he never fought for the Taliban nor supported Al Qaeda in any way.

On October 11, 2004, the U.S. government finally released Hamdi after subjecting him to nearly three years solitary confinement as an "enemy combatant."

Hamdi's case is deeply troubling. Even if we were to accept the government's allegations against him, he was never presented as more than an individual who participated in hostilities on behalf of the Taliban forces. By releasing Hamdi under this agreement, the government has now acknowledged that he was—*at worst*—a soldier fighting for the enemy's army, and therefore, under the Geneva Conventions, a prisoner of war.

More importantly, the government cannot possibly claim that Hamdi was a major national security threat or even a potential source of intelligence about Al Qaeda operations. Nevertheless, it saw fit to argue in court that permitting him to meet with his attorney would "jeopardize compelling national security interests" and "irreparably harm the military's ongoing efforts to gather intelligence." These bald—and as it turns out wholly unsupported—allegations were made in a two-page affidavit submitted by a Defense Department bureaucrat who had no personal knowledge of Hamdi's background or capture. Yet, these statements were used to justify the most startling deprivation of Hamdi's constitutional rights. Despite his U.S. citizenship, for nearly three years he was held incommunicado and prevented from meeting with his lawyer and getting access to any court. Unable to present his own account of his actions in Afghanistan as long as he remained in custody, he remained helpless in the face of the U.S. government's baseless and needlessly aggressive position. And in the end, when confronted with a Supreme Court decision requiring it to establish even the most basic fact justifying any wartime detention—that Hamdi took up arms against the United States—the Justice Department folded. None of the government's accusations will ever be evaluated by a court. Hamdi's release now under the agreed-upon terms paints in bold relief the horrific consequences for liberty and justice when the executive branch is permitted to act unchecked.

Padilla's case adds to Hamdi's stark portrait of the effects of arbitrary and unlawful executive action. At every juncture in the case when it appeared that a federal court might make a determination adverse to the administration, the nature of the accusation and the detention was changed. For example, when the Justice Department became concerned that the court might determine that Padilla could not be held indefinitely as a material witness under that federal statute (because a sister court in the district had so ruled), Padilla was declared an "enemy combatant" and transferred to military custody.[86]

The Justice Department was confronted with an imminent showdown in the Supreme Court when Padilla's attorneys filed an appeal with the Court on October 25, 2005, seeking a determination on the fundamental issue: "Does the President have the power to seize American citizens in civilian settings on American soil and subject them to indefinite military detention without criminal charge or trial?"[87] The Bush administration's response was entirely in keeping with its strategy of avoiding Supreme Court rulings on the scope of the president's power to fight the "war on terror." Rather than respond to Padilla's Supreme Court appeal, the Justice Department filed criminal charges against him and the president ordered that Padilla be released from military detention and transferred to the control of the Attorney General for criminal proceedings.[88]

What conclusions can be drawn from the administration's effort to try to avoid a Supreme Court confrontation with Padilla's attorneys? It is certainly difficult to divine much from the government's ever-changing characterizations of the nature of Padilla's threat to national security. On June 10, 2002, John Ashcroft, then attorney general, announced to the world that the administration had foiled a terrorist plot to explode a radioactive bomb in the United States by catching Jose Padilla.[89] However, within days of Padilla's designation as an "enemy combatant" and his transfer to solitary confinement in a naval brig in South Carolina, Deputy Secretary of State Paul Wolfowitz was already revising those allegations downward to "some fairly loose talk."[90] Two years later, Deputy Attorney General James Comey would again change directions, stating that Padilla had been planning to kill hundreds of people by destroying an apartment building that uses natural gas. Interestingly, by the time that the administration filed criminal charges against Padilla in November 2005, his indictment did not include *any* of the government's earlier allegations that he had planned to carry out attacks in the United States; there was nothing about the administration's very public accusations that Padilla intended to detonate a "dirty bomb" or cause an "apartment explosion."

At the time of this writing, Padilla stands charged with an indictment that holds no mention of Al Qaeda. Instead, it states that Padilla was one of five men who may have helped to raise money and recruit volunteers in the 1990s to go overseas to countries including Chechnya, Bosnia, Somalia, and Kosovo.

Padilla's role in this alleged conspiracy appears very minor; while he is accused of going to a training camp in Afghanistan, there is no statement that he ever engaged in terrorist activity or planned attacks of any kind inside the United States.[91]

How do we interpret these changes in direction? There are several possibilities. It could be that the Bush administration's intelligence was completely wrong from the outset. Or that its unconstitutional treatment of Padilla destroyed the opportunity for any legitimate prosecution of him on the charges originally alleged. Or perhaps the Bush administration has finally decided to trust this country's legal institutions, which have served us well for more than two hundred years. But we certainly should not be left to guess what happened here. In June 2004, the Justice Department sent a report discussing the Padilla case to the Senate Judiciary Committee. Even a partial release of this report or of the underlying investigative files would permit us to judge for ourselves whether we approve of the basis for Padilla's seizure, the methods of interrogation used on him, the imposition of punishment without trial, or the conditions of confinement he endured.

On December 21, 2005, the U.S. Fourth Circuit Court of Appeals denied the government's application to transfer Padilla to Florida for criminal proceedings and to vacate the court's opinion. In a sharp rebuke, the court stated that the government's "actions may be to avoid consideration of our decision by the Supreme Court [and] have left not only the impression that Padilla may have been held for these years, even if justifiably, by mistake—an impression we would have, though the government could ill afford to leave extant. . . . And these impressions have been left, we fear, at what may ultimately prove to be substantial cost to the government's credibility before the courts."[92]

In January 2006, however, The Supreme Court reversed the Fourth Circuit decision and approved Padilla's transfer to Florida.[93] On April 3, 2006, the Court declined to hear Padilla's second appeal of his case, filed as *Padilla v. Hanft* (05-533). While only three of the necessary four justices voted to hear the case, the Court declined to dismiss the case as moot. By refusing to dismiss the case, the Court left in place the decision of the Fourth Circuit Court of Appeals. Little media attention was paid to this aspect of the decision, perhaps because it seems a subtle legal distinction. In fact, it may have serious implications for American citizens. The previous decision in Padilla's case upheld the president's wartime power to seize an American inside the U.S., indefinitely detain him in military custody as an "enemy combatant" without charges, and without access to a lawyer (at least for a very extended period) or a court. This rule still stands in America.

Will the Bush administration and those that follow continue to hold fast to the legal position that the president has the power to arrest American citizens on U.S. soil, relegate them to confinement in military custody, and strip them of virtually all of their constitutional rights? Do we all still potentially face a presidential declaration of "enemy combatant" status that would permit the executive to place any of us in solitary confinement to languish for years before it decides to make its case against us openly, in a court of law?[94]

WHAT DO THE SUPREME COURT'S DECISIONS IN THE HAMDI AND PADILLA CASES REALLY MEAN?

While at first glance the requirements set forth in the *Hamdi* decision seem to provide citizens with protection should they be declared an "enemy combatant," the review procedure established by the Supreme Court actually offers little comfort to those detained on such grounds. The review scheme only applies to those citizens who are caught in a situation of military hostilities in which their role—which side they are fighting for—is in doubt. Also, the neutral tribunal to which "enemy combatants" must be allowed to appeal to challenge their detention need not be a federal court. The Court allowed the government to establish military hearings to decide these cases. Further, the rules governing what evidence would be acceptable in such hearings are much more favorable to the government than are the evidentiary rules for criminal proceedings. For example, hearsay evidence—uncorroborated statements made by people not testifying in court—would be permitted in the military hearings and could be the basis for a citizen's continued detention. Most troubling is Justice O'Connor's statement that the Constitution would permit the government to create a presumption in its favor so that the detainee would be compelled to prove that he is *not* an "enemy combatant." By turning the foundational principle of our criminal justice system on its head, the plurality has built a mountain that few detainees could ever successfully climb.

The Bush administration's "enemy combatant" designation automatically strips citizens of all the most significant constitutional rights incident to citizenship—a power that the Fourteenth Amendment to the Constitution denies to all branches of government.[95] The designation also denies detainees the rights accorded all persons under international law that exist regardless of one's citizenship. Despite the fact that no law whatsoever—save edicts issued by executive fiat under totalitarian regimes—supports the government's position, it has, nevertheless, asserted the right to hold "enemy combatants" like Padilla for the duration of the "war on terror"—a war that the Bush administration has repeatedly stated is not a temporary state of hostilities but rather a permanent new reality. The cases of *Padilla* and *Hamdi* establish terrible and terrifying precedents—even in the wake of the Supreme Court's *Hamdi* decision—that the government may seize and detain any U.S. citizen whom the president decides to place on the country's enemies list. In essence, once you are designated, you are immediately placed in military custody where the government need not ever charge you with a crime nor provide you with a criminal trial. And while the Supreme Court has stated that you will be entitled to some sort of due process hearing, it is not clear when such a hearing must occur or what it will look like. Pursuant to the president's "enemy combatant" power, then, an American citizen can be stripped of all constitutional rights, detained indefinitely, held incommunicado, and subjected to relentless interrogation unchecked by any of the conventional norms of due process. In a very real sense, the designation of "enemy combatant" status itself constitutes a detainee's charge, trial, conviction, and passing of sentence.

How concerned should we be about how these two apparently unique cases have been decided? First, they are not unique. As of early 2005, there has been at least one other American, John Walker Lindh, who has been designated as an "enemy combatant." Padilla's and Hamdi's confinement in indefinite executive detention as "enemy combatants" contrasts greatly with the government's decision to prosecute Lindh, an American citizen who was arrested while fighting for the Taliban government on the battlefield in Afghanistan. Inexplicably, Lindh was prosecuted in the criminal justice system rather than being remanded to indefinite executive detention.[96]

Second, as the differential treatment of these individuals makes clear, the government has established the malleable category of "enemy combatant" status that may be molded so as to include anyone deemed guilty of a range of "offenses" from specific, statutorily defined military offenses, to crimes, to inchoate speculations about an individual's intention to act at some point in the future.[97] In fact, even the small number of designations to date indicates that the definition of "enemy combatant" covers a wide spectrum of activities, from fighting for foreign armies against the United States in Afghanistan to merely contemplating the commission of criminal acts within this country's borders.

Third, the decision to treat individuals such as Hamdi and Lindh so differently, despite the fact that they were apprehended in similar circumstances, indicates the presence not only of wholly unfettered executive discretion but also the almost unimaginably arbitrary exercise of such discretion. What can possibly be the basis for the difference in treatment of these two individuals? We are left to speculate that the government had sufficient evidence to prosecute Lindh criminally and did not have evidence to support a criminal case against Hamdi. The government's refusal to provide Hamdi with any of the protections of the criminal justice system tends to show, then, a nefarious motive.

Fourth, John Ashcroft, then attorney general, made some very disconcerting statements in 2002 regarding his plan to create a military detention camp for U.S. citizens deemed by the administration to be "enemy combatants."[98] Under that plan, the military alone would have the right to make the designation, and internees in this special camp would be treated in the same manner as Padilla and Hamdi. Under another plan, a committee comprising the U.S. attorney general, the secretary of defense, and the director of the CIA would decide which citizens could be interned and subjected to indefinite military detention.[99]

While it is unclear whether the Ashcroft plan remains under consideration, even the mere suggestion of such a group detention facility should cause us deep concern. It indicates that the Bush administration is, or at least was, proposing to keep the "enemy combatant" designation as a permanent legal category, and was considering using this new citizen "enemy combatant" detention program on a larger scale. And because the "war on terror" has no geographic or temporal boundaries, this plan could continue indefinitely and be invoked to seize citizens anywhere in the world, including within the United States.

Most disturbing however, is the fact that the Supreme Court's *Hamdi* decision did not specifically deny the president this power; it merely required the government to put forth some minimal amount of evidence to justify the military detention. In this regard, the Supreme Court's definition of the term "enemy combatant" in the *Hamdi* case becomes absolutely critical for civil rights lawyers seeking to prevent the government's expansion of this power. Justice O'Connor defines the "enemy combatant" category as one comprising people who are "part of or supporting forces hostile to the United States or coalition partners in Afghanistan *and* who engaged in an armed conflict against the United States *there.*"[100] Under this definition, in order to be designated an "enemy combatant," a person must be part of the forces fighting the United States or its partners in Afghanistan and must have also taken up arms against the United States in Afghanistan. The Supreme Court's definition appears to completely exclude people, like Padilla, who have never been accused of taking up arms against the United States in Afghanistan. By extension then, at least in theory, there should be little risk for people who have never engaged in the armed conflict at all. Another important limitation exists: the Supreme Court has authorized "enemy combatant" military detention only for the duration of the particular conflict in which the detainees were captured. This certainly leaves open the possibility that a person may challenge his or her detention on the ground that the conflict has ended.

International humanitarian law makes clear that the Supreme Court's definition of participation in military hostilities as a prerequisite for military detention is entirely appropriate. The Geneva Conventions, along with Additional Protocol I, set forth in detail the rights of people caught up in armed conflict. Combatants who are "members of the armed forces of a Party to a conflict" are lawful military targets, while non-combatants are not.[101] When a civilian takes up arms in the zone of combat, he or she becomes a lawful target of attack, but only insofar and for as long as he or she is taking a "direct part in hostilities."[102] A civilian does not become a "combatant" or a lawful target for attack merely because an opposing commander suspects that the civilian might, at some point in the future, plot to engage in violent acts.[103] Thus, a civilian who supports the enemy's cause off the battlefield, contemplates taking part in the battle in the future, or sympathizes with the enemy's plight may not be considered to be taking a "direct part in hostilities" under the laws of war. He or she could, however, be detained and punished under domestic criminal laws for engaging in those acts, provided that all procedural safeguards are observed.[104] Thus, Jose Padilla, who was never alleged to have been a member of any regular armed force, to have participated directly (or even indirectly) in any battle, or to have played any role in the conflict between the United States and the armed forces of Afghanistan's Taliban government, cannot be considered a combatant of any sort.[105]

The Bush administration's newly created category constituted a radical break with U.S. military practice and a dramatic extension of the laws of war to persons wholly unconnected to any armed conflict. And all of this has been done without reference to any pertinent precedent in U.S. history or a single concession to any limiting principle. An examination of United States practice dating from the Civil War to the present reveals that *only* those persons who were members of conventionally armed forces or who were found to have actively engaged in combat on the battlefield have been deemed "combatants" who could be kept in military custody without trial in civilian courts.[106] During the Civil War, the Supreme Court ruled that a man accused of conspiring to overthrow the United States government could not be detained until the war's end as a prisoner of war or tried by a military commission, because he had not taken part in hostilities against the government.[107] Similarly, during World War I, the government tried members of the German army who had entered the United States as part of an espionage plot in courts-martial[108] but tried the American citizens who conspired with them in civilian court for treason.[109]

The executive policies discussed here and in chapter 2—the use of the material witness statute, minor immigration violations, and the newly created "enemy combatant" designation as grounds for indefinite investigative or preventive detention—all attest to a very haphazard and at the same time extremely broad response to a range of issues engendered by the September 11 attacks. The government's use of the material witness statute in the *Padilla* case led to a judicial decision that established certain parameters but failed to articulate an appropriate standard for judges to use when they are reviewing a challenge to a detention under that statute. Similarly, the Supreme Court's decision in the *Hamdi* case set forth some of the rules governing a challenge to the detention of a person who has been designated an "enemy combatant," but it did not specify what form the process would take; it did not articulate the evidentiary rules that would apply; and it did not declare which entity would be the proper decision maker to rule upon the legality of such a detention.[110]

While the Supreme Court's response indicates that the exercise of these executive powers should be restrained and that our civil liberties should be better protected, it seems all too likely that another terrorist attack would engender an even more extreme reaction from this administration. It is incumbent upon us to engage in a thoughtful effort to address the problems identified now, before that happens.

The Bush administration's "enemy combatant" policy is eroding the foundations of democracy in this country. In creating this policy, the executive branch disregarded the Non-Detention Act, an act of Congress passed in 1971 for the express purpose of preventing the president from arresting and detaining Americans in the manner that had been undertaken during World War II.[111] Much more concerning, it also undermines the right to habeas corpus—the right to test the legality of one's detention in court—which is a constitutional guarantee that only Congress has the right to suspend in cases of extreme necessity. This understanding of the writ as a vehicle to ensure due process informed the Framers when they crafted the Constitution and Bill of Rights.[112] The Framers believed that the writ of habeas corpus would provide "greater securities to liberty" than other provisions of the Constitution, because "the practice of arbitrary imprisonments [has] been, in all ages, [one of] the favorite and most formidable instruments of tyranny."[113]

The Framers determined that *only Congress* could suspend the right to judicial review of executive detention,[114] and even then only "when in Cases of Rebellion or Invasion the public safety may require it."[115] By granting this power to Congress, as opposed to the president, the Framers ensured that no branch of government had the unilateral power to deprive a person of liberty. Moreover, by vesting this authority in Article I, the Framers ensured that this important decision would be made by the more representative and deliberative branch of government. Indeed, the Framers specifically contemplated circumstances where grave national emergencies might justify the temporary abridgement of individual liberties.[116] In light of their experience with executive abuses, however, they deemed the legislature to be the branch best entrusted with the power to suspend the writ of habeas corpus.[117]

In the famous case *Youngstown Sheet & Tube Co. v. Sawyer*, which involved a challenge to President Truman's attempt to seize the nation's steel mills during the Korean War, the Supreme Court made clear that the separation of powers between the president and Congress is clearly demarcated in the Constitution: "In the framework of our Constitution, the President's power to see that the laws are faithfully executed refutes the idea that his is to be a lawmaker. The Constitution limits his functions in the lawmaking process to the recommending of laws he thinks wise and the vetoing of laws he thinks bad. And the Constitution is neither silent nor equivocal about who shall make the laws which the President is to execute."[118] The Constitution states that only Congress has the authority to make the law.[119] The executive, by contrast, "shall take care that [those] Laws be faithfully executed."[120] Furthermore, the principle that Congress cannot delegate legislative power to the president is universally recognized as vital to the integrity and maintenance of the checks and balances system ordained by the Constitution.[121] Even when national security is invoked, "[c]onvenience and political considerations of the moment do not justify a departure from the principles of our system of government."[122]

For this reason, the Authorization of the Use of Military Force in Afghanistan (AUMF) passed by Congress on September 18, 2001, does nothing to change that result.[123] That legislation does not authorize the capture and detention of civilians, either in the United States, or from allied nations thousands of miles from the battlefield, particularly when the allegations have nothing whatsoever to do with the terrorist attacks of September 11. The AUMF specifically authorized President Bush to use force against: "Nations, organizations, or persons . . . [that] *planned, authorized, committed or aided the terrorist attacks on September 11, 2001,* or [that] harbored such organizations or persons in order to prevent any future acts of international terrorism against the United States by such nations, organizations, or persons."[124] The Supreme Court has made clear that the language of the AUMF limits the executive's authority to use force against only those individuals with a connection to the terrorist attacks of September 11.[125]

While the president, acting in his role as commander in chief, may invoke laws to "exercise the authority conferred upon him by Congress"[126] and "direct the performance of those functions which may constitutionally be performed by the military arm of the nation in a time of war,"[127] he cannot do what he is doing now: invent a vaguely defined category of individuals who may be plucked from their homes and businesses anywhere on earth, and detained, without charge, indefinitely. Nor can the executive branch, long after it has arrested and detained individuals deemed to fall within this category, invent for itself a status determination procedure in order to validate its decision that the detainees have been properly placed within its specially created category. By doing so, the executive has unlawfully usurped Congress's constitutionally delegated lawmaking function[128] and violated these detainees' due process rights.

The president's ability to transform his power to conduct military operations abroad into expansive authority to usurp congressional and judicial authority over domestic affairs is constrained for another reason as well. The executive cannot extend his war power to intrude upon internal affairs. The Constitution and the Supreme Court have long recognized the distinction between internal and external governmental affairs as a critical factor in assessing the scope of power of a given branch of government, particularly the president's war power.[129] As Justice Jackson of the Supreme Court declared in the *Youngstown* case, "no doctrine that the Court could promulgate would seem to me more sinister and alarming than a doctrine in which a president—whose conduct of foreign affairs is so largely uncontrolled, and often even is unknown—can vastly enlarge his mastery over the internal affairs of the country by his own commitment of the nation's armed force to some foreign venture."[130] The president's military powers were never intended to supersede representative government of internal affairs, a proposition that Justice Jackson found obvious from the Constitution and from elementary American history.[131]

From the founding of this country, the idea of military control over civilian society has been an anathema to our constitutional system. Indeed, one of the chief complaints of the colonists against the British throne was, as stated in the Declaration of Independence, that King George III had "affected to render the Military independent of and superior to the Civil power."[132] As the structure of the Constitution makes clear, one of our core concepts is that of civilian control over the military: Congress regulates the military and declares war; and the president, a civilian, is the commander in chief of the military. Addressing this issue, the Supreme Court has stated: "The established principle of every free people is, that the law shall alone govern; and to it the military must always yield."[133]

Plainly, the military seizure and imprisonment of American citizens like Jose Padilla violates the basic premise of civilian supremacy prohibiting military control over civilians. Padilla, a citizen who is not a member of the military, cannot constitutionally have military law applied to him under the present circumstances. No military authority exists to confine him.[134] Yet, on the president's order he was kept imprisoned in a naval brig in South Carolina for more than three years.

In a frontal attack on another branch of government, the judiciary, the Bush administration has contended throughout the proceedings in these American "enemy combatant" cases that because we are "at war," the courts have no role to play in reviewing any of the executive branch's actions. The Bush administration's attempt to wrestle power from the executive's co-equal branches of government, along with its deliberate erosion of the line between civilian and military authority plainly places at risk all of the principles embodied in our constitutional system.

CHAPTER FOUR

Guantánamo: The Legal Black Hole

Conformity with international human rights and humanitarian law is not a weakness in the fight against terrorism but a weapon, ensuring the widest international support for actions and avoiding situations which could provoke misplaced sympathy for terrorists or their causes. . . . [T]he Assembly considers that the U.S. Government has betrayed its own highest principles in the zeal with which it has attempted to pursue the "war on terror." These errors have perhaps been the most manifest in relation to Guantánamo Bay.

—Parliamentary Assembly of the Council of Europe, April 26, 2005

THE FIRST DETAINEES ARRIVE AT GUANTÁNAMO

On January 11, 2002, the first 110 men and boys were flown, blind-folded and shackled to the floor of cargo planes, to the U.S. Naval Base in Guantánamo Bay, Cuba (Guantánamo), and locked in a makeshift set of small wire cages called Camp X-Ray.[1] These "cells" had no running water, toilet, beds, protective covering or clothing. Detainees were provided only a thin mat.[2] The mesh cages were like those used in dog kennels with open, chain-link fencing on all four sides, a top secured by spirals of razor wire, and a concrete slab as the floor, leaving detainees little protection from the elements or the scorpions and rats that came to visit them at night.[3] These hastily constructed cells were used for months while more permanent facilities were being built to house those seized from countries all over the world in the "war on terror."[4]

The Guantánamo facility is a forty-five square-mile base enclosed by seventeen and one-half miles of fencing and surrounded by soon-to-be stadium-bright lights. A relic of another era, when a Cuban invasion on the facility was thought to be a possibility, the facility was also originally surrounded by an extensive minefield. The U.S. side of the base was demined in 1999 on the orders of President Bill Clinton, but the Cuban side still contains numerous landmines. According to Navy Captain Mark Leary, the fence and bright lights—and presumably also the landmines—are now intended "to prevent incursions by outsiders . . . such as some Christian activists who wanted to stage a human-rights protest at the base."[5]

Shortly after the first detainees were transported to the base, the Bush administration announced its position that the U.S. facilities at Guantánamo were beyond the reach of American law and the laws of war. According to the White House lawyers advising the president—including, most prominently, then White House counsel Alberto Gonzales—if the men captured were designated "enemy combatants" rather than prisoners of war, they would not be covered by the Geneva Conventions. Wholly unprepared for the rapid influx of detainees and without policies and procedures in place for how to treat them, the military personnel at Guantánamo were given tremendous leeway to improvise and change the rules governing detention.

Denied not only all constitutional protections, but all international law protections as well, the men detained at Guantánamo were immediately subjected to interrogation under extreme conditions that included physical and psychological torture and abuse. How and why were these individuals stripped of their dignity and human rights? From the Bush administration's perspective, the calculus was quite simple: they had been deemed "enemy combatants." The administration designated *all* people seized during the war in Afghanistan as "enemy combatants." The treatment that could be meted out to an "enemy combatant" was literally without boundary. The designation carries with it a prescribed set of confinement conditions that deprive so-called "enemy combatants" of all of their human rights. In the detainees' reality, the designation was—and is—not merely a "combatant status category," it is an accusation, a trial, a conviction, the determination of a sentence, and the imposition of a punishment all rolled into one.

WHO IS REALLY IMPRISONED IN THE CELLS OF GUANTÁNAMO?

Military commanders have now openly conceded[6] that there was a very imprecise screening of the men and boys captured in Afghanistan; and that as a result they "just didn't get the right folks" and wound up with many detainees who neither posed any threat to the U.S. nor possessed any significant information about Al Qaeda or the Taliban.[7] It is now clear that the vast majority of the men held at Guantánamo have no connection to terrorism. Brigadier General Martin Lucenti was quoted in the *Financial Times* as stating "[o]f the 550 [detainees] that we have, I would say most of them, the majority of them, will either be released or transferred to their own countries. . . . Most of these guys weren't fighting. They were running."[8] While the government has sought to retreat from General Lucenti's admission, his comments are consistent with many of the statements made by Defense Department officials.[9] An active duty intelligence officer at Guantánamo was also recently quoted as agreeing that "the United States is holding dozens of prisoners at the U.S. Navy Base at Guantánamo who have no meaningful connection to al-Qaida or the Taliban and is denying them access to legal representation. . . . There are a large number of people at Guantánamo who shouldn't be there."[10]

Nevertheless, to this day—more than five years after Camp X-Ray was opened—the detention camps and the inmates confined in them remain enshrouded in a cloak of secrecy. The expanded prison facilities at Guantánamo can now hold more than seven hundred detainees—the peak number it has held to date.[11] During the period from January 2002 until January 2006, an unknown number of inmates were released or transferred into detention in their home countries while others replaced them at Guantánamo,[12] with the last new detainees arriving in the fall of 2004. The government has never publicly acknowledged the identities of all of the Guantánamo detainees. In fact, it was not until May 2006 that any list of the detainees' names and their countries of origin was disclosed. Even then, the government only released the information because it was compelled to do so by the Court as part of a Freedom of Information Act lawsuit brought by the Associated Press. There is no indication of whether the May 2006 list of 759 people contains the names of everyone who has ever been detained at Guantánamo, and there can be no definitive statement of who remains at the facility without a list detailing who has been released or transferred. At the time of this writing, efforts to identify every detainee held in Guantánamo continue.

The lack of concern for the families of people seized and sent to Guantánamo is evinced by the Bush administration's apparent failure to keep accurate and complete records. During argument in federal court for the case of Falen Gherebi, a Libyan national held at Guantánamo, Justice Department lawyers stated that the administration had kept neither an exact count nor a complete listing of the names of the many hundreds of people detained at the naval base.[13] Perhaps this is the reason that no list of current Guantánamo detainees has ever been released?

While some information can be gleaned from the government's reluctant production of information in the detainees' habeas proceedings and other Freedom of Information Act lawsuits, additional facts have recently come to light through the statements of released detainees, the public testimony of detainees' family members, and the statements of consular officials who have had limited contact with the detainees.[14] The account of the seizures and treatment of two detainees whose family members brought the lawsuit *Rasul v. Bush*[15]—the challenge to the Bush administration's decision to hold detainees indefinitely without charge, trial, or access to a court—illustrates the plight of at least some of the people sent to Guantánamo. These two men and a third friend were named the "Tipton Three" by the British media, and their stories were brought to popular attention in the U.S. by the release of a docudrama film entitled "The Road to Guantánamo."

Asif Iqbal traveled to Pakistan from his home in the small town of Tipton, Britain after September 11, intending to marry a woman from his father's small village there. Two of Iqbal's friends, Shafiq Rasul and Rhuhel Ahmed, also traveled to Pakistan to visit their relatives, explore their families' cultural background, and attend Iqbal's wedding. Rasul also wanted to continue his computer studies. Shortly before his marriage, Iqbal's father allowed him to leave the village briefly and he and his friends crossed into Afghanistan. They were ultimately detained by the Northern Alliance and turned over to United States military forces in December 2001.

In 2002, the men were transported to Guantánamo. Nearly two years later, in March 2004, Iqbal, Rasul, and Ahmed were released from prison and sent home to Britain. They had consistently and vehemently denied any involvement in any terrorist activity for nearly all of the long period they had been detained. Ultimately, however, under extreme duress caused by hundreds of hours of interrogation, long periods of isolation, and physical and psychological abuse, the men falsely confessed to having been in a terrorist training camp in Afghanistan, and to appearing in a videotape with Osama bin Laden made in August 2000. Rasul explained that he had been held in complete isolation for two long periods—many months—when an interrogator showed him the video of bin Laden, and he agreed that he was one of the people in it. "I could not bear another day of isolation, let alone the prospect of another year," he said.[16]

The British intelligence agency MI5 undertook an investigation to determine the veracity of the men's Guantánamo confessions. It took the agency less than twenty-four hours to determine definitively that "the men had been in England when the video was shot and during the time they were supposed to have been in Al Qaeda training camps."[17] The three men maintain today that they never had any involvement in terrorist activities and that they are innocent of any wrongdoing. The United States has never presented any valid evidence to the contrary.

GUANTÁNAMO: NOT ONLY FOR BATTLEFIELD DETAINEES

We now know that the population imprisoned at Guantánamo is far more diverse than the Bush administration's portrayal in the media and before the courts. The men incarcerated at Guantánamo were arrested in a wide variety of contexts, and had the U.S. government complied with the law, both international and domestic law would have dictated how they were to be treated. For example, under international humanitarian law, individuals fighting for the Taliban government who were captured on or near the battlefield would likely have been accorded POW status, even if only temporarily until an impartial tribunal could be convened expeditiously to determine their proper status.[18] Persons fighting for Al Qaeda, on the other hand, would have been treated as criminals or war criminals, and likely transferred to the United States through the extradition process and then tried in our criminal courts. Civilians unlawfully participating in the military hostilities on behalf of the Taliban would also have been subject to prosecution for their unlawful actions. And civilians, like the "Tipton Three," who played no role in the military hostilities at all, but were swept up in the fog of war, would have been released.

Although these different statuses encountered in the battlefield zone—prisoner of war, criminal, war criminal, and innocent civilian—would seem to cover the universe of individuals who have been sent to Guantánamo by the U.S. government, they do not. Among those seized and sent there were children—juvenile detainees—who, depending on their age, were housed either in a separate prison called Camp Iguana or with adult detainees. Although the three youngest detainees, aged seven to eleven, were sent home within a few months of their arrival at Guantánamo, at least eight others, age thirteen to fifteen, were held for far longer. According to Amnesty International, thirteen-year-old Mohammed Ismail Agha was seized in Afghanistan in late 2002 and held for more than a year without charge or trial, first at the U.S. Air Force's Bagram Air Base in Afghanistan, and later at Guantánamo. During his imprisonment at Guantánamo, Mohammed was held in solitary confinement and was subjected to sleep deprivation techniques—intended to aid interrogations—in the same manner as the adult detainees.[19] "Seventeen-year-old Akhtar Mohammed told Amnesty [International] that he was kept in solitary confinement in a shipping container for eight days in Afghanistan in January 2002."[20] Children's statements regarding the torture they suffered while in U.S. custody, collected by Amnesty International and other human rights groups, have been corroborated by accounts given by soldiers who either witnessed or participated in the abuse.

Although international law draws the line between childhood and maturity at eighteen, the U.S. Defense Department has apparently set its own standard at sixteen years of age. Because of this disparity, we will likely never know how many children were being held—or are now being held—in American custody in "war on terror" detention centers in Iraq, Afghanistan, and other unknown places around the world. According to the *New York Times*, a memo sent to Defense Secretary Donald Rumsfeld shortly after the 2001 invasion of Afghanistan, recently uncovered by the journalist Seymour Hersh, stated that there were "800–900 Pakistani boys 13–15 years of age in custody" at that time.[21] "A Pentagon spokesman told Hersh that juveniles received some special care, but added, 'Age is not a determining factor in detention.'"[22] The ICRC reported registering more than one hundred juvenile detainees under eighteen years of age during visits to coalition prisons in 2001, with some of the children as young as eight years old.[23]

There seems little doubt that while there may have been children who picked up a gun during the conflict in Afghanistan, there were likely many more who were merely swept up with their families in dragnets precipitated by unreliable tips. How have these children dealt with their seizure and transport to an island prison for indefinite detention and interrogation, so far from home and so far away from their parents? We don't know, and we will likely never know what has happened to them because of the government's refusal to provide complete identifying information for its "war on terror" detainees. Without information about released detainees, no one will be able to find out what happened to these children. Isn't this our responsibility—not only to find them but to offer assistance and compensation where appropriate?

How has the rest of the world viewed our treatment of this group of "enemy combatants"? Even our allies in the "war on terror" have expressed their outrage at our actions. The nations of the world are "virtually unanimous" in their adherence to the principle that children deserve special protection.[24] The most widely ratified human rights treaty to date, the Convention on the Rights of the Child (CRC) adopted by the United Nations in 1989,[25] defines "child," for the purposes of its protection, to mean "every human being below the age of 18 years."[26] International standards recognize that children under the age of eighteen are a particularly vulnerable group and are entitled to special care and protection because they are still developing physically, mentally, and emotionally. Key principles incorporated in these standards include using detention solely as a measure of last resort, ensuring the rights of children to maintain contact with their families, and guaranteeing the right to a prompt determination of their case.

According to a report by Human Rights Watch, a spokesperson for the U.S. military confirmed that the children detained as "enemy combatants" at Guantánamo "are being interrogated because they have potential to provide important information."[27] But the possibility that they might provide information cannot justify the continued detention of these children. If the children were to be questioned, this should have been done promptly upon arrest in their home country. If the U.S. government believed that the children detained at Guantánamo committed specific offenses, then it should have provided them with counsel and ensured that their cases were adjudicated in a court with the proper authority to apply to established juvenile justice standards. If the children were not going to be charged with any offense, then they should immediately have been returned to the custody of their parents or guardians.

According to experts, the conditions at Guantánamo likely posed serious risks for the children confined there. These include "long periods of time in virtual isolation due to their small numbers"; no access to their families and severely restricted access to their legal counsel; "interrogation without the benefit of family members or legal counsel; the lack of staff trained in the rights and special needs of children; and indefinite detention with no clear information regarding the timing of their release."[28] These conditions are all especially detrimental to the well-being of children and violate international standards regarding the child's right to maintain contact with his or her family through correspondence and visits while deprived of his or her liberty. International standards also mandate that a child's case be resolved expeditiously and without unnecessary delay. The imperative for timely action on a child's case is even more pronounced when the child is detained, isolated from his or her family and community, and denied appropriate educational and recreational programs.[29]

Despite worldwide consensus on these principles, the U.S. government did not, and has not, provided the juvenile detainees with access to their families or with proper psychological treatment or educational programs. Worse yet, the government has done everything in its power to prevent the lawyers for the juvenile detainees from moving their cases anywhere near a court for resolution.[30] The government's recent decision to charge and prosecute one juvenile detainee, who is now nineteen after nearly four years in confinement, is the most disconcerting. Despite the Canadian government's repeated request that the U.S. formally agree to take the death penalty off the table for the young Canadian detained in Guantánamo who now faces trial by a military commission, the government has refused to do so, stating only that it does not "intend" to seek the death penalty at this time.[31] Both U.S. law under the March 2005 Supreme Court ruling in the case *Roper v. Simmons*[32] and international law under the International Convention for Civil and Political Rights prohibit the death penalty for crimes committed when the offender was a juvenile under age eighteen.[33] Given the law on the books, by what right does the Bush administration reserve the power to even *consider* this sentence for a juvenile offender?

In addition to the unlikely population of children at Guantánamo, there are those who found themselves detained there despite *not having been anywhere near the part of the world in which the United States was fighting*. Among detainees still held in Guantánamo are Jamil El-Banna and Bisher Al-Rawi, two permanent residents of the United Kingdom (UK) who were arrested in the African nation The Gambia[34] and then sent, by way of Afghanistan, to the U.S. naval base in Cuba.

Jamil El-Banna was born in Palestine and is a Jordanian national. He arrived in the United Kingdom in 1994 and was given indefinite permission to remain in the country as a refugee. Jamil's five young children are all UK nationals and are being raised by their mother there. Bisher Al-Rawi was born in Iraq and immigrated to the UK with his family in 1983. All of his relatives living in the country are also UK nationals.

Jamil El-Banna and Bisher Al-Rawi, along with Bisher's brother, Wahab Al-Rawi, and a friend, Abdullah El-Janoudi, had been planning for some time to start a peanut oil manufacturing plant in The Gambia. Wahab Al-Rawi had traveled to The Gambia ahead of his three partners in order to secure the necessary business permits for the plant.

On November 2, 2002, El-Banna, El-Janoudi, and Bisher Al-Rawi were arrested at London's Gatwick Airport as they were about to board their flight to The Gambia. According the UK authorities, the three men were detained and questioned for two days about their alleged involvement with international terrorism because a suspect device—a modified battery charger—was found in Bisher Al-Rawi's luggage. Unbeknownst to the men, a telegram containing false information was sent that day by MI5 to the CIA, stating that the men had been arrested under the anti-terrorism act, that Bisher Al-Rawi was an Islamist extremist,[35] and that his luggage contained an improvised electronic device which could be used as a component of a home-made bomb.[36] Upon investigation, the police determined that the device was only a battery charger, and released the three men without charge and told them that they were free to travel to Africa.[37] However, the CIA apparently was not informed of this determination; the "allegations concerning this 'device' reappeared in [the men's] 'trial' before the CSRT (Combatant Status Review Tribunal) as 'evidence' that they were 'enemy combatants.'"[38]

On November 8, the three men flew to The Gambia to set up their peanut processing business. Upon arrival, however, the three men, along with Wahab Al-Rawi who had come to the airport to meet them, were arrested by the Gambian National Intelligence Agency (GNIA) and taken to GNIA headquarters in Banjul. The four men were questioned by GNIA agents regarding the purpose of their visit. They explained their business venture and that the project had received approval from the Gambian government and had been properly registered with the Gambian authorities.[39] Not long after this first interrogation session, U.S. agents took over the questioning and the men were moved to several different undisclosed prison locations in the area.[40] The interrogations involved threats of beatings and rape and the use of "stress and duress" techniques later to become a familiar part of the interrogation regime at Guantánamo. According to Amnesty International, "[o]ne of the men was reportedly threatened by U.S. agents and told that unless he co-operated he would be handed over to Gambian police who would beat and rape him."[41]

On December 5, 2002, after being detained and interrogated for nearly a month, El-Janoudi and Wahab Al-Rawi were released without charge and permitted to return to the UK. However, El-Banna and Bisher Al-Rawi remained in Gambian detention.[42] They were held incommunicado for over a month in Banjul and were relentlessly questioned by U.S. agents about their alleged links with Al Qaeda.[43]

In early 2003, British counsel for the two men were advised that they had been secretly transferred from The Gambia to Afghanistan, first to the "Dark Prison" in Kabul, and then two weeks later to the U.S. forces-controlled Bagram Air Base, where they were held for an additional two months. From Bagram, they were flown to Guantánamo.

The treatment the men suffered during the flight to Kabul echoes that suffered by other victims of the CIA extraordinary rendition program: "[t]hey were dressed in diapers, wore hoods without eye-holes, had their ears blocked up, their legs shackled and their hands painfully handcuffed behind their backs, and were denied access to toilets."[44] The transfer took place before the men were allowed to speak with a lawyer, before a court could undertake an independent review of any evidence against them, and despite the fact that a habeas corpus petition on their behalf had already been filed by human rights lawyers and was pending in the High Court in The Gambia.[45] The conditions in the "Dark Prison" were also shockingly inhumane: there was no light, no means to wash nor any toilet, the cells were unbearably cold and the prisoners were given inadequate clothing, the food was rotten, and the men were frequently beaten.[46]

When they arrived in Guantánamo, El-Banna and Al-Rawi were allowed to write a letter to their respective families, which the International Committee of the Red Cross delivered. When their families learned that they were in custody, they contacted attorneys. Apart from this sporadic, censored mail from their families and the visits of their attorney, the detainees have absolutely no contact with the outside world. Yet, neither of these men has been charged with any criminal offense or any violation of the laws of war.

They have not appeared before any proper military or civilian tribunal. Not only have they *not* been informed of their rights under domestic or international law, the government contends they *need not* be so informed.

Neither of the two men had ever been to Afghanistan or Pakistan before their arrest. Neither had ever taken part in any military action against the United States. Nevertheless, as of this writing, they have remained imprisoned at Guantánamo since January 2003.

Disturbingly, the circumstances of Jamil El-Banna and Bisher Al-Rawi are not uncommon among the Guantánamo detainees. Another Guantánamo habeas case involves the detention of Algerian-born Bosnian citizens who were arrested in Bosnia. Lakhdar Boumedienne and Mohammed Nechla were taken into custody in the fall of 2001 by Bosnian-Herzegovinian authorities, on order of the Bosnia-Herzegovina Federation Supreme Court in connection with the U.S. government's assertions that they were planning to target the UK and U.S. embassies in Bosnia-Herzegovina.[47] At the time of their arrest, these men were more than two thousand miles from any battlefield in Afghanistan, and none of them had been involved in the United States' military efforts there or in any activities related to planning or carrying out the September 11 attacks.[48]

The Bosnian authorities held the two men, along with four other people who had been taken into custody in connection with the same allegations, for three months while they investigated the allegations made by the United States. On January 17, 2002, at the conclusion of that investigation, the Supreme Court of the Federation of Bosnia-Herzegovina, on the recommendation of the Bosnian federal prosecutor, ordered the release of all six men.[49] Despite the Federation's Supreme Court Order, immediately upon their release in the early morning hours of January 18, 2002, the detainees, at the urging of the U.S. government, were taken into custody by the Bosnia-Herzegovina Federation and then handed over to the United States.[50] They were then transported to Guantánamo.

In September 2002, the Bosnia-Herzegovina Human Rights Chamber Court heard the applications of three of the detainees alleging that, by allowing U.S. forces to abduct them, Bosnia-Herzegovina had violated the

European Convention on Human Rights. Specifically, they alleged that the handover to the U.S. government violated Articles 1 (safeguards regarding the expulsion of aliens); 3 (prohibiting expulsion of nationals); 5 (the right to liberty and security); and that delivery into U.S. custody created the potential for violations of Article 2 (use of the death penalty); 3 (prohibiting torture); and 6 (right to a fair trial).[51] The Human Rights Chamber Court found, among other things, that Bosnia-Herzegovina and the Federation of Bosnia-Herzegovina had violated Article 1 and Protocols 6 and 7 to the European Convention on Human Rights.[52] Despite these rulings, the men have been held in Guantánamo for nearly four years. No charges have been brought against them.

In addition to these "enemy combatants" seized far from any battlefield, there is yet another group of people whose one-way trip to Guantánamo did not originate with any role in the armed conflict between the United States and Afghanistan: bounty victims. According to media reports, Afghani intelligence officers began offering financial rewards the day after they participated in a five-hour meeting with U.S. Special Forces.[53] That day, loudspeaker announcements were made from buildings and helicopters traveling all across the Afghan mountains promising "the big prize" to people who turned in Al Qaeda fighters to the military.[54] Leaflets were distributed with such statements as:

> You can receive millions of dollars. . . . This is enough to take care of your family, your village, your tribe for the rest of your life—pay for livestock and doctors and school books and housing for all your people.

Bounty rewards were also publicized by radio spots and the circulation of posters and matchbooks in remote villages in Pakistan and Indonesia.

In the end, it appears that "[m]ost Guantánamo detainees were rounded up by the Northern Alliance, Afghani warlords or Pakistanis and turned in for generous U.S. bounties. . . ."[55] Former CIA intelligence officer Gary Schroen stated that he personally traveled to Afghanistan with a suitcase filled with $3 million in cash to pay warlords like General Rashid Dostum for their assistance to U.S. forces. Schroen has said "[i]t may be that we were giving rewards to people like Dostum because his guys were capturing a lot of Taliban and Al Qaida."[56] Documents provided to the Associated Press by the U.S. government reveal testimony from dozens of detainees about bounties ranging from $3,000 to $25,000. These sums were paid by tribal leaders to Pakistani and Afghani tribesmen, who then turned the men in to the American military.[57] Nasser al-Mutairi—a Kuwaiti detainee released from Guantánamo—said that General Dostum's forces sold him and other Kuwaitis for $5,000 each to Pakistani authorities, who then sold them to the Americans.[58] Uighurs (ethnic Chinese Muslims) detained at Guantánamo also have stated they were sold by a tribal group for $5,000 each.[59]

The State Department has since confirmed the existence of the "U.S. Rewards for Justice" program, which it states has paid out more than $60 million for information leading to the capture of suspected terrorists.[60] While acknowledging that money cannot buy off people who are driven by ideology, the U.S. continues to offer high bounties for key figures, such as the $10 million bounty for Taliban leader Mullah Mohammad Omar, a suspect in the 2002 Bali bombing.

The arrests of individuals from all over the world, who were nowhere near the battlefield in Afghanistan, illuminate a fully implemented new policy of the Bush administration. *The executive branch now claims the unfettered right to seize and indefinitely detain without charge or trial any individual it deems to be of risk to the United States, regardless of whether the person seized was directly involved in any military hostilities against the United States.* The government claims that these people—deemed "enemy combatants," no matter where they are arrested or what they were doing at the time of their arrest—are not entitled to the protections of the Geneva Conventions. According to the Bush administration, an "enemy combatant" can be held until the executive branch determines either that he has no further intelligence value or the global "war on terror" ends. Yet at the same time, government officials have publicly acknowledged that at least some of the detainees at Guantánamo were victims of circumstance and are probably innocent.[61]

THE CONDITIONS AT THE GUANTÁNAMO DETENTION CAMPS

In February 2002, at a time when no other human rights organization was willing to directly challenge the government's actions, the Center for Constitutional Rights (CCR) filed habeas corpus petitions on behalf of four individuals detained at Guantánamo, seeking a hearing in federal court to test the basis for their detention. Despite multiple adverse rulings in the lower federal courts, in April 2004, CCR prevailed in bringing the Guantánamo detainees' case *Rasul v. Bush* before the U.S. Supreme Court. The *Rasul* case became the first major test of whether the executive branch had exceeded its powers in the "war on terror" by asserting that Guantánamo was outside the jurisdiction of any court and beyond the reach of any law. In a momentous six-to-three decision issued on June 28, 2004, the justices found that the Guantánamo detainees *do* have the right to contest the basis for their detention in U.S. courts.

Within a day after the July 2004 Supreme Court decision in *Rasul*, counsel for the detainees at the Center for Constitutional Rights were overwhelmed by calls and e-mails from lawyers and law firms across the country offering to volunteer their time to assist in the representation of the Guantánamo detainees. Regardless of their political stripes, they were appalled at the Bush administration's repudiation of the rule of law. Conversations between Republicans and Democrats, conservatives and liberals, all revealed a deep and serious concern about the direction the administration was taking our country. How could a sitting president argue that he had completely unfettered control over other human beings? How could a presidential administration proclaim that it had created a court to which no law applied? Attorneys from eleven law firms decided to jump into the representation on a moment's notice and filed habeas petitions on behalf of fifty-three detainees. The lawyers for this initial wave of cases first opened the doors of Guantánamo to reveal it to the world.

Although the government has consistently endeavored to limit counsel visits and has "allowed [only] tightly controlled media visits"[62] at Guantánamo, we have been able to learn a number of things about the daily operations at the naval base since the first "enemy combatants" were transferred there for detention. As of 2003, the majority of the inmates were held in three camps described by the government as maximum-security facilities. Modeled after our supermaximum security prisons used for the confinement of ostensibly uncontrollable inmates, conditions at Camp Delta are, by all accounts, far harsher. At the beginning of the detention process, the facility was designed so that: "[e]ach prisoner [would] live in a separate cell that is 6 feet 8 inches by 8 feet. The doors and walls are made of a tight mesh. . . . Unless rewarded for good behavior, each prisoner [would be] allowed out of the cell only three times a week for 20 minutes of solitary exercise in a concrete-floored cage, followed by a 5-minute shower."[63] For many detainees, the "[l]ights are kept on 24 hours a day, and guards pace the rows constantly. Inside each cell, detainees have a hole-in-the-ground toilet, a sink with running water low enough to make washing feet for prayers easy, and an elevated shelf-bunk with a mattress."[64]

THE TORTURE AND ABUSE OF THE GUANTÁNAMO DETAINEES

The treatment detainees endure during interrogations is horrendous and constitutes torture under international law. Asif Iqbal and Shafiq Rasul, two of the three British citizens from Tipton discussed previously, report that during some of the interrogations detainees are "short-shackled"—meaning that their hands and feet are shackled together in a manner that forces them to stand crouched over—from seven to forty-eight hours at a time.

Their accounts include descriptions of a variety of other serious physical and psychological assaults. The treatment Iqbal and Rasul received at the hands of their American captors and their surrogates was not an aberration. Information from a range of sources, including over one hundred thousand government documents produced to the Center for Constitutional Rights and other organizations through their Freedom of Information Act lawsuit,[65] shows a systematic pattern of torture and abuse of people seized and held in U.S. custody in the "war on terror." The evidence comes from the detainees themselves (as told to their lawyers); FBI and other government agency documents (from the Freedom of Information Act lawsuit); physicians who examined the medical records of the detainees; and military personnel who made the decision to tell the world about this shocking abuse.[66]

Under U.S. policy, Guantánamo detainees have been beaten; subjected to religious insults (including being forced to watch pages ripped out of the Qur'an or the Qur'an itself thrown into a detainees' toilet buckets); intimidated by dogs; stripped naked, hooded, and blindfolded; exposed to extreme heat and cold; denied basic necessities, such as blankets, clothing, or soap; routinely "short-shackled" or chained in a "hog-tie" position or otherwise forced into painful stress positions for hours and even days during interrogations; sprayed with pepper spray; stripped; forcibly shaved of their hair and beards; given forcible body cavity searches; threatened with rendition to third countries where they would be subjected to torture; denied the use of toilet facilities during interrogations in order to force them to soil themselves; subjected to loud music for lengthy periods; denied rest or sleep; deprived of food or water; subjected to total isolation and sensory deprivation for prolonged periods; threatened with death or with the torture or death of their families and relatives; sexually humiliated (for instance by the parading of partially unclothed women in front of more devout prisoners); raped or threatened with rape; subjected to mock drowning; and deprived of medical treatment for serious conditions, or allowed treatment only on the condition that they "cooperate" with interrogators.[67]

In their own words, Iqbal and Rasul describe the interrogation practices they suffered as follows:

> Our interrogations in Guantánamo . . . were conducted with us chained to the floor for hours on end in circumstances so prolonged that it was the practice to have plastic chairs . . . that could be easily hosed off because prisoners would be forced to urinate during the course of them and were not allowed to go to the toilet. . . . One practice . . . was "short shackling" where we were forced to squat without a chair with our hands chained between our legs and chained to the floor. If we fell over, the chains would cut into our hands. We

would be left in this position for hours before an interrogation, during the interrogations (which could last as long as 12 hours), and sometimes for hours while the interrogators left the room. The air conditioning was turned up so high that within minutes we would be freezing. There was strobe lighting and loud music played that was itself a form of torture. Sometimes dogs were brought in to frighten us. . . . Sometimes detainees would be taken to the interrogation room day after day and kept short-shackled without interrogation ever happening, sometimes for weeks on end.[68]

Interrogators at Guantánamo keep detainees in isolation units so the only human contact they have is with their interrogators. In solitary confinement, detainees are deliberately exposed to extreme temperatures. The metal cells have little air circulation and become very hot during the day. At night, the cells are extremely cold and the air-conditioning is turned on to lower the temperature even further. Interrogators repeatedly pressure detainees to confess to having an association with Al Qaeda. How many detainees, like the "Tipton Three," may have given false confessions out of a desperate attempt to end the torture of the interrogations?

The experience of a detainee named Al Dossari further details how mistreatment and torture techniques have been used at Guantánamo. On one occasion, while in the interrogation room, an MP trained a rifle directly on Al Dossari at close range, despite the fact that Al Dossari was shackled to the floor. On another occasion, an interrogator in civilian clothing threatened to send Al Dossari to a prison with murderers, where he said Al Dossari would be raped. During another interrogation, a woman banged Al Dossari's head on a table, and a chain wrapped around his waist was tightened until it caused him to vomit.[69]

Another detainee, Al Murbati, described the following experience to his attorney:

Within a few days of arriving at Guantánamo, two older interrogators dressed in civilian clothing showed [him] a document. The interrogators told [him] that the document was a transcription of an audiotape made of a high-ranking Al Qaeda member from Kuwait that described potential targets. The interrogators asked [him] where the next attack would occur. When [he] was unable to respond he was put in solitary confinement and threatened with a transfer to Egypt where, he was told, he would be tortured.

Typically, [his] interrogations in Camp Delta were conducted from approximately 6 a.m. until 4 p.m., or from 10 p.m. until 4 a.m. For the entirety of most of the sessions, he was made to sit on the floor with his ankles shackled to the floor and with his hands pulled under his legs and also shackled to the floor.

During certain interrogations, the air conditioning was set very high, making the interrogation room quite cold. At other times, there would be no air conditioning, making the interrogation room very hot. On multiple occasions, the floor of the interrogation room had been treated by what appeared to be a mixture of water and a powerful cleaning agent. This mixture would be thrown on [his] face and body, causing great irritation. Because he would be shackled when this occurred, [he] was unable to do anything to alleviate the irritation. Especially when the air conditioning was turned off, the cleaning agent that was put on the floor would make breathing difficult. The cleaning agent also caused mucous discharges from [his] nose.

Several days after a contentious interrogation, [he] was taken from Camp Three to Camp One. There, in an interrogation room, he was shackled to the floor by his hands and feet, with his hands pulled underneath his legs. For approximately twelve hours, very loud music and white noise was played through six speakers arranged close to [his] head. . . . In certain sessions, multiple flashing strobe lights were used as well; these lights were so strong that [he] had to keep his eyes closed. The interrogation rooms were always cold when the music and strobe lights were employed. Generally, [he] was not asked any specific questions during these sessions, although sometimes he was told that he needed to cooperate generally.

When [he] was not in the interrogation room during this period, he was moved from cell to cell . . ., typically on an hourly basis. As such, [he] was never able to sleep for more than short periods even when not in the interrogation rooms… At other times, when [he] was shackled and facing away from the door someone would enter the room quietly and then blow a very loud horn in [his] ear.[70]

Recounting how they witnessed the beating of Bahraini detainee Jummah Al-Dousari, Rasul and Iqbal stated that Al-Dousari, a man they described as ill and "psychiatrically disturbed," was "lying on the floor of his cage immediately near to us when a group of eight or nine guards known as the ERF team (Extreme Reaction Force) entered his cage. . . . They stamped on his neck, kicking him in the stomach even though he had metal rods there as a result of an operation, and they picked up his head and smashed his face into the floor. One female officer was ordered to go into the cell and kick him and beat him which she did, in his stomach. This is known as 'ERFing.'"[71]

The mistreatment of detainees frequently began long before their arrival at Guantánamo. The "Tipton Three" have described in detail their treatment at the hands of U.S. military personnel and Afghani civilian authorities during the time of their detention in Afghanistan in late 2001. According to the three men, they were detained in northern Afghanistan on November 28, 2001, by forces loyal to General Dostum. When they were loaded into containers to be transported to Sherbegan prison, U.S. forces were present:

The three men were packed into the containers together with almost 200 others. Asif became unconscious and awoke to find that in an attempt to allow air into the containers Dostum's forces had fired machine guns into the sides of the containers. Asif was struck in the arm by a bullet as a result. The journey to Sherbegan [prison] took nearly 18 hours and the containers were not opened until they reached the prison. All three men remained in the containers amongst the dead and dying throughout this time. Asif reports that to get water he had to lick the side of the container or wipe a cloth on the top of the container where the condensation had collected and squeeze the drips of water into his mouth. On arrival at Sherbegan of the 200 originally in the container only 20 were alive, some of them seriously injured. . . .

Conditions in Sherbegan were appalling, Asif says; "in the first week the only food we got was a tiny portion of bread per day and a very small amount of water. This was to last us the whole day." . . . The weather was freezing. Shafiq says "I had a pair of flimsy shoes supplied by the Red Cross but no socks. At this time I was extremely weak. I was suffering from dysentery and my clothes were extremely thin and provided very little protection from the weather. We were all covered in hair and body lice and I had not washed for at least 6 weeks and I was filthy."

[At the Khandahar facility,] Asif explains, his second interview was also with an American but on this occasion he was badly beaten by his interrogator and the guard. He states that, "My second interview took place a couple of days later. I was taken away from the others, with my hood on and walked (bent double) by some soldiers to a tent. An American came into the tent and shouted at me telling me I was Al Qaeda. I said I was not involved in Al Qaeda and did not support them. At this, he started to punch me violently and then when he knocked me to the floor started to kick me around my back and in my stomach. My face was swollen and cut as a result of this attack. The kicks to my back aggravated the injuries I had received from the soldier striking me with a rifle butt. After a few moments the guards dragged me back to the tent. Whilst he was attacking me, the interrogator didn't ask me any other questions but just kept swearing at me and hitting me."[72]

The extreme emotional and physical toll visited upon the detainees as a result of their indefinite detention and torture during interrogations has become increasingly visible, and has lead to protests in the form of mass hunger strikes and waves of suicide attempts.

THE GUANTÁNAMO HUNGER STRIKES

The mental condition of the detainees is to the point where the detainees are all participating in a hunger strike. The detainees are upset with the way they are being treated by the guards. They are upset because they are being held as prisoners without being charged with a crime or released. The detainees think America is intentionally keeping people in custody for no other reason than as an attack on Muslims. The detainees are going to strike by not changing their clothes, not eating food, not drinking water more than absolutely necessary. If one person starts a strike then all of the men will follow. In the last six days, [redacted] has not taken more than three ounces of water per day. He has not for eaten six days. He has not changed his clothes in a week. He wants to be charged with a crime or released.
—Summary of FBI Interview of Detainee at Guantánamo Bay[73]

Internal government memoranda released in response to litigated FOIA requests, client interviews by pro bono habeas counsel, and court records reveal that the prisoners at Guantánamo have been engaged since the beginning of 2002 in substantial, and at many times life-threatening hunger strikes (resulting in an unknown number of detainees slipping into comas). These strikes are deliberate, mass protests by the detainees against their indefinite detention without trial and their inhumane treatment. For over five years the U.S. government has successfully blocked all but one habeas corpus hearing for two detainees, even after the Supreme Court issued its decision in *Rasul* affirming the prisoners' right to challenge the lawfulness of their detention. The hunger strikes are the detainees' response to the government's open defiance of the rule of law.

No public source identifies the precise date of the first hunger strike held at Guantánamo. But according to media reports, the most widespread of the early strikes took place from late February through early May 2002, and was a coordinated large-scale mass protest. It was started when a military police officer removed a homemade turban from a prisoner while he was saying his prayers.[74]

At first, the military attempted to minimize the seriousness of the strike. Joint Task Force public affairs officer Marine Major Steve Cox offered a prepared statement saying that "[b]y no means is this an organized, concerted effort by the camp's detainee population."[75] However, as the hunger strike expanded to a peak of 194 participants over a two-month period, it became a focused protest of the prisoners' indefinite detention without any legal process and their harsh living conditions. By mid-March, three detainees who had refused food and water for fourteen days were forcibly given intravenous fluids.[76] By this date, military officials were finally acknowledging that the prisoners were protesting "the fact that they don't know what is happening to them"[77] and that the hunger strikers primary concern was "their murky future."[78] As a result of the force feeding, participation diminished until the last two remaining strikers were force-fed in order to end their protest. One man was returned to Camp Delta on May 2nd, ending his sixty-three day strike and another man returned on May 10th, his seventy-one days of fasting having ended when he was fed through a tube forcibly inserted into his nose.[79] There is evidence from several sources, including internal government memoranda, of another mass strike that took place in the fall of 2002. By the end of that year, the detainees' protests had grown more urgent. During at least three FBI interviews taken at that time, prisoners stated that there were also discussions about a mass suicide effort, in part "for the purpose of protesting the treatment at Camp Delta and to protest keeping innocent men at Camp Delta."[80]

In the summer of 2005, while the Defense Department was conducting misleading "show tours" of the detention center at Guantánamo for U.S. senators, up to two hundred prisoners were engaged in a hunger strike to protest their inhumane treatment. During the tours, senators were prohibited from speaking directly to the detainees. After observing only the detainees housed in Camp Four—where a small number of prisoners clothed in white jumpsuits are cooperating with interrogators—the senators were left with an extremely inaccurate view of the detainees' living conditions and treatment. Senator Pat Roberts (R-KS), for example, stated on July 11, 2005, that "it is really hard for me to imagine any better treatment that this country could provide for those kind of people. They are treated humanely and respectfully."[81]

It was on July 20, 2005, just shortly after Senator Roberts' statement, that the June/July 2005 Hunger Strike was first publicly announced by two Afghani citizens, Habir Russol and Moheb Ullah Borekzai, who had been released from Guantánamo two days earlier.[82] The Center for Constitutional Rights subsequently confirmed that the mass protest had been planned and begun in June 2005 and had occurred across all five camps. Once again, government officials at first denied the existence of the protests, but over the course of the week following Russol and Borekzai's public announcement, the Defense Department was forced to admit that yet another strike was ongoing. Imprisoned British resident Omar Deghayes gave this description of the protest, "[t]hey began on June 21, 2005, by rejecting one meal each day for a week. On June 28, they began to reject two meals. On July 2, 2005, they began rejecting all food. . . . A majority of Camp Five are taking part in the hunger strike."[83]

Camp Five, which still remains closed to outside visitors including political representatives, houses nearly one hundred prisoners. While the Defense Department touted the relatively benevolent living conditions at Camp Four to touring Senators, the vast majority of detainees lived in appalling conditions in the other camps. Several prisoners explained to their attorneys the seriousness of the hunger strikers' requests for a fair hearing and humane treatment. Jarallah Al-Marri was hospitalized as a result of his participation in the strike and a deteriorating heart condition. He told his attorney, Jonathan Hafetz of the Brennan Law Center, that he had been in solitary confinement for over sixteen months and often goes as long as three weeks without being allowed outside his cell for recreation. The lights in Al-Marri's cell remain on twenty-four hours a day, seven days a week, and he has been denied adequate bedding and clothing. As a result, Al-Marri is able to sleep only two hours a night, and both his physical condition and mental state have deteriorated significantly.[84]   During the June/July 2005 Hunger Strike, the condition of fifty of the strikers became so grave that the Defense Department was forced to provide the men with intravenous treatment. Because of the increase in treatment needs, medics were unable to manage the detention center's medical calls and elected to stop making routine medical calls. Violence against the protesters was also reported. In one incident on July 9, 2005, O.K., an individual seized by the U.S. when he was a juvenile, was kicked by military police approximately ten times when he collapsed on the ground from weakness after being transported back from the hospital. The same officer then placed a finger on a pressure point on O.K.'s neck and applied strong pressure for approximately one minute, causing O.K. severe pain and restricting his ability to breathe.

The military only acknowledged the participation of fifty-two prisoners in the June/July 2005 Hunger Strike, while consistent and reliable reports by habeas counsel indicate that nearly two hundred prisoners participated. Although the Defense Department has refused to provide accurate public information about the conditions at Guantánamo, the breadth and severity of the June/July 2005 Hunger Strike did force the department to permit the creation of a prisoners' representative committee (Prisoners Council) to negotiate with prison officials concerning the protesters' demands. Military officials responded to some protests regarding the lack of basic human necessities by, for example, agreeing to provide prisoners with clean bottled water. Based upon Defense Department's promise to bring the detention center into compliance with the spirit of the Geneva Conventions, the strike was ended on July 28, 2005. The August 2005 Hunger Strike began at Guantánamo after the Defense Department almost immediately reneged on its promises to the Prisoners Council. Confirming fears expressed by the attorneys for the prisoners, as soon as the Defense Department believed that it was out from under public scrutiny, abuse and mistreatment began anew. Reports have been made that several prisoners were beaten by military personnel in early August 2005. For example, British resident Binyam Mohammed recounted to his attorney Clive Stafford Smith how a Kuwaiti prisoner had been violently assaulted by the military's Extreme Reaction Force and then subjected to psychological abuse.

A statement made by Binyam Mohammed to his counsel on August 11, 2005, expresses the detainees' clear and limited demand that the U.S. government fulfill its promise to abide by rule of law: "We ask only for justice: treat us, as promised, under the rules of the Geneva Conventions for Civilian Prisoners while we are held, and either try us fairly for a valid criminal charge or set us free."[85] According to detainee Shaker Aamer, when the August 2005 hunger strike began, instead of negotiating with the Prisoners Council, the Defense Department placed its members in isolation. The department also refused to publicly discuss the detainees' conditions and flatly resisted habeas counsel's attempts to visit their clients, several of whom had recently suffered the beatings and other psychological abuses that had provoked the protest. It took emergency hearings held in the federal district court in Washington, D.C., on August 30 and 31, 2005, for the court to order the Defense Department to provide attorneys from Shearman & Sterling with access to four of their clients, three of whom the department had already confirmed were participating in the hunger strike.

It wasn't until September 2, 2005, that the Defense Department issued its first public acknowledgement of the protest, when military spokesman Army Colonel Brad Blackner confirmed that a hunger strike had been ongoing since August 8th and that nine men had been hospitalized.[86] The military claimed, however, that only seventy-six detainees were refusing food, and denied reports that detainees had been assaulted or abused by military police or interrogators.[87] Army Col. Blackner stated that "We continue to monitor them 24 hours a day."[88] The government had apparently decided not to inform prisoners' counsel or their families of the strike or the status of detainees' health, though as Blackner's statement shows they were clearly aware of the significant health concerns.

While habeas counsel have continuously voiced concern for their clients' health given the length of their detention without trial and the conditions of their confinement, the situation has now become acutely dangerous. It is unclear how many detainees are on hunger strike at the time of this writing. It took a second emergency court hearing after the August 2005 hunger strike started simply to address counsel's right to information regarding the health status and medical treatment of their clients participating in the hunger strikes. Julia Tarver, an attorney with the New York City-based law firm of Paul, Weiss, Rifkind, Wharton & Garrison LLP, sought and obtained public release of her declaration regarding the situation at the naval base. Tarver's notes detail interviews she conducted with three clients at Guantánamo engaged in a hunger strike: Yousef Al Shehri, Abduhl-Rahman Shalabi, and Majid Al Joudi. The declassified notes reveal the dire conditions of these men. According to Tarver's sworn declaration:

> Force-feedings resulted in prisoners "vomiting up substantial amounts of blood. When they vomited up blood, the soldiers mocked and cursed at them, and taunted them with statements like 'look what your religion has brought you.'"
>
> "Large tubes—the thickness of a finger—were viewed by detainees as objects of torture. They were forcibly shoved up the detainees' noses and down into their stomachs. Again, no anesthesia or sedative was provided. . . . [R]iot guards . . . forcibly removed these NG tubes by placing a foot on one end of the tube and yanking the detainee's head back by his hair causing the tube to be painfully ejected from the detainee's nose."
>
> "[D]etainees were verbally abused and insulted and were restrained from head to toe. They had shackles or other restraints on their arms, legs, waist, chest, knees, and head . . . with these restraints in place, they were given intravenous medication (often quite painfully, as inexperienced medical professionals seemed incapable of locating appropriate veins). Their arms were swollen from multiple attempts to stick them with IV needles. . . . If detainees moved, they were hit in the chest/heart."
>
> "In front of Guantánamo physicians—including the head of the detainee hospital—the guards took NG tubes from one detainee, and with *no sanitization whatsoever*, reinserted it into the nose of a different detainee. When these tubes were reinserted, the detainees could see the blood and stomach bile from other detainees remaining on the tubes. A person detainees only know as Dr. [redacted] stood by and watched these procedures, doing nothing to intervene."
>
> One of the detainees, Abdul-Rahman, stated that, "one Navy doctor came and put the tube in his nose and down his throat and then

just kept moving the tube up and down, until finally Abdul-Rahman started violently throwing up blood. Abdul-Rahman tried to resist the 'torture' from this physician, but he could not breathe."

The detainees had been complying with nasal tube feeding orders only because they had been told—falsely—that it had been ordered by a U.S. court.[89]

After years in U.S. custody without formal charges or a hearing on the legality of their detention—despite a Supreme Court ruling in their favor—the hunger-striking detainees at Guantánamo have come to the conclusion that, according to Abdul-Rahman, "now after four years in captivity, life and death are the same."[90] The government has chosen not to give the men the supportive communications from their families and religious advisers urging them to end the strike, but instead isolated the men and inflicted physical and psychological pain to break their wills and crush the protest.

It was not until February 2006 that the U.S. military admitted that it had instituted more aggressive measures to deter prisoners from participating in long-term hunger strikes to protest their incarceration at Guantánamo.[91] In response to media inquiries, officials at the base acknowledged that guards had initiated the practices of strapping striking detainees into "restraint chairs" for hours a day to force-feed them and then placing them in isolation for extended periods to prevent them from receiving any encouragement by other detainees. General Bantz Craddock, head of the United States Southern Command, while stating that use of the restraint chairs was "not inhumane," also "left no doubt, however, that commanders had decided to try to make life less comfortable for the hunger strikers. . . ."[92] Attorney Julia Tarver's expression of her concerns after her October 2005 trip to visit her clients offers a response to the government's continued rationalizations of its treatment of the strikers:

What we learned on our last trip to Guantánamo was troubling to us as lawyers, as human beings, and as Americans. We never thought we would see the day when this sort of treatment took place at a facility run by the United States government. It is inconsistent with the rule of law this country was founded upon, and it is inconsistent with the spirit and values of the American people.[93]

THE SUICIDES AT GUANTÁNAMO

The torture and abuse visited upon the men imprisoned at Guantánamo without access to justice has begun taking its final toll. In the first year and a half after the prison opened, eighteen individuals engaged in twenty-eight suicide attempts,[94] and since the prison opened, there have been at least thirty-six attempted suicides, likely more; the exact number is not known owing to the government's change in reporting practices.[95] Even relatively early into their detention (by the end of 2002), fifty-seven prisoners were being treated for serious mental illnesses, with many of them taking antidepressants or antipsychotic medication.[96]

Guantánamo officials belatedly confirmed to the press in January 2005 that between August 18 and August 26th, twenty-three Guantánamo detainees had used pieces of clothing and "tried to hang or strangle themselves at the U.S. military base . . . during a mass protest in 2003."[97] This included a mass suicide attempt by ten detainees on August 22nd. The long delay in reporting these significant events raises questions about a cover-up, particularly in light of the International Committee of the Red Cross's public statement about the psychological impact of indefinite detention and solitary confinement. The incidents occurred not long after Major General Geoffrey Miller took command of the prison with "a mandate to get more information from prisoners accused of links to al-Qaida or the ousted Afghan Taliban regime that sheltered it."[98]

Military officials described the suicide attempts as "a coordinated effort to disrupt camp operations and challenge a new group of security guards" who had recently assumed duties at the detention center.[99] The Defense Department also differentiated between a "suicide attempt in which a detainee could have died without intervention, and a 'gesture' aimed at getting attention." On this basis, Guantánamo medical staff characterized only two of the twenty-three suicide attempts over a nine-day period in August 2003 as genuine suicide attempts and classified the remaining twenty-one as "manipulative, self-injurious behavior."[100] The twenty-three suicide incidents were among the three hundred and fifty "self-harm" incidents recorded by the military in 2003.[101]

Tragically, since the belated reports first surfaced, many more Guantánamo detainees have since given up hope, after suffering almost five years of desperation, extreme isolation, and anticipation of confinement without end. On June 10, 2006, three men,[102] Yasser Talal al-Zahrani, a twenty-one-year-old man from Saudi Arabia, Mani Shamani Turki al-Habardi al-Utaybi, a thirty-year-old Saudi citizen, and Ali Abdullah Ahmed, a twenty-eight-year-old young man from Yemen, committed suicide by hanging themselves with nooses made of bed sheets and clothing.[103] The three young men, like many of their fellow prisoners, had recently been brutally force-fed, strapped into a six-point restraint metal chair while a nasal-gastric tube was inserted through their noses into their stomachs. According to the Pentagon, one of the men, al-Utaybi, was scheduled to be released from Guantánamo within days, but had not been told by Defense Department or military officials because the U.S. had not yet decided to which country he would be transferred.[104]

Given the secrecy surrounding their deaths and the circumstances of their detention and treatment at Guantánamo, the public is left to speculate as to the reasons for the three individuals' decisions to end their lives. One thing is certain though, the prison's rules forbidding all personal contact with families, making communication with attorneys extraordinarily difficult, and permitting extremely abusive interrogations and various forms of psychological pressure, when combined with isolation and indeterminate confinement, created fertile conditions for severe depression and hopelessness. Even more alarming, in response to the suicides, military officials at the base immediately clamped down on the prisoners, curtailing existing policies on the length of meals, recreation time, prison lighting, and increasing the frequency of cell-block patrols, and immediate enforcement of disciplinary rules.[105] One of the most undermining punitive measures taken was the seizure of detainees' legal files, which they had been permitted to keep in boxes outside of their cells and to read when granted permission. Military officials at the base decided that the three men who died had been communicating with each other and might have enlisted the assistance of their attorneys in facilitating the conversation. Habeas attorneys were immediately banned from the base, and the facility was closed for a week while the detainees were moved to different cells so that friendships were disrupted. The government's accusations of conspiracy stand unresolved at the time of this writing.[106]

The government's response to inquiries from the press has continued to echo its incredibly callous response to the first wave of suicides. Rear Admiral Harry Harris, the current commander of the camps at Guantánamo, called the more recent deaths "an act of asymmetric warfare against [us],"[107] and Colleen Graff, U.S. Deputy Assistant Secretary of State for Public Diplomacy, referred to the prisoners' suicides as "a good PR [public relations] move."[108]

The government's distorted characterization of the motives behind the men's deaths is disingenuous given that the military's list of criteria for sending men to Guantánamo included consideration of whether the seized men might be at risk for suicide.[109] According to one military official, the personnel stationed at Guantánamo were prepared for suicide attempts: "[r]ight from the start, it was known there were individuals capable and willing to harm themselves. One of the reasons they were brought there was because it was thought they would be a harm to themselves."[110]

THE LAW'S ABSOLUTE PROHIBITION OF THE INTERROGATION TECHNIQUES USED AT GUANTÁNAMO

Torture and inhumane treatment are absolutely prohibited in all forms of armed conflicts by the customary and conventional rules of international humanitarian law. The Third and Fourth Geneva Conventions mandate that prisoners of war and civilian detainees be treated humanely at all times.[111] Both conventions also make the killing, torture, or inhuman treatment of protected persons "grave breaches" which may be prosecuted as serious war crimes.[112]

International human rights law is also unequivocal in its ban on torture. Article 7 of the International Covenant on Civil and Political Rights[113] absolutely prohibits torture or cruel, inhuman and degrading treatment or punishment, and the prohibition allows no exception under any circumstances.[114] Article 2 of the Convention Against Torture (CAT) declares that "no exceptional circumstances whatsoever, whether a state of war or a threat of war, internal political instability or any other public emergency, may be involved as a justification of torture."[115] Article 4 defines the ban as an obligation from which no derogation may be made even in the *context of a national emergency so severe as to threaten the life of the nation*.[116] The U.N. Human Rights Committee has stated that the prohibition is a peremptory norm of international law, non-derogable, and binding on all states,[117] and the European Court of Human Rights has affirmed the U.N. committee's statements by Article 3[118] of the European Convention on Human Rights which states that the protection against torture is absolute—*even in the context of efforts to combat the scourge of international terrorism*.[119]

The U.N. Committee Against Torture has stated that the threat of torture, severe sleep deprivation, forcing a person to sleep on the floor handcuffed after interrogation, physically restraining a person in very painful conditions, and hooding can each constitute inhuman treatment. The U.N. Special Rapporteur on Torture has identified certain actions as involving the infliction of suffering severe enough to constitute torture, including, among other things: suspension; exposure to excessive light, noise, or temperature extremes; sexual aggression; prolonged denial of rest or sleep, sufficient hygiene or medical assistance; total isolation and sensory deprivation; and threats to torture or kill relatives.[120]

Under U.S. law, the due process clause of the Fifth Amendment to the Constitution, which is applicable to both interrogation procedures and the conditions of detention, prohibits actions taken under color of law (actions taken with governmental authority) that are "so brutal and offensive to human dignity" that they "shock the conscience."[121] The Eighth Amendment's prohibition on cruel and unusual punishment has a fluid definition, which the Supreme Court has said "must draw its meaning from the evolving standards of decency that mark the progress of a maturing society,"[122] and applies only to convicted persons and to pretrial detainees.[123] The Eighth Amendment's prohibitions have been held to include disproportionate punishments, non-physical forms of cruel and unusual punishment, and wanton or unnecessary infliction of pain.[124]

In 2006, five U.N. human rights experts[125] undertook a rare collaborative investigation of the detention conditions at Guantánamo and issued a report (Human Rights Commission Report)[126] which concluded that the solitary confinement of people indefinitely without charge or judicial trial constitutes inhuman treatment[127] and that the Defense Department's authorized interrogation techniques and the force-feeding of Guantánamo hunger strike detainees constitutes torture.[128] Another report, issued by the U.N. Committee against Torture,[129] roundly criticized the United States for its failure to register detainees caught in its "war on terror," for its practice of transferring detainees to countries with records of state-sponsored torture, and for its practice of indefinitely detaining prisoners at Guantánamo.[130] Just after issuance of the two reports, the European Parliament recommended that Guantánamo be replaced by an international tribunal.[131]

Despite the worldwide consensus on the absolute prohibition of torture and cruel and inhuman treatment, the Bush administration deliberately chose to authorize such treatment in Guantánamo as well as in every other place it has held its "war on terror" captives outside of U.S. territory: in Afghanistan, in Iraq, and in secret sites around the world.

THE ADMINISTRATION'S SELECTIVE COMPLIANCE WITH INTERNATIONAL LAW

One of the Bush administration's first strategic moves in the wake of the September 11 attacks was its decision to develop a system to fight terrorism which acknowledged and utilized only those principles of humanitarian and human rights law that would serve the administration's ends. Through its shrewd selection process and a slick media campaign, the administration successfully accomplished a number of astounding—if horrifying—goals. First, it managed, virtually without notice among the public, to conflate the international armed conflict with Afghanistan with the law enforcement actions taken against Al Qaeda members and sum them together to form a "war" that it claimed was not governed by the laws of war.

Afghanistan and the United States are high contracting parties to the

Geneva Conventions, and thus when the two governments were engaged in an international armed conflict, both sides should have been bound by the Geneva Conventions' rules regarding POW status and the treatment of civilians and POWs. Somehow though, the Bush administration created enough confusion so that the regular soldiers of the Taliban—the recognized government of Afghanistan at the time—were deprived of these protections. Then, when the international armed conflict with Afghanistan formally ended in late 2002—by the United States' recognition of the new provisional government—and the conflict changed into a non-international armed conflict, the Bush administration began to refer to its continued efforts there as part of the widening "war on terror" against Al Qaeda and its associated organizations.

The use of the "war" nomenclature has been the foundation for President Bush's invocation of the commander-in-chief powers from the initial period of massive air strikes against Afghanistan through to the present day. However, the Bush administration carefully picks and chooses what rules the U.S. government will obey in its "war on terror." Though President Bush has asserted his right to use the commander-in-chief power, he does not acknowledge any limitations on its use. While he asserts the power to imprison "war on terror" captives, he eschews the Geneva Convention rules governing the captives' treatment and conditions of confinement. The power to hold prisoners of war until hostilities cease is claimed, but none of the POW or civilian protections are afforded the captives by the Bush administration, and the administration sees no end to its "war on terror" such that release will ever likely be warranted. Other contradictions, violations, and outright war crimes in the Bush administration's "war on terror" are discussed below.

THE ADMINISTRATION'S DECISION TO THROW OUT THE GENEVA CONVENTIONS

One of the first principles of the Bush administration's new legal regime was announced just after the start of the war in Afghanistan. Within days of publicizing the capture and detention of people near the battlefield, the administration without further explanation announced that it would not follow the mandates of the Geneva Conventions with regard to the treatment of people captured in or around the zone of military hostilities.[132] For those of us unschooled in the rules of the laws of war, this likely had little impact; but for those aware of the import of the Geneva Conventions, the Bush administration's decision was shocking.

It was shocking because the Geneva Conventions have the force of law and cannot simply be ignored at the president's whim. Nearly half a century ago, the nations of the world came together to ratify the Geneva Conventions in response to the horror, brutality, and torture visited upon soldiers captured during the two world wars.[133] The United States signed and ratified all four of the Geneva Conventions, making them part of the highest law of the United States.[134] Under the supremacy clause of the Constitution, ratified treaties have constitutional force as binding federal law.[135] In addition, Article III of the Constitution expressly gives the federal courts the power to decide cases involving treaties: "The judicial Power shall extend to all Cases, in Law and Equity, arising under this Constitution, the Laws of the United States, *and Treaties made*, or which shall be made under their Authority."[136] Finally, the U.S. military has adopted regulations that expressly incorporate requirements of the Third Geneva Convention.[137] Simply put, all of this means that the government is legally bound to comply with the mandates of the Geneva Conventions.[138]

The Third Geneva Convention gives soldiers many different types of protections designed to curb a detaining power's basest impulses. Article 3 of the Third Geneva Convention delineates the basic standard of treatment for POWs, indicating that they "must at all times be humanely treated,"[139] and specifically mandates that they must not be killed or endangered, physically mutilated, or subjected to medical or scientific experiment.[140] Article 13 requires that POWs be protected from violence, intimidation, insults, and public curiosity.[141] Article 17 states that POWs may not be coerced into supplying information to the capturing power; they are only bound to supply their names, ranks, and numbers,[142] and Article 22 requires that they not be interned in unhealthy areas or where the climate is injurious to them.[143] The Third Geneva Convention clearly reflects that the world community has learned from its mistakes. The United States, too, once took seriously the obligations of and protections provided by the Geneva Conventions.[144] In fact, our own military regulations incorporate the procedures set forth in the Third Geneva Convention for convening a competent tribunal to determine an individual's status. The regulations further guarantee the detainees' right to attend the hearing, present witnesses, and address the panel.[145]

Our Constitution, laws, and regulations require the government to comply with the Geneva Conventions and the rules established by our military laws during wartime. By expressly disavowing these legal requirements, the Bush administration has deliberately circumvented the strictures of international law as well as our domestic laws that incorporate these international principles. In addition, the Bush administration not only disregarded the law, it tossed aside more than fifty years of consistent military practice. The United States has adhered to the requirements of the Third Geneva Convention in nearly every conflict since World War II and has strenuously urged other nations to do the same. For example, during the 1991 Persian Gulf War, the U.S. Army convened 1,196 tribunals to resolve the status of individuals detained during Operation Desert Storm.[146] With the exception of specific instances during the Vietnam War, the U.S. military has endeavored to comply with the requirement that "a tribunal is required whenever a captive who has participated in hostilities asserts the right to be a POW."[147]

HOW AND WHEN DID THE BUSH ADMINISTRATION'S DECISION COME ABOUT?

In the summer of 2004, after several internal executive branch memoranda were leaked to the press, the Bush administration decided to release a number of White House documents written by senior administration officials and attorneys working in the Office of Legal Counsel. From these and other subsequently released documents, it is now possible to trace the development of the administration's policy decision to circumvent the Geneva Conventions and other treaties and conventions. It began with a series of discussions and legal memoranda between the Justice Department and the Office of White House Counsel in late 2001.

Secretary Rumsfeld has repeatedly expressed the opinion that the Geneva Conventions may not be relevant to military operations against the Taliban and Al Qaeda because they involve circumstances that were not considered when "the Geneva Conventions were fashioned"[148]—an opinion that plainly echoes the earlier stated positions articulated in the Justice Department memos on these issues. For example, on January 25, 2002, Attorney General Alberto Gonzales, then White House counsel, submitted a memorandum to President Bush in which he urged the president to take the public position that the Taliban forces and Al Qaeda operatives in Afghanistan fall outside the coverage of the Geneva Conventions.[149] Gonzales made clear that he thought that such a position, which was based on a formal legal opinion issued by the Justice Department,[150] would provide the government with the "flexibility" it needed in the war against terrorism, which in his opinion "render[ed] obsolete Geneva's strict limitations on questioning enemy prisoners."[151] In addition, Gonzales made the case that the president's disavowal of the Geneva Conventions would "substantially reduce the threat of domestic criminal prosecution under the War Crimes Act"[152] for U.S. officials involved in harsh interrogation techniques.[153] Although Gonzales noted some of the objections raised by military leaders about this position—including the country's long history of military compliance with the Geneva Conventions, the government's inability to invoke the conventions in the future if enemy forces mistreated our soldiers, the likely condemnation it would inspire in our allies, and the bad example it would set for other nations in future conflicts—he flatly rejected them as unpersuasive.[154]

Secretary of State Colin Powell's objections—laid out in his January 26, 2002 memo—were dismissed just as easily. After noting that the Gonzales memorandum failed to set forth what he believed to be the pros and cons of the options noted, Powell reached the conclusion that the best course was for the president to acknowledge that the Geneva Conventions applied to the conflict.[155] A two-page letter dated February 1, 2002 to the president from John Ashcroft seeks to counter Powell's position and evaluates the issue in the stark terms of potential criminal liability for American military officials. Ashcroft states that a decision by the president that the Geneva Conventions do not apply to the conflict in Afghanistan would minimize the "various legal risks of liability, litigation, and criminal prosecution" and would ensure that no court would entertain charges that American military or intelligence officials "violated Geneva Convention rules regarding field conduct, detention conduct or interrogation of detainees." Under this option, Ashcroft concludes, the War Crimes Act, which criminalizes some violations of the Geneva Conventions would not be a concern.[156]

By the time—only one week later on February 7, 2002—that Assistant Attorney General Jay Bybee of the Office of Legal Counsel submitted his analysis to Gonzales classifying the Taliban forces as falling outside of the conventions' protection, the administration's path had been chosen. The objections of career military officers and State Department counsel were simply tossed aside by senior Bush administration lawyers who thought that the new "war on terror" rendered long-standing international treaties "obsolete."

On February 7, 2002, President Bush announced that while the U.S. government would apply the "principles of the Third Geneva Convention" to captured members of the Taliban army, it would not consider or treat any of them as prisoners of war as required by the Third Geneva Convention because, in the government's view, they did not meet the requirements of an armed force. The president also made clear that he had decided that captured persons alleged to be members of Al Qaeda would not be entitled to the protections of the conventions, but also noted that such captives would be treated "humanely . . . to the extent appropriate and consistent with military necessity."[157] Unfortunately, no mention was made in the president's memorandum—or in that of Attorney General Gonzales—that the United States was also bound by obligations it had undertaken when it signed and ratified the International Covenant on Civil and Political Rights and the Convention Against Torture, both of which also prohibit all forms of torture and cruel, inhuman, or degrading treatment or punishment at all times—in peace and in war. Moreover, the president's admonishment to the armed forces in his February memorandum that they must treat alleged Al Qaeda and Taliban detainees "humanely"—an obligation that apparently was not thought to constrain the CIA's detention practices—does not seem to square with the techniques used on the detainees. The administration conveniently failed to define what it meant by "humane treatment."[158] According to former deputy White House counsel Timothy Flanigan, the Bush administration did not believe that the phrase "inhumane treatment" was "susceptible to a succinct definition" and therefore provided no guidance on how this prohibition should be adhered to.[159]

THE EFFECTS OF THE NEW POLICY

By labeling the Guantánamo detainees "enemy combatants" in early January 2002, Defense Secretary Rumsfeld publicly signaled the start of the administration's plan to override the long-standing U.S. military practice of applying the Geneva Conventions and according the explicit protections provided by them to all persons captured in an armed conflict.[160] It also signaled the administration's decision to place civilians—persons not participating in any hostilities or persons arrested far from any battlefield—in military custody, treat them as enemy soldiers, and deprive them of all of the international human rights protections to which they were—and still are—entitled. The effect of these decisions was to automatically deny all of the detainees sent to Guantánamo—military personnel, alleged terrorists and criminals, and innocent civilians, including young children and the very elderly—the international human rights protections which they otherwise would have been accorded, including the rights to humane treatment, adequate living conditions, and medical treatment.

Although the Bush administration announced that it was complying with the spirit of the Geneva Conventions,[161] in fact, it had already determined that the Geneva Conventions' most important protections would be ignored: the rights of detainees in military custody to be free from torture, humiliating and degrading treatment, and other forms of coercive interrogation. The stage had therefore been set early on by the administration for the use of unlawful and inhumane methods designed to extract information from the detainees. In fact, even before internal administration briefings on the applicability of the Geneva Conventions had begun, the issue of the status of noncitizens held at Guantánamo and its implications for the possibility of seeking judicial review of the detentions was being discussed. On December 28, 2001, Patrick Philbin and John Yoo, two deputy assistant attorneys general, submitted a memorandum to William J. Haynes II, general counsel for the Department of Defense, addressing the issue of whether any federal court would have the authority to consider claims raised by noncitizen detainees held at Guantánamo.[162] The memo also addressed the "potential legal exposure if a detainee successfully convinces a federal district court to exercise habeas jurisdiction" to consider the legality of the individual's detention.[163] With the Justice Department's decision that the federal courts would *not* be able to review actions taken by the military at Guantánamo, the administration began to act as if, in fact, *no law at all* applied to the offshore, off-limits detention camp at Guantánamo.

The newly created "enemy combatant" category seemed to solve a number of difficult problems with a single phrase. It magically invested the executive with the authority to detain these people, regardless of the context of the seizure or actions of the individuals. At the same time, because their status demanded detention in Guantánamo, it also magically stripped these men, charged with no crime, of all legal rights or protections. In short, the administration believed that its creation of the new "enemy combatant" category, along with its decision to confine every person seized as part of the "war on terror" at Guantánamo, created the perfect lawless enclave that could shield the administration's actions from the scrutiny of the courts, the public, and the world.

In truth, the administration's calculated attempt to evade the reach of international law and domestic constitutional and military law seems stunning not only because it reveals a naked grab for power, but also because it disavows the importance of nearly every principle that the people of this country hold dear. Any respect for the balance of power achieved by our system of three coequal branches of government was tossed aside. Just as easily discarded were the promises made to the people of this country that we all understood to be part of the moral fabric of our constitutional democracy. And finally, ignored without so much as a second thought were the obligations and commitments made to the other nations of the world regarding our respect for the rule of law and human dignity.

In the administration's new "enemy combatant" category are those subhumans who are entitled to no legal protections at all. The decision to authorize the use of torture on the Guantánamo detainees made clear that administration officials did not believe that they were bound to honor, or even acknowledge, the basic human dignity of these prisoners. This final piece of the framework designed to circumvent the law fell into place with the declaration by Justice Department lawyers that torturing Al Qaeda detainees in captivity abroad "may be justified" and that international prohibitions of torture might actually be, themselves, unlawful. According to the Justice Department, these prohibitions could be deemed unconstitutional "if applied to interrogations" conducted in the "war on terror."[164] The key supporting analysis for this position was written for Alberto Gonzales by Jay Bybee from the Office of Legal Counsel within the Justice Department—the notorious "Bybee Torture Memo."[165]

The Bybee Memo of August 1, 2002, (Bybee Memo) evaluates how certain acts might be interpreted under the War Crimes Act and the Convention Against Torture in order to assess whether persons who either engage in those acts in the field or authorize others to engage in them might be subject to criminal prosecution for their roles.[166] According to Bybee, the statutory definition of "torture" should be redefined in order to enable the administration to accomplish its objectives: "Physical pain amounting to torture must be the equivalent in intensity to the pain accompanying serious physical injury, such as organ failure, impairment of bodily function, or even death. For purely mental pain or suffering to amount to torture under [the War Crimes law], it must result in significant psychological harm or significant duration, e.g., lasting for months or years."[167]

Indeed, Bybee's argument went even a step further. He stated that in order for the law to be violated, the "defendant would have to act with the specific intent to inflict severe pain, and the infliction of such pain must be the defen-

dant's precise objective."[168] According to the Bybee Memo, under this requirement, even if a person *knows* that severe and unbearable pain will result from
his or her actions, if he or she does not intend to cause that particular harm—
i.e., if it is not his or her objective—then he or she lacks the requisite intent
required to be prosecuted even though he or she does not act in good faith.[169]
This also means that if defendants can show that they acted in the good-faith
belief that their conduct would not produce the result that the law prohibits,
they cannot be penalized for their acts.[170] A similar conclusion is reached in
the Bybee Memo with respect to the reach of the Convention Against Torture: "CAT not only defines torture as involving severe pain and suffering, but
also it makes clear that such pain and suffering is at the extreme end of the
spectrum of acts by reserving criminal penalties solely for torture. Executive
interpretations confirm our view that the treaty . . . prohibits only the worst
forms of cruel, inhuman, or degrading treatment or punishment."[171]

The Bybee Memo, written in response to a specific CIA request for a legal
opinion on the boundaries of government liability for engaging in torture, also
develops some of the defenses that might be used to negate claims that certain
interrogation methods violate the War Crimes statute. Among the defenses
researched and recommended is the defense of "necessity." The Bybee Memo
concludes that the "necessity" defense—the defense that there was no other
action available to the defendant—could be successfully used even if the harm
the defendant inflicted was intentional homicide.[172] Under the Justice Department's calculus, a defendant could raise that defense successfully because "a
detainee may possess information that could enable the United States to prevent attacks that potentially could equal or surpass the September 11 attacks
in their magnitude. Clearly, any harm that might occur during an interrogation would pale to insignificance compared to the harm avoided by preventing
such an attack, which could take hundreds or thousands of lives."[173] In short-
hand, the defendant interrogator "had to torture" the detainee, because he or
she knew that the person had critically important information about a great
and imminent threat. In case it is not recognizable framed in this way, this is
merely the criminal expression of the ticking-bomb scenario invoked by those
who seek to justify our path down the grim road of immorality.

Along with the defense of necessity, the Bybee Memo argues that the doctrine of "self-defense"—which traditionally permits a person to use force to prevent imminent harm to another person—could also successfully be invoked.[174] According to Bybee, the use of this defense is justified even though "an enemy combatant *in detention* does not himself present a threat of harm," because the defendant/interrogator has the right to invoke the nation's right to self-defense.[175]

The extremely narrow definition of torture discussed in the Bybee Memo is unequivocally contravened by international treaties signed and ratified by the United States. The Convention Against Torture bars not only torture but also "cruel, inhuman, or degrading treatment or punishment," actions which are not deemed the equivalent of torture."[176] More importantly, the Convention Against Torture provides that "[n]o exceptional circumstances whatsoever, whether a state of war or a threat of war, internal political instability or any other public emergency, may be invoked as a justification of torture."[177] The International Covenant on Civil and Political Rights, which also bans torture and other abuse and mistreatment, states that the right to be free from torture and other cruel, inhuman, or degrading treatment can never be suspended by a country, even during episodes of public emergency.[178] *Torture is simply not permitted for any reason, at any time, in peacetime or in war.*

Unfortunately, before the Bybee Memo was eventually repudiated by the Justice Department on December 30, 2004,[179] its legal reasoning was adopted in whole by the participants in the Working Group on Detainee Interrogations in the Global War on Terrorism, a group appointed by Defense Department General Counsel William J. Haynes II and headed by Air Force General Counsel Mary L. Walker. The Working Group comprised representatives of the Office of the Undersecretary of Defense; the Defense Intelligence Agency; the general counsels of the Air Force, Army, and Navy; the counsel to the commandant of the Marine Corps; the judge advocates general of the Air Force, Army, Navy, and Marines; and the Joint Staff Legal Counsel.[180] According to the Walker Working Group Report, the proposition that the president has the authority as commander in chief to approve the use of torture in interrogations in order to obtain "intelligence vital to the protection of untold thousands of American citizens" was not controversial at all. The report concluded that the president could issue a directive stating that subordinates charged with torture could submit as evidence that their actions were authorized by the president, because the authority to set aside the laws during wartime is "inherent in the President."[181]

On April 4, 2003, the Walker Working Group issued its recommended interrogation techniques for the Guantánamo detainees. The approved techniques included hooding, mild physical contact, dietary and environmental manipulation, sleep adjustment, false flag (leading detainees to believe that the interrogator is from another country), isolation, and threats of transfer to a third country where the detainee knows there is risk of torture or death.[182] All techniques, except for hooding, mild physical contact, and threats of third country transfer to torture, were approved by Secretary Rumsfeld.[183] Nine specific techniques were recommended "for use with unlawful combatants outside the United States."[184] These included use of prolonged interrogations, prolonged standing, forced grooming, sleep deprivation, physical training, face or stomach slaps, removal of clothing (forced prolonged nudity), isolation, and increasing anxiety by use of aversion (presence of dogs).[185]

By August 2003, military intelligence officers and interrogators working in Iraq sought approval for a similar list of interrogation techniques, including: the use of low voltage electrocution, phone book strikes, muscle fatigue inducement, sleep deprivation, closed-fist strikes, and other "coercive" techniques that would "cause no permanent harm to the subject . . . [but] often call for medical personnel to be on call for unforeseen complications."[186] The abusive interrogation methods the Defense Department employed in Guantánamo had migrated to Iraq.[187]

In the years since the 2004 Defense Department memo was written, the Bush administration has staunchly maintained its position that torture and other abusive interrogation techniques are critical to its prosecution of the "war on terror." In fact, during his confirmation hearings in 2005, White House counsel and then Attorney General designate Alberto Gonzales asserted that the Convention Against Torture's prohibition of cruel, inhuman, or degrading treatment *does not apply* to U.S. personnel who are involved in the detention and interrogation of noncitizens held outside of U.S. territory.[188] Even more recently, in May 2006, State Department Legal Adviser John B. Bellinger III stated during the United States' formal report to the U.N. Committee Against Torture that the U.S. government will continue to adhere to its position that the Convention Against Torture does not apply to actions taken against persons held outside the geographic boundaries of the United States.[189]

The notion that the president's authority as commander in chief permits him to ignore this country's laws, treaties, and Constitution and shield military officials and civilians who, acting on his authority, violate domestic and international law by their interrogation methods, is not only outrageous and unprecedented—it is indisputably unlawful. The Supreme Court decisions, constitutional provisions, federal statutes, and international treaties it violates—beyond those already discussed—are just too numerous to recite here.

Clearly, the legal positions advocated by the Justice Department and subsequently adopted by the Working Group became the foundation for the decisions made to use methods in the "war on terror" that violate domestic and international law. Still, it is difficult to understand how such long-established and universally accepted moral and legal principles were so easily cast aside. The techniques approved by the Bush administration and implemented by orders from the Defense Department are *precisely* those that this country has strongly condemned in its annual State Department Country Reports for countries in which there is state-sponsored torture. That hypocrisy has not been lost on any person, organization, or country that has paid attention to the U.S. position on the human rights compliance of other countries. The credibility of the U.S. claim to any sort of moral high ground is thoroughly undermined. While the ultimate repudiation of the Bybee Memo may mollify some of our allies, it cannot undo the years of abuse and terrible suffering of the people who were subjected to our new "war on terror" strategies.

This new position—the United States had never before officially sanctioned torture—was vehemently opposed by the FBI, high-ranking members of our own armed forces, civil and human rights groups, civilian law enforcement groups, and intelligence officers.[190] While not all these groups agreed on the grounds for their opposition, many agreed that the new policy meant an inescapable corruption of the morality of the American military and would result in a very significant alienation of international opinion. Furthermore, and significantly, none of the law enforcement agencies believed that such methods were successful in garnering worthwhile information from the interrogated person. FBI officers present at Guantánamo interrogations refused to participate in such techniques and firmly stated their position that their own investigative techniques could produce much more information.[191]

Why then did the administration authorize such horrible and inhuman practices? Although we should all be loathe to believe it, one explanation somehow rings true: that these terrible practices, which have permanently damaged people, were implemented not for intelligence-gathering purposes at all, but *solely* for the purpose of intimidation.[192] Pehaps our government has done these unspeakable things to human beings in order to show the world that it will stop at nothing—including the bankrupting of our morality and democratic ideals—to conquer those who we believe have wronged us.

THE LEGAL CHALLENGES

The administration's argument that the "war on terror" has unleashed the president's inherent commander-in-chief power that permits him to declare persons "enemy combatants" and detain them without charge or trial leads inexorably to its claim that there is now an unreviewable executive detention power that may operate indefinitely given the projected duration of the global "war on terror." By this power, the United States government claims the right to seize any person, from any country, at any time, and declare that individual an "enemy combatant" who may be held until the government declares that the hostilities have ended.

Two legal challenges to the Guantánamo detentions were filed in response to these outrageous claims made by the government. One case was filed on behalf of four men—two of the three British citizens from Tipton, Shafiq Rasul and Asif Iqbal, along with Mamdouh Habib and David Hicks, two Australian citizens. The other case has been filed on behalf of twelve Kuwaiti

citizens. The form of the pleading in the *Rasul* case was that of habeas corpus
(a Latin phrase meaning "to bring the body before the court"), a specific type
of complaint asking for a person's relief from unlawful detention. The *Rasul*
petition alleged that the four men had been seized in connection with hostilities in Afghanistan and that after being turned over by Northern Alliances
forces, they were transferred to United States custody and eventually flown to
the detention camps at Guantánamo Bay. At Guantánamo, the four men were
confined for more than two years without charges, access to counsel or courts,
or recourse to any legal process. The executive branch presented no evidence
to justify their detention and, in fact, claimed that it was under no obligation
to do so. It also claims the right to hold the Guantánamo detainees indefi
nitely.

The *Rasul* petitioners argued that the district court had the authority to
hear their case pursuant to the federal statute that codifies the Great Writ of
Habeas Corpus.[193] The statute grants the federal courts power to review executive detentions that are "in violation of the Constitution or laws or treaties of
the United States."[194]

The executive branch argued that the federal courts are powerless to review
the petitioners' detention because they are foreign nationals imprisoned beyond
the "ultimate sovereignty" of the United States. In essence, the government
claimed that it had created a prison on Guantánamo Bay that operates entirely
outside the law. Within the walls of this prison, foreign nationals may be held
indefinitely, without charges or evidence of wrongdoing, without access to family, friends, or legal counsel, and with no opportunity to establish their
innocence. According to the executive branch, no court in the country has jurisdiction to review the cause for their detention.

The federal trial court agreed with the government's position. It held that
foreign nationals outside United States sovereignty have no constitutional
rights that may be vindicated in federal trial court, regardless of their circum
stances. According to the court, the government is free to act without legal
restriction on Guantánamo because the detainees enjoyed no enforceable
rights, "under the due process clause or otherwise," so long as they have not set
foot within the "ultimate sovereignty" of the United States. In other words,

because the Guantánamo detainees were not U.S. citizens, and because they were not being held on territory owned in the most complete sense by the United States, the courts had no power to hear their claims. In short, though the United States had held the detainees without legal process for approximately eighteen months, far from any theater of military operations and in an area over which the United States exercises exclusive jurisdiction and control, the lower trial court held that they had no rights that could be vindicated in federal court.

THE SUPREME COURT'S DECISION

The Supreme Court, in *Rasul v. Bush*,[195] held that federal courts have the authority to hear cases arising from Guantánamo pursuant to the power granted to them by the habeas statute. The Court found that habeas jurisdiction extends not just to the sovereign territory of the United States, but also to "a territory over which the United States exercises plenary and exclusive jurisdiction."[196] On this issue, the Court could have reached no other conclusion given the facts presented to it.

In 1903, in withdrawing its forces after the Spanish-American War, the United States entered into a lease with the newly formed Republic of Cuba for the territory that now comprises the naval base at Guantánamo Bay. The government occupies Guantánamo Bay pursuant to a lease that grants the United States "complete jurisdiction and control," while Cuba retains "ultimate sovereignty."[197] The lease continues in perpetuity unless both parties agree to terminate it. The United States has made clear its intention to continue the lease indefinitely.

Guantánamo's land mass exceeds more than forty-five square miles. It is a self-sufficient and fully American enclave, larger than Manhattan, with thousands of military and civilian residents who enjoy the trappings of a small American city. The base operates its own schools, power system, water supply, and internal transportation system. Nearly seven thousand people, including soldiers and civilians, American and foreign nationals, live on the base under U.S. authority. The government controls all entry to the base, and no one may enter or leave without approval from the United States. On its official Web site, the United States Navy has described Guantánamo as a "Naval reservation, which, for all practical purposes, is American territory. Under the [lease] agreements, the United States has for approximately [ninety] years exercised the essential elements of sovereignty over this territory, without actually owning it."[198] In fact, Congress has repeatedly extended federal statutes to the base,[199] and federal courts have heard cases arising from there involving both citizens and foreign nationals.[200] The Court therefore held that habeas jurisdiction extends not just to the sovereign territory of the United States but also to "a territory over which the United States exercises plenary and exclusive jurisdiction."[201]

The Court further held that the habeas statute[202] did not intend to distinguish in its geographical coverage between U.S. citizens and foreign nationals.[203] Finally, the Court found that the district court has jurisdiction to hear petitioners' claims arising under the Alien Tort Statute,[204] a law that specifically gives aliens the right to sue for a "tort [injury] . . . committed in violation of the law of nations or a treaty of the United States."[205]

WHAT DOES THE SUPREME COURT'S DECISION IN RASUL V. BUSH REALLY MEAN?

The Bush administration essentially argued that the Supreme Court must sanction the creation of a prison wholly outside of the law because it must defer to the executive's decisions made within the context of the "war on terror." The government claimed that the Guantánamo detainees do not enjoy *any* substantive protections as a matter of right, but only as a matter of convenience, and only to the extent permitted by the government. The administration and the Defense Department viewed the detainees as being held in a law-free zone, possessing only those rights under military or civilian law that the government deigned to extend.

But no decision, law, or rule authorized the executive branch to imprison the detainees indefinitely at its sole discretion without any legal process or justification for its actions. The government's disdain for the principles of justice and the rule of law is unprecedented in our history.

Had the Bush administration's position in the *Rasul* litigation been adopted by the Supreme Court, it would have meant that the executive branch had authority to elevate itself above both Congress and the judicial branch and that it could circumvent all domestic and international law in the pursuit of its objectives in the global "war on terror." The risks thus posed by the Bush administration's position in *Rasul* to our democratic institutions were significant.

On June 28, 2004, the United States Supreme Court rejected the government's argument that the Guantánamo detainees, because they are noncitizens confined outside the United States, had no right to access to the U.S. courts. The Court held unequivocally that "[a]liens held at the [Guantánamo] base, no less than American citizens, are entitled to invoke the federal courts' authority" under the habeas statute to test the lawfulness of their detentions and to pursue their other claims for relief in U.S. courts.[206] The Court rejected the government's argument that Guantánamo is an area beyond the reach of U.S. law, explicitly ruling that it is "within the 'territorial jurisdiction' of the United States."[207] The Court also flatly rejected the government's argument that petitioners have no constitutional, statutory, or treaty-based rights that could be vindicated in federal court, declaring instead that petitioners' allegations that they are innocent civilians detained without due process or access to counsel "unquestionably" describe detention in violation of the Constitution, laws, or treaties of the United States.[208] The Court further held that the federal courts' obligation to determine the legality of petitioners' detentions is unaffected by the government's invocation of the president's war powers, as it is the courts—and not the executive—that have the obligation to determine the legality of "Executive detention in wartime as well as in times of peace."[209]

Within two or three days after the decision, the district court judge before whom the *Rasul* case had initially begun called the parties together by teleconference to discuss implementing the decision and arranging for counsel for the detainees to meet with their clients in Guantánamo. Apparently unprepared for the loss in court, the government's lawyers tentatively took the position that while the detainees might have the right to bring a habeas corpus proceeding in federal court, they had no right to access to counsel to assist them in bringing such a case. Seemingly surprised at the government's position, the judge gave the government one week to come up with a firm response. After this short delay, the government assured counsel for the detainees and the judge that it would permit counsel to go to Guantánamo to meet with their clients and would arrange for such visits as quickly as possible. By the end of July 2004, however, it was apparent that the government intended to do no such thing.

After many delays, the government filed a brief with the district court stating that although the Guantánamo detainees have the right to go to court to challenge the bases for their imprisonment, they have no right to the assistance of counsel in doing so. In other words, detainees from more than forty-nine different countries would be required to bring their own lawsuits without any knowledge of the American judicial system and, for many detainees, without any command of English.

Plainly, the Supreme Court intended for the detainees to have access to counsel in order to pursue their cases; no one could expect those detained to negotiate within a completely unknown court system, operating in a foreign language, from a position of solitary confinement thousands of miles away from the proceedings. The right of access to counsel is so firmly entrenched in our constitutional and statutory structure that even in wartime the Supreme Court has never accepted the proposition that a court can adjudicate a habeas petition without giving the petitioner the ability to present facts in support of his or her case.[210] The Supreme Court has made clear that "the state and its officers may not abridge or impair petitioner's right to apply to a federal court for a writ of habeas corpus."[211] It is hard to imagine a more direct violation of the detainees' right to habeas corpus than holding them incommunicado without access to counsel. A detainee who cannot communicate with counsel simply cannot pursue his or her rights by means of a petition for a writ of habeas corpus.

In the end, the government's position boiled down to the contention that if the detainees had no right to access to counsel, then any conditions the government chose to place on that access would be permissible. The government's argument that it would allow the detainees to communicate with their lawyers only "as a matter of grace" thus permitted it to propose an extremely onerous set of conditions restricting counsels' access to Guantánamo, attorney-client communications, the circumstances under which the different detainees' attorneys may share their work product, and the classified treatment of documents to be used in the cases.

On October 20, 2004, United States District Judge Colleen Kollar-Kotelly issued a ruling in the *Rasul v. Bush* case holding that the detainees are entitled to be represented by counsel under the federal habeas statute and the Criminal Justice Act. The district court also ruled that all of the detainees' claims alleged in their petitions and complaint could be pursued by them in federal court. Finally, on one of the critical conditions issues, the court held that the government may not seek to breach the attorney-client privilege by monitoring communications.

In September 2004, the chief administrative judge for the United States District Court for the District of Columbia decided to assign the issues common to all of the habeas cases to a single judge for determination. That autumn, thirteen habeas cases were brought together before Judge Joyce Hens Green on issues ranging from the government's refusal to provide security clearance applications to the detainees' lawyers so that they could visit Guantánamo to the parties' negotiation of a protective order that would govern all information derived from meetings held among attorneys and clients at the base.

While attorney visits to their clients at Guantánamo began in November and December 2004, the parties filed yet another round of briefing. When counsel for the detainees sought to compel the government to provide its explanation for the detention of their clients, the government balked. Then, while complying with the court's order to provide this required information, the government moved to dismiss all thirteen habeas petitions on the same grounds that it had raised previously and lost in the *Rasul* case before the Supreme Court, along with the new argument that the Supreme Court had failed to set forth the standards under which the detainees' rights were to be decided. The dismissal motion for eleven of the habeas cases was heard by Judge Green and the dismissal motion for two of the cases was heard by Judge Leon. In January 2005, the rulings came down, with the two judges reaching nearly opposite conclusions; Judge Leon ruled in favor of the government following the reasoning of the court of appeals decision that had been overturned by the Supreme Court's decision in *Rasul v. Bush,* while Judge Green followed the reasoning of the Supreme Court's decision in *Rasul* and upheld the fundamental human rights of the detainees.

In her opinion, Judge Green refuses to turn away either from the evidence of torture or from the deficiencies in the purported "due process" procedures established by the government in the wake of the *Rasul* ruling. In particular, she was concerned that the evidence upon which the Combatant Status Review Tribunals—military tribunals in which the detainees, unrepresented by counsel, were given the chance to disprove the government's determination that they were "enemy combatants" without access to witnesses or evidence—relied was tainted by evidence coerced from detainees under torture. Judge Green specifically mentioned the cases of Mamdouh Habib, the Egyptian-born Australian citizen who has alleged that he was tortured in Egypt prior to his transfer to Guantánamo, and that of Murat Kurnaz, a Turkish national and German resident, who was not permitted to see the evidence relied upon for his classification as an "enemy combatant" in the first instance, and like the others could not have an attorney to assist him. This problem was exacerbated, the judge opined, because the "personal representatives" appointed to the detainees instead of lawyers were military officers whose primary allegiance was to their commanding officers and not their "client" detainee, instead of lawyers whose allegiance would be to their clients.[212]

With regard to the evidence of torture and mistreatment of Guantánamo detainees, the judge referred to statements made by an FBI agent corroborating the detainees' claims of abuse:

On a couple of occassions [*sic*], I entered interview rooms to find a detainee chained hand and foot in a fetal position to the floor, with no chair, food or water. Most times they had urinated or defacated [*sic*] on themselves and had been left there for 18, 24 hours or more. On one occassion [*sic*], the air conditioning had been turned down so far and the temperature was so cold in the room, that the barefooted detainee was shaking with cold. When I asked the MPs what was going on, I was told that interrogators from the day prior had ordered this treatment, and the detainee was not to be moved. On another occassion [*sic*], the A/C had been turned off, making the temperature in the unventilated room probably well over 100 degrees. The detainee was almost unconscious on the floor with a pile of hair next to him. He had apparently been literally pulling his own hair out throughout the night. On another occassion [*sic*], not only was the temperature unbearably hot, but extremely loud rap music was being played in the room, and had been since the day before, with the detainee chained hand and foot in the fetal position on the tile floor.[213]

The conflicting opinions of Judges Green and Leon have now been appealed by both sides to the D.C. Circuit Court of Appeals. The government has made two arguments on appeal. First, it argues that the president's constitutional war powers include a grant of plenary authority to detain "enemy combatants," to determine the scope of that new category, to concoct whatever process he sees fit for determining who falls within that category, and to apply that process free of judicial constraints, with the courts having no authority to review the president's decisions on these matters. Second, the government argues that, regardless of whether the detainees are innocent and no matter how the government treats them, they have no rights under the Constitution, treaties, or laws of the United States that can be vindicated in court because they are aliens detained at Guantánamo, an area outside the sovereign territory of the United States. The administration makes these arguments now despite the fact that they are precisely the same arguments it made—and lost—before the Supreme Court in *Rasul.*

While this appeal may take another year to reach resolution—which will likely happen in the Supreme Court—the detainees remain in legal limbo and their families in distress. At the time of this writing, the *Rasul v. Bush* decision still has unfortunately had little effect in terms of actually providing detainees with access to U.S. courts to hear their cases. Among the numerous obstacles blocking progress is the United States' refusal to identify all of the men currently detained at Guantánamo. As of November 2006 only about three hundred and forty of the four hundred and thirty-five prisoners remaining there had habeas petitions filed on their behalf.

CSRTS AND ARBS: NEW OBSTACLES BUILT TO KEEP DETAINEES FROM A FAIR COURT TRIAL

While the detainees' lawyers were busy battling for their clients' rights in the Supreme Court, the Bush administration was busy constructing a new series of administrative hurdles to place in front of any detainee who might get close to having his day in court. In July 2004, the Defense Department announced the creation of Combatant Status Review Tribunals (CSRTs) and Administrative Review Board Tribunals (ARBs). The CSRTs and ARBs were the administration's very delayed effort—years after capture, thousands of miles from the combat zone, and after repeated, abusive interrogations—to paint a false picture of its due process procedures for the detainees.

The Bush administration contends that these forums offer detainees the ability to plead their case for release from detention. Neither forum however provides even the most basic and fundamental due process protections. The administration purportedly created these new procedures as a substitute for the Geneva Convention Article 5 tribunals that are to take place on or near the battlefield immediately after capture and swiftly determine the captive's legal status. Soldiers fighting for the enemy are designated as prisoners of war and may be referred for prosecution for war crimes or civilian criminal violations; those who are innocent and have had no part in the hostilities are returned to the place of their capture and released to freedom. The expeditious Article 5 hearings are summary in form because each type of detainee is subsequently entitled to additional due process in accordance with his determined status. The administration's tribunals bear no resemblance at all to the Geneva Convention hearings.

The administration's plan to conduct CSRTs for the Guantánamo detainees was announced on July 7, 2004—just about one week after the Supreme

Court issued its decision in *Rasul* granting the detainees the right to challenge their detentions in federal court—in an order issued by Deputy Secretary of Defense Paul Wolfowitz (CSRT Order).[214] The CSRT Order was issued more than two and a half years after the first men were transferred to Guantánamo for imprisonment. This delay alone renders any attempted parallel with the Geneva Conventions Article 5 hearing unsound.

In addition, the CSRT procedures are deeply flawed and wholly inadequate in terms of ensuring that due process is afforded the detainees.[215] They do not include the participation of an impartial decision maker; in fact, the government has acknowledged that the *very purpose* of the CSRTs is *not* to provide an impartial determination of *whether* detainees are "enemy combatants" but rather to *confirm* the government's longstanding conclusion that the detainees are "enemy combatants." The CSRT Order itself states that: "Each detainee subject to this Order *has been determined* to be an enemy combatant through multiple levels of review by officers of the Department of Defense."[216] Essentially, the CSRT procedures appoint low-ranking military officials to the task of confirming the long-maintained determinations of their superiors, a process which cannot possibly be characterized as an impartial review.[217] Moreover, final review of the decisions of the CSRT process is retained by the secretary of defense, who has already prejudged the outcomes.[218]

Furthermore, according to published reports, the primary evidence presented at CSRTs by the military to confirm the detainees' "enemy combatant" status comes from the detainees' own interrogations at Guantánamo, interrogations which have included extreme abuse and been shown to produce false confessions. Introduction of evidence derived from such interrogations renders the CSRT proceedings irretrievably beyond the bounds of due process.[219] A study analyzing the records of the hearings held for 393 detainees (out of a total of 558 hearings held) revealed that the government produced no live witnesses in any of the hearings.[220]

In addition, the CSRTs do not afford detainees a "fair opportunity" to rebut the government's allegations. First, detainees are not provided with any documentary evidence prior to the hearing. They are only provided with a summary discussing the reasons for their "enemy combatant" designation. The military refuses all detainee requests to inspect the classified evidence against them, permitting them to see only summaries of this evidence as well.[221] Second, the procedures provide little or no opportunity for the detainees to present their own evidence or call witnesses in their defense. The CSRT Order provides that the detainees are allowed to call witnesses *only* if the government concludes, in its unreviewable discretion, that the witnesses are "reasonably available,"[222] and the procedures provide no mechanism by which the detainees may gather any evidence not provided to them by the government. The military has refused all detainee requests to call defense witnesses who are not detained at Guantánamo, and denied 74 percent of requests to call witnesses who are detained at the prison.[223] Third, the procedures establish a presumption of guilt. In addition to the fact that the detainees have already been determined to be "enemy combatants," the CSRT procedures put the burden on the detainees to rebut the existing presumption in favor of the government's evidence.[224] Fourth, by design, the CSRTs may accept hearsay and other unreliable evidence, including statements that may have been made under coercive conditions.

Despite two Supreme Court rulings, the CSRT procedures also bar detainees from choosing their own independent counsel. The *Hamdi* ruling states that a detainee, as an "enemy combatant," "unquestionably has the right to access to counsel," and the court's decision in the *Rasul* case holds that the *Hamdi* ruling applies equally to the Guantánamo detainees, because they, "no less than American citizens, are entitled to invoke the federal court's authority."[225] The CSRT procedures state that the military chooses a "personal representative" to assist each of the detainees. These personal representatives are not lawyers and need not even have any legal training, and therefore may not be familiar with the special laws governing wartime detentions. Moreover, these military-assigned personal representatives do not establish a confidential lawyer-client relationship with the detainees. Instead, they remain free to communicate any information they glean from their conversations with the detainees to the members of the tribunal or any other military officials. Yet, while the government will not allow detainees' chosen counsel to attend the proceedings, they have decided to allow the press to attend certain CSRT hearings, confirming that the CSRTs are merely show trials.[226]

Finally, the CSRTs use an overly expansive and unsanctioned definition of the term "enemy combatant." In the *Hamdi* decision, the United States Supreme Court accepted the government's definition of "enemy combatant" as "an individual who . . . was part of or supporting forces hostile to the United States or coalition partners in Afghanistan and who engaged in an armed conflict against the United States there."[227] The CSRT Order, in contrast, defines the category expansively to include any person who "was part of or supporting Taliban or Al Qaeda forces, or associated forces."[228] Under the government's newly-minted category of persons it may detain indefinitely and without due process, an individual may be an "enemy combatant" without having engaged in combat in any sense. Instead, anyone whom the government declares to have "supported" the Taliban, at the time the legitimate government of Afghanistan, in any fashion (including cooks, secretaries, taxi drivers, school teachers, and nurses) may be indefinitely detained by the United States as an "enemy combatant," even if they never took up arms against the United States or supported international terrorism.

Apparently, as a result of this expansive definition of "enemy combatant," detainees are not even entitled to present evidence at their CSRTs that they were *forced* to work for the Taliban. According to an Associated Press report, one Afghani detainee sought to call four witnesses to confirm his claim that he had been forced to work for the Taliban as a cook. The presiding CSRT officer denied the request, declaring: "Whether or not the detainee was forced to join the Taliban, or in what role they served in the Taliban, is not relevant."[229] Another detainee stated that the Taliban "came to my house and took me by force. I joined the Taliban by force, not by my own choice . . . Everybody in Afghanistan knows that if the government asks you, you can't say no." The CSRT panel also denied this detainee's request to call witnesses, concluding that how or why a detainee joined the Taliban is irrelevant.[230]

The egregious due process deficiencies of the CSRT process have gained in significance in the last few months. With the passage of two laws, the Detainee Treatment Act of 2005 and the Military Commissions Act of 2006, Congress has apparently codified the replacement of the "war on terror" detainees' right to a hearing in federal court on their petition for a writ of habeas corpus with a limited review of the CSRTs' findings in the D.C. Circuit Court of Appeals. Under this new scenario, detainees' access to civilian courts may be severely restricted. The administration now seeks to block the presentation of even factual evidence of innocence in the new Court of Appeals review of the CSRT findings. If the CSRTs are to be the detainees' main legal recourse, then we will have sanctioned a decision to provide these men—some of whom were legitimate Taliban soldiers, others of whom are innocent—with a kangaroo court. And we will have nothing to say when the same is done to our soldiers by other countries in future conflicts.

The executive branch also set up the Administrative Review Board as a second administrative body to review detainees' status. The ARB determines—also based on classified evidence that may have been obtained under coercion—whether an individual should remain in U.S. custody, be transferred to detention in another country, or be released to freedom in his home country.[231] The determination is purportedly made on the basis of whether the administration believes that the individual presents a danger to the U.S. or its allies and whether the individual has any remaining intelligence value. However, the ARBs provide no guidance to the panel as to how to best make these important determinations about a detainees' future and future safety. The findings may be suspended or amended at any time. Perhaps most troubling, the ARB Order contemplates that detainees may even be held in detention despite a low threat assessment, "if there is any other reason that it is in the interest of the United States and its allies." The only potential "other reason" explained in the regulations concerns a detainee's intelligence value, and yet here too the regulations do not include any standards to guide the ARB panel's determination of this question.

In the ARBs the detainees are also presumed guilty from the outset and assumed to pose a threat to the United States or its allies. As in the CSRT proceedings, detainees are not permitted to have access to lawyers;[232] they are somehow supposed to gather the evidence to support their claims to innocence while they are kept incommunicado, with little or no contact with the outside world. Finally, there is no review of the ARB's findings at all outside of the executive branch. The president has once again declared the Defense Department the sole witness, judge, jury, and enforcer at Guantánamo.[233]

TRANSFERS TO INDEFINITE EXECUTIVE DETENTION ELSEWHERE

Detainees who have been found eligible by the Defense Department to leave Guantánamo must face yet another very serious problem: the likelihood that they will be transferred to detention back in their home country. Since the military began transferring people to Guantánamo for detention in January 2002, the Defense Department has transferred approximately three hundred detainees to other countries.[234] But a transfer does not necessarily mean that the men who have been cleared (either through the CSRT or ARB processes) will be released to freedom upon their arrival in their country of origin. Although some detainees appear to have been freed upon their release, the U.S. government has transferred the majority of the three hundred or more released detainees to the custody of another country with the understanding that the receiving country's government has an independent law enforcement interest in detainees and with the agreement that the detainees will be detained under conditions similar to those imposed in Guantánamo.[235] At the time of this writing, more than one hundred and fifty detainees—and likely many more in the future—have been transferred to the control of other countries for continued detention there.[236] And while the U.S. government has claimed that it has sought and received "diplomatic assurances" from officials with these foreign governments that the transferred men will not be tortured,[237] the Bush administration has refused to provide either the detainees' lawyers or the judges in any of the cases with "any details about the type or form of 'assurances' given, the scope of the monitoring that takes place after transfer, or the consequences of noncompliance."[238]

Detainees' counsel have good reason to be concerned because many of the released detainees have been transferred to countries—such as Pakistan, Saudi Arabia, Morocco, and Yemen—that our own State Department has confirmed torture prisoners.[239] Of course, under such circumstances the only means of ascertaining the circumstances of released detainees is to undertake an investigation in the receiving country—a task not always easily accomplished given the U.S. government's partners in the transfer program. We are left with very little information about the fate of those detainees who were not represented by counsel when they were transferred from Guantánamo. Media accounts have provided some anecdotal details about the few former Guantánamo detainees who were released to apparent freedom in the UK, Australia, Turkey, and Russia. However, a horrifying picture was painted for attorneys and detainees alike when a small group of habeas counsel traveled to one country in order to investigate what happened to the men whom the U.S. government had transferred there.

In the early summer of 2005, Tina Foster, a Center for Constitutional Rights attorney, traveled to Yemen and spoke with Walid Muhammad Shahir Muhammad Al Qadasi, a detainee who was released from Guantánamo and forcibly "repatriated" to Yemen.

Al Qadasi was originally taken into custody by Iranian officials while traveling in Iran in late 2001. The Iranians held him for several months before "selling" him to the U.S.-allied Afghani authorities, who were informed that Al Qadasi was a member of Al Qaeda. As noted previously, following the 2002 U.S. invasion of Afghanistan, the practice of "selling" foreign nationals arrested in or near Afghanistan to the U.S. military for thousands of dollars in bounty money was common place.[240] In U.S. custody, Al Qadasi was sent to a prison in Kabul, where he was interrogated under torture for approximately three months, then transferred to U.S. forces-controlled Bagram Air Base, where he received routine beatings in aid of interrogation. On an unknown date, the United States military transferred Al Qadasi to Guantánamo, where he was held for nearly two years.[241]

In early April 2004, Al Qadasi was injected with an unknown substance by military personnel at Guantánamo. After receiving the injection, he experienced long periods of loss of consciousness for the next four days. During periods of consciousness, Al Qadasi reported suffering from hallucinations. On about the fifth day after the injection, Al Qadasi awoke and discovered that he was no longer clothed in a Guantánamo detainee uniform, but instead was wearing a pair of jeans, a sweater, and a jacket. He had also been given a bag containing personal hygiene items like a blanket, a toothbrush and toothpaste, soap, and shampoo. After overcoming his confusion, Al Qadasi learned that he was in a prison in Sana'a, Yemen. He had never been informed that he would be transferred to Yemen.

At the time of this writing, Al Qadasi remains in prison without charge and without access to any court. He has never been accused of a crime by Yemeni authorities. He was first detained in Sana'a for thirteen months, where he was held in solitary confinement without light in an underground cell and suffered constant beatings and verbal abuse from prison guards. He was given rotten food and became ill after meals. He was not allowed to use toilet facilities.

He was subsequently transferred to the Ta'iz prison in the city of Ta'iz, Yemen. When he was transferred, he was starving, but the prison officials in Ta'iz also refused to feed him. His father was forced to drive several hours every day to deliver food to him. Al Qadasi said that without his father's help, he would have been allowed to starve to death. He continued to suffer interrogations and beatings in Ta'iz prison. Then, in late June 2005, he was transferred back to the Sana'a.

Al Qadasi's accounts of his brutal treatment are well corroborated by human rights reports on Yemeni prisons.[242] The State Department has reported that Yemeni prisons are extremely overcrowded, sanitary conditions are poor, and food and healthcare are inadequate to non-existent,[243] and Human Rights Watch has stated that there have been credible reports of torture, including beating with cudgels and immersions in water to create the experience of near drowning.[244]

Because of the great risk of harm for detainees upon transfer to countries with poor human rights records, the majority of the federal judges ruling on the detainees' urgent requests for assistance have held that the government must provide the court and the detainees with thirty days' advance notice of any intended removal from Guantánamo. The detainees' hope is that in that time they will be able to ascertain the receiving country, decide whether transfer to that country would be dangerous, and if so, lodge a challenge to that decision in court. However, because of the continued difficulty in identifying all of the detainees, many men do not have this protection and remain at risk of transfer to detention and torture.

THE FUTURE OF THE GUANTÁNAMO PRISONS

Bush administration officials appear to be proceeding with their plan to indefinitely imprison suspected terrorists in a permanent prison facility currently being built in Guantánamo. Media reports indicate that the Pentagon and the CIA sought White House approval in 2005 for the lifetime detention there of hundreds of people now in military and CIA custody. Most of these are people whom the government cannot prosecute in civilian or military courts either because there is not enough evidence against them to make a case[245] or because the only—or primary—evidence that could be submitted would be tainted by its unlawful origin.

Despite the outcry from Congress[246] and human rights organizations[247] about the creation of a prison to hold detainees who have not been accorded any due process with regard to the allegations made against them, the Bush administration awarded the Halliburton Company a contract to build the new detention facility at Guantánamo.[248] The prison, now referred to as Detention Camp 6, is planned to house up to 220 men, and has cost an estimated $42 million.[249] With the establishment of this permanent prison, the United States will place itself in the company of regimes deplored throughout history for their unlawful imprisonment and disappearance of people deemed, without evidence, to be enemies of the state.

HOW IS GUANTÁNAMO VIEWED BY THE INTERNATIONAL COMMUNITY?

Few canons of international law are more universally accepted than the prohibition against prolonged, arbitrary detention. For centuries, the law in Anglo-American countries not only has prohibited indefinite detention without legal process but also has allowed prisoners to challenge that detention by means of habeas corpus.[250] The common-law tradition of respect for the principle of judicial review is reflected in the holding of the Supreme Court of Canada. In the 1998 case *R. v. Cook*,[251] that court held that the Canadian constitution protects foreign nationals outside Canadian territory, so long as the conduct in question is that of Canadian government officials, and the application of the constitution will not interfere with the sovereign authority of a foreign state.[252] Even before the Supreme Court's ruling in *Rasul v. Bush*, the executive branch's position that the prisoners at Guantánamo occupied a law-free zone prompted the English Court of Appeal to note its "deep concern that, in apparent contravention of fundamental principles of law, [the prisoners] may be subject to indefinite detention in territory over which the United States has exclusive control with no opportunity to challenge the legitimacy of [their] detention before any court or tribunal."[253] A senior judge in the United Kingdom described the detentions on Guantánamo as "a monstrous failure of justice."[254]

Judicial review of executive detentions is not limited to common-law jurisdictions. This principle is enshrined in the constitutions of nearly every country in the civilized world,[255] as well as every major human rights instrument in force today, including the Universal Declaration of Human Rights,[256] the International Covenant on Civil and Political Rights,[257] and the American Declaration of the Rights and Duties of Man.[258]

War does not alter this settled principle of international law. The International Court of Justice has observed that "the protection of the [ICCPR] does not cease in times of war."[259] The United Nations Human Rights Committee, the body that monitors compliance with the ICCPR, has held that Articles 9(1) (prohibiting arbitrary detentions) and 9(4) (guaranteeing judicial review of detentions) apply to all deprivations of liberty, and that Article 9(4) is non-derogable (cannot be taken away), even in times of armed conflict.[260] The United States did not, and still has not, declared any derogation from the International Covenant on Civil and Political Rights.[261] No statement of intent to deviate from the norms set forth in the ICCPR has been made by the Bush administration in its prosecution of the "war on terror."

International humanitarian law similarly provides that even during hostilities, prisoners may not be held without legal process. More than 190 countries, including the United States, are parties to the Geneva Conventions.[262] The Official Commentary to the Fourth Geneva Convention[263] makes clear that "every person in enemy hands must have some status under international law. . . . [N]obody in enemy hands can be outside the law."[264]

In light of these settled principles, it is not surprising that the detentions at Guantánamo have been sharply criticized by the international community, including the International Committee of the Red Cross, the United Nations, and the European Parliament. In 2002, the Inter-American Commission on Human Rights of the Organization of American States, of which the United States is a member, decided that the Guantánamo prisoners may not be held "entirely at the unfettered discretion of the United States Government" and that the government must convene competent tribunals to determine the legal status of the prisoners under its control.[265]

In the wake of the most recent 2006 U.N. human rights reports,[266] religious leaders and heads of state from around the world began calling upon the Bush administration to close the detention facilities at Guantánamo. On October 5, 2004, Archbishop Desmond Tutu stated that the detentions there were "illegal" and "immoral";[267] on July 30, 2005, former President Jimmy Carter stated that the detention and abuse of terror suspects at Guantánamo was "an embarrassment" and has "give[n] terrorists an unwarranted excuse to use despicable means to hurt innocent people";[268] and on March 3, 2006, Dr. Rowan Williams, the Archbishop of Canterbury, also demanded closure, calling the prison camp "an extraordinary legal anomaly" that "sets a precedent for tyrants" around the world.[269] By June 21 2006, Anders Fogh Rasmussen, the Danish Prime Minister, had called Guantánamo a violation of "the very principle of the rule of law," and even British Prime Minister Tony Blair,[270] one of the Bush administration's closest allies in its "war on terror," had called for the closure of Guantánamo.

CHAPTER FIVE

America's Not-So-Secret Military Court

[C]ivil liberty and . . . martial law cannot endure together; the antagonism is irreconcilable; and, in the conflict, one or the other must perish.

—*United States Supreme Court in the case Duncan v. Kahanamoku,*
327 U.S. 304, 324 (1946)

Martial rule can never exist where the courts are open, and in the proper and unobstructed exercise of their jurisdiction [because the] Constitution of the United States is the law for rulers and people, equally in war and peace, covers with the shield of its protection all classes of men, at all times, and under all circumstances.

—*United States Supreme Court in the case Ex parte Milligan, 71 U.S.*
2, 120-21 (1866)

THE BUSH ADMINISTRATION'S UNCEASING EFFORTS TO EVADE JUDICIAL SCRUTINY

It was nearly five years ago when President Bush first declared that he had the power as commander in chief in the "war on terror" to try foreign detainees before special military commissions of his own design and reject both the civilian and military court systems in this country.[1] The president's November 2001 Military Order (Military Order) authorized the secretary of defense to try by military commission any noncitizen whom the president determines in writing: is a current or former member of Al Qaeda; has aided or abetted terrorist acts against the U.S.; or has knowingly harbored persons who fit either of the two previous descriptions—provided that the president also determines that "it is in the interest of the United States that such individual be subject to this order."[2]

While these military commissions may take place either inside or outside the United States, they will all almost certainly take place outside of the cardinal guarantees of both the American criminal justice system and our military justice system. With one signature, President Bush replaced our traditional, open legal system with that of a makeshift and secretive terrorist trial system in which he is rule maker, law maker, investigator, accuser, prosecutor, judge, jury, sentencing court, reviewing court, and jailer or executioner. This new system radically and recklessly forsakes the most fundamental constitutional protections guaranteed by our judicial system: the rights to an independent judiciary, to trial by jury, to public proceedings, to due process, and to appeals to an independent court. In the president's newly fabricated military commission system, all of these safeguards would be gone. This was the administration's plan.

The Military Order granted the secretary of defense significant discretion in establishing the evidentiary rules for the military commission trials, authorizing the reliance on secret evidence, the use of closed proceedings, and the imposition of the death penalty by a less-than-unanimous vote of a three-person military commission.[3] No court of any jurisdiction—state, federal, or international—would be allowed to review the decision of the military commission; only the president or the Secretary of Defense would have the authority to rule on the detainee's final appeal and the sentence.[4]

From the time of the publication of the Military Order in November 2001 until July 2006, the Defense Department made every effort to move these unlawful military commission proceedings forward. Fortunately for the ten men designated and charged with crimes to be tried by the commissions—as well as for those of us concerned with maintaining the rule of law and the values underpinning our democracy—this makeshift military commission structure has proven vulnerable to attack. Lawyers for the men designated for trial filed challenges before their commission panels and the federal courts on numerous issues: the commission's lack of authority to hear cases about offenses that are not recognized war crimes; the lack of expertise of commission panel members (only one of whom was required to be an attorney); the use of procedures that would have permitted prosecutors to withhold exculpatory evidence and investigatory resources from the defense team; the existence of ethical conflicts (for commission panel members who had served in the war in Afghanistan); the use of secret evidence and exclusion of the defendant from certain sessions of the proceedings; and the lack of adequately trained translators.

In sum, the picture the new commission structure painted resembled the historical Star Chamber Court. In England in the 1500s, the Court of Star Chamber was a political weapon for bringing actions against opponents to the policies of Henry VIII and his cabinet and parliament. The sessions of the court were held in secret, with no indictments, no right of appeal, no juries, and no witnesses. By the time of Charles I, the Star Chamber had become completely synonymous with the misuse and abuse of power by the king. The parallels with the administration's military commissions are perhaps too close for comfort.

Even before the first case concerning the military commissions was heard by the Supreme Court, harsh criticism had already come from the military prosecutors charged with the responsibility of representing the government in the military commissions. In early 2005, an Australian broadcasting company obtained leaked e-mails from two former military commission prosecutors.[5] In an e-mail from prosecutor Major Robert Preston to his supervisor, Preston wrote that he "consider[s] the insistence on pressing ahead with cases that would be marginal even if properly prepared to be a severe threat to the reputation of the military justice system and even a fraud on the American people."[6] He concluded his e-mail by saying that he "cannot continue to work on a process he considers morally, ethically and professionally intolerable"—in a process that is neither full nor fair.[7] Captain John Carr, another prosecutor assigned to the military commissions who also left the Department, stated outright that the commissions were rigged:

When I volunteered to assist with this process and was assigned to this office, I expected there would at least be a minimal effort to establish a fair process and diligently prepare cases against significant accused. Instead, I find a half-hearted and disorganized effort by a skeleton group of relatively inexperienced attorneys to prosecute fairly low-level accused in a process that appears to be rigged.[8]

Carr wrote that the chief prosecutor had told him outright that the outcome of the commission trials had been predetermined: "You have repeatedly said to the office that the military panel will be handpicked and will not acquit these detainees and that we only needed to worry about building a record for the review panel."[9]

These attacks, as well as those by civilian defense counsel representing the detainees, delayed the proceedings such that none of the trials of the men charged were anywhere near conclusion at the time the first federal court challenge was heard in the case *Hamdan v. Rumsfeld*.[10]

GOING AFTER BIN LADEN'S CHAUFFEUR

By July 2003, the Defense Department had designated six Guantánamo detainees to be the first men tried before the military commissions. From February to July 2004, charges were referred to military commissions impaneled in four cases; the other two detainees were released without trial. Preliminary hearings began for the four men in August 2004, but all proceedings were abruptly halted in November 2004, when a decision was rendered by Federal Judge James Robertson in the case of Salim Ahmed Hamdan holding that the military commissions violated U.S. and international law.[11] Hamdan, a thirty-four-year-old Yemeni national, had been captured by Afghani forces and handed over to the U.S. military in Afghanistan in November 2001. Alleged to have served as Osama Bin Laden's personal driver, he was charged with conspiracy to commit terrorist acts merely because of his driving duties and alleged knowledge of Al Qaeda's nefarious objectives, and he was held in solitary confinement at Guantánamo from early 2002 until his commission proceedings began in August 2004.

From the very beginning of Hamdan's military commission, the prosecution tried to exclude him from the courtroom during the testimony of witnesses against him. Although the Defense Department's commission regulations permitted this type of secret testimony, no constitutional, federal, or international law permitted it. When Hamdan's defense team challenged the secrecy and exclusion in federal court—in the lawsuit that Hamdan had originally filed challenging the legality of the commissions—and sought an injunction to prevent the commission trial from going forward, the judge in the case, Judge James Robertson, agreed with Hamdan, noting that the Constitution gave defendants the right to confront the witnesses against them and that the Geneva Conventions provided analogous fair trial protections for prisoners of war.

Judge Robertson's decision also stated that military commissions could only hear cases regarding offenses that were triable under the laws of war (which include the Geneva Conventions); that Hamdan was entitled to a Geneva Convention Article 5 hearing to determine his legal status—i.e., whether he is a civilian, prisoner of war, or unauthorized war participant—that until he was given such a hearing, he was entitled to POW protections; and that the commissions must conform to the procedures laid out in the Uniform Code of Military Justice (UCMJ), our domestic code of laws governing military activities.[12] Although Hamdan won his challenge to the legality of President Bush's military commission system, the district court did not resolve the question of the legality of Hamdan's indefinite detention. And so Salim Hamdan remains imprisoned at Guantánamo.

The government immediately filed an appeal of the district court's ruling that the military commissions were unlawful. And on July 15, 2004, the Court of Appeals for the District of Columbia Circuit reversed Judge Robertson's decision, holding instead that the commissions had been implicitly authorized by Congress under the UCMJ when Congress passed the Authorization for the Use of Force.[13] The Court of Appeals also held that the president's newly created military commission system could not be judged by the standards codified in the Geneva Conventions because none of the protections set out in the conventions could be enforced in court by a person who has been mistreated, only countries which had signed the conventions could enforce the personal protections given to civilians and POWs through diplomatic means.[14]

The Supreme Court agreed to hear Hamdan's appeal from that decision on November 7, 2005, and oral arguments were heard by the Court on March 28, 2006.[15] In addition to the original questions of whether the president lacked the constitutional power to create the military commissions and whether they violated the Geneva Conventions, by the time the Supreme Court was to hear argument in the case, it faced yet another daunting question: whether the Court itself had the authority to hear Hamdan's case *at all* given the new restrictions imposed by the Detainee Treatment Act of 2005 (DTA).[16]

PASSAGE OF THE DETAINEE TREATMENT ACT OF 2005

Signed into law by President Bush on December 30, 2005, the DTA was an administration initiative intended to strip the federal district courts (the trial courts in the federal court system) of the power to hear any challenges raised by the Guantánamo detainees. According to the Bush administration's interpretation, under the new law only the District of Columbia Circuit Court of Appeals is authorized to hear detainee cases, and even then, its review role is narrowly circumscribed to permit only a limited review of the military's Combatant Status Review Tribunal decisions. This narrow scope of review could be interpreted to mean that detainees would be prohibited from challenging the facts behind their designation as "enemy combatants," even if the (often classified) information relied upon was tainted by torture or other mistreatment during interrogation, *and even if new evidence comes to light which could exonerate them.*

In addition, while the DTA includes a prohibition against mistreatment, it simultaneously bars detainees from filing any action against the United States regarding any aspect of their detention.[17] So while one provision in the

DTA may seem to proclaim a ban on torture, another provision in the law prevents detainees from seeking the courts' assistance to stop the torture or abuse they may be suffering while in U.S. custody. In fact, this terrible scenario has already come to fruition: the government moved to dismiss a detainee's claim that the force feeding methods being used by the military at Guantánamo were tantamount to torture on the ground that the DTA prohibits the federal district court from hearing any application brought by any of the detainees.[18] In short, the DTA's prohibition against mistreatment is unenforceable.

In the wake of an intensive White House-led legislative campaign aimed at portraying the Guantánamo cases as clogging up the courts with trivial requests on behalf of the detainees, Congress—doing the Bush administration's bidding—passed the DTA in a naked and unvarnished effort to accomplish the administration's plan to get every detainee case thrown out of court. The DTA was an attempt to replace the detainees' authorized habeas corpus hearings with a superficial review of the military's CSRT determinations in the Court of Appeals. As noted in chapter 4, the Defense Department has stated that by the time a detainee was given his CSRT, his case had already been "through multiple levels of review" and that he had been determined to be an "enemy combatant."[19] The purpose of the CSRT therefore is solely to decide whether this determination should be upheld for each detainee.[20]

In addition to moving detainees' cases from the trial courts to the court of appeal, the DTA also severely limited the scope of judicial review of the military commission trial decisions. The Court of Appeals is limited to reviewing final commission decisions *only* when a sentence of ten years or more is imposed. The Bush administration also takes the view that the DTA limits the scope of the Court of Appeal's review to the sole question of whether the final commission decision was consistent with the procedural rules created by the Defense Department.

Attorneys acting as habeas counsel, who come from many of the nation's largest and most prestigious law firms and law schools, and legislative advocates from human and civil rights organizations across the country fought tooth and nail against the passage of the DTA. These people saw clearly that the act was an effort to get Congress to authorize indefinite executive detention and deny the Guantánamo prisoners the means to challenge the factual and legal grounds for their detention. Despite this seemingly narrow objective, the law nevertheless would have the effect of rolling the United States backward in history to a time when the Great Writ of Habeas Corpus had not yet been invented, to the 12th century. This indeed may have been the Bush administration's objective notwithstanding the fact that the petition for a writ of habeas corpus[21] has long been the *primary* means by which prisoners seek judicial review and release from unlawful imprisonment, and that the writ of habeas corpus[22] continues to be one of the most important mechanisms safeguarding individual freedom against arbitrary state action. Looking at the DTA in this light, we cannot help but be utterly shocked at the direction in which the Bush administration has taken us.

Seeking to immediately enforce its new powers, on January 12, 2006, the administration filed a motion in the Supreme Court to dismiss the *Hamdan* case on the ground that the DTA divested the nation's highest court of its power to hear Hamdan's challenge to his detention and trial before the military commissions. At the same time, the administration also filed a motion to dismiss every single habeas corpus case that had been filed on behalf the hundreds of men imprisoned at Guantánamo.

Upon signing the DTA, President Bush had indicated his intention to use the new law to dismiss all of the pending Guantánamo cases.[23] In line with that objective, within days after the bill became law the Justice Department gave notice to habeas counsel and the district courts of its intention to move to dismiss all of the pending habeas cases filed on behalf of the detainees. And then, on January 12, 2006, the administration moved to dismiss the first Guantánamo detainee case that had made it to the Supreme Court, *Hamdan v. Rumsfeld*, in which Salim Hamdan sought to challenge the legality of the military commission system, established to try the Guantánamo detainees for newly created war crimes.[24] The government also moved to dismiss the appeal of the two joined cases, *Al Odah* and *Boumedienne*, which comprise the first thirteen habeas petitions filed on behalf of fifty-three Guantánamo detainees.

Once again, just like the arguments made in the *Rasul* and *Hamdi* cases, the courts were confronted with the Bush administration's argument that the judicial branch of the federal government had no authority to review challenges to either the Guantánamo detentions or the military commission trials of the "war on terror" detainees.

The Supreme Court heard argument in the *Hamdan* case on March 28, 2006. On June 29, 2006, the Court issued a 5-3 decision reversing the decision of the United States Court of Appeals for the District of Columbia in *Hamdan v. Rumsfeld.* The Supreme Court was first called upon to address the issue of its own authority to hear the case before it. The Court held that it retained that power—and that the lower courts retained their power as well to hear the detainees' challenges—because the DTA did not apply retroactively to bar courts from reviewing the cases that had already been filed before the new law was enacted.[25] The Supreme Court found that the time-honored principle of allowing a person to challenge the legality of their detention before a neutral judge was the most crucial means of safeguarding the right to personal liberty and that it could not be so easily discarded. The administration's and Congress's attempt to use the DTA to toss out all of the Guantánamo detainees' cases with a swipe of the pen had failed. Despite the fact that the Supreme Court in *Hamdan* soundly affirmed the continued viability of the detainees' habeas cases however, the District of Columbia Circuit Court of Appeals, upon urging by the Justice Department, requested yet another round of briefing. As each issued is raised and briefed and decided and appealed, the Guantánamo detainees remain incommunicado, locked in prison without charge or trial, unable to even speak with their families.

The Supreme Court's decision in *Hamdan v. Rumsfeld* did more than just ensure that the Guantánamo detainees' cases could proceed, it also invalidated the president's military commission system as it had been initially crafted.[26] The Court found that Hamdan's attacks on the military commissions were correct on nearly every ground asserted. It ruled that President Bush did not have the authority to set up a military commission trial system on his own without congressional authorization, and that the system in place at Guantánamo was illegal under our own domestic military law—the Uniform Code of Military Justice (UCMJ)—and the Geneva Conventions, the international laws of war. While the UCMJ authorizes the president to create military commissions, it requires that the regulations governing such commissions use the legal principles of law and rules of evidence that the federal courts use in regular criminal cases,[27] and to follow other relevant provisions of the UCMJ. The Supreme Court found that President Bush's military commission system failed this test because, among other things, the defendant would have been excluded from the proceedings when classified evidence was to be discussed (in contravention of § 839(b) of the UCMJ) and evidence obtained by coercion would have been allowed into the record (in contravention of § 831).

The Supreme Court also made clear that the Bush administration's decision that the Geneva Conventions applied to suspected members of Al Qaeda and protected suspected Taliban members, and that the administration's position on these matters—a position which would no doubt have gigantic international implications—was wrong. Sweeping aside the administration's contention that there should be no judicial review of the president's decision to set aside the Geneva Conventions, the Court found that "none of the overt acts that Hamdan is alleged to have committed violates the law of war" and that "there is no allegation that Hamdan had any command responsibilities, played a leadership role, or participated in the planning of any activity."[28]

Going even further, the Court held that the administration had violated both U.S. military law and international law when it failed to obey the requirements of Article 3 of the four Geneva Conventions, and thereby punctured a central concept of the administration's policy in the "war on terror": that the Geneva Conventions could be disregarded on the president's whim. The Bush administration has always argued that the conflict with Al Qaeda— i.e., the "war on terror"—is an international conflict, but that is not governed by the Geneva Conventions because Al Qaeda is not a state that can be a high contracting party to the conventions. This argument, in the administration's view, enables President Bush to employ his commander-in-chief powers around the world to seize and detain suspected terrorists from any country, while at the same time, frees the president from the constraints imposed by the Geneva Conventions. But the Supreme Court said this theory simply does not cut it.

Article 3 of the Geneva Conventions—which incorporates human rights law principles applicable to armed conflicts—guarantees to every human being the right to certain minimum standards of humane treatment and fair trial rights. The Supreme Court held that since the United States' conflict with Al Qaeda is not a conflict between nations, it is not an international conflict, and therefore it was governed by Article 3. One of the Article 3 guarantees is the right to have your case brought before "a regularly constituted court affording all judicial guarantees which are recognized as indispensable to civilized people." The Court felt that the administration's military commission system contained far too many compromises to critical rights—such as the right to confront your witnesses—that such "courts" did not meet the Article 3 requirements. By holding the United States to the most fundamental of international human rights standards, the Supreme Court sent a message for all of us to the rest of the world—even if it was only a relatively small message in comparison to our government's tragic errors that we must eventually account for—that our democracy is still functioning and that the moral principles it was founded upon continue to breathe even today. Not all of us have abandoned our commitment to these principles and our promises to the world.

The Supreme Court in *Hamdan* also pointedly rejected the Bush administration's argument that Congress's 2001 Authorization for the Use of Military Force and the DTA provided the required congressional authorization for the military commissions. A key to the Supreme Court's position in this case can be found in this statement from Justice Steven's opinion: "[I]n undertaking to try Hamdan and subject him to criminal punishment, the Executive is bound to comply with the Rule of Law that prevails in this jurisdiction."[29]

STARTING ROUND FOUR: THE ADMINISTRATION TRIES AGAIN AFTER LOSING IN THE RASUL, HAMDI, AND HAMDAN CASES

Unfortunately, the victory for Salim Hamdan and the other men charged before the commissions apparently never stood on solid political ground. Literally within hours after the Supreme Court decision had been made public, the Bush administration issued its own announcement stating that it intended to draft and push through legislation to amend the military commission system supposedly so that it would comply with the Supreme Court's ruling. Even more disconcerting, as the days passed from the date of the June decision in *Hamdan v. Rumsfeld,* the administration's position continued to harden, so that by the time that Congress was preparing for its August 2006 recess, the draft administration bill that had been leaked to the press proposed a military commission structure that made very few changes from the prior system that had just been found unconstitutional.[30] And in the end, the bill ultimately passed by Congress and signed by the president on October 17, 2006, the Military Commissions Act of 2006,[31] did not stray far from that initial administration proposal.

Although in early June 2006—prior to the *Hamdan* decision—President Bush had stated that the detainees should be tried in the courts in the United States and that the Guantánamo facility should be closed,[32] by the time the Supreme Court issued its decision in the *Hamdan* case, the administration had switched tracks and returned to its earlier position that cases involving "terrorist unlawful combatants" were not appropriate for either civilian or military American courts.[33] Somehow interpreting the *Hamdan* decision as one in which the Supreme Court had agreed with its idea of a global "war on terror" and permitted it to expand President Bush's commander-in-chief "war powers" beyond all recognition,[34] the administration drafted a proposal for military commission trials that would enable the U.S. to hold someone in executive detention "until the cessation of hostilities" in the admittedly unending "war on terror."

THE MILITARY COMMISSIONS ACT OF 2006

The impetus behind the passage of the MCA is no secret. Republican senators made their intention plain. According to Senator Cornyn (R-TX), "once . . . [the MCA] is effective, Congress will finally accomplish what it sought to do through the [DTA] last year. It will finally get the lawyers out of Guantánamo Bay."[35]

At bottom, however, the administration's real concern was not with how many cases the lawyers have filed—habeas petitions name more than one person so there are approximately two hundred petitions for more than four hundred and fifty people—it was with the fact that if detainees actually got their day in court and were able to present their full cases to judges, then the judiciary would be able to peer into the reasons for the detentions of so many people that had nothing to do with any battle or terrorist activities against the United States. The Bush administration hoped that the DTA and the MCA would seal off from scrutinizing judicial eyes decisions made regarding the seizure and detention of people from around the world by an administration that claimed the world as its battlefield.

WHO DOES THE MCA COVER?

Far from being a narrowly-focused law that merely sets the rules for the administration's second version of the military commission system, the Military Commissions Act of 2006 is one of the most sweeping acts ever enacted in this country's history on the powers of the president to seize, detain, interrogate, and try people that he considers to be a threat to the country. Unlike the Detainee Treatment Act of 2005, the MCA's provisions—stating who may be declared an "unlawful enemy combatant," how long they may be detained, what rules apply to their treatment, what access they may have to our judicial system, and who may be held responsible for their mistreatment—are no longer anchored in the idea that the Defense Department is seeking to capture and arrest people who have participated in armed conflicts against the United States or have been participants in terrorist activities.

Depending upon the courts' interpretation of the MCA, the designation "unlawful enemy combatant" now may include people who have "purposefully and materially" supported "hostilities" against the United States, even if they did not take part in any hostilities themselves and even if they have never been anywhere near a battlefield.[36] Because there are no definitions in the MCA for the terms "hostilities" or "material support," an ordinary civilian who sends money to the charitable arm of a banned organization may be declared an "unlawful enemy combatant," placed in military custody at Guantánamo or in another "war on terror" prison somewhere else, and tried in front of a military commission. In the absence of sharply defined terms, a word like "hostilities" could be used to make a credible argument that any number of previously constitutionally-protected First Amendment activities fit the bill. Could your own participation in civil disobedience in support of an unpopular cause be the basis for an "unlawful enemy combatant" designation? Others who may risk the same fate include any person who has been determined to be an "unlawful enemy combatant" by a CSRT or other "competent tribunal" created by the president or the secretary of defense. Here again, the law fails to specify by what criteria these status determination tribunals will judge a person brought before them.[37]

The statuses and definitions in the MCA (and prior "war on terror" laws and rules) have been wholly invented by the Bush administration; they have no basis in international humanitarian law. They are dangerous for this reason as well. They represent the piece-by-piece dissection and destruction of the laws of war. While the Bush administration claims the MCA is intended to implement the laws of war, the act appears to undermine one of the key pillars of the Geneva Conventions: the distinctions between armed conflict and criminal activity, and those between combatants and non-combatants. These distinctions are critical: in armed conflict, the special laws of war apply and only combatants may engage in hostilities and are subject to attack; domestic criminal laws apply otherwise and the protections accorded people in the various circumstance situations and categories differ significantly.

The familiar language and structure of some of the act's provisions seem intended to hide the fact that the MCA thoroughly unravels our country's commitment to the Geneva Conventions, and by likely extension, that of many other nation's as well. What was once fairly a well-defined boundary between armed conflict and the daily operation of civil society has now been obscured to the point where no such distinction can be made at all. Under the MCA, an individual's conduct that might run him afoul of the act and result in a designation of "unlawful enemy combatant" status need not occur during a declared war, an international armed conflict, or an armed conflict of any sort, nor must it consist of taking up arms against the United States or its allies.

The lack of any geographic limitation restricting the use of the "unlawful enemy combatant" designation to persons seized in a zone of military hostilities adds yet another layer of concern. On what basis are we now permitted to subject the citizens of other countries that are not engaged in any armed conflict with the United States to military custody and trials? Are our military forces or intelligence agencies now permitted to ignore countries' sovereignty and snatch their citizens out of their lives at will?

Deeply worrying as well is the fact that a person's eligibility for this status of "otherness" appears to have no temporal limitations. The MCA proclaims that an "unlawful enemy combatant" is any person "who *has engaged* in hostilities or who *has purposefully and materially supported hostilities* against the United States or its co-belligerents" or "who, *before, on, or after the date of the enactment* of the [MCA], *has been determined to be an unlawful enemy combatant* by a Combatant Status Review Tribunal or another competent tribunal established under the authority of the President or Secretary of Defense."

Neither of the two categories of "unlawful enemy combatants" appears to limit eligibility for this unsavory designation to people who commit prohibited acts after the law becomes effective and neither specifies any end-date for eligibility. In fact, to the contrary, the act's language appears to have been crafted specifically to sweep in as many people as possible who might have acted in some fashion against the interests of the United States (or "its co-belligerents") at some point in the past—i.e., "has engaged in hostilities" and "before . . . the date of enactment"—or who might do so at some time in the future. It seems entirely likely that the Bush administration would argue that actions taken many years ago by a political opponent, but which have only recently come to light, could be the basis for an "unlawful enemy combatant" designation. It seems equally plausible that the administration would advance an argument that any misconduct committed by a person today could become the basis for such designation many, many years in the future when the next "competent tribunal" is established by the president or the secretary of defense. In fact, there does not seem to be any way to expand these categories; they sweep in as possible "enemies of the state" people from all over the world for actions that they may have already taken or have yet to even plan.

WHAT PROTECTIONS AND RIGHTS DO "UNLAWFUL ENEMY COMBATANTS" HAVE UNDER THE MCA?

Like the "enemy combatant" designation power, the detention, treatment, and trial provisions of the MCA also are not applicable solely to the men detained at Guantánamo. The MCA expands the scope of the president's powers under the concept of a global "war on terror" so that the entire world is now the battlefield. These new rules are intended to apply to people held in U.S. military custody around the globe. For example, even though congressional debate and media presentations focused on the military commission trials planned for anywhere from twenty-five to sixty Guantánamo detainees, the MCA takes away from *all noncitizens living in the United States*—including this country's more than twelve million permanent residents[38]—the right to go to court if they are declared "unlawful enemy combatants," even if they are arrested and imprisoned inside the United States. This section of the MCA marks the first time that Congress has passed a law depriving millions of people living here on American soil of the right to file a petition for a writ of habeas in a court of law in order to challenge their detention. Over a few short weeks in September and October 2006, the Bush administration and Congress have tried to erase from the law books our long-honored democratic principle that all who are present within this country's borders are entitled to the protections of the Constitution.

What happens to such unfortunate souls now? Well, although the MCA does not explicitly address the question of detention, there is nothing in the act that would require the government to bring a person declared an "unlawful enemy combatant" to trial. Although three primary authors of the MCA have said that the category refers only to the fact that such individuals may be tried by military commission,[39] the possibility nevertheless remains that people may be held indefinitely.

And what has happened to detainees' ability to challenge their detention in court? While the Detainee Treatment Act prevents post-DTA and future Guantánamo detainees (i.e., all Guantánamo detainees who file challenges after the DTA was signed into law) from bringing habeas corpus cases or any other lawsuits challenging the conditions of their imprisonment, the MCA is intended to extend these court-stripping provisions backward in time (to reach all of the cases already filed on behalf of hundreds of detainees and now pending before the courts) and forward in time to apply them to noncitizens in U.S. custody anywhere around the world. If the administration's interpretation of the law survives review in the courts, then no person in these dire circumstances will even be able to seek relief from mistreatment from a court independent of the military.

Worst yet, a detainee held in military custody under the "unlawful enemy combatant" designation who is given neither a combatant status review tribunal nor a military commission trial has no way of getting any court to hear his case at all. This person would be resigned to executive detention in U.S. military custody *indefinitely*. Even after a detainee has been released from military custody, the MCA prevents him from seeking any sort of redress or compensation from a U.S. court no matter how unjust his imprisonment and how greatly he suffered.

For detainees held in military detention but not scheduled to be tried before a military commission, the court review intended to take the place of a habeas corpus hearing would limit appeal of their tribunal determinations with no possibility of introducing any factual evidence, even factual evidence that could conclusively demonstrate innocence. Examples of what such outrageous injustice would look like already exist. The Algerian men noted in chapter 4, who were wrongly accused of terrorist activities in Bosnia and sent to Guantánamo, were acquitted of all charges and freed by the Bosnian Supreme Court. However, they were not permitted to present the Bosnian court's decision as evidence in their Combatant Status Review Tribunals. Now, under the new legal regime sought by the administration, even the court of appeals sitting in review of the CSRT ruling would not be permitted to receive such evidence as part of its review and the men could remain unjustly imprisoned forever.

For detainees who will be tried before a military commission, the situation is also very bleak. The MCA would allow commission trials to take place with few of the fair trial guarantees provided by either our civilian or military justice systems. Among the most disturbing provisions are those that would: permit the use of evidence obtained through coercive interrogations without any opportunity for the defendant to confront his accusers; permit the exclusion of the defendant from the proceedings in certain circumstances; limit the defendant's right to see any classified evidence even if it is exculpatory; prevent the defendant from claiming rights and protections granted to him under the Geneva Conventions; seek to hold the defendant criminally responsible for offenses that are not war crimes and for acts that were not crimes at the time they were committed; and authorize imposition of the death penalty or any period of imprisonment.

Each of these provisions threatens our democracy. That the MCA appears to extend the jurisdiction of the military commissions beyond trials concerning "violations of the laws of war" is troubling.[40] As we authorize military commissions to try people for terrorism-related activities and other crimes that have always been tried in our criminal courts, we shift the terrorism-related prosecutions of noncitizens to a court system that deprives defendants of the most basic due process rights. This concept could be invoked to use military commissions to try people for crimes with no relationship to any terrorist activity and at the same time bypass our civilian criminal justice system with all of its constitutional guarantees. The Bush administration offers no justification for exempting common criminal cases from our criminal justice system,[41] although one reason seems clear enough: the looser rules of the military commission system mean that convictions will be far easier to accomplish.

Nor has the administration or Congress offered any explanation as to why immigrants are to be denied their basic fundamental rights as compared to citizens. In passing the MCA, Congress has aided the administration in the creation of a two-tier system of justice for the world with the top tier reserved for American citizens and the bottom tier reserved for everyone else. The differential treatment broadcasts to the world what is plainly the administration's true position: all noncitizens are to be viewed with suspicion, and may be denied—at the sole discretion of the president—the constitutional protections that we have *always afforded to every person* accused of a crime in this country. Our commitment to equal treatment has been undermined without so much as a nod to judicial precedent or public opinion. This country has never advanced the idea that only citizens are entitled to the benefits of our constitutional guarantees when they are subject to criminal prosecution.[42] In fact, the United States Supreme Court has held steadfast to this principle of equal protection even in those periods in which the country sought to impose harsh measures to address threats to national security. For example, more than a century ago Congress enacted a statute that subjected Chinese immigrants caught without proper documents to one year of hard labor without providing them with proper criminal trial protections. On appeal to the Supreme Court in the case *Wong Wing v. United States*,[43] the Court struck down the statute, finding that it was an unlawful deprivation of the immigrants' constitutional rights. The Supreme Court again emphasized our Constitution's commitment to this key democratic principle in 2001, when it held in *Zadvydas v. Davis*,[44] that "the Due Process Clause applies to all 'persons' within the United States, including aliens, whether their presence here is lawful, unlawful, temporary, or permanent."[45]

The breadth of the military commission's authority is further augmented by the definitions used in specifying the offenses that are triable by the commissions, as well as by the inclusion of offenses that have never been recognized as "war crimes." The offense of "conspiracy" falls within this category. A defendant may be tried for "conspiracy" if he "conspires to commit one or more substantive offenses triable by military commission. . . ."[46] This means that one can be tried for conspiracy even if the underlying unlawful act is not a violation of the law of war and therefore is outside the scope of the military commission. As human rights experts have appropriately noted, "[t]he issue here is not whether international acts genuinely constituting participation, conspiracy, or providing material support to terrorist activities should be criminalized; U.S. civilian law already criminalizes such acts. The question is whether such offenses are war crimes, and whether defendants charged with such acts, including longstanding U.S. residents, should be sidelined from the civilian criminal justice system, and so denied the normal rights associated with the presumption of innocence."[47] The Supreme Court in *Hamdan* said that the Constitution precludes military commissions from prosecuting crimes that lie outside of the laws of war. According to Justice Stevens in *Hamdan*, the government must prosecute crimes in federal courts whenever those courts are open and functioning.

The ambiguity of the elements of the MCA's named offenses means that no one will be able to ascertain exactly what is forbidden and, thus, what behavior is to be avoided. In this country, no criminal law that provided punishment to a person on the basis of such vague and ambiguous terms would ever pass muster under our Constitution. The Supreme Court has long adhered to the principle that a law is unconstitutional if it is so ambiguous that a person of common understanding cannot know what conduct is forbidden.[48] Furthermore, in the absence of more clear and precise definitions of the covered offenses, we cannot gauge whether individuals brought before the military commissions are being treated equally in terms of the offenses they are charged with, the type of evidence that is used against them, or the rulings made in their individual cases. We have no means of ensuring consistency in charging, trying, convicting, or sentencing those persons brought before the military commissions. Free of democratic accountability and invested with the power to order executions in secret, the president and the secretary of defense have indeed granted these commissions the totalitarian powers of the Star Chamber.

Finally, because there are no statutes of limitations governing the president's determination of who is to be charged and tried by military commission, presumably any person who ever committed an act deemed to fall within that very large and undefined category of "hostilities," could many years later find themselves suspected of being a terrorist and being dragged into the black hole of the military commissions.

WHAT ELSE DOES THE MCA DO?

The MCA also authorizes coercive interrogation tactics and creates retroactive immunity from prosecution for war crimes. None of the publicized debates in Congress and few of the mainstream media stories on the MCA focused on what may have been one of the Bush administration's chief motivations behind passage of the act. It waters down the War Crimes Act of 1996, the federal law that makes certain violations of the laws of war felonies if they are committed against or by a U.S. citizen. It a crime to mistreat detainees in violation of the Geneva Conventions. Although no one has ever been prosecuted under this law to date, CIA operatives and civilian personnel, including civilians working for the military, are vulnerable to prosecution under the War Crimes Act. Members of the armed forces must face prosecution by a court-martial under the Uniform Code of Military Justice.

Why was it necessary to limit the reach of the War Crimes Act by decriminalizing certain behavior and eliminating any possibility for accountability for past violations of the law? The answer seems clear enough. Beginning as far back as January 2002, the Bush administration was worried about prosecutions that could be brought for detainee mistreatment by a future administration, and in particular about prosecutions brought in cases where detainees died while in U.S. custody. There is no statute of limitations in cases where the mistreatment results in death, raising the specter of prosecution of administration officials far into the future. Some political analysts have even surmised that then White House Counsel Alberto Gonzales recommended against applying the Geneva Conventions to the war in Afghanistan because, the theory goes, if the conventions did not apply, then the War Crimes Act which criminalizes their violation would not apply either.[49]

Prior to the MCA, the War Crimes Act criminalized all violations of Article 3 of the Geneva Conventions (prohibiting cruel and inhuman treatment), as well as other grave breaches of the Geneva Conventions. This prohibition has now been replaced by a very short, specific list of "grave breaches" of Article 3 that now constitute war crimes. Nine offenses make this list, but certain key offenses are left out. For example, prior to the MCA amendments to the War Crimes Act, it was a war crime to deprive a detainee of the rights of a fair trial. Now, subjecting a detainee to an unfair trial is no longer a war crime. Nor is "degrading and humiliating treatment," such as the sexual taunting, forced nudity, and similar interrogation techniques invented at Guantánamo and exported to the Abu Ghraib Prison in Iraq. The International Committee of the Red Cross has expressed deep concern over these omissions from the list of violations considered war crimes under domestic U.S. law, noting as well that the new law contains no explicit prohibition on the use of coerced testimony as evidence.[50]

Not only has the list of violations been shortened, but the threshold for what constitutes a war crime is now much higher. While "cruel and inhuman treatment" is listed as offense, only conduct that causes serious physical or mental pain or suffering qualifies as cruel and inhuman treatment. Disturbingly, this type of pain or suffering is defined as existing only where there is "extreme" pain, substantial risk of death, or significant impairment of a body part, organ or mental faculty. According to administration officials, this definition means that certain of the "special" interrogation techniques approved by the president and Secretary Rumsfeld, such as prolonged sleep deprivation, extended exposure to temperature extremes, and waterboarding (simulated drowning) are not prohibited as cruel and inhuman treatment because they do not cause "prolonged suffering."

Have we decided that we will permit a president to knowingly violate the Constitution, criminal laws, and international treaties—so long as Congress is willing to go along with a request to create retroactive immunity? The MCA provides the president with the greatest array of legal powers that has ever been vested in a single person, office, or branch of government since the birth of this nation, a stunning abandonment of the doctrine of separation of powers. In this regard, the Bush administration's military commission structure is entirely consistent with the administration's persistent—and largely effective—efforts to usurp power from the other branches of government. And its successful shepherding of the MCA through Congress represents the culmination of its efforts to shred the Geneva Conventions. If the law passes scrutiny, the administration will then have succeeded in making real Attorney General Alberto Gonzales's comment that the Geneva Conventions are outdated and irrelevant.

THE AVALANCHE THAT LED UP TO THE CREATION OF AN EXTRACONSTITUTIONAL MILITARY COURT

As discussed in previous chapters, by the time the November 13, 2001, Military Order was signed, the Justice Department had already detained more than two thousand immigrants and was in the process of authorizing local law enforcement agencies to question five thousand young men of Middle Eastern descent who had entered the country legally after January 1, 2000, about their political associations. These executive actions came on the heels of the Justice Department's October 30, 2001, decision to authorize governmental monitoring of communications between individuals detained by the federal government and their lawyers when the attorney general believes that intercepting the communication may be helpful in deterring acts of violence or terrorism.[51] This unprecedented intrusion on the attorney-client privilege permitted such eavesdropping without prior judicial approval, *regardless* of whether anyone has been charged with a crime. The new policy was widely criticized because of its chilling effect on attorney-client communications, its impairment of the attorney-client privilege, and its subversion of the Sixth Amendment's guarantee of effective assistance of counsel in criminal cases.[52]

Over the past five years, the Bush administration has claimed the unprecedented executive power to engage in "war on terror" seizure, detention, and interrogation operations, without any involvement or oversight by either Congress or the courts. By as early as February 2002, President Bush and his legal advisers had concluded that he had the power to unilaterally suspend the operation of the Geneva Conventions and place "war on terror" detainees in places where courts could not reach. Since the Supreme Court issued its decision in *Rasul v. Bush* holding that the Guantánamo detainees have the right to test the legality of their detention in court, the Bush administration has consistently refused to acknowledge that decision and has argued vehemently that the federal courts do not have jurisdiction in any case involving the president's detention and trial of people he has declared "enemy combatants." This position—one which utterly disavows the separation of powers doctrine and undermines the key constitutional principle that the judiciary must act as a check on the executive—remains the hallmark of the Bush administration's tenure. In December 2003, in an argument before the Ninth Circuit Court of Appeals, Justice Department lawyers argued that the administration could detain any person it deemed to be an "enemy combatant" and that there could be no judicial review of the person's detention even if there were allegations of torture or summary execution. In April 2004, then solicitor general Ted Olsen told the nine justices of the Supreme Court in the *Rasul* case that they too did not have the power to review such detentions and that the Court should "not try to micromanage the war on terror." Later on, Justice Department lawyers would repeat this refrain before the district court judges assigned to handle detainees' habeas corpus cases, arguing that President Bush's power to pick up any person, from any country, at any time, and place that person in indefinite executive detention, was not subject to any constitutional constraint, including judicial review.

These new policies constitute only a small piece of what is becoming the most sweeping and sustained governmental effort to investigate and prosecute perceived "enemies" of the state since the McCarthy era. The implications of such changes are so antithetical to democratic principles that immediate public scrutiny and debate are needed to assess the degree to which these policies have violated the Constitution, our federal law, and our international treaty obligations to respect human rights. The creation of these broad investigatory, adjudicatory, and sentencing powers have already exacted a staggering price in terms of our rights and freedoms, yet the Bush administration maintains that such sacrifices are needed to counter the new security risks posed by terrorism.[53] Citizens, policy makers, educators, lawyers, and civil rights activists have all expressed grave concerns about the toll these measures have taken on our democratic institutions, our credibility in the international community, and our ability to defend and advance human rights around the world. Could this be a price that we are willing to pay? We won't know until we, *the People*—fully informed of the facts and determined to participate—engage in the open and rigorous discourse that is the hallmark of democracy.

WITH THE MCA IN PLACE, DOES THE PRESIDENT NOW HAVE THE LEGAL AUTHORITY TO CREATE MILITARY COMMISSIONS TO TRY TERRORISM SUSPECTS?

The Bush administration originally claimed that the Military Order is constitutional, politically necessary, and morally justified. It points to three sources of federal authority for the Military Order: (1) the president's constitutional authority as commander in chief of the armed forces of the United States;[54] (2) the Congressional Joint Resolution Authorizing the Use of Military Force;[55] and (3) two provisions of the Uniform Code of Military Justice.[56] After the *Hamdan* decision, we now know that none of these sources actually granted the president the authority that he claimed. The military commission system was found to be unlawful under U.S. law and unprecedented in our history, and to conflict with international legal standards.

America's use of military commissions in the past provides no support whatsoever for the way military commissions are presently configured under the MCA. As previously discussed, the Bush administration has pointed to the World War II *Quirin* case as historical support for its position. In *Quirin*,[57] the Court upheld the propriety of a trial of eight German saboteurs by military commission.[58] In fact, that decision does not support the administration's position. At the time of the *Quirin* case, Congress had issued a formal declaration of war and had expressly authorized the trial by military commission of "enemy aliens" who violate the law of war—i.e., citizens of a state with which the United States is at war—in two statutes, Articles 81 and 82 of the Articles of War.[59] The Supreme Court based its decision in the case on the international law of war as it existed at the time, and upheld the authority of the military commission to try enemy-state combatants for their unlawful actions within the United States during a *declared* international armed conflict.

The circumstances under which the Court decided the *Quirin* case are simply not present today. None of the proposed defendants can be charged with violations of the law of war committed in the context of a declared armed conflict because Congress has not made a formal declaration of war. Even if it had, any international armed conflict ended with the U.S. recognition of the provisional government of Afghanistan. Nor are members of Al Qaeda "enemy aliens" within the meaning of international law because they are not combatants or soldiers from an enemy state's army.[60]

International treaty law defines the specific circumstances in which the laws of war apply and the United States has accepted and adopted these rules.[61] Under the Geneva Conventions, a state of war exists only when a conflict arises between nation-states.[62] While the Geneva Conventions also spell out rules of war that apply for "non-international armed conflicts" or noncountry conflicts, they clearly provide that such rules apply only to conflicts between a state's armed forces and dissident groups within that state that are under responsible command and that exercise authority over a part of the state's territory.[63] Plainly, neither of these definitions applies to the current situation. On September 18, 2001, Congress authorized military action, but it did not issue a declaration of war. Moreover, even if the United States' actions with regard to Afghanistan and the Taliban government amounted to a declaration of war against those entities, the same conclusion can not be drawn with respect to a group like Al Qaeda that is neither a nation nor a government.[64] In fact, the people being held by the Bush administration on suspicion of terrorism may be citizens of as many as forty-seven different nations. A number of these nations are close allies with the United States, such as France, Spain, and Egypt. The *Quirin* decision cannot stretch to cover the present circumstances or the current standards of the international law of war.

Furthermore, the Court's decision in *Quirin* is now widely recognized as an abysmal miscarriage of fairness and justice. Historians who have analyzed FBI records declassified in the 1960s, as well as prosecutors who actually participated in the proceedings, have reached a consensus that the 1942 tribunals were deeply flawed and the fates of those tried were sealed long before the confused proceedings were held.[65] Undoubtedly, those tribunals should not constitute the model for how the U.S. tries any person for any offense.

Although Congress enacted legislation authorizing the use of courts-martial after World War II, such tribunals have limited jurisdiction and have never been used to try offenses committed by civilians.[66] The Supreme Court addressed this issue many years ago in *Milligan,* a Civil War–era case in which the Court overturned a conviction of a civilian by a military tribunal because the tribunal had not been authorized by either the Constitution or Congress.[67] Speaking to the issue of presidential authority, the Court stressed that the use of military tribunals for civilians "cannot [be] justif[ied] on the mandate of the President; because he is controlled by law, and has his appropriate sphere of duty, which is to execute, not to make, the laws; and there is no unwritten criminal code to which resort can be had as a source of jurisdiction."[68] The Supreme Court in the *Milligan* case also expressly rejected the government's contention that the use of a military tribunal was necessary given the exigencies of the Civil War. The Court stressed, "The Constitution of the United States is a law for rulers and people, equally in war and in peace, and covers with the shield of its protection all classes of men, at all times, and under all circumstances."[69] Surely the president cannot argue that terrorism poses a greater threat to our nation than the Civil War.

DOES THE MILITARY COMMISSION SYSTEM CONTEMPLATED BY THE MCA VIOLATE INTERNATIONAL LAW?

To the extent that any military commissions could legally hear cases at all, they would have to be limited solely to combatants alleged to have violated the laws of war.[70] By definition, the laws of war are only violated during an armed conflict by persons who are acting on behalf of a state or as part of an insurgency that rises to the level of a civil war. Therefore, in order to assess the current situation in terms of international law, we must first determine whether the attacks of September 11, 2001, can be considered acts of war committed by state actors.

Although under the principles of international law the United States cannot be at war with bands of terrorists, with regard to those fighting on behalf of the Taliban regime, the situation is different. The Taliban regime was the acting government of Afghanistan, whether formally recognized by the United States or not, and once the United States attacked that country, a "war"—or an international armed conflict—under international law was started. Therefore, Taliban fighters captured on the battlefield must be treated in accordance with the requirements of the Geneva Conventions, and if they are accused of committing war crimes, they must be tried before courts-martial and not military tribunals.

Whether the current situation constitutes a "war" or "international armed conflict" within the meaning of international law is of great importance in determining the legal status of those persons involved in the hostilities, the forum in which they can be tried for their actions, and the nature of the charges that can be brought against them. While civilians can be prosecuted for their mere involvement in hostilities, combatants cannot. The status of those captured under international law will be either that of a prisoner of war protected under the Third Geneva Convention or that of a civilian or "unprivileged combatant" protected under the Fourth Geneva Convention. The rights afforded to POWs on the one hand, and civilians and unprivileged combatants on the other, differ significantly. For this reason, the question of whether the present state of affairs amounts to a war or armed conflict must be addressed first.

American officials have used the word "war" euphemistically to refer to a wide range of governmental programs designed to address major social and political problems—e.g., the "war on poverty" or the "war on drugs." But historically the word's accepted meaning has been that of a conflict between traditional nations that have defined borders and organized military forces, the success of which is measured in terms of the achievement of geographical objectives. It is from this historical understanding that the international law definition is derived.

International humanitarian law imposes rights and obligations on all parties to international and internal (non-international) armed conflicts. Under the Geneva Conventions and their two protocols,[71] "war" or "armed conflict" can only arise between two or more nation-states or a nation-state and an insurgent group within that state.[72] A "state," for purposes of international law, is "an entity that has a defined territory and a permanent population, under the control of its own government, and that engages in, or has capacity to engage in, formal relations with other such entities."[73] States are the principal entities that have a legal personality in the international legal order; they have the capacity to make agreements and treaties, and they have rights and corresponding obligations under them.

The answer to the question of whether the United States can in fact be "at war" with Al Qaeda or any other group of terrorists is clear in light of these international law principles. Terrorist organizations like Al Qaeda plainly do not fit within the definition of a state: members of the network are reportedly dispersed throughout countries all over the world and are not associated with any distinct territory. So our fight with Al Qaeda is not a "war" or "armed conflict" of any sort under international law.

The international humanitarian law analysis differs for those captured on the battlefield in Afghanistan. Individuals who meet the "combatant" criteria and who are captured in the course of an armed conflict are afforded POW status, with rights and protections commensurate with the respect accorded their military status as soldiers. The protections of the Geneva Conventions provide that POWs must be quartered in conditions that meet the same general standards as the quarters available to the captor's force, i.e., the U.S. armed forces. The legal rights of POWs include the right to attack military objectives (e.g., armed forces personnel, bases, equipment) and the right not to be prosecuted for legitimate military actions (e.g., taking up arms against other combatants). Those POWs whom the government wishes to prosecute for war crimes (such as the murder of civilians) are entitled to certain minimum standards of due process in judicial proceedings and must be tried by the same court under the same rules as those used for the detaining country's armed forces.[74] In that light, a captured Taliban soldier who fought for the regular armed forces of Afghanistan should be deemed a POW and should not be tried by the military commissions. If warranted, however, a Taliban soldier could be tried by an American court-martial for violations of the laws of war.

Some of the people captured in Afghanistan and detained by the U.S. government may not be POWs. Under the Geneva Conventions, only those who were members of the armed forces or were part of an identifiable militia group that complied with the formal requirements of combatant status may be considered POWs. In circumstances where there is doubt about a prisoner's status, the Geneva Conventions and U.S. military regulations require that the prisoner be considered a POW and treated as such until a "competent tribunal" can make a determination.[75] The presumption that a person captured on a battlefield has POW status provides protections that, after World War II, all nations thought necessary to protect all people, including American servicemen and women, captured in war.

Again, as discussed, the Geneva Conventions require the humane treatment of *all* persons captured during armed conflict. Every captured person is entitled to basic shelter, food, clothing, and medical attention.[76] No detainee may be subjected to torture, corporal punishment, or humiliating or degrading treatment. These rules apply regardless of whether one is found to have POW status. If the United States government fails to show respect for the Geneva Conventions, it will be in no position to demand that captured American soldiers be treated any better.[77]

The MCA would also empower the president to violate the United States' binding international treaty obligations. The International Covenant on Civil and Political Rights (ICCPR) obligates all signatories to protect the due process rights of all persons subject to any criminal proceeding. Once these treaty obligations were ratified by the United States, they became the "supreme Law of the Land" under the U.S. Constitution, and must be applied by all courts in proceedings that are brought under them. U.S. treaty obligations simply cannot lawfully be overturned or ignored by a president who grants himself powers above the law.

The MCA raises significant concerns regarding whether the United States will comply with its obligations under the ICCPR.[78] Like other agreements ensuring the protection of human rights, the ICCPR permits a country to deviate from some of these obligations in times of public emergencies.[79] However, the covenant also provides that certain rights and freedoms are so fundamental that they may not be suspended even in a time of public emergency. These rights include, among many others: the right to live your life (Article 6); the prohibition against torture and cruel, inhuman, and degrading treatment or punishment (Article 7); the prohibition against convictions based on retroactive laws (Article 15); and the right of religious freedom (Article 18).[80]

The ICCPR sets forth a specific procedure that must be followed when a state wishes to intentionally infringe upon any of those rights.[81] Under this procedure, the state must immediately inform other parties to the covenant of the specific provisions from which it has deviated, and it must use as intermediary the secretary general of the United Nations. A state must explain its reasons for the transgression and must state the date upon which it will resume observing the provision. Finally, a state may deviate from its obligations under the ICCPR only "to the extent strictly required by the exigencies of the situation" and only provided that such measures are not inconsistent with its other obligations under international law. Nothing done to date by the Bush administration meets the high standard for deviating from the human rights guarantees of the ICCPR.

The MCA sharply curtails the right to liberty and security of the person as guaranteed by Article 9 and the right to a fair trial as guaranteed by Article 14 of the covenant. Because the MCA fails to specify the nature of all of the outlawed conduct, it violates the Article 9 prohibition against arbitrary arrest and detention. Under Article 9, an individual detained on a criminal charge must be brought promptly before a judge or officer and trial must be held within a reasonable time. Anyone who is detained pending trial has the right to have the lawfulness of the detention determined by a court. But under the MCA, there is no requirement that all persons detained be told the reason for their arrest or the charges against them and there is no requirement that they be brought before a judicial authority to determine the lawfulness of their detention. In fact, to the contrary, the MCA expressly negates the right of a detainee to challenge the lawfulness of his detention. The MCA also violates the Article 14 guarantees of the right to due process and to a fair and public hearing by a competent, independent, and impartial tribunal. The act does not provide for a trial by an independent and impartial judge or for a public trial. The accused has no real privilege against self-incrimination, nor is he guaranteed full access to the evidence submitted against him.

AMERICA'S CONDEMNATION OF MILITARY TRIBUNALS LIKE THOSE IMPLEMENTED BY THE MCA

In virtually every instance in which other countries have used military tribunals to try civilians, the State Department has strongly criticized the practice on the specific ground that the elimination of due process guarantees undermines the basic human right to a fair, public trial. Take a look at the following examples of U.S. pronouncements on this issue:

China: In its annual Country Report on Human Rights Practices, the State Department recently criticized the Chinese justice system in part because defendants there are not provided with certain due process guarantees, including the presumption of innocence, proof of guilt beyond a reasonable doubt, and habeas corpus relief. In particular, the State Department finds problematic that the Chinese government has broad authority to define crimes that endanger "state security"; that trials involving national security may be conducted in secret; that police can monitor attorney-client meetings; and that defendants are not always permitted to confront their accusers. Most recently, the State Department concluded that the lack of due process is particularly egregious in death penalty cases.

Egypt: In its Country Reports for 2002 and 2003, the State Department severely criticized the manner in which military tribunals were used in Egypt to try offenses ranging from nonviolent political dissent to acts of terrorism. The State Department's specific objections included aspects that are now cause for concern in the United States: civilians may be tried by the military tribunal; the judges are military officers appointed by the Ministry of Defense; and verdicts may not be appealed. The State Department's year 2000 annual Country Report expressly noted that "this use of military courts . . . has deprived hundreds of civilian defendants of their constitutional right to be tried by a civilian judge." The 2000 report also stated that "military courts do not ensure civilian defendants due process before an independent tribunal" and that the judges "are neither as independent nor as qualified as civilian judges in applying the civilian Penal Code."

In both of these cases, the United States has rightfully and repeatedly refused to accept the rationalizations offered by foreign governments for dispensing with due process rights and convening secret military tribunals to try civilians. Now political leaders and human rights advocates from inside and outside of the United States have begun to urge Americans to call the Bush administration to account for putting forth the same unconvincing justifications for engaging in the same lawless behavior.[82]

The Bush administration has articulated a threefold rationale for its shocking disregard of foreign policy pronouncements in this area. According to President Bush, Vice President Cheney, and Secretary Rumsfeld, the military commission system is necessary because it will ensure swift and uncomplicated justice and allow the government to "use intelligence information that could not be used in a regular court proceeding"[83] due to concerns about the safety of sources and the confidentiality of intelligence measures; and ensure the safety of jurors and witnesses. However, none of these arguments can truly justify abandoning our constitutional court system, which is *not* based upon speed, simplicity, and deference to the desires of the government. To the contrary, it recognizes that unless it thoroughly protects the interests of the accused in the face of the demands of the mob, then the justice system is not worthy of that name.

To justify the Bush administration's desire to depart from the principles of the Constitution at home, it now echoes some of the same reasoning that it criticized regarding the use of military tribunals abroad. But such pleas ring hollow. History demonstrates that our federal courts are fully capable of handling cases involving crimes of terrorism against the United States.[84] Following public trials that conformed to all constitutional requirements, those charged with the 1998 bombings of the American embassies in Kenya and Tanzania as well as with the 1993 attack on the World Trade Center were convicted in our federal courts. Furthermore, Congress has recently expanded the criminal jurisdiction of our federal courts in a deliberate effort to cover a broader range of terrorism offenses.[85] That terrorists have been successfully prosecuted in civilian courts belies the administration's call for the use of military tribunals. And because federal courts can restrict public disclosure of sensitive information and hold defendants without bond if their release could harm national security or endanger the community, neither of these prosecutions jeopardized our intelligence sources or put jurors or witnesses at risk.[86]

The U.S. court system is often acknowledged as a model for transparent justice in a democratic society. We need not sacrifice our constitutional principles nor abandon our commitment to human rights in order to try and punish those accused of terrorism.

Full implementation of the military commission system will undermine our collective ideals in three ways. First, the government would communicate to the world that it values secrecy and expediency over justice by permitting one person to play all of the prosecutorial and judgment roles, with little accountability to the other branches of government or to the people. Second, by implementing the MCA, the United States creates a model for military (and indeed even civilian) trials that conveys that due process rights cannot withstand the pressure of the times and so must be replaced by a system of secret proceedings in which the charges, the evidence, the verdicts, and the punishments would never have to be revealed to the public. We will have burned the rule book of American justice and replaced it with a totalitarian code of vengeance. Third, as reflected in the MCA, the administration's disdain for adherence to fundamental human rights principles in our own country irrevocably damages our ability to exert moral leadership and champion human rights around the world. We will be giving license to the most repressive regimes in the world to violate the human and civil rights of their citizens because that is the model we have advertised and exported to the world.

By implementing this new system, the United States will deal a stunning blow to the institutions of international law, communicating to the world that it will not comply with the international treaties that it has signed and ratified. We will etch in bold relief our dismissal of global collaborative efforts and our contempt for the results of these efforts. As a result, Americans living abroad will be placed at risk. Once we use these tribunals, our government will be unable to protest effectively when other countries use similar measures against American civilians, peacekeepers, diplomats, or soldiers who are accused of terrorist activities. In taking this treacherous step, the United States announces that it rejects our history as a country developed by and for immigrants seeking a better life. We announce that this country is no longer a haven for those who seek refuge from oppression and violence around the globe. We announce to the world that any person not born in this country is inherently suspect.

Yet we remain, mostly, a nation of courageous, open, and tolerant people who have not forgotten how recently our own families came to this country for the promise of a better life. And we are neither so ignorant nor so blind as to equate the word "immigrant" with the word "terrorist." We will not stray from the path of justice if we are brave and careful and wise and generous and if we embrace our responsibilities to our communities and to those struggling for freedom around the world. Only then will we reject the devil's bargain that the government offers and refuse to sacrifice our commitment to civil and human rights out of fear. We must embrace the truth of our principles and our best teachings, and refuse to abandon the ideals that we love best: justice, equality, and truth.

CHAPTER SIX

Kidnapping for Preventive Detention and Interrogation under Torture

All told, more than 3,000 suspected terrorists have been arrested in many countries. Many others have met a different fate. Let's put it this way—they are no longer a problem to the United States and our friends and allies. . . . We have the terrorists on the run. We're keeping them on the run. One by one, the terrorists are learning the meaning of American Justice.

—President George W. Bush, State of the Union Address, January 28, 2003

We don't kick the [expletive] out of them. We send them to other countries so they can kick the [expletive] out of them.

—Unnamed U.S. government official[1]

THE RENDITION PROGRAM: ILLEGAL, IMMORAL, AND EXTRAORDINARY

Even after the belated U.S. Army investigations into complaints regarding the use of torture and other abusive methods at Guantánamo and U.S. detention facilities in Afghanistan and Iraq, another covert tactic has recently taken the spotlight in the public debate about the strategies used by the government in its global "war on terror": the Bush administration's f program.

The term "rendition" has been used in government agency parlance for many years to refer to the transfer of an individual from one country to another without recourse to any of the standard legal procedures of extradition, immigration removal, or exclusion. For some time, the U.S. government has engaged in the "regular" rendition of alleged criminals that it wanted to stand trial in U.S. courts against the wishes of their host government. The case of General Manuel Noriega offers an interesting example of this strategy.

According to the U.S. government's allegations, Manuel Noriega exploited his position as a general in the Republic of Panama's army to obtain personal profit, offering narcotics traffickers the safe use of Panama as a location for shipment of large loads of cocaine destined for the United States, providing protection for laboratory facilities for the manufacture of cocaine, and allowing the deposit of millions of dollars of narcotics proceeds in Panamanian banks. The United States accused Noriega of participating in a racketeering enterprise designed to facilitate the manufacture and transportation of large quantities of cocaine destined for the United States and to launder narcotics proceeds.

On February 14, 1988, a federal grand jury sitting in Miami, Florida, returned a twelve-count indictment charging General Noriega with participating in an international conspiracy to import cocaine and materials used in producing cocaine into and out of the United States. Shortly after these charges against Noriega were brought, Noriega delivered a widely publicized speech in which he denounced the United States. Subsequently, on December 15, 1989, he declared that a "state of war" existed between Panama and the United States. Tensions increased between the two countries, and on December 20, 1989, President George H. W. Bush ordered U.S. troops into combat in Panama City on a mission whose stated goals were to restore democracy, preserve the Panama Canal treaties, and seize General Noriega to face federal drug charges in the United States. Noriega successfully eluded American forces for several days, prompting the United States government to offer a one million dollar bounty for his capture. Eventually, he took sanctuary in the Papal Nunciature in Panama City, touching off a diplomatic impasse when Vatican officials refused to turn Noriega over to the United States. After an eleven-day standoff, Noriega surrendered to American forces on January 3,

1990. He was flown to Florida and formally arrested by agents of the Drug Enforcement Agency.

Responding to Noriega's contention that the military action which brought about his arrest was "shocking to the conscience" and that due process considerations required the court to divest itself of authority over him, the court held that the principle was "well settled that the manner by which a defendant is brought before the court normally does not affect the ability of the government to try him." The court relied for support on the *Ker-Frisbie* doctrine, which holds that a court is not deprived of jurisdiction to try a defendant on the ground that the defendant's presence before the court was procured by unlawful means.[2]

Before the September 11 attacks, executive orders[3] authorized the CIA to carry out renditions under restrictive rules that included interagency oversight and review by the White House and that authorized renditions for the *purpose* of bringing prisoners to this country to face criminal charges in a court of law.[4] Ostensibly, "regular" renditions or "renditions to justice" were intended to subject the individual kidnapped and transferred to United States territory the full and fair process of the federal courts. The Interim Report issued by the 9/11 Commission characterized this pre-September 11 rendition program as follows:

> The role of diplomacy was to gain the cooperation of other governments in bringing terrorists to justice. PDD 39 stated: "When terrorists wanted for violation of U.S. law are at large overseas, their return for prosecution should be a matter of the highest priority and shall be a continuing central issue in bilateral relations with any state that harbors or assists them." If extradition procedures were unavailable or put aside, the United States could seek the local country's assistance in a rendition, secretly putting the fugitive in a plane back to America or some third country for trial.[5]

The Bush administration's extraordinary rendition program now uses this practice to achieve different objectives: indefinite preventive detention of a terrorism suspect in a foreign country that is willing to incarcerate someone without trial; or interrogation under torture and other abusive measures that would not be legally or morally permissible in this country. Although administration officials have defended the program as only a slight variation from its antecedent, the plain fact is that it looks nothing like the "rendition to justice" policy. There is no longer any corresponding intention to achieve justice either for society or for the individual rendered. Today, the U.S. government contemplates sending in military special forces teams to violate other nations' sovereignty by snatching civilians literally off the streets, blindfolding and shackling the "targets" or "packages" and flying them to third countries to hand them over to secret police or intelligence interrogation teams, depriving them of the protections of the Geneva Conventions as required by the laws of war, and hiding them from the International Committee of the Red Cross, then ordering either that the individuals be held indefinitely without charge or trial or that they be "prepared" for U.S. transport to Guantánamo or a secret CIA-run facility for indefinite detention.

After initial denials, the United States government now openly defends its secret extraordinary rendition program as a legitimate and effective counterterrorism technique, despite its violation of domestic constitutional law and international prohibitions against *refoulement*, torture, and cruel, inhuman, or degrading treatment.[6] Former CIA director George Tenet stated that rendition is one of the United States' key counterterrorism policies, and publicly confirmed that the practice had even been successfully used by the CIA even before September 11.[7] Responding to early inquiries about the changed rendition policy and the role of torture reportedly involved in such transfers, former Defense Department general counsel William Haynes, in a June 2004 letter to Senator Patrick Leahy (D-VT), stated that: "United States policy is to obtain specific assurances from the receiving country that it will not torture the individual being transferred to that country. We can assure you that the United States would take steps to investigate credible allegations of torture and take appropriate action if there were reason to believe that those assurances were not being honored."[8] However, Haynes claims cannot be verified because the process by which diplomatic assurances are obtained is kept secret.[9]

As more details about the program were made public in 2005 and 2006, government officials from Attorney General Alberto Gonzales to Secretary of State Condoleezza Rice have echoed Haynes's false promise by emphatically declaring that the program's *purpose* is not to send detainees "to countries where we believe or we know that they're going to be tortured"[10] and then by softly noting that the United States seeks "diplomatic assurances" if the country receiving the individual has a long history of state-sponsored torture.[11] Although he acknowledged that the United States cannot control what other countries will do, it is what Attorney General Gonzales *did not say* that is of importance. He did not say—and in fact he cannot say truthfully—that the United States takes any steps to monitor whether countries receiving detainees comply with the "diplomatic assurances" that they purportedly offer. He did not say that the United States knowingly condones the torture and abuse of detainees in these countries by providing dossiers with suggested questions as part of the "diplomatic package" sent with the men it transfers, and then sits back and waits for the foreign intelligence interrogators to extract the information requested from the prisoners by whatever methods they find most expedient.[12]

HOW DID WE GET INTO THIS BUSINESS?

How did our "rendition to justice policy"—as flawed as it already was—morph into the nefarious program that is in operation today? Although administration officials have put forth the idea that the Bush extraordinary rendition program is only a slight variation from its antecedent, the plain fact is that it looks nothing like it. People are not being seized on the basis of an existing criminal indictment and they are not being flown to the United States and placed before a federal court for trial with all of the due process protections the Constitution requires. Now justice plays no part in this American policy.

How did this change actually occur? The extraordinary rendition program was adopted as part of a very large, very secret intelligence program authorized by President Bush within six days of the September 11 attacks and without congressional comment or approval.[13] Known publicly only as "GST," an abbreviation of a classified code name, our government is now running one of the largest covert intelligence-gathering programs in this country's history, with an infrastructure that literally spans the globe.[14] Among the GST initiative's clandestine programs include those allowing the CIA to seize terrorism suspects from foreign countries (sometimes with help from foreign intelligence agencies) and transport them to other countries for indefinite detention or interrogation; to create and oversee a web of secret prisons abroad; to use inhumane and immoral interrogation techniques that violate domestic and international law; and to operate an aircraft fleet to accomplish these ends.[15] According to published reports, the top secret presidential order even empowered the CIA to commit assassinations: to hunt down and kill designated persons around the world. This authorization, like the rest of the covert order, is justified by the Bush administration as an act of "self-defense" that was tacitly endorsed by Congress when it passed the Authorization for the Use of Military Force in Afghanistan on September 14, 2001.[16]

Confirmation of the intelligence community's use of these ghastly practices has come from many sources. Intelligence officials within the CIA have confirmed that former CIA director George Tenet "had the authority on who was going to get it."[17] He then "delegated most of the decision making on lethal action to the CIA's Counterterrorism Center."[18] The specific legal authorization for such action came from the Bush administration, which asked for reinterpretations of laws and policies that had been banned under the congressional reforms in the 1970s.[19] In one example of such reinterpretation, the targeting and killing of Hamza Rabia, accused of being an operational planner for Al Qaeda, was classified as an act of self-defense, not as an assassination.[20]

When the CIA wanted approval to use new—and unlawful—methods of interrogation, the White House delegated the task of providing the justification to a small coterie of like-minded lawyers in the Justice Department's Office of Legal Counsel. This group included, among others, Jay Bybee, now a federal judge with lifetime tenure who sits on the Ninth Circuit Court of Appeals, and Jack Goldsmith and John Yoo, now law professors at Harvard and the University of California at Berkeley, respectively. These renegade legal scholars believed fervently in the idea of an all-powerful presidency, answerable to no other branch of government. The unitary executive theory is quite controversial. It in essence dispenses with our familiar notion of the separation of powers and argues in its place that the power of Congress to divest the president of control of the executive branch is limited. The theory proposes that the president possesses *all* of the executive power and controls all agencies within the executive branch. Under this notion, the authority of Congress and the Supreme Court to impose checks and balances on the president's decision making is severely constrained. Discretionary executive power is reserved solely for the president.[21] Possible legal disputes of the president's actions are disallowed because "the executive cannot sue himself" under this theory.[22] The Bush Justice Department has proffered the unitary executive theory not only in support of its extraordinary rendition program but also, for instance, in its determination that the Environmental Protection Agency may not sue the U.S. military for its failure to comply with federal environmental laws (because the only party in the suit would be the president).[23]

The theory takes a distorted, revisionist view of the Founders' intentions. The phrase "unitary executive" in the discussion of the original drafting at the 1787 Constitutional Convention referred merely to the practice of having a single individual fill the office of the president, as opposed to the idea proposed in the Virginia Plan to house several executives in the office of the president.[24] Though the Supreme Court has never ruled on the "unitary executive theory," constitutional law experts have noted that the theory falls quite a bit short given the plain language of the Constitution and the unchallenged history of its framing. The Constitution grants to Congress the exclusive power to "make all Laws which shall be necessary and proper for carrying into Execution . . . all . . . Powers vested by this Constitution in the Government of the United States, or in any Department or Officer thereof," and the exclusive power "To make Rules for the Government and Regulation of the land and naval Forces." Where "Laws" are defined as that which the Congress has the exclusive power to pass, the president is specifically obligated to "take Care that the Laws be faithfully executed." In every Supreme Court case involving a statutory restriction of the power of the president, the statute has been upheld, including those involving statutes that were found only to *imply* the limitation on presidential power.

The Bush administration's commitment to one of the most aggressive interpretation's of presidential power in American history has meant not only that the president has relied *solely* on the advice of the close inner circle of individuals who crafted the legal analysis, political rationales, and plan for implementation, but also that he has excluded the usual governmental players from the process. State Department officials and Justice Department criminal division attorneys, who had previously dealt with international terrorism, were completely locked out of the policy formation process. In fact, the advice of many experienced governmental advisers in these departments, as well as that of high-level officials in the military, was completely ignored.[25] It was left to the CIA and White House Office of Legal Counsel lawyers to write the justifications for seizing suspects far from any battlefield without an order of extradition, detaining them without providing access to counsel or a court, depriving them of all other due process rights, depriving them of the protections of the Geneva Conventions as required by the laws of war, and hiding them from the International Committee of the Red Cross. And it was the members of this same inner presidential planning group who decided that it was legal for suspects to be seized and secretly held in one country and then transported to another for the express purpose of interrogating them under torture or holding them indefinitely, and thereby authorized the new policy of extraordinary rendition.

The CIA policy of outsourcing torture steadily expanded over the years since the September 11 attacks.[26] From the many, often detailed accounts that have now been collected from detainees by their legal counsel or leaked from government officials to news media, it seems that the U.S. government is quite willing to secretly ask the same countries that it openly castigates for their human rights records to do our dirty work for us.[27]

THE VICTIMS OF EXTRAORDINARY RENDITION

Because of the secretive nature of the extraordinary rendition program, the inaccessibility or "disappearance" of many of its victims, and the less than forthright responses of the U.S. and foreign governments participating in the transfers, the facts of many cases are difficult to pin down. Yet as time goes on, more details come to light. There is no longer any doubt that some suspected terrorists have been sent to CIA-run secret detention centers around the world, and that others have been transported for interrogation purposes to third countries including Egypt, Jordan, Syria, and Saudi Arabia.[28] In fact, in a May 2005 television interview, Ahmed Nazif, Prime Minister of Egypt, acknowledged that the Egyptian government had worked since September 11 with the United States to facilitate the rendition of sixty to seventy terrorism suspects to Egypt alone.[29] This collaboration was undertaken despite the fact that the State Department Human Rights Report for Egypt has consistently stated that the use of torture during interrogations in Egypt is "common and persistent."[30] Despite claims that they seek "diplomatic assurances," it appears that U.S. officials are far from concerned about the records of collaborating countries like Egypt. In fact, U.S. officials appear to have deliberately selected countries known for their use of torture in order to ease any constraints on the interrogation of suspects. One unnamed government official told the Washington Post that he had supervised the capture and transfer of accused terrorists, and said that "[i]f you don't violate someone's human rights some of the time, you probably aren't doing your job . . . I don't think we want to be promoting a view of zero tolerance on this."[31]

Our current understanding of the CIA's extraordinary rendition program covers several variations of the unlawful practice of seizing men and flying them to third countries where they are subjected to additional crimes including torture, enforced disappearance, and indefinite detention. One variation of the practice involves the *seizure of men from countries that were not involved in any way in the international armed conflict between Afghanistan and the United States and had no connection to the Taliban government or Al Qaeda.* Despite the countries' lack of any connection to military hostilities or armed resistance against the United States, their citizens were kidnapped and sent to prisons in Afghanistan, Syria, Egypt, or some other cooperating country for interrogation under torture prior to being flown to Guantánamo for detention there.

Mamdouh Habib is one person who suffered this fate. Habib's case utterly belies the Bush administration's claim that the program is justified by congressional approval of the 2001 Authorization of the Use of Military Force in Afghanistan. Habib, an Australian citizen of Egyptian descent, traveled to Pakistan in August 2001 to look for schools for his teenage children to attend. When he learned of the imminent attack planned by the United States for the neighboring country, he made arrangements to cut his trip short and return home. He never made that return flight. In October 2001, Habib was arrested by Pakistani police, who then transferred him to U.S. agents in Pakistan, who in turn transported him to Egypt.

Upon his arrival in Egypt, Habib was taken into secret custody and held in a barren, 6-foot-by-8-foot cell, where he was forced to sleep on the concrete floor with only one blanket. There, he was interrogated under merciless torture. Reports indicate he was hung by his arms from hooks on the wall and "repeatedly kicked, punched, beaten with a stick, rammed with an electric cattle prod, and doused with cold water when he fell asleep; . . . told that if he didn't confess to belonging to Al Qaeda he would be anally raped by specially trained dogs; [and] shackled and forced to stand in three torture chambers: one room was filled with water up to his chin, requiring him to stand on tiptoe for hours; another chamber, filled with water up to his knees [with] a ceiling so low that he was forced into a prolonged, painful stoop; [the third with] water up to his ankles, and within sight of an electric switch and a generator, which his jailers said would be used to electrocute him if he didn't confess."[32] In one ingenious method of cruelty, Habib was suspended with his feet resting on the side of a cylindrical drum that was connected to a battery, and "when Mr. Habib did not give the answers his interrogators wanted, they threw a switch and a jolt of electricity went through the drum. . . . The action of Mr. Habib 'dancing' on the drum forced it to rotate, and his feet constantly slipped, leaving him suspended by only the hooks on the wall."[33] After six months of such torture, U.S. agents retrieved Habib and transported him to

Guantánamo, where he was detained as an "enemy combatant" until his release to freedom in Australia in 2005. There are many other victims who suffered similar crimes as Mamdouh Habib and who still remain locked in the island prison.

There are victims of the CIA's program who fall into another category: men who have been abducted by U.S. special forces from various countries around the world and transported to CIA "black sites" in Eastern Europe, Africa, or elsewhere—prisons into which no court has yet been able to peer.[34] The case of Muhammad Haydar Zammar sheds only a little light on this dark practice. Zammar is a German national who was seized in December 2001 while he was traveling in Morocco. He was held for several weeks there without charge and them flown to Syria, where German intelligence and law enforcement officials interrogated him at the request of U.S. officials. Zammar's family received their last communication from him by letter dated June 8, 2005, which was transmitted to them by the International Committee of the Red Cross (ICRC) in Damascus. Zammar's whereabouts remain unknown to his family.[35]

As discussed in chapter 4, detainees imprisoned at Guantánamo face yet another variation of rendition: the possibility of transfer to a country acknowledged by the U.S. government to practice torture. These so-called "repatriation" transfers to the country of a detainee's birth are carried out regardless of the victim's most recent country of residence or even of their political asylum status. Habib's release to freedom in Australia sadly seems to represent the exception. Many unfortunate souls have been subjected to the government's "transfer" policy; the Defense Department has confirmed that over three hundred persons have been transferred out of Guantánamo,[36] with very few of the transfers resulting in release to freedom.[37] In 2003, Human Rights Watch urged the government to abandon its plans to send Uighur detainees back to China where they would very likely face torture and trial for crimes against the state.[38] Since then, the State Department has stated that although it is willing to release the twenty-two Uighurs to freedom, they cannot be returned to their country of origin because to do so would place them at great risk of torture and possibly death.[39] However, the State Department's concern for the men's well-being may have more to do with the international furor that greeted its plans to return them to China, given that other Guantánamo detainees have been returned to countries such as Tajikistan where it is equally likely they would be subject to torture.[40] In October 2005, a wheelchair-bound Egyptian detainee, Sami al-Laithi, was transferred to Egypt four months after the Defense Department cleared him of being an "enemy combatant." The State Department's latest Country Report on Egypt stated that "torture and abuse of detainees by police, security personnel, and prison guards remained common and persistent," and detailed numerous cases.[41]

That the government is operating primarily out of expediency rather any concern for human rights is illustrated well by its action on May 5, 2006, transporting five Uighur men from Guantánamo to Tirana, Albania, a country with no Uighur community, a skyrocketing unemployment rate, and the acknowledged inability to keep the men safe from extradition—legal or otherwise—to China for trial.[42] The transfer was made on the evening before argument was scheduled in the Court of Appeals in Washington, D.C., on the question of how the Defense Department could justify keeping the men imprisoned in Guantánamo when the department itself had found them innocent more than a year before. Rather than facing the court, the Defense Department ordered the transfer to Albania without consulting the men's habeas counsel—scuttling completely the negotiations under way for the five men to be accepted for asylum and resettlement in one of two countries with Uighur communities. The men now face continual threats from China's increasingly strident demands for their extradition.[43]

Some of these transfers may be taking place as a result of individual or group negotiations between the U.S. and the governments of the detainees' nationality; others, however, are undertaken pursuant to secret bilateral agreements reached between the United States and these countries. Perhaps the best evidence of such agreements, with the exception of the drafts shown briefly to the press in 2005,[44] is the prison that the United States is building in Afghanistan.[45] Just outside of the capital in Kabul, Policharki Prison is reportedly being readied, with the benefit of U.S. funding, in anticipation of the return of Afghani suspects from Guantánamo.[46] Often, as it appears in the case of Al Qadasi in Yemen, the U.S. government has pressured the receiving country into keeping the transferred individual confined indefinitely without charge or trial until the Defense Department determines that the individual no longer poses any threat.[47]

The Bush administration announced in 2005 that it intended to transfer hundreds of Guantánamo detainees to prisons in three countries: Saudi Arabia, Yemen, and Afghanistan, all with troubling human rights records.[48] If it were not for the quick reaction of habeas counsel for the detainees, many more of their clients might be lost and languishing in foreign prisons. Almost unanimously, the courts have ruled that the government's attempt to remove detainees to countries that would afford no due process or Geneva Convention protections would violate the Supreme Court's ruling in the *Rasul* case and the lower courts' own power to determine whether the detentions are legal. To date, no transferred Guantánamo detainee has been charged with any crime by the United States, a fact that the government refuses to acknowledge.

THE CASE OF MAHER ARAR

A close look at the crimes suffered by Maher Arar demonstrates both the inner workings of the extraordinary rendition program and the pernicious effect it has on its victims. Maher Arar is a Canadian citizen in his mid-thirties who was born in Syria and emigrated to Canada with his family when he was a teenager. He was educated in Canada and has worked both in Canada and the United States as a software engineer. He currently lives there with his wife and two children. At no point in his life has Arar ever been charged with a crime.

In September 2002, while on a family vacation, Arar received an e-mail from his former employer, The MathWorks, asking if he was willing to return from his vacation early to consult with a prospective client in Ottawa. Thinking that it would be good to take the job, on September 25, 2002, Arar took a flight to Zurich, leaving his wife and two children behind to enjoy the rest of the vacation. After stopping overnight in Zurich, he boarded a flight to Montreal, with a transfer in JFK Airport in New York City to a connecting flight.

At around noon on September 26, 2002, Arar's flight landed at JFK Airport, and he disembarked in order to catch his connecting flight to Ottawa. Although Arar was not attempting to enter the United States, the law requires that upon arriving from Zurich people traveling further have to pass through U.S. immigration. At the immigration booth, Arar presented a valid Canadian passport to the inspector on duty. After reviewing Arar's passport, the inspector instructed him to wait nearby. At about 2 p.m., an immigration officer brought Arar to an office to be fingerprinted and photographed. Shortly thereafter, two uniformed men searched Arar's wallet, carry-on bags, and luggage without his consent. Concerned that he would miss his connecting flight, Arar repeatedly asked to make a telephone call home. His requests were ignored.

In the late afternoon, several men arrived in the area where Arar was being detained. One of them told him that he wanted to ask him some questions. He assured Arar that he would be permitted to make his connecting flight after answering the questions. When Arar asked them if he could call a lawyer, they told him that only U.S. citizens were entitled to lawyers. An FBI agent then interrogated Arar for nearly five hours. The agent constantly yelled and swore at Arar, calling him a "fucking smart guy" with a "fucking selective memory." When Arar took more than a few seconds to respond to the rapid-fire questioning, the agent became angry. Referring to a report not provided to Arar, the FBI agent questioned him about his work and travel in the United States and his relationships with specific individuals, including one man in particular. Arar explained that the man was a casual acquaintance of his from Ottawa and that in 1997 the man had witnessed an apartment rental agreement signed by Arar.

Following the five-hour interrogation, Arar was questioned for another three hours, this time by an immigration officer who asked him about his membership in or affiliation with various terrorist groups. Arar vehemently denied any such connections. This second interrogation ended at about midnight. Arar was then chained, shackled, and driven to another building at the airport, where he was locked away alone. There was no bed. The lights remained on all night and Arar could not sleep. The next morning, September 27, 2002, two FBI agents interrogated Arar for another five hours, asking him about Osama bin Laden, Iraq, and Palestine, among other things. During the interrogation, the agents repeatedly yelled and swore at Arar, yet he continued to deny any affiliation with terrorists or terrorist activity. He repeatedly asked to see a lawyer and to make a telephone call, but these requests were again denied.

Many hours later, Arar was taken back to his cell, chained and shackled. He was given a cold McDonald's meal—his first food in almost two days. Early that evening, an immigration officer came to Arar's cell and asked him to "volunteer" to be sent to Syria. Arar refused, insisting that he be sent to Canada or Switzerland. Angered by his response, the officer stated that the United States government had a "special interest" in him and instructed Arar to sign a form. Even though he was not permitted to read the form, Arar signed it, fearing adverse consequences if he did not do so.

Later that evening, Arar was taken from his cell in chains and shackles, put in a vehicle, and driven from the airport to the Metropolitan Detention Center (MDC) a federal prison facility located in Brooklyn, New York. There, he was strip-searched, given an orange jumpsuit to wear, and placed in solitary confinement in a small cell.

Over the next three days, until October 1, 2002, Arar repeatedly asked to see a lawyer and to make a telephone call, but every one of these requests was ignored. On October 1, 2002, an MDC official handed him a document stating that the INS had found that he was "inadmissible" to the United States (an immigration determination making him immediately deportable) because he belonged to an organization designated by the secretary of state as a Foreign Terrorist Organization, namely, Al Qaeda. Arar was never given the opportunity to contest this finding.

On the same day, Arar was finally permitted to make a telephone call. He called his mother-in-law in Ottawa. Arar's family had been frantically searching for him since his disappearance. Upon learning that he was detained at MDC, his in-laws contacted the Office for Canadian Consular Affairs, which had not been informed by the United States of Arar's detention. They also retained a New York City immigration attorney for him.

The next day, October 2, 2002, two immigration officers visited Arar's cell. They asked him to designate in writing the country to which he wished to be removed. He designated Canada. On October 3, 2002, Arar was visited by Maureen Girvan, an official from the Canadian Consulate. He showed Girvan the document finding him inadmissible to the United States and expressed concern that he might be removed to Syria. Girvan assured him that this could not happen because he was a Canadian citizen.

On the evening of Saturday, October 5, 2002, Arar was visited for the first time by his lawyer, who had requested permission from the MDC warden the day before to meet with him. Late the next evening, Sunday, October 6, 2002, Arar was taken in chains and shackles to a room where about eight INS officials questioned him about his opposition to being sent to Syria. Arar had had no prior notice of this interrogation, and the only notice given to his lawyer was a message left by a government official on her voicemail at work that very evening, Sunday. Initially, Arar told his interrogators that he would not answer questions without his lawyer, but he reluctantly agreed to respond after being falsely told by his interrogators that his lawyer had chosen not to attend the meeting. Arar told his interrogators that he feared that he would be tortured if he was to be sent to Syria. His claims in this regard would later be fully substantiated.

Day thirteen of Arar's detention began with the continuation of the previous night's interrogation, which lasted for six hours, until 3 a.m. on October 7, 2002. Throughout the ordeal, his interrogators informed him that they were discussing the issue with "Washington D.C." but gave him no information about his fate. Arar was asked to sign what appeared to be a transcript. He declined to do so, and they took him back to his cell in chains and shackles.

Later that Monday morning, Arar's lawyer retrieved the voicemail message that had been left for her on Sunday night—long after the interrogation had ended. Later that same day, she received a call from an INS agent falsely notifying her that Arar had been taken to the INS's New York City Varick Street offices "for processing" and was en route to a detention facility in New Jersey. She then received another call from the INS falsely notifying her that Arar had arrived at the detention facility. She was told to call back the next day for the exact location. The INS officials had lied; Arar remained confined at MDC during this entire period.

Very early on Monday, October 8, 2002, at approximately 4 a.m., Arar was taken, chained and shackled, to a room where two INS officials told him that, based on classified information, the INS regional director had decided to remove him to Syria, and that the government had determined that his removal to Syria would be consistent with Article 3 of the Convention Against Torture. When Arar repeated his concerns about being tortured in Syria, the officials simply stated that the INS is not governed by the "Geneva Convention." They also told him that he was barred from reentering the United States for five years. On October 8, 2002, an order was signed by the Justice Department removing Arar to Syria.

Arar was then taken from MDC in chains and shackles to a New Jersey airstrip, placed on a small private jet, and flown to Washington, D.C. From there, his captors flew him to Amman, Jordan, where they handed him over to Jordanian authorities on October 9, 2002. His custodians in Jordan beat Arar brutally before turning him over to authorities in Syria.

President Bush has described Syria as having a "legacy of torture, oppression, misery and ruin." Those remarks are consistent with the United States' long-held recognition that Syria is a nation that practices torture. The State Department's 2002 Country Report on Human Rights Practices in Syria makes plain that according to evidence collected by the United States:

> [S]ecurity forces continued to use torture, although to a lesser extent than in previous years. Former prisoners, detainees, and the London-based Syrian Human Rights Organization reported that torture methods included administering electrical shocks; pulling out fingernails; forcing objects into the rectum; beating, sometimes while the victim is suspended from the ceiling; hyperextending the spine; bending the detainees into the frame of a wheel and whipping exposed body parts; and using a chair that bends backwards to asphyxiate the victim or fracture the victim's spine. In 2001 AI published a report

claiming that authorities at Tadmur Prison regularly tortured prisoners, or forced prisoners to torture each other. Although it occurs in prisons, *torture was most likely to occur while detainees were being held at one of the many detention centers run by the various security services throughout the country, especially while the authorities were attempting to extract a confession.*[49]

In addition to the very real practice of torture in Syrian prisons, the State Department also concluded that Syrian "[p]rison conditions generally were poor and did not meet international standards for health and sanitation. . . . Facilities for political or national security prisoners generally were worse than those for common criminals."[50] Despite this legacy of torture, or more likely because of it, Arar was turned over to the Syrian security forces, where for the next ten months, until August 19, 2003, he was detained in the Falastine Branch of Syrian Military Intelligence (Falastine Branch).

Arar was interrogated for almost eighteen hours each day. He was also subjected to physical and psychological torture. Syrian security officers beat him on the palms, hips, and lower back using a two-inch thick electric cable. They also regularly struck him in the stomach, face, and back of the neck with their fists, causing excruciating pain.

While the severity of the physical beatings eventually diminished, Syrian security officers continued to subject Arar to intense psychological torture. They placed him in a room where he could hear the screams of other detainees being tortured. The officers repeatedly threatened to place him in the spine-breaking "chair," hang him upside down in a "tyre" and beat him, and give him electric shocks. In order to minimize the torture, Arar falsely confessed, among other things, to having trained with terrorists in Afghanistan. In fact, he has never been to Afghanistan in his life and has never been involved in any terrorist activity.

The questions Syrian security officers asked him were strikingly similar to those asked him by the FBI agents at JFK Airport in September 2002. Presumably, U.S. officials provided their Syrian counterparts with a dossier and questions to be posed to Arar, compiled at least in part from his interrogation in U.S. custody. It is difficult to imagine why Syria would be interested in interrogating a law-abiding Syrian-born Canadian accused of no crime, but for the U.S. government's insistence on sending him there to be questioned using methods that we would find immoral and abhorrent in this country.

When he was not being interrogated, Arar was placed in a tiny underground cell—which he calls the "grave"—measuring approximately seven feet long, seven feet high, and three feet wide—with hardly enough room to move. The cell was damp and cold, especially during the winter months, and the only light there was came through a small aperture in the ceiling above through which cats often urinated on him. Sanitary conditions were woefully abysmal. He was allowed to bathe—in cold water—once a week. He was not permitted to exercise, and the food was barely edible. While detained at the Falastine Branch, he lost forty pounds.

The intensive interrogations and severe physical beatings ceased on October 20, 2002, the same day that the Canadian Embassy officials in Syria inquired about him. Between October 23, 2002, and August 14, 2003, Syrian officials allowed Canadian Consular officials to visit Arar at the Falastine Branch on seven occasions. Prior to each visit, Syrian security officers threatened Arar with additional torture if he complained about his abuse to his visitors. He complied with their prohibition until August 14, 2003. On that date, unable to bear the mistreatment any longer, he yelled out to a Canadian Consular official that he had been tortured and was being kept in a grave. Approximately five days later, he was briefly transferred to the Syrian Military Intelligence's Investigations Branch, and from there to Sednaya Prison, an overcrowded prison where he remained for six weeks. On September 28, 2003, Arar was transferred back to the Falastine Branch where he was held in solitary confinement for another week.

Syria ultimately released Arar without filing a single charge against him. As Syria's highest-ranking diplomat in Washington, Imad Moustapha, explained: "We did our investigations. We traced links. We traced relations. We tried to find anything. We couldn't."[51] On October 5, 2003, Arar was taken to the Syrian Supreme State Security Court where a prosecutor told him that he would be released without criminal charges into the custody of Canadian officials.

On October 6, 2003, Arar returned home to Ottawa and to his family, whom he had not seen in more than a year. Although Arar has received apologies from the Canadian government, he has been unable to rest until he understands fully what had happened to him and why. He wants to clear his name, but more importantly, he wants to ensure that no one else ever suffers in the same way. Toward this end, Arar lobbied the Parliament of Canada until it announced the convening of a Public Inquiry into the actions of Canadian officials dealing with his detention in the United States, his deportation, his imprisonment and treatment in Syria, and his return to Canada.[52] The inquiry's other purposes are to make recommendations for changes in the law and policies of the country and to suggest a structure for an independent, arm's-length review mechanism for the Royal Canadian Mounted Police's activities with respect to national security.[53]

The United States declined Canada's request that it participate in the Public Inquiry. Despite the U.S. government's reluctance to reveal its role in Arar's rendition to torture, a number of government officials have admitted anonymously that his case falls within the covert extraordinary rendition program.[54] In the chilling words of one official, "The temptation is to have these folks in other hands because they have different standards. . . . Someone might be able to get information that we can't from the detainees."[55] Cofer Black, a former director of counterterrorism at the CIA, noted that the CIA has long maintained a secret intelligence relationship with Syria. This relationship apparently continues despite the Bush administration's *public* condemnations of Syria's human rights record.[56]

On September 18, 2006, the Canadian Commission of Inquiry issued its report, concluding that "categorically that there is no evidence to indicate that Arar has committed any offence or that his activities constitute a threat to the security of Canada." Canadian investigators exhaustively investigated Arar, and found no information that could implicate him in any terrorist activities. The commission also found no evidence that Canadian officials acquiesced in the U.S. decision to detain and remove Arar to Syria, but found it very likely that the United States had relied on inaccurate and unfair information about Arar provided by Canadian officials.

In January 2004, Arar, represented by lawyers from the Center for Constitutional Rights (CCR), filed a federal civil rights lawsuit in the United States against the U.S. government officials whom he believes participated in his rendition to torture, alleging violations of his due process rights and his right not to be *sent to torture*—a right protected by a relatively new statute, the Torture Victims Protection Act. In February 2005, after filing numerous motions to dismiss the lawsuit, the government officials filed a motion alleging that the entire case constitutes a "state secret" and therefore should not be permitted to proceed at all in any forum. The state secrets doctrine is an evidentiary privilege designed to shield the public disclosure of sensitive evidence; it was not intended to provide a means to block access to the courts altogether, nor to be a tool to prevent unpalatable truths from being revealed. There are very few past instances when courts have granted the dismissal of an entire lawsuit on the basis of this privilege prior to the parties' engaging in evidence gathering and identifying specific documents that should be individually evaluated for their sensitivity. The government in the *Arar* case is following the same strategy as it used in the whistle-blower case of Sibel Edmonds, now being appealed to the U.S. Supreme Court: attempting to use an evidentiary privilege to hide egregious government wrongdoing.[57]

In the end, the government's state secrets argument was unnecessary. On February 16, 2006, Federal Court Judge David Trager dismissed the lawsuit, finding that national security and foreign policy considerations prevented him from holding the officials liable for carrying out an extraordinary rendition even if such conduct violates our treaty obligations or customary international law. According to Maria LaHood, one of the CCR attorneys leading the case, "[t]his ruling sets frightening precedent. U.S. officials sent Maher Arar to Syria to be detained and interrogated through torture. To allow the Bush Administration to continue to evade accountability and continue to hide behind the smokescreen of 'national security' is to do grave and irreparable damage to the Constitution and the guarantee of human rights that people in this country could once be proud of."

Of course, the question of whether government officials can send a human being to another country to be tortured is not a political question. It is a legal question appropriate for resolution by the courts. Torture is absolutely prohibited by both domestic and international law. If our courts are not willing to protect individuals like Arar, who will? The CIA's extraordinary rendition program also presents us with a moral question. Does this kind of program represent the values that we, *the People*, have chosen to live by? If not, when will we, *the People*, take the necessary actions to bring our government's practices back in line with the values that this country was founded upon?

At the time of this writing, Arar's attorneys are in the process of filing his appeal of the district court's decision to the Second Circuit Court of Appeals.

THE CASE OF KHALED EL-MASRI

In 2005, the well-documented case of German resident Khaled El-Masri captured the attention of the international media. The crimes committed against El-Masri also deserve a closer look. His heart-wrenching personal testimony exposes the cruel secret mechanisms of the CIA's extraordinary rendition program and demonstrates the shocking lack of concern and remorse shown by U.S. government officials—even when it becomes clear that the government kidnapped and tortured "the wrong man" in a case of mistaken identity. El-Masri's claims have been substantiated by an investigation undertaken by German prosecutors, who have said that they believe that he was abducted because his name is similar to that of an Al Qaeda suspect, Khalid Masri.[58] We now know that CIA officials were aware that they had kidnapped the wrong man not long after El-Masri had been transported from Europe to a U.S.-run prison in Afghanistan. *Yet, the U.S. government nevertheless kept him—an innocent man—in unlawful detention for at least two additional months.*[59]

In December 2003, after a difficult fight with his wife, El-Masri left Germany for a short trip to Skopje, the capital of Macedonia. By the time he made it back home on the morning of May 29, 2004, having been released after five months of detention and interrogation under torture in a secret prison, his house was empty. He had been held in complete secrecy, unable to even let his family know he was still alive. His wife feared that he'd left her for another woman and, not knowing if he'd ever return, had taken their children to her family's home in Lebanon.[60]

El-Masri was stopped at the Macedonian border on New Year's Eve and was taken into custody after immigration officials took a "close look at his passport." The bus driver on the route to Skopje confirmed to investigators that El-Masri had been on board and was taken away by border guards.[61] El-Masri reports he was held at gunpoint in a hotel room in Skopje for twenty-three days by men he believed were from the Directorate for Security and Counter-Intelligence.[62] He was interrogated in English, a language that he does not understand, about Islamist organizations and his alleged attendance at a "terrorist training camp" in Jalalabad, Afghanistan. El-Masri repeatedly asked to see the German ambassador or another official in charge:

> I was guarded at all times, the curtains were always drawn, I was never permitted to leave the room, I was threatened with guns, and I was not allowed to contact anyone. At the hotel, I was repeatedly questioned about my activities in Ulm [Germany], my associates, my mosque, meetings with people that had never occurred, or associations with people I had never met.[63]

At the end of this ordeal, El-Masri was driven to Skopje airport, where he was beaten by men dressed in black and wearing hoods and gloves:

> Someone sliced the clothes off my body, and when I would not remove my underwear, I was beaten again until someone forcibly removed them from me. I was thrown on the floor, my hands were pulled behind me, and someone's boot was placed on my back. Then I felt something firm being forced inside my anus.[64]

Before taking off, El-Masri was dressed in plastic underpants and a tracksuit, and a plastic bag was placed over his head, ostensibly to foster sensory deprivation. He was secured to the floor of the plane with his arms and legs attached to the walls such that he could not move in any direction.[65] He was flown first to Baghdad and then to Afghanistan where he was taken to the "Salt Pit" in Kabul, an abandoned brick factory run as a prison by the CIA.[66] According to Amnesty International, El-Masri was detained there in a dark cellar, beaten, and given insufficient food. He was interrogated numerous times by United States agents.[67] El-Masri reports that it was only after going on a hunger strike that his captives relented, and he was finally released.[68] He has never been charged with a crime or brought before any court.[69]

On May 28, 2004, El-Masri was told that he would be flown to some European country, not Germany. When the flight landed, he was driven in a car for about six hours, and was eventually joined by three men. When he was let out of the car, his blindfold and handcuffs were removed, and he was given his suitcase. He was told by the men to walk down a nearby path without looking back. It was dark, and "as [he] walked [he] feared that [he] was about to be shot in the back and left to die."[70] On the path, El-Masri was met by three armed men in uniform. After being told that he had entered Albania illegally, the men drove him to the Mother Teresa International Airport near Tirana, Albania. A ticket was purchased for him for a flight to Frankfurt, Germany.[71] The extraordinary manner of his return home highlights the utter disregard that the United States and partnering foreign states have shown for human rights in implimenting the CIA's extraordinary rendition program.

On December 6, 2005, the American Civil Liberties Union (ACLU) filed a lawsuit for Khaled El-Masri in a federal district court against former CIA director George Tenet, three CIA-linked air transport companies, and twenty unnamed employees of the CIA. As the *Washington Post* reported in 2005:

> Flight logs also support El-Masri's claims that he was flown out of Macedonia by U.S. secret agents. Aviation records show a U.S.-registered Boeing jet arrived in Skopje at 9 p.m. on January 23, 2004, and departed about six hours later. Masri had provided German investigators with the same time and date. . . . The jet, with tail number N313P, was registered to a U.S. firm, Premier Transport Services, Inc., that records suggest is a CIA front company. The same firm

owned another aircraft, a Gulfstream jet that has been used in other rendition cases.[72]

On May 12, 2006, Khaled El-Masri's case was preemptively dismissed on state secrets grounds. The government argued that by requiring it to reveal what had happened to El-Masri, the lawsuit would jeopardize our national security interests by exposing CIA methods to the general public.[73] In dismissing the case, however, the judge noted that:

> [I]f El-Masri's allegations are true or essentially true, then all fair-minded people, including those who believe that state secrets must be protected, that this lawsuit cannot proceed, and that renditions are a necessary step to take in this war, must also agree that El-Masri has suffered injuries as a result of our country's mistake and deserves a remedy. Yet, it is also clear from the result reached here that the only sources of that remedy must be the Executive Branch or the Legislative Branch, not the Judicial Branch.[74]

The ACLU has stated that it is committed to pursuing the case and seeking a fair hearing for El-Masri.[75]

Despite the international public outcry following revelations in the media of the horrifying experiences of innocent men like Khaled El-Masri, Maher Arar, and others, the CIA extraordinary rendition program apparently continues. Most of its secret victims may never be revealed, while those few men who have been brave enough to speak out have thus far been barred from justice.

WHAT LAWS ARE WE VIOLATING WHEN WE RENDER PEOPLE TO DETENTION, INTERROGATION AND TORTURE?

Because the Bush administration has determined that the practice of rendition is a "vital tool in combating transnational terrorism,"[76] it has attempted, when pressed on the issue, to justify its practice of sending suspects to countries that the United States itself considers human rights violators by announcing its use of diplomatic assurances. At the same time, however, Attorney General Alberto Gonzales has openly acknowledged that it is not possible to "fully control" the actions of other nations.[77]

Under international human rights treaties and customary international law, states are under an obligation not to transfer any person to another country if this would result in exposing the individual to serious human rights violations, including torture. This rule, called the principle of *nonrefoulement*, is enshrined in the 1951 Convention relating to the Status of Refugees, the Convention Against Torture, the International Covenant on Civil and Political Rights, and the Geneva Conventions, among many others. The United States is a party to each of these treaties and is bound by them.

In addition, the prohibition of *refoulement* to a risk of torture is also a part of customary international law, which is part of our federal law by virtue of Supreme Court decisions addressing the issue. The prohibition has attained the rank of a peremptory norm of international law; it imposes an absolute ban on any form of forcible return to a danger of torture that is binding on all countries, including those which have not become a party to the treaties codifying this rule.[78]

Despite the clarity of domestic and international law, the United States has refused to comply with the prohibitions against torture, abuse, and *refoulement*, choosing instead to take the positions that

> ➤ the Convention Against Torture (CAT) is non-self-executing and therefore cannot be enforced without legislation that codifies the prohibition on torture and makes it enforceable by individuals in court;

> ➤ pursuant to its "Understanding"—a declaration at the time of ratification of the U.S. government's unique interpretation of the CAT provision—the term "torture" has been redefined such that "an act must be specifically intended to inflict severe physical or mental pain or suffering" in order to constitute "torture";[79]

> ➤ the CAT's prohibition of cruel, inhuman, or degrading treatment does not apply to U.S. personnel's treatment of noncitizens when it occurs outside of U.S. territory;[80]

➤ pursuant to its "Reservation" to Article 16—another means of exempting the United States from having to fully comply with the CAT—the United States "considers itself bound to prevent 'cruel, inhuman, or degrading treatment or punishment'" only to the extent such treatment is prohibited "by the Fifth, Eighth, and/or Fourteenth Amendments to the Constitution of the United States";[81] and

➤ "diplomatic assurances" reduce the risk of torture and therefore absolve the United States of all responsibility for violations of the prohibition against torture and *refoulement* committed when a captive is rendered to a third country for detention and interrogation.

As discussed in previous chapters, the Bush administration's five positions work together to create gigantic loopholes in the net of human rights protections created by treaties, covenants, and customary international law. For example, utterly disregarding the convention's absolute ban on torture, the Defense Department relied on the Bush administration's declaration that the CAT is not self-executing when it developed the interrogation techniques to be used on detainees at Guantánamo. The Walker Working Group Report stated:

> Article 2 also provides that acts of torture cannot be justified on the grounds of exigent circumstances, such as state of war or public emergency, or on orders from superior officer or public authority. The United States did not have an Understanding or Reservation relating to this prohibition (however, the U.S. issued a declaration stating that Article 2 is not self-executing).[82]

The administration has used the requirement that an act of torture must be "specifically intended," though the CAT contains no such limitation, to *narrow the definition of torture* and build a defense against any allegations of torture that may be made by "war on terror" detainees. A letter from the Justice Department to the White House, dated August 1, 2002, stated that the U.S. "understanding" on torture "accomplished two things":

First, it made crystal clear that the intent requirement for torture was specific intent. By its terms, the Torture Convention might be read to require only general intent. . . . Second, it added form and substance to the otherwise amorphous concept of mental pain or suffering. In so doing, this understanding ensured that mental torture would rise to a severity comparable to that required in the context of physical torture.[83]

The August 2002 Bybee Memo cited the U.S. reservations to the CAT and proposed that torture occurs only when its physical effect becomes "equivalent in intensity to the pain accompanying serious physical injury, such as organ failure, death, or major impairment of bodily functions."[84] Though the Bybee Memo was replaced by the Justice Department in December 2004, the revised memorandum does not define torture or prohibit cruel, inhuman, or degrading treatment, nor does it disavow Bybee's unprecedented interpretation that the president's commander-in-chief powers authorize him to permit the use of torture.[85]

Statements made by Attorney General Gonzales further attest to the fact that the Justice Department's position is that *the United States is free to subject noncitizens to cruel, inhuman, or degrading treatment when it acts outside of U.S. territory.* In January 2005, Gonzales, then White House counsel, responded to questions put to him in his senate confirmation hearings by stating that:

[T]he only legal prohibition on cruel, inhuman, or degrading treatment comes from the international legal obligation created by the CAT itself . . . The Senate's reservation, however, limited Article 16 to requiring the United States to prevent conduct already prohibited by the Fifth, Eighth, and Fourteenth Amendments. Those amendments, moreover, are themselves limited in application. The Fourteenth Amendment [right to equality before the law] does not apply to the federal government, but rather to the States. The Eighth Amendment [prohibition on cruel and unusual punishments] has long been held by the Supreme Court to apply solely to punishment imposed in the criminal justice system. Finally, the Supreme Court has squarely held that the Fifth Amendment [right to due process] does not provide rights for aliens unconnected to the United States who are overseas. Thus, as a direct result of the reservation the Senate attached to the CAT, the Department of Justice has concluded that under Article 16 there is no legal obligation under the CAT on cruel, inhuman, or degrading treatment with respect to aliens overseas.[86]

In short, despite the fact that detainees held by the United States at Guantánamo, who are considered to be within United States territory under the Supreme Court's decision in *Rasul*, and that detainees held at locations outside of U.S. territory, who are wholly within the power and effective control of U.S. forces, are all covered by the CAT as determined by the U.N. Committee Against Torture,[87] the Bush administration has decided to treat these individuals as falling wholly outside all domestic and international human rights protections.

Diplomatic assurances contain no mechanism for enforcement or any legal remedy for a detainee if the country he is sent to fails to comply with their assurances. Because such assurances are only sought when the sending country *perceives a need for guarantees* with regard to the treatment of the person concerned, it is difficult to imagine a situation in which a nation could in fact rely on diplomatic assurances while still fulfilling its *nonrefoulement* obligations. For these reasons, courts, human rights treaty bodies, and international law experts examining extradition, deportation, and expulsion to countries where there is a danger of torture or other forms of abuse have stated that diplomatic assurances do not adequately eliminate the risks involved.

The U.N. Committee Against Torture in its May 2006 report noted its concern that the United States considers that the *nonrefoulement* obligation of Article 3 of the convention does not extend to a person detained outside its territory, and therefore feels free to engage in the rendition of suspects, without any judicial procedure, to states where they face a real risk of torture. The committee also stated that the United States' use of "diplomatic assurances" or other kinds of guarantees is troubling given the secrecy surrounding these procedures, the absence of judicial scrutiny, and the lack of monitoring mechanisms to assess whether the assurances have been honored. The committee concluded its findings with the following recommendation: "The State party should apply the *nonrefoulement* guarantee to all detainees in its custody, cease the rendition of suspects, in particular by its intelligence agencies, to States where they face a real risk of torture, in order to comply with its obligations under Article 3 of the convention. The State party should always ensure that suspects have the possibility to challenge decisions of *refoulement.*"[88]

The United Nations Special Rapporteur on Torture also stated recently that "in circumstances where there is a consistent pattern of gross, flagrant or mass violations of human rights, or of systematic practice of torture, the principle of *nonrefoulement* must be strictly observed and diplomatic assurances should not be resorted to."[89] Yet, that is precisely what our government is doing. Although "diplomatic assurances" are undertaken in secret,[90] inherently unreliable, not legally binding, and provide no recourse for the person transferred, the United States considers them sufficient to fulfill its *nonrefoulement* obligations.

Thus, the Bush administration's positions limiting its obligations under the CAT have provided its legitimizing argument for the CIA's extraordinary rendition program. According to the Bush administration, so long as the Convention Against Torture is not enforceable in U.S. courts, *and* no one specifically intended for Maher Arar to be tortured in Syria, *and* the CAT's prohibition of cruel, inhuman, or degrading treatment does not apply to American personnel's treatment of noncitizens outside of United States territory, *and* the government officials involved sought "diplomatic assurances" from Syria before they transported Arar there for interrogation, the United States is not responsible for Arar's ten-month ordeal at the hands of the Syrian secret police.

What good are the arguments constructed by our government to justify horrendous and immoral acts when it is obvious to the rest of the world that we have merely decided to ignore the absolute prohibition against torture and deny our moral and legal obligations to humanity? Why are we permitting the Bush administration to take us down this dark road?

CHAPTER SEVEN

Floating Prisons, Ghost Detainees, and the Nameless

The various detention facilities operated by the 800th MP Brigade have routinely held persons brought to them by Other Government Agencies (OGAs) [i.e. the CIA] without accounting for them, knowing their identities, or even the reason for their detention. The Joint Interrogation and Debriefing Center (JIDC) at Abu Ghraib called these detainees "ghost detainees." . . . they moved around within the facility to hide them from a visiting International Committee of the Red Cross (ICRC) survey team. This maneuver was deceptive, contrary to Army Doctrine, and in violation of international law.

—*Major General Antonio Taguba, Army Investigator for the Article 15-6 Investigation of the 800th Military Police Brigade*[1]

By December 2004, the media had already reported on the existence of a secret CIA detention facility within the Guantánamo prison compound created to house captives thought to possess valuable information about Al Qaeda operations. According to these initial reports, the CIA had been authorized by a presidential directive to capture and detain certain types of suspects without acknowledging their existence to the public or accounting for them to the ICRC or revealing the rules governing their treatment.[2] Within a year of this report, the Bush administration, apparently after being outed by disclosures made by a CIA official,[3] was forced to admit to the existence of a covert prison system set up by the CIA in 2001 to hold "war on terror" suspects in complete isolation from the outside world.[4] Although the contours of the CIA's global internment program are still emerging, U.S. intelligence officials have confirmed that "most of the facilities were built and are being maintained with congressionally appropriated funds" and that the hidden network included sites in eight countries, including Thailand, Afghanistan, and several small Eastern European countries.[5] Authorization for the creation of the "black site" prison network came from the Presidential Finding authorizing covert action, signed by President Bush on September 17, 2001.[6] Because few in this country are privy to the details of the CIA program, virtually nothing is known about who has been—or may still be—kept in these facilities; what interrogation methods have been used with them; or how decisions are made about when to release the detainees.

Of the many disturbing practices that have been undertaken or condoned by the U.S. government in the name of protecting national security through the "war on terror," the forced disappearance and long-term incommunicado detention of terrorism suspects in undisclosed locations may present the most fundamental challenge to our constitutional democracy and the foundations of American society. The government's endorsement and employment of such methods strips us of our identity as a nation ruled by law. The United States' torture and disappearance of its adversaries and perceived adversaries relegates it to the same section of the history books as those unsavory regimes that have used these practices to quell dissent and to which the United States has ostensibly placed itself in opposition. More troubling than this hypocrisy, however, is the knowledge that our country's actions will be cited as an example of what is permissible by any country that seeks to justify violations of human rights in an effort to movements for greater political or social freedoms under the guise of ensuring national security.

In the same way as the administration chose Guantánamo as a detention center because it was thought to be beyond the jurisdiction of the U.S. courts, the ghost detainee policy represents an effort to hide interrogation practices beyond all public scrutiny. In fact, it seems likely that these two policies have developed from the same secret internal memorandum authored by Justice Department lawyers and approved by senior Bush administration officials. As previously discussed, the Bybee Memo of August 2002, written in response to the CIA's request for guidance on the permissible boundaries of interrogation methods, stated that international laws against torture "may be unconstitutional if applied to interrogations" conducted in the "war on terror," thereby opening the door to practices unlawful under both the Constitution and international law.[7]

The Geneva Conventions require that all enemy prisoners be promptly registered and be permitted visits from international organizations such as the International Committee for the Red Cross. Governments are allowed to prevent ICRC access to detainees only in extreme circumstances, such as when the detention facility is directly under attack or when providing access to the detainee would put one of the parties engaged in the military dispute in immediate danger. Although President Bush has stated publicly that the Geneva Conventions apply to all combatants in Iraq, Defense Secretary Rumsfeld nevertheless gave approval to former CIA director George Tenet to secretly detain and interrogate individuals captured in the "war on terror" and the war in Iraq,[8] and President Bush signed the September 17, 2001, Presidential Finding granting "exceptional authorities" to the CIA in the "war on terror." The Presidential Finding authorized the creation of secret detention facilities and permitted the use of extremely harsh interrogation techniques.[9]

While the full population of the CIA's web of secret detention facilities has not yet been definitively ascertained, media reports, along with the reports of several leading human rights groups, indicate that the government may be holding in excess of fourteen thousand people at more than three dozen detention centers around the world, at least half of which operate in secret.[10]

HIDING DETAINEES: REVELATIONS ABOUT GHOSTS

The Ghosts at Guantánamo

Amnesty International recently expressed their fears about "war on terror" detainees apparently "disappeared" at Guantánamo:

> On 12 March 2005, the Pentagon announced that the transfer of three detainees to Afghanistan, Maldives and Pakistan left "approximately 540" detainees in Guantánamo. This is exactly what it said

five days earlier on 7 March, when announcing the transfer of three detainees to France. Prior to that, the last figure it gave was "approximately 545" when it announced on 28 January 2005 that the transfer of Mamdouh Habib to Australia left "approximately 545" detainees in the base. This was the same figure it gave a few days earlier after four British detainees were returned to the UK on 25 January. The imprecision of the Pentagon's figures allows the possibility that individual detainees could be transferred to and from the base without being reflected in the figures.[11]

Indeed, reports now confirm that the CIA operated a secret facility-within-a-facility in Guantánamo, where they housed detainees who were never registered on the internee rolls or identified to the ICRC.[12]

The Ghosts in the War in Iraq

The CIA has been repeatedly "allowed to operate under different rules," according to the report of the Independent Panel to Review Department of Defense (DOD) Detention Operations, which was chaired by former defense secretary James Schlesinger. This includes in the treatment of prisoners of war captured in the war in Iraq. Reports of U.S. Army investigations into the intelligence activities at Abu Ghraib also found that "the perception that non-DOD agencies [the CIA] had different rules regarding interrogation and detention operations was evident."[13] The perception, shown to be widely held within the military, is that the Bush administration has assured the CIA that it need not abide by international law—and that if the CIA is not burdened by the Geneva Conventions, why should other branches of the military comply in their treatment of detainees in the "war on terror"? Investigators have confirmed that the unbridled authority given to the CIA created an atmosphere of lawlessness. They found that "The lack of OGA [CIA] adherence to the practices and procedures established for accounting for detainees eroded the necessity in the minds of soldiers and civilians for them to follow Army rules. . . . CIA detention and interrogation practices led to a loss of accountability, abuse, reduced interagency cooperation and an unhealthy mystique that further poisoned the atmosphere at Abu Ghraib."[14]

In Iraq, "ghost detainees" are thought to be held in Camp Cropper near Baghdad International Airport, Camp Bucca near Basra, close to the Kuwaiti border, Camps Redemption and Ganci located at Abu Ghraib, and nine other temporary holding facilities run by military divisions or brigade commands.[15] Although there are official databases listing Iraqi detainees, they are neither centralized, comprehensive, nor accurate.[16] Estimates of the number of detainees held at these facilities range from ten thousand to twelve thousand prisoners.[17] In U.S. prisons in Iraq, as in Afghanistan, U.S. detention policy is constantly in flux; while at one point the Defense Department stated that the Geneva Conventions would be applied to Iraqi detainees, at another, they were designated "unlawful combatants." Most recently, they have been deemed "security detainees"—yet another new category unrecognized under either existing U.S. Army rules or the laws of war. In addition, the Defense Department has stated that its "security detainees" may also be lawfully "transferred out of the country for indefinite detention elsewhere"—a policy decision obviously in keeping with the CIA's extraordinary rendition program.[18]

This practice plainly violates the Fourth Geneva Convention's prohibition of the forcible transfer of protected persons outside of occupied territory.[19] In March 2004, Jack L. Goldsmith III, then an assistant attorney general, drafted a memorandum in which he attempted to craft a legal argument justifying the transfer of certain persons seized in Iraq to locations outside of Iraq for interrogation. However, there is simply no way around the Fourth Geneva Convention's absolute prohibition of the forcible transfer or deportation of protected persons outside of the occupied territory.[20]

In mid-June 2004, *U.S. News & World Report* first reported the story of an Iraqi man who was picked up by the Kurdish military in June 2003 and turned over to the CIA. According to reports, the man was taken by CIA officials to an undisclosed location outside of Iraq for interrogation.[21] During the time of his interrogation and his later detention at Camp Cropper, the man's name was deliberately kept off of the list of the camp's detainees and was not presented to the ICRC. Several months later, a CIA legal analysis revealed that the detainee had been considered an "unlawful combatant" and therefore, according to the agency, not entitled to the protections of the Geneva Conventions.[22] In the wake of this story, further investigation by reporters revealed a much broader problem. On June 18, 2004, Secretary Rumsfeld admitted in an afternoon news briefing at the Pentagon that, upon a request by then CIA director George Tenet, he had ordered many other detainees to be held secretly.[23] Secretary Rumsfeld refused, however, to provide any reason for failing to register detainees with the ICRC, stating only that such explanations were classified.

The Taguba Report—an investigative report issued on June 7, 2004, and written by Major General Antonio Taguba, documenting the results of an Army investigation into the abuses that occurred at Baghdad's Abu Ghraib Prison—found that the military police at Abu Ghraib frequently held persons incommunicado and off the internee rolls. Military police moved these "ghost detainees" around the prison to hide them from visiting Red Cross delegations.[24] The report concludes that these practices are "deceptive, contrary to Army doctrine, and in violation of international law."[25]

Another Army inquiry into the situation at Abu Ghraib, led by General Paul J. Kern, again confirmed the existence of numerous ghost detainees in Iraq. Testifying before two congressional committees in September 2004, General Kern, the senior investigating Army official, stated that "the number [of ghost detainees] is in the dozens, to perhaps up to 100."[26] Precise numbers could not be given, he noted, because no records were kept on the CIA detainees.[27] Despite repeated requests made by Major General George Fay, another Army investigator, intelligence officials still have not confirmed whether all of the ghost detainees have been handed over to the military and properly registered with the ICRC.[28] News media and human rights organizations such as Human Rights Watch have made requests for information regarding the location, legal status, conditions of detention, and plans for release for these detainees, but they have also gone unanswered.[29]

The Ghosts in Afghanistan

Prison facilities in Afghanistan, like those in Iraq, hold many "war on terror" detainees who, although their presence is acknowledged by the U.S. government, nevertheless are inaccessible to the ICRC and their families either because there are no official detainee lists or the existing lists are inaccurate. While U.S. Army regulations require the creation of a detainee database that includes the name, date and place of capture, person to be notified in the event of capture, and other personal information for each detainee, to date, no such comprehensive database has been established for the detainees in Afghanistan.[30] Families seeking information about their relatives in U.S. detention have little to aid them in their endeavor

According to the Defense Department, two out of the original twenty-five U.S. military detention facilities are still in operation in Afghanistan: one located at the U.S. Air Force's Bagram Air Base and another at the U.S. Air Force's Kandahar Air Base.[31] Human rights reports added the CIA run facility known as the "Salt Pit" in Kabul to that list, though it has now been closed following reports of the death of an Afghani detainee (described below).[32] In addition to these facilities, United States Central Command (CENTCOM), the U.S. unified military command with operational control over U.S. combat forces, has confirmed that there are a number of "transient" holding facilities scattered throughout Afghanistan that are used to hold detainees until they are transferred to either the Bagram or Kandahar facilities.[33] These U.S. facilities include prisons in or near Asadabad, Gereshk, Jalalabad, Tycze, Gardez, and Khost.[34]

According to a report issued by the Army inspector general, the conditions at these "transient" facilities make them unacceptable for holding detainees for more than two weeks.[35] Yet, reports from detainees themselves indicate that prisoners have been kept in such facilities for months and have been held in large areas without roofs, exposed to extremes of heat and cold, depending on the season.[36]

Estimates of the total number of detainees held in Afghani facilities as of January 2005 range from 550 to 700.[37] The administration's position regarding the legal status of these detainees has not changed since February 7, 2002, when President Bush declared that Taliban soldiers are not entitled to the protections of the Geneva Conventions and that Al Qaeda members are not covered by the Geneva Conventions at all.[38] In the Bush administration's view, the detainees' lack of any legal status under the laws of war and our own domestic military justice code allows that the rules regarding their treatment become entirely a matter of executive discretion. This situation has led to torture and abuse.[39]

The Nameless: Reports of Ghosts from Around the World

The ICRC's repeated requests for information on all the locations holding ghost detainees have been rebuffed, as the agency made clear in a March 2004 public statement: "Beyond Bagram and Guantánamo Bay, the ICRC is increasingly concerned about the fate of an unknown number of people captured as part of the so-called global war on terror and held in undisclosed locations . . . obtaining information on these detainees and access to them is an important humanitarian priority."[40] In a statement issued four months later, the ICRC noted that it remained "more and more concerned about the lot of the unknown number of people captured in the context of what we would call the "war against terror" and detained in secret places. . . . We have asked for information on these people and access to them. Until now we have received no response from the Americans."[41]

The U.S. government will also not acknowledge the reported existence of detention facilities or interrogation centers operating in Pakistan,[42] Jordan,[43] on the island of Diego Garcia,[44] or on two U.S. ships, the USS *Bataan* and USS *Peleliu*.[45] Evidence of these facilities has been confirmed however from several other sources. A report of a U.S. Army investigation recounts an inquiry into the abuse of an Afghani detainee held in U.S. custody in Peshawar, Pakistan, the closest major city to Kohat and Alizai.[46] In an October 2004 article in the Israeli daily newspaper *Ha'aretz*, a longtime national security reporter described the CIA's operation in a Jordan facility, noting that at least eleven high-level Al Qaeda prisoners were being held there for interrogation.[47] Other investigative reporters have confirmed that the Al Jafir Prison in the southern Jordanian desert is used as a CIA interrogation facility for terrorism suspects.[48]

The most basic questions remained unanswered. How many people are now being held in U.S. custody by *all* U.S. agencies? Where are these people being held? Are they being listed on the ICRC rolls? What is the legal basis being asserted by the United States for their detention, and what rights do the detainees have under the law?

REPORTS OF TORTURE, ABUSE, AND DEATH: THE FATE OF THE NAMELESS

The president's decision to allow the CIA unfettered discretion to run their secret detentions operation created fertile ground for serious human rights abuses. Accounts of brutal treatment and deaths of detainees while in CIA custody continue to surface on a regular basis. This soldier's statement regarding the death of a CIA "ghost detainee" was released in Freedom of Information Act litigation brought by a coalition of civil and human rights groups: "The OGA [CIA] then packed the detainee in ice and placed him in a local taxi. The taxi driver was paid to take the body away. . . . [redacted material] allowed OGA to house their detainees at the AG facility in 'ghost cells' in block 1A."[49] Major General George Fay's report on intelligence activities at Abu Ghraib refers to the same case, noting that the detainee was brought to the prison by CIA agents and was never registered with the military guards at the facility.[50] Media reports have confirmed other deaths, such as that of an Afghani detainee who was held in the "Salt Pit" in Kabul. He was purportedly stripped, chained to the floor, assaulted, and left out overnight without covering. He died from exposure.[51] According to human rights groups, the Afghani detainee was never registered on any detainee logs, including the CIA's own ghost detainee log. Though the "Salt Pit" is now closed, no one has been able to uncover the fate of the many other detainees reportedly held there.[52]

At the time of this writing in 2006, U.S. government, media, and human rights organizations' reports have already confirmed that more than one hundred detainees have died in U.S. military and CIA custody.[53] The government has publicly stated that at least twenty-seven of these deaths have been investigated as homicides.[54] According to the ACLU, of the forty-four autopsy reports produced by the Army that it has reviewed, twenty-one appear to show that the detainee was a homicide victim.[55] Some of these reports—which list the causes of death as "strangulation," "hypothermia," "asphyxiation," and "blunt force injuries"—appear to show the homicides were the result of the abusive interrogation techniques used by the CIA, Navy Seals, or Military Intelligence personnel.[56] Yet, the blatant illegality of the secret actions taken by military jailers in Afghanistan, Guantánamo, and Iraq at the behest of the CIA has not been seriously challenged by *any* military officer or by *any* politician from either side of the aisle, despite the fact that it is precisely such secrecy that creates the conditions in which abuse is more likely to occur. To date, only one CIA contractor has been charged in regard to the death of a detainee,[57] and no officials with the agency have yet been seriously called to account for these unconscionable human rights and humanitarian law violations.[58] Meanwhile, the secrecy that incubates these heinous acts continues.

Given what we are learning about the scope of the CIA's extraordinary rendition program (as discussed in detail in chapter 6), it seems likely that there will be additional revelations of detainee torture, abuse, and even murder in the future. According to a preliminary report issued by the Council of Europe's Parliamentary Assembly Committee on Legal Affairs and Human Rights, the CIA conducted more than a thousand secret flights over European territory since 2001.[59]

THE LEGACY OF THE NAMELESS: CONSEQUENCES OF HIDING DETAINEES IN VIOLATION OF DOMESTIC AND INTERNATIONAL LAW

By the U.S. government's illegal, secret actions in the "war on terror," immeasurable damage has been done to this country's reputation and to its moral credibility in calling for compliance with human rights norms in the future. The unconscionable treatment of "ghost detainees" also practically invites similar treatment of captured Americans. Representative John Kline (R-MN), a retired Marine colonel, summed up his view of the situation in this way: "We had a gigantic failure of leadership—one that a year ago, I would have said was impossible to have in the United States Army."[60]

Under international law, enforced disappearances are considered one of the most serious human rights violations: they are deemed "a grave and abominable offense against the inherent dignity of the human being."[61] The General Assembly of the United Nations has stated that enforced disappearance "constitutes an offense to human dignity, a grave and flagrant violation of human rights and fundamental freedoms . . . and a violation of the rules of international law."[62]

Because "disappeared" detainees are cut off from the outside world, they are outside any protection of the law. There is no way for outsiders to intervene, and with no judicial or ICRC oversight, the conditions create a significant risk of torture. In 2004, the Special Rapporteur of the U.N. Commission on Human Rights "remind[ed] all States that prolonged incommunicado detention may facilitate the perpetration of torture and can in itself constitute a form of cruel, inhuman, or degrading treatment or even torture, and urges all States to respect the safeguards concerning the liberty, security and dignity of the person."[63]

THE RESPONSE BY CONGRESS AND OUR RESPONSIBILITY AS CITIZENS

In order to ensure that we are fulfilling our obligations under the Geneva Conventions, our own domestic military law has also long required that Congress be provided with an accurate accounting of the detainees captured by U.S. Armed Forces and the ICRC be given access to prisoners in U.S. custody. For more than fifty years, these principles have been codified both in binding military regulations and the individual armed forces field manuals governing our soldiers' conduct.

For example, Defense Department Directive 2310.1 affirms the United States' obligation to comply with the Geneva Conventions and creates a framework for information disclosure. Pursuant to this directive, the secretary of the Army has two major sets of responsibilities. First, he or she must develop plans for the treatment, care, accountability, legal status, and administrative procedures to be followed with regard to persons captured or detained by, or transferred from the custody of the U.S. Military Services.[64] Second, the secretary must develop and operate a POW and civilian internment information center that accounts for all people who pass through the custody and control of the U.S. military in order to comply with the United States' Geneva Conventions obligations.[65]

To meet these obligations, the Army established the National Prisoner of War Information Center (NPWIC),[66] charged with maintaining records for both prisoners of war and detained civilians. The NPWIC must ensure that there is a full accounting of every person who passes into U.S. hands,[67] and the center operated during the 1991 Gulf War and other military operations since. W. Hays Parks, Special Assistant to the Army JAG, maintained that the NPWIC would be used in Iraq. The Taguba Report, however, stated that the reporting systems in Iraq that would typically provide information to the NPWIC were significantly underutilized and did not give an accurate picture of the detainee population in U.S. custody at any point in time during the war.[68] Former defense secretary James Schlesinger also found that the failure to implement a required comprehensive detainee collection database delayed both the interrogation of detainees and the release of innocent men.[69]

In October 2004, the Army published a new, interim field manual intended to affirm its obligation to account for all person held in U.S. custody regardless of their legal status. Congress also took action in October 2004, enacting as part of the Ronald W. Reagan National Defense Authorization Act provisions requiring the secretary of defense to report to Congress on U.S. compliance with these basic standards. The statute requires the secretary to prescribe detailed regulations for Defense Department personnel, including contractors, to ensure that all detainees held in Defense Department custody receive humane treatment in accordance with U.S. and international law.[70] The law also requires that detainees receive information in their own language regarding the Geneva Conventions protections due them; it provides for inspections of detention facilities; and requires the secretary to accurately report on the status of detainees wherever they are held in U.S. custody. The law further requires that the Senate and House Armed Services Committees are provided annual reports disclosing investigations into violations of domestic or international law regarding detainee treatment; general information on foreign national detainees in Defense Department custody, including the numbers, nationalities, and average length of detention of such detainees; as well as information regarding detainees released during the year and detainees transferred to the jurisdiction of other countries.[71]

The Bush administration must be held accountable to the international and domestic laws affirmed by Congress. There must be a public accounting of all of the people held by the U.S. government or at its behest around the world. The abuse of prisoners in U.S. custody in Iraq, Afghanistan, and Guantánamo—and in other undisclosed locations—cannot be allowed to continue. It is unacceptable for people in U.S. custody to simply disappear. We, *the People*, must make sure that the country that was long considered the world's preeminent democracy holds true to the principles upon which it was founded.

CHAPTER EIGHT

Hiding the Truth in Plain Sight

The government being the people's business, it necessarily follows that its operations should be at all times open to the public view. Publicity is therefore as essential to honest administration as freedom of speech is to representative government. "Equal rights to all and special privileges to none" is the maxim which should control in all departments of government.

—*Secretary of State William Jennings Bryan, "Bryan's Rules for the New Voter,"* Baltimore Sun *(April 25, 1915)*

One of our democracy's bedrock principles is that the operations of government must be open for all to see. Our system of checks and balances depends on the public and Congress having access to information about the activities of the executive branch; when government operates behind closed doors there can be no oversight and no accountability to the people.

Through its extraordinary expansion of government secrecy, the Bush administration has launched an unprecedented assault on this country's commitment to the principle of open government.[1] It has consistently narrowed laws that are designed to promote public access to information, expanded laws that permit the government to withhold information or operate in secret, and used executive orders and other measures which enable the executive branch to avoid public scrutiny to change federal policies and practices. In short, it has worked hard to operate without public or congressional scrutiny of its actions. As a result of the administration's increasing restrictions on access to information, Congress, the media, and public interest watchdog groups have been greatly hindered in their efforts to monitor executive branch activities.[2] The veil of secrecy grows daily to cover an ever-expanding territory of government action

THE EROSION OF THE FREEDOM OF INFORMATION ACT

A key component of the Bush administration's assault on open government has been its continual efforts to narrow the public's access to information under the federal Freedom of Information Act.[3]

The Freedom of Information Act (FOIA) was passed in 1966 to facilitate public access to information held by the executive branch.[4] Prior to FOIA's adoption, individuals seeking government records had to establish that they had a special entitlement to the requested records.[5] The act, intended to provide the public with broad access to government records, overturned this hurdle. The law was designed "to pierce the veil of administrative secrecy and to open agency action to the light of public scrutiny."[6] Toward that end, FOIA creates a strong presumption in favor of disclosure[7] and places the burden on the government agency to justify withholding any of the requested documents or information.[8] An agency's refusal to provide requested information must fall under one of the specific exemptions that FOIA provides to the disclosure requirements,[9] and individuals requesting information can appeal and then seek judicial review if the government ultimately denies the request.

Under the Bush administration, the Freedom of Information Act's reach has been significantly restricted.[10] Through a series of policy actions, the administration has issued guidance to agencies advising them to reverse the presumption that government documents should be disclosed whenever possible and directing them to withhold a new category of documents—those that are "sensitive but unclassified."[11] It has adopted regulations that block the release of specific types of FOIA information and pursued legislation to create new categories of information to be made exempt from disclosure. Finally, the administration has applied FOIA exemptions inappropriately to withhold documents and has engaged in litigation to contest the public's right to information. Experts on government openness and information policy have noted that the Bush administration has reduced the public's right to know more than any other administration in modern history.[12] The Bush administration has drained the spirit out of FOIA in its effort to conceal the workings of government from the people.

From citizens' first efforts requesting documents under FOIA, one of the key issues in the struggle over secrecy has been agency claims of exemption from disclosure. In an attempt to broaden the public's access in this regard, the Clinton administration formally adopted the position that there is a "presumption of disclosure" for exempt materials that could be overcome only if the agency could establish that it "reasonably foresees that disclosure would be harmful to an interest protected by that exemption."[13] In short, under Clinton, even when technical grounds for withholding a document existed, agencies were advised to release the document unless they could show that there would be foreseeable harm from doing so.

The Bush administration reversed the Clinton presumption on October 21, 2001. John Ashcroft, then attorney general, in a memorandum to the heads of all federal agencies and departments, affirmatively stated that the Justice Department would defend agencies' assertions of FOIA exemptions "unless they lack a sound legal basis."[14] Ashcroft admonished agencies to fully consider the variety of countervailing interests before making any FOIA disclosure. The directions could not have been any clearer with regard to discouraging agencies from releasing information to the public. No longer was a showing required of the actual harm expected from the release of documents; instead, documents were simply automatically withheld.

We have already seen some of the results of the Ashcroft policy in chapter 2 when we looked at the attorney general's denial of a FOIA request seeking information about the names of the immigration detainees arrested after the September 11 attacks. Subsequently, Andrew Card, assistant to the president and chief of staff, circulated a memorandum in March 2002 intended to further reduce public access to information. The Card Memorandum primarily did two things: it urged agencies to use their discretion to withhold from disclosure records regarding weapons of mass destruction and "other information that could be misused to harm the security of our Nation and the safety of our people";[15] and it directed all federal agencies to review their record management procedures to ensure that they were in compliance with specifications of the executive guidance encouraging agencies to protect "sensitive but unclassified information." No definition was provided for the new term "sensitive" information. The Card Memorandum and accompanying guidance made clear that even though such documents were not "classified" they nevertheless should be withheld.[16] In order to accomplish this goal, the guidance recommended that agencies invoke FOIA exemption 2,[17] which exempts from release government records "related solely to the internal personnel rules and practices of an agency"—an exemption historically interpreted to protect information regarding employment or law enforcement matters.[18]

FOIA exemption 4, which protects trade secrets and confidential commercial or financial information provided to the government by the private sector, is another exemption recommended by the guidance for use in order to preclude disclosure. Rather than limiting the use of exemption 4 to that end, however, the guidance encourages agencies to invoke that exemption to shield from public scrutiny *all* information voluntarily submitted to the government by industry.[19]

While examples of agency use of the administration's strategies for evasion abound, two examples probably suffice to illustrate the point here. In one case, relying on the Card Memorandum, the Defense Department refused a FOIA request submitted by the Federation of American Scientists seeking the release of an unclassified report on what the government had learned from the 2001 anthrax attacks regarding the improvements needed in the areas of detection, response, and emergency preparedness. The report, written by the Center for Strategic and International Studies from publicly available documents, was unclassified, rendering a national security exemption claim difficult to make. Instead, the Defense Department invoked exemption 2 covering records relating to internal personnel rules.[20] Despite the federation's contention that releasing the report would build consensus in the United States for augmenting bio-preparedness in order to correct the identified vulnerabilities,[21] the Defense Department refused to release it. Only after the Federation of American Scientists appealed the denial did the Defense Department decide to release a redacted version of the report—nearly two years after the request.[22]

In the second case, pursuant to a FOIA request made by the United Mine Workers Association, the federal Mine Safety and Health Administration (MSHA) provided heavily redacted notes documenting a September 2002 meeting between MSHA officials and representatives of the Ohio Valley Coal Company. Also present at the meeting was the company's president and Robert Murray, a major Republican campaign contributor.[23] The released copies of the meeting notes were so heavily redacted that the text of the notes was incomprehensible.[24] The MSHA cited FOIA's law enforcement exemptions—which apply to records which if released could interfere with enforcement proceedings or cause an unwarranted invasion of privacy—as well as the deliberative process privilege—that covers documents prepared by agency staff and attorneys in anticipation of litigation. However, an investigation by Representative Henry Waxman revealed that "the meeting had no apparent law enforcement purpose, and even if it had, it is unclear how release of the redacted material [which revealed threats made by Ohio Valley Coal Company representatives to MSHA officials] could have either interfered with enforcement or constituted an unwarranted invasion of privacy."[25] Furthermore, the deliberative process privilege was not properly invoked, given that the conversation recorded was not one involving solely agency personnel but rather one between agency officials and outside parties.

In addition to encouraging the increasingly expansive and often inappropriate use of exemptions, the Bush administration is responsible for the creation of the Critical Infrastructure Information Act of 2002, which exempts from FOIA information related to the security of the country's "vital infrastructure" that is voluntarily provided to the federal government by private parties. The act creates a gigantic exemption from information disclosure under FOIA. The definition of the term "critical infrastructure" is very broad and includes "systems and assets, whether physical or virtual, whose destruction would have a "debilitating impact on security, national economic security, or national public health or safety."[26] Information submitted voluntarily by the private sector to the Department of Homeland Security (DHS), with a statement identifying it as "critical infrastructure information," is thus automatically protected from disclosure unless DHS determines otherwise. Under this scheme, then, the exemption could be manipulated by companies to operate as a shield preventing them from having to release evidence of errors, crimes, or other misconduct.[27]

Finally, although there are a number of other mechanisms creatively employed by the Bush administration to suppress the release of government information, one particularly stands out: the denial of fee waivers. Agency costs related to the search, duplication, and review of the documents requested may be charged to requesters who intend to use the records for a commercial purpose.[28] The statute provides for fee waivers for members of the media, public interest organizations, and the general public when the records are not sought for a commercial use and the request is made by "an educational or noncommercial scientific institution, whose purpose is scholarly or scientific research; or a representative of the news media."[29] A fee waiver is also mandated when "disclosure of the information is in the public interest because it is likely to contribute significantly to public understanding of the operations or activities of government and is not primarily in the commercial interest of the requester."[30]

The Bush administration has adopted a tough policy of challenging and denying FOIA requesters' eligibility for fee waivers, including contesting requesters' claim to "preferred status" and their assertions that the information is likely to contribute significantly to public understanding of government activities.[31] Among the newest objections raised by federal agencies is the contention that freelance journalists are not representatives of the news media,[32] and that education organizations that publish reports and newsletters do not qualify as media organizations if they are not "both organized and operated [solely] to disseminate information."[33]

In a recent case, the agency denied a fee waiver on the ground that the information sought would not contribute significantly to the public's understanding of government operations—in essence it was deciding what the public needed to know. In that case, the Brady Center to Prevent Gun Violence requested inspection reports on a firearms dealer who allegedly sold a gun that had been used to shoot two police officers.[34] The Bureau of Alcohol, Tobacco and Firearms denied the fee waiver request on the grounds that the

Brady Center had already received similar information about other firearms dealers and therefore there would be no benefit to releasing the information on this particular dealer.[35]

THE INCREASING NATIONAL SECURITY CLASSIFICATION OF GOVERNMENT RECORDS

In another reversal of the trend toward openness begun by President Clinton, the Bush administration has drastically decreased the volume of classified information to be made available to the public.

Safeguarding national security information is achieved by means of presidential executive orders. Under such orders, information is classified as either "confidential"—meaning that release is expected to cause damage to national security; "secret"—meaning that release is expected to cause serious damage; and "top secret"—meaning that release is expected to cause exceptionally grave damage.[36] In addition, specific agencies, such as the CIA, the National Security Agency, and the Defense Department, among others, have the authority to establish different classification levels for information that falls within the areas of their respective responsibilities.

By means of Executive Order 12958,[37] President Clinton sought to change the systemwide default toward secrecy among federal agencies and departments that had developed during the Cold War. The Clinton executive order achieved this by creating a presumption against classification in cases of significant doubt;[38] authorizing challenges to classification decisions; limiting the duration of classification to ten years; and requiring the automatic declassification of historically valuable records within five years of the order.[39] Within the first six years following the order, the number of records declassified increased more than five times the number declassified in the fourteen-year period from 1980 to 1994.[40]

President Bush abruptly closed this avenue of public access with the adoption of Executive Order 13292 on March 25, 2003. This executive order overturned both the presumption against classification and the requirement of classification at a lower level when there is doubt as to the appropriate level,[41] and it also permitted agencies to set a period of up to twenty-five years for an original classification if they determine that the duration is required owing to the sensitivity of the information.[42] In addition, Executive Order 13292 lowered the showing required to exempt records from declassification and pushed back the deadline for when the automatic declassification was to take place from April 2003 to December 2006.[43]

Three other changes accomplished by the Bush executive order bear mentioning here. First, the authority of the Interagency Security Classification Appeals Panel (ISCAP), the body that reviews agency decisions to exempt documents from automatic declassification and adjudicates challenges to classification decisions, was weakened by the transfer of its power to the director of Central Intelligence. Now, ISCAP decisions can be overridden by the CIA director, whose decisions, in turn, can only be overridden by the president.[44] Second, the Bush executive order significantly expanded the number of individuals who can make the original determination to designate documents as classified, adding the secretary of health and human services, the administrator of the Environmental Protection Agency, and the secretary of agriculture.[45] Third, the order expands agency authority to reclassify information that had previously been declassified. While Clinton had ordered that "information may not be reclassified after it has been declassified and released to the public under proper authority,"[46] the Bush executive order permits agency heads to reclassify such documents if the information "may reasonably be recovered."[47]

Finally, the Bush administration has expanded the protection of "sensitive security information," a category of unclassified information regarding the aviation industry that is exempt from disclosure under FOIA.[48] When Congress—at the request of the White House—enacted the Aviation and Transportation Act, it transferred responsibility for aviation security to the newly established Transportation Security Administration.[49] In the same act, Congress also expanded the law authorizing the designation of sensitive security information to cover all modes of transportation.[50]

The effect of the administration's decision to broaden agency authority to classify documents and prevent their release has been dramatic. The average number of original classification decisions per year during the period from 2001 to 2003 has increased fifty percent over the average for the previous five years.[51] Meanwhile, the declassification of documents has significantly decreased—by sixty percent from the volume declassified under the Clinton administration.[52] The great increase in classification decisions and decrease in declassification decisions should cause us even more concern given testimony by counterintelligence and security officials that makes clear that many disregard,[53] misinterpret, or misapply the rules regarding classification[54] and that, as a result, as many as half of all government secrets are improperly classified.[55]

This means that the volume of information about the operations of government hidden from public view has grown exponentially under President Bush. One example illustrates the stark reality of this problem. The Taguba Report detailing the unlawful mistreatment of Iraqi war prisoners in U.S. custody was originally classified in its entirety by the Defense Department. When one reporter who had read a leaked copy of the report asked Defense Secretary Donald Rumsfeld why the report was classified given that no information included in it was inherently secret, Secretary Rumsfeld answered: "[Y]ou'd have to ask the classifier."[56] Of course, the fact that the classification decision violated the prohibition against classification decisions made to conceal violations of the law was never mentioned.

Beyond the legal violation that the misclassification represented, experts have noted that the concealment of misconduct is always counterproductive. J. William Leonard, the Director of the Information Security Oversight Office, commenting on the classification of the Taguba Report, stated the following:

> And what is to be gained by classifying such activity? Our values as a society are such that they will invariably serve as a self-correcting measure when confronted with such abuses—thus the inevitability that such information will become widely known. At the same time, the initial act of classification can negatively impact the timeliness and completeness of notifications provided to certain Government officials, thus impairing their ability to deal with ensuing issues. In

the final analysis, we only succeed in keeping the information from those who need to know it most—the American people and their leaders—and even then, we only delay the inevitable.[57]

STRETCHING COURT PRECEDENT TO EXPAND THE COVER OF SECRECY

The Freedom of Information Act, like each state's analogous freedom of information law, is a valuable tool for every person who wants to know how her or his government operates and what it is doing with regard to a particular issue. Because the act also creates exemptions from disclosure to balance the public's right to know against competing interests such as individuals' privacy rights or national security, when a request for information under the act is denied and the denial is challenged by the information seeker, the courts are called upon to reconcile the competing interests in that case.

With increasing frequency over the last fifteen years, the courts have chosen privacy over openness when weighing the competing interests in FOIA cases. Several Supreme Court decisions have tipped the balance significantly in favor of privacy, restricting access to information that could have shed light on disreputable governmental activities. In *Department of Justice v. Reporters Committee for Freedom of the Press*, a 1989 decision, the Supreme Court held that federal agencies may withhold from public disclosure on privacy grounds "rap sheets" (a person's history of arrests, indictments, convictions, and acquittals) from public disclosure, even though all of the information included on the sheets is publicly accessible elsewhere.[58] The Court, upholding the exemption of all rap sheets, interpreted the law as requiring those seeking the information to prove that they would use it only to examine the conduct of the agency in possession of the requested records.[59]

Seven years after this decision, Congress amended FOIA to undo the Court's restrictive definition of what objective qualifies as being sufficiently in the "public interest" to warrant disclosure.[60] The amendment made clear that FOIA was intended to serve *any* purpose, and a requesting party's motive is no longer a basis for a denial of disclosure. As we have seen, however, under the influence of the Bush administration, federal agencies have revived this unlawful objection to disclosure.

The courts, however, continue to interpret FOIA exemptions broadly, and they uphold agency decisions refusing requests with regularity. In a troubling case also involving the FOIA privacy exemption, *United States Department of State v. Ray*,[61] the Supreme Court allowed the State Department to withhold the agency's records identifying Haitian refugees who were denied political asylum in this country and involuntarily returned to Haiti. President Reagan had issued an executive order that directed the State Department to intercept ships carrying undocumented would-be immigrants and return them to their countries of origin. As part of this plan, the secretary of state was supposed to obtain an assurance from the Haitian government that interdicted Haitians would not be subject to prosecution for their illegal departure. In order to monitor compliance with that assurance, the State Department conducted confidential interviews with unsuccessful emigrants six months after their involuntary return. Plaintiffs in the *Ray* case sought records of these interviews in order to show that their fears of persecution were well-founded.[62] Citing the privacy exemption, the Supreme Court overturned the court of appeals' decision requiring disclosure and upheld the State Department's refusal to release the documents. Strangely, the Court reasoned that the release of the identifying information might expose to persecution the Haitians who had been interviewed, even though the Haitian government *already had* the information sought.[63]

More recently, in March 2004, the Supreme Court was called upon in *National Archives and Records Administration v. Favish*,[64] to decide whether a citizen would be entitled to access information collected by the government during its investigation of the death of Vincent Foster Jr., deputy counsel to President Clinton. Skeptical of the government's conclusion that Foster had committed suicide, Allan Favish, associate counsel for Accuracy in Media, filed a FOIA request seeking, among other things, eleven photographs taken of Foster's body. Overturning the decision of the Ninth Circuit Court of Appeals, which ordered disclosure of the photos, the Supreme Court ruled that the death-scene photographs were "records or information compiled for law enforcement purposes," as defined in exemption 7(c) of the act and that the Court was therefore required to evaluate whether disclosure of them would "constitute an unwarranted invasion of personal privacy."[65] Concluding that the term "personal privacy" covered Foster's relatives' privacy interests in controlling images of his death, and that this interest outweighed Favish's interest, the Court held that Favish was not entitled to the photographs. The Court stated that in cases requiring a balancing of the competing interests of privacy and disclosure, the person requesting the information had to establish a sufficient reason for the disclosure. In order to satisfy exemption 7(c)'s public interest requirement, the Court held, the requester must "show the investigative agency or other responsible officials acted negligently or otherwise improperly in the performance of their duties."[66] The result of this decision is paradoxical: agencies will consider releasing law enforcement records *only* if the person requesting them can provide evidence of government wrongdoing that the sought-after information might reveal. Furthermore, the evidence must be strong enough to convince "a reasonable man" that the government likely acted improperly. In other words, only if you have the evidence of wrongdoing already in hand will you have even a chance at seeing the government files.

One First Amendment advocacy group has noted that the Bush administration is already stretching the decision in *Favish* to argue for even greater restrictions on the public's access to information. In a brief to the Supreme Court in a case that does not involve FOIA or the issue of personal privacy, according to the Reporters Committee for Freedom of the Press, the government cited the *Favish* decision for the proposition that any person seeking information about the government must show that the government is engaged in some wrongdoing in order to learn about the government's activities.[67]

According to the OpenTheGovernment.org report on the increase in secrecy under the Bush administration,[68] the government spent "$6.5 billion last year [2003] creating 14 million new classified documents and securing accumulated secrets—more than it has for at least the past decade."[69] With more than four thousand federal employees having the authority to classify information, a significant cultural imperative tending toward overclassification, and an administration with a political agenda mandating the same, the result is overwhelming government secrecy.

Far beyond the monetary cost of this culture of secrecy are its ramifications for our national security. According to the National Commission on Terrorist Attacks upon the United States (commonly known as the 9/11 Commission), both overclassification and incorrect classification have led to the "excessive compartmentalization of information among agencies," and this is an impediment to information sharing among agencies. In the final analysis, the 9/11 Commission concluded that, "excessive secrecy in government sabotaged attempts to find, track, and catch the terrorists."[70]

BLOCKING CONGRESS'S ACCESS TO INFORMATION

The congressional oversight of executive branch activities that is set forth in the Constitution[71] and mandated by our system of checks and balances invests in Congress the authority to investigate, review, and monitor federal agencies' policies and activities.[72] During the Bush administration, however, Congress has rarely invoked these powers, at least in part because of the partisan political population of the House and the Senate. In addition to Republican resistance to investigations of any allegations of misconduct by those in the White House, administration officials have erected a wall to block members of Congress who seek to investigate and review administration activities. Nearly every institutional mechanism by which Congress exercises its oversight function has been peremptorily shut off by the Bush administration, including the U.S. Government Accountability Office (GAO), the House Government Reform Committee, and congressionally established investigative commissions.

The GAO is the nonpartisan, investigative arm of Congress; it is the accountability watchdog and a key congressional tool used to fulfill its oversight function. The GAO has the authority, by statute,[73] to investigate all matters related to the use of public money, and its reports are released both to Congress and the public. Very early on in the Bush administration, officials challenged the basic authority of the GAO when it sought information on the energy task force chaired by Vice President Dick Cheney.[74] Congressman Henry Waxman asked the GAO to investigate the task force after hearing reports that major campaign contributors had special access to the task force while the public, including environmental and consumer advocacy groups, was locked out.[75] Although Congressman Waxman's request to the GAO was perfectly appropriate and within the GAO's authority, the vice president, nevertheless, refused to comply, stating that the inquiry "would unconstitutionally interfere with the functioning of the Executive branch."[76] When the refusal led to a lawsuit, however, it was the GAO that lost the battle. The federal court dismissed the GAO's suit, holding that the comptroller general did not have the authority to sue and that only congressional committees could bring such a suit.[77] The GAO's decision not to appeal the ruling means that there has been another victory for the administration in its push for secret government. In the past, the GAO has often relied on the threat of a lawsuit as an enforcement mechanism to be used in its investigations of the executive branch.[78] That leverage is now gone.

The Bush administration levied a similar challenge to the investigative power of the Committee on Government Reform, a congressional committee that in 1928 was given the power to require executive agencies to provide information. Under the Seven Member Rule Act, when any seven members of the committee request information, the agency must comply with the request.[79] The current administration, however, forced the Committee on Government Reform to begin litigation on two occasions to enforce its authority. One of these lawsuits involved a request for the complete data set for the 2000 Decennial Census from the Department of Commerce; the agency refused to reveal the data set that showed the sampling errors made in the census calculations. In this case, unlike that of the GAO, the Committee on Government Reform won the battle, and the federal court ruled against the Bush administration.[80] On appeal, the case was combined with a FOIA lawsuit seeking the same information, and the Ninth Circuit Court of Appeals ordered the Commerce Department to release the adjusted census data under FOIA. Despite Congress's victory in this case, the administration continues to resist complying with the Seven Member Rule in nearly every case.[81]

Information requests made to the Bush administration by ranking members of congressional committees have met with the same stonewalling. When the ranking members of eight House committees wrote to President Bush on June 3, 2004, to advise him of their intention to investigate the prison abuses at Abu Ghraib and other facilities being used in the "war on terror" and to request the documents necessary to commence their investigation, they received no response whatsoever.[82] Congressman Henry Waxman's written requests to President Bush and then National Security Advisor Condoleezza Rice, seeking documents regarding the president's false statement made in the State of the Union address that Iraq was seeking to import uranium from Africa, also received no response.[83] Apparently, the president thinks that he owes no explanation to Congress or the American public for any of his actions.

Perhaps the most disturbing executive branch effort to block congressional oversight is the administration's refusal to cooperate with Congress's effort to investigate the September 11 attacks. In November 2002, Congress enacted a law creating the 9/11 Commission to examine the "facts and causes relating to the terrorist attacks," and "report to the President and Congress on its findings, conclusions, and recommendations for corrective measures that can be taken to prevent acts of terrorism."[84] The Bush administration's resistance to the 9/11 Commission's inquiry is by now well known. In July 2003, the 9/11 Commission's Republican Chairman Thomas Kean and its Democratic Chairman Lee Hamilton issued a joint statement objecting to the Defense and Justice Departments' failure to provide requested information as well as the administration's insistence that administration personnel be present at all interviews with intelligence officials.[85] From the fall of 2003 until April 2004, 9/11 Commission efforts to get key presidential intelligence briefing documents—including the August 6, 2001, President's Daily Brief, which had warned of the Al Qaeda threat—were repeatedly blocked by the White House. The White House allowed the 9/11 Commission to see the document in April 2004 only after it became a topic of widespread public discussion. And in the spring of 2004, the White House sought to block the 9/11 Commission's efforts to compel Condoleezza Rice from testifying under oath before the 9/11 Commission.[86] Once again, only public pressure compelled the White House to relent. How can President Bush credibly state that his major objective is ensuring national security when he consistently resisted cooperating with the 9/11 Commission's inquiry?

In short, the Bush administration has obstructed Congress's access to administration officials and documents in nearly every area of inquiry undertaken. Perhaps most tellingly, this obstruction operated to hinder the 9/11 Commission's investigation as well.

CHAPTER NINE

Secret Cases and State Secrets

The public's right to know has suffered. The Bush-Cheney administration has systematically ushered in a new era of government secrecy
through policies and directives that weaken transparency laws and
avoid accountability.

—*Senator Patrick Leahy*[1]

The growing trend toward secrecy extends beyond the context of military proceedings—it is happening here and now, in routine immigration hearings, in
law enforcement applications made for intelligence investigations, and in cases
that have made their way through the civil legal system all the way to the
Supreme Court. All with hardly a soul knowing.

THE NON-EXISTENT CASE OF M.K.B.

In February 2004, the U.S. Supreme Court declined to hear a case brought
by twenty-three media and public interest organizations[2] challenging federal
court orders to keep the habeas corpus case of Mohamed Kamel Bellahouel
completely secret. The ruling also denied a request by the Reporters Committee for Freedom of the Press, a nonprofit First Amendment advocacy group, to
intervene in the case as a party in order to raise the secrecy issue.

Bellahouel is an Algerian who is married to an American citizen, and who
was detained on an immigration charge one month after September 11.[3]
While no criminal charges were ever filed against him, Bellahouel was impris-

oned for five months during which time he was asked to testify before a federal grand jury. With the assistance of a public defender, Bellahouel filed a habeas corpus petition seeking to challenge the lawfulness of his detention in court. At the government's request, the federal district court judge entered an order closing the case from all public scrutiny. The Eleventh Circuit Court of Appeals upheld the order, and the entire case proceeded in secret; all parties were placed under a "gag order," and all court documents were sealed. So completely was the case cloaked by the courts' orders that its very existence was publicly unknown and likely would not have been discovered had an appeals court clerk not left references to the "M.K.B." matter on the court's calendar.[4] Reporters check court dockets to find out what cases have been filed in the courts around the country, and the dockets enable people to track the progress of a case through the judicial system. They show the number assigned to the case by the court, the names of the parties in the lawsuit, their lawyers' names and contact information, and a brief summary of each document filed in the case or actions taken by the court (such as hearings or conferences scheduled and orders entered). So, but for the chance appearance on the docket, the public likely still would not know anything about this case.

During Bellahouel's appeal, the issue of his challenge to his detention became moot, because the government, apparently believing that the man represented no national security threat, permitted him to post a $10,000 bond and then released him from custody while he waited for the completion of his immigration hearing on whether he had overstayed a student visa.[5]

When the courts refused to open the case to public view, the Chief of Appeals for the federal public defender's office in Miami, Paul Rashkind, sought U.S. Supreme Court review of those decisions. Amazingly, when considering whether to hear the matter, the Court extended the extraordinary secrecy enveloping the case to *its own proceedings*, and permitted then-Solicitor General Theodore B. Olson to file the government's papers in opposition to the request for review entirely under the seal of secrecy. According to First Amendment expert Floyd Abrams, the Supreme Court's action in the case is unprecedented. He noted that even during the 1971 Pentagon Papers case, which concerned the publication of a top-secret government study of the Vietnam War, the government had filed two briefs, one under seal and one for the public.[6] In the *M.K.B. v. Warden* case, by contrast, the government has not posted its position in any place that the public can access; it has simply not publicly stated the reasons for its position. Under these conditions, the people are utterly unable to assess the position taken by the government and consequently cannot hold the government accountable.

According to the Reporters Committee for Freedom of the Press, the most recent examples of secret dockets involve cases against alleged terrorists. While the Justice Department has held fast to its policy of not even providing the numbers of individuals arrested on terrorism charges, it has occasionally revealed the existence of plea agreements after resourceful journalists uncover a secret case. One example is the case of Iyman Faris, who pleaded guilty to a charge of providing material support to Al Qaeda. When two *Newsweek* reporters discovered the case, the Justice Department admitted the existence of the plea bargain and noted only that its "need to keep it secret had dissipated."[7] Why secrecy was required in the first place remains unclear.

While the government has stated that providing the number of individuals arrested on terrorism charges would "give a road map to the terrorists," because it could theoretically monitor the government's progress in the "war on terror," it has never explained how a terrorist operative could be in U.S. custody for months without the terrorist organization knowing that its operative is missing.[8] As many have aptly noted, this inconsistency raises the question about whether such secrecy is really needed to protect national security or is being used instead to shield the government from public scrutiny.[9]

The secret docketing of the *Bellahouel* case points to a troubling trend that has largely escaped public attention. While courts have always exercised their authority to seal specific documents or files in a particular case to protect trade secrets or other matters deemed too sensitive for public scrutiny, there has been little analysis of the courts' power to seal an entire case so that the case literally disappears from public view. A recent battle over this issue in Connecticut eventually led to a rule that prohibits courts from removing a case from the docket. However, because the issue is dealt with independently by each state, practices differ across the country. In fact, some state statutes require that certain types of cases—like custody cases—be kept secret, and others provide for the erasure of court records after the elapse of a specific period of time from judgment. There is no basis for such secrecy. Little harm could be done by the adoption of a rule providing public notice of requests to seal a case so that the media could seek to intervene in the case and, if appropriate, challenge the sealing motion. Such a rule would not prevent the court from balancing the privacy or national security needs against the public interest in knowing about the issues and outcome of a case.

Similar rules could also govern the range of other measures judges use to shield court proceedings from the media and the public, including sealed search warrants, broad gag orders imposed on attorneys, the excessive sealing of court documents, and the secret selection of jurors. With the increasing use of these measures, our right to observe the operation of the judicial system is being eroded by leaps and bounds. Until recently, the use of anonymous juries had been a rare occurrence, reserved primarily for situations in which jurors' safety is at risk, such as cases involving organized crime figures.[10] The expansion of this practice to its use in celebrity trials, such as that of Martha Stewart's illegal stock sale case, creates a dangerous precedent. Fortunately, in that case, a challenge brought by seventeen news organizations to fight the judge's secrecy order was successful in the Second Circuit Court of Appeals. Three weeks into the trial, the court ruled that "[t]he burden is heavy on those who seek to restrict access to the media, a vital means to open justice. . . . Here, the government has failed to overcome the presumption of openness. The mere fact of intense media coverage of a celebrity defendant, without further compelling justification, is simply not enough to justify closure."[11] In the end, however, the trial judge kept the jurors' names secret until after the verdict was handed down.

HOW THE BUSH ADMINISTRATION IS EXTINGUISHING CASES: THE STATE SECRETS PRIVILEGE

The Bush administration has come up with a uniquely powerful way of dissolving cases that it does not want the public to see, the courts to analyze, or the plaintiffs to win. Since 2001, the administration has reinvigorated and inflated the "state secrets" evidentiary privilege and wielded it as a weapon to snuff out legal challenges to some of the most draconian policies it has employed in the "war on terror" including the CIA's extraordinary rendition program involving the covert transfer of terrorism suspects to countries known to commit state-sanctioned torture, and the clandestine electronic surveillance of thousands of Americans' communications and commercial transactions.

The state secrets privilege is a common-law evidentiary rule that permits the government to block discovery (the pre-trial request for relevant information by either party in a case) of "any information that, if disclosed, would adversely affect national security."[12] It is intended to protect against the release of information that might impair "the nation's defense capabilities . . . intelligence-gathering methods or capabilities," or disrupt "diplomatic relations with foreign governments."[13] The courts have also made plain, however, that this privilege must be narrowly construed so that it is not used to "defeat worthy claims of violations of rights,"[14] or to deny plaintiffs a constitutionally provided judicial forum for resolving dispute.[15] For this reason, the courts have ruled that the privilege may not be used to "shield any material not strictly necessary to prevent injury to national security. . . ."[16]

The Supreme Court outlined the proper use of the state secrets privilege fifty years ago in *Reynolds v. United States,* 345 U.S. 1 (1953), a lawsuit in which the family members of three civilians who died in the crash of a military plane in Georgia sued for damages. In response to a discovery request for the flight accident report, the government invoked the state secrets privilege, stating that because secret military equipment was being tested on the aircraft during the fatal flight and the report contained information about the equipment, it could not be compelled to produce the report. The Supreme Court upheld the government's claim of privilege over the accident report, but did not dismiss the suit. Instead, it sent the case back down to the federal district court for further proceedings, explaining that:

> There is nothing to suggest that the electronic equipment, in this case, had any causal connection with the accident. Therefore, it should be

possible for respondents to adduce the essential facts as to causation without resort to material touching upon military secrets. Respondents were given a reasonable opportunity to do just that, when petitioner formally offered to make the surviving crew members available for examination. We think that offer should have been accepted.[17]

Upon remand to the district court, plaintiff's counsel deposed the surviving crew members, and ultimately settled the case.[18]

The state secrets privilege is properly used as shield to prevent the disclosure of legitimately determined sensitive evidence, not as a sword to justify the premature dismissal of serious claims. The Supreme Court recently reinforced the principle that the privilege should not be used to bar claims at the outset of any litigation in the case *Tenet v. Doe*, 544 U.S. 1 (2005), in which the Court distinguished the *Totten* rule, which may require outright dismissal of a lawsuit at the very first stage of the case if it involves unacknowledged espionage agreements, from the state secrets evidentiary privilege, which may be invoked to prevent the disclosure of specific evidence during the discovery process.

In the five decades between the *Reynolds* decision and the start of the Bush administration's "war on terror," America has maintained this balance between security and the right to an open, democratic court system. The typical result when the states secrets privilege has been successfully invoked by the government has been for the court to remove the privileged evidence from the case and permit the case to proceed without use of or reference to that evidence.[19] The courts have consistently held that use of the privilege must be weighed against "American concerns for democracy, openness, and separation of powers,"[20] and the privilege's narrow contours require that "whenever possible, sensitive information must be disentangled from nonsensitive information to allow for the release of the latter."[21]

Because neither the parties nor the court can predict whether the privileged evidence will be necessary or even relevant to the case, there is no categorical rule mandating the dismissal of lawsuits prior to discovery. Wholesale dismissal of a case is permitted at the outset of a case *only* where a court can devise *no process whatsoever* that would enable the case to proceed without revelation of state secrets. Otherwise, the proper course is to proceed and let the court determine the claims of privilege as (and if) they arise during discovery. If, *after discovery* and full consideration of the non-privileged evidence, the court finds that the plaintiff is unable to establish a prima facie case (a case with sufficient evidence to proceed), or if the defendant is unable to press a valid defense without relying on the privileged evidence, *only then* may dismissal of the case become appropriate.[22]

Because of the injustice and finality of a dismissal, courts have used creative alternatives to permit an injured party to vindicate his or her rights while it simultaneously protects state secrets from disclosure. For example, in *Heine v. Raus,* a case involving sensitive CIA information, the Fourth Circuit Court of Appeals directed the district court to review *in camera* (privately in the judge's chambers) any discovery material that might arguably fall within the privilege.[23] A court could conduct an entire trial *in camera*.[24]

Despite fifty years of such sound and balanced precedent, none of these alternatives are given a moment's thought by the lawyers for the Bush administration. The idea of scrubbing a case of sensitive evidence seems totally inefficient given that the government can wipe the case completely off the docket by claiming that proceeding with any aspect of the case would jeopardize national security. The state secrets privilege has now become a powerful tool used to drastic result.

Experts have confirmed not only that the Bush administration is asserting the privilege at a significantly higher rate than any other administration before it, but also that it is using it in a manner radically different from how it was used in the past.[25] The state secrets privilege was invoked "just four times in the first 23 years following the 1953 decision," and "after that, state secrets claims were filed at a fairly even pace during the Cold War and beyond, once or twice per year, under Democratic and Republican presidents alike."[26] According to the National Security Archive at George Washington University, lawyers representing the administration have requested that federal judges dismiss at the outset at least twenty-one cases in the past five years. Even these unprecedented figures are shaky given that some cases may be entirely under seal and kept secret from the public.[27]

Invoking the state secrets privilege in case after case, government lawyers have aimed to shoot down nearly every challenge to the Bush administration's unlawful policies involving indefinite detention, brutal interrogation, extraordinary rendition, and domestic surveillance. The suppression of these cases has put the vitality of our legal and moral principles at grave risk.

Khaled El-Masri's rendition to detention and interrogation under torture in Afghanistan by U.S. agents represents one of the most widely known examples of the publicly acknowledged CIA extraordinary rendition program.[28] In its motion to dismiss the entire case at the pleading stage, the government contended that it was unable to either confirm or deny the allegations made in the complaint about the secret extraordinary rendition program. The government made this argument to the court, despite the fact that the world's leading media outlets corroborated El-Masri's allegations, and the government itself—through the statements of former CIA director George Tenet and Secretary of State Condoleezza Rice—repeatedly confirmed the existence of the rendition program. Nevertheless, the government contended that it could not answer a single question in the litigation without being compelled to violate the privilege and therefore the case should be dismissed in its entirety from the outset. Though the leap of logic here is suspect at best, the government's manuevering was unfortunately successful. The suit was dismissed on the ground that further legal proceedings might expose state secrets and jeopardize national security.[29]

At the time this book goes to press, there are three cases challenging the Bush administration's domestic spying efforts—the "terrorist surveillance program," discussed in full in chapter 10. In each of these cases, government lawyers have attempted to employ the tactic successfully used in El-Masri's case. However, the assault against democracy that was deemed permissible by the courts in dismissing the torture of a foreign national was finally halted when the privacy of Americans was threatened. In the case of *Hepting v. AT&T*, the administration's lawyers argued for dismissal of a class action lawsuit brought against AT&T for secretly providing customer information to the government in the name of battling terrorists. The government argued that any continuation of the case would compel it to confirm or deny the *exis-*

tence of domestic surveillance operations.[30] The acknowledgement of the existence of the surveillance program by senior administration officials apparently did not alter the government's analysis in any way. Ultimately, in July 2006, the court declined to dismiss the suit.[31]

The arguments made in the *Hepting v. AT&T* case reveal the most dangerous aspect of the Bush administration's use of the state secret evidentiary privilege. In short, lawyers for the administration are arguing that not only are the courts precluded from adjudicating cases like these, but that *Congress is powerless* to do anything to halt the administration's unlawful activities. At issue in the *Hepting* case is whether AT&T secretly provided customers' telephone call information to the administration as part of its "terrorist surveillance program"[32] without the constitutionally and statutorily required court authorization.

The Bush administration's use of the state secret privilege to block all judicial scrutiny of its actions in its national security and counterterrorism program is part of a direct assault on the judiciary which began at the start of the administration. Aggressive use of the state secrets privilege is a critical part of the administration's plan for the continual expansion of executive power to the point of obliterating all judicial checks on its tightly held "war on terror" tactics.[33]

Our judicial system has always operated on the presumption of openness, a position that the Supreme Court—until recently—has consistently endorsed. Not only do the measures that limit public information about the operation of the judicial system threaten to undermine our First Amendment rights, they also threaten the fundamental constitutional guarantee of a public trial. Our Constitution presumes that public scrutiny and discussion ensure fair trials. As the Supreme Court has aptly noted, "[p]ublic confidence cannot long be maintained where important judicial decisions are being made behind closed doors and then announced in conclusive terms to the public, with the record supporting the court's decision sealed from the public view."[34] How can we trust decisions made on the basis of information hidden from us? How can we trust the decision makers?

In 2003, Senator Herb Kohl (D-WI) introduced the Sunshine in Litigation Act of 2003 (Sunshine Act) to deal with some of these issues. The Sunshine Act would restrict the use of protective orders and sealed records in federal civil actions. It would bar courts from entering orders restricting the disclosure of information obtained through discovery and from approving settlement agreements that restrict such disclosure. The Sunshine Act would also prohibit courts from restricting access to court records unless the judge makes specific findings that the order sealing records would not restrict the disclosure of information relevant to public health or safety, that the public interest in disclosure is outweighed by a specific and substantial interest in maintaining confidentiality, and that the order is no broader than necessary. The bill[35] was referred to the Senate Judiciary Committee in April 2003, but that committee has never acted upon it.

We must demand that the president respect the limitations that the Constitution imposes on the office under our system of checks and balances and honor the essential roles of Congress and the Judicial Branch in ensuring that our nation's security is protected in a manner consistent with our constitutional guarantees. These proceedings must be open to the public and conducted in a manner that provides *the People* with a clear account of what happened and who is responsible.

CHAPTER TEN

Living under the Watchful Eye

Imagine these scenarios:

> ➤ Robert Greene, an investigative reporter for the *Atlanta Journal Constitution*, contacts Jamil Hussain, a foreign graduate student attending Georgia State University, to get his views on whether he has felt any post September 11 backlash as a Muslim student here on a student visa. Unknown to Greene, Jamil is the subject of a roving wiretap authorized under the PATRIOT Act. Because the roving wiretap gives law enforcement and intelligence officers the power to eavesdrop on Jamil's telephone conversations and e-mail correspondence, the government is listening in on and recording Greene's conversations with Jamil, his investigative source. In addition, by contacting someone who is the subject of foreign intelligence surveillance, Greene has made himself vulnerable to having a pen register or tap-and-trace device placed on his telephone and e-mail accounts. All the government must do is go to the secret FISA court and certify that the information likely to be obtained would be relevant to an ongoing foreign intelligence investigation.[1] Once

approved, the devices would provide government investigators with access to every e-mail address and telephone number that Greene contacts.

➤ You are a graduate student attending New York University, studying political science. After reading about certain provisions of the PATRIOT Act, you remember an American history course you took in college and decide to go to a neighborhood used bookstore and see if you can find any books on the McCarthy era. While you are in the bookstore, you find a bunch of books that look interesting on that subject as well as the subjects of government repression of freedom of speech and association. You also find that the store has for sale a poster with a composite image of President George W. Bush and Senator Joseph McCarthy shaking hands. You decide to buy the books and the poster. When you go to the register, the store owner asks you if you would like to attend a meeting of a peace group that evening at 8:00 p.m. You decide to go to the meeting and learn about what the group is doing. Two weeks later, you are in your apartment in faculty housing working on your thesis paper, when a loud knock comes at your door, making you jump out of your seat. At your door are two Secret Service agents. They have come to ask you some questions about your book purchases, the poster on your wall, and your attendance at the peace meeting because someone has called in an anonymous tip.

Do these scenarios sound far fetched to you? Well they did, at least initially, to me. But guess what, both of these scenarios actually took place here in America under the Bush administration. In fact, in mid-December 2005, NBC News reported on the existence of a secret Defense Department document that listed dozens of anti-war meetings and demonstrations as "suspicious incidents" which demanded further investigation.[2] Subsequent media reports confirmed that the Counterintelligence Field Activity Agency (CIFA), a division of the Defense Department whose size, budget, and scope of operations remain secret, has been collecting information about domestic organizations' lawful, peaceful political activities.[3] This revelation caused considerable consternation from many people all across the political spectrum.[4] In response, the Defense Department ordered a review of the Pentagon's Threat and Local Observation Notice (TALON) intelligence database to determine if information on citizens who posed no threat to national security had been improperly retained in the system.[5]

We now know that such constitutionally-protected, democratic activities as anti-war and counter-recruitment protests were captured in the Pentagon's TALON database as possible "domestic threats." The Pentagon has monitored such organizations as the United for Peace and Justice (UFPJ), a coalition of more than thirteen hundred local and national groups throughout the United States that joined together to oppose the war in Iraq. A demonstration organized by UFPJ near a recruiting station in Fayetteville, North Carolina on the second anniversary of the start of the war was listed in the "threat" database.[6] Groups such as Truth Project, Inc., a Florida not-for-profit group comprised of peace and social justice activists who meet in a Quaker church in Lake Worth, Florida, had apparently made the grade as well. The Truth Project's planning meetings during 2004 and 2005 were listed in the Pentagon's database of suspected domestic "threats."[7] The Rhode Island Community Coalition for Peace and their December 2004 protest in front of the Rhode Island National Guard Office, calling for immediate troop withdrawal from Iraq, were also listed in the Pentagon's database of suspected domestic "threats."[8]

The TALON data collection program was started in 2003 by former deputy defense secretary Paul Wolfowitz to track groups and individuals with possible links to terrorism, an issue that the Bush administration has now placed squarely under the control of the Defense Department. Under the program, the Pentagon has gathered information on Americans engaged in traditional First Amendment activities and then shared that information with other government agencies through the database.[9] This abuse of power, purportedly intended to protect citizens but used instead to monitor critics of the Iraq war and other Bush administration policies, is doubly disturbing. It not only has a chilling effect on people who merely seek to exercise their free speech and association rights, it also dangerously blurs the historically critical line between the military and civil society. There is simply no constitutional role for the military to play in monitoring the First Amendment activities of Americans. The Pentagon's secret surveillance of antiwar organizations, peaceful protests, and group gatherings marks a trend of encroachment that must be stemmed immediately before more of our rights fall prey to military oversight and enforcement—our rights as free citizens are at serious peril.

THE UNCHECKED GROWTH OF GOVERNMENT SURVEILLANCE

Most Americans know that the PATRIOT Act expanded the federal government's surveillance, detention, and investigative powers in some fashion. What is far less widely known, however, is the extent of the government's investigative powers *prior* to the passage of the PATRIOT Act and how far that Act extended those powers. To understand the full scope of the government's ability to investigate us now we need to look back a little in time.

THE EROSION OF THE LEVI GUIDELINES

The Ford administration created the Levi Guidelines after the 1970s Church Committee hearings revealed decades of FBI abuses from the days of the Palmer Raids through COINTELPRO. During the 1950s and 1960s, in the midst of the politically charged atmosphere of the Cold War and the McCarthy era, the FBI routinely installed electronic surveillance devices on private property in order to monitor the conversations and meetings of suspected communists.[10] During the 1970s, the country was shocked by revelations of how the FBI's COINTELPRO program, authorized by President Nixon, wiretapped Martin Luther King Jr. and other dissidents solely because of their political beliefs, violated the privacy of thousands of American citizens who opposed the Vietnam War, and sought to subvert the activities of lawful political groups.[11] Media accounts of the CIA's Operation

CHAOS, which involved the illegal surveillance of Americans involved in the peace movement, student activists, and black nationalists, added fuel to the fire.[12] The Church Committee Report, issued in 1976 by the Senate Select Committee charged with investigating the CIA's illegal surveillance, concluded that "[u]nless new and tighter controls are established by legislation, domestic intelligence activities threaten to undermine our democratic society and fundamentally alter its nature."[13]

Congressional pressure and the public outcry over these abuses played a large role in pushing the FBI to vow to limit its domestic surveillance activities to situations in which criminal activity was suspected.[14] Although the Levi Guidelines were self-imposed, for nearly three decades the FBI complied with these restrictions in the name of the constitutional values they protected. The idea that government monitoring of political activity would chill people's discussions and dissolve their organizations apparently was enough to keep the FBI on course. No longer.

On November 30, 2001, John Ashcroft, then attorney general, commenced the Bush administration's initiative aimed at strengthening the hand of domestic law enforcement agencies by announcing his intention to relax the restrictions on the FBI's surveillance activities.[15] According to Ashcroft and FBI Director Robert Mueller, the Levi Guidelines were obsolete and hindered the FBI's counterterrorism investigations.[16] So, in May 2002, Ashcroft unilaterally decided upon and announced new guidelines for the FBI's domestic intelligence investigations. The guidelines summarily abandoned the long-standing civil liberties protections that had been put into place after the Church hearings documented specific FBI abuses against civil rights leaders and other activists opposed to U.S. involvement in the Vietnam War. Under Ashcroft's new guidelines, the FBI has the authority to launch a preliminary investigation on any person without more than the merest hint of evidence. These investigations can be maintained for up to one year, and the limitations on the surveillance techniques that can be used are few.

Loosening the guidelines is part of a larger plan designed to fundamentally alter the FBI's mission, from crime solving to domestic intelligence gathering; a change Ashcroft and Mueller and others in the administration deemed necessary to create an intelligence apparatus aggressive enough to thwart terror-ism.[17] The relaxation of the restrictions freed up the FBI to conduct domestic spying operations and begin surveillance of religious and political organiza-tions. FBI agents can now monitor political activities even when the activities are unconnected to the investigation of any crime, and decisions to initiate counterterrorism inquiries can be made by special agents in charge of field offices rather than only by directors situated at headquarters in Washington, D.C.[18] Without even basic supervision from within the agency, there are now no mechanisms to monitor how FBI agents exercise their discretion to start a counterterrorism investigation.

What is the cost to our open and free society if we must be concerned about who is listening in on our meetings and conversations? And where is the evidence that paying this cost is worthwhile in terms of our increased safety? Will policing lawful political activities assist the FBI in stopping ter-rorist acts? None of the nineteen perpetrators of the September 11 attacks were overtly political or expressed dissident views in any public place.[19] While these questions have not been answered, the rules have already been changed and we have begun to see the effects of that change.

Despite this country's rich tradition of dissent—from the Boston Tea Party to the Selma March—challenging us to reach for the highest moral standards of constitutional democracy, the government is trampling our freedoms and the protections that we have come to take for granted. Although dissent is essential to our democratic tradition, within the last four years the govern-ment has harassed and intimidated citizens exercising their free speech rights and has even directly suppressed free speech.[20] Several examples illustrate this trend. On November 23, 2003, in the wake of public protests in Miami, Florida over the proposed Free Trade Area of the Americas, the *New York Times* published an article detailing the FBI's activities collecting information on the organization, training, and strategies of antiwar demonstrators and groups, and advising local law enforcement officials to report any suspicious activity to the Bureau's counterterrorism squad.[21] A confidential memorandum circu-lated by the FBI to local law enforcement agencies in Washington and San Francisco on October 15, 2003, in anticipation of antiwar demonstrations in those cities, analyzed how peace groups recruit demonstrators, rehearse for demonstrations, and use the Internet to raise money.[22] In interviews with the media, FBI officials said that the intelligence-gathering activities documented in the memorandum were "aimed at identifying anarchists and extremist elements plotting violence," not at monitoring the protected political speech of antiwar demonstrators.[23] Nevertheless, the memorandum warned local law enforcement officials about protest activities that present a threat, such as forming human chains, and discussed demonstrators "innovative strategies" such as videotaping arrests in order to "intimidate" the police.[24] The memorandum also noted that protestors often raise money to pay for lawyers for those arrested during a protest.[25] But no reference was made to the fact that every single one of the actions noted is a constitutionally protected activity—not only protected, but revered by the people of this country.

Where does this FBI advice lead? Perhaps to the issuance of a subpoena like the one served on Drake University by a federal prosecutor[26] seeking information regarding the student organizers and attendees at an antiwar conference held at the college on November 15, 2003. Or maybe to the extensive questioning of hundreds of antiwar protestors about their political activities and associations like that done by New York City police in 2003.[27] Or perhaps the FBI's advice leads to the establishment of highly suspect preventative tools like the "no fly" list, which subjected the peace activists on the list—including ministers, nuns, and political cartoonists—to either a complete bar on flying or an extremely thorough (and invasive) security screening every time they fly.[28]

Perhaps the most troubling aspect of the increase in surveillance, however, is that the intelligence information included in the FBI's October 2003 Memorandum was collected, at least in part, through firsthand observation and informants. At the same time, FBI officials said that the purpose of their surveillance of antiwar groups and their protest activities "was not to monitor the protestors but to gather intelligence.[29] The connection being drawn between political protests and terrorist activities is an extremely dangerous one. A single protest by animal rights activists that involved trespassing and releasing laboratory animals to freedom was not treated as a criminal act but was instead prosecuted as Animal Enterprise Terrorism. The defendant now faces federal charges that could lead to a sentence of more than eighty years in prison.[30] What transformed what would ordinarily be deemed criminal acts, such as trespass and theft, into an act of terrorism? The U.S. attorney involved in this particular case stated that the defendant was a terrorist because he tried to impose his will on others by using violence.[31] Is the difference then whether one intended to send a message to people by committing the crime? It seems plain then that the government is now criminalizing dissent. Do we really want to go back to the days of J. Edgar Hoover, when the FBI was permitted to engage in political spying and to outlaw all dissent? Are we willing to give up our hard-won civil liberties without a question about whether there are other ways to achieve greater security?

At the same time that the FBI is getting into the spy game, the CIA is getting into the domestic law enforcement game. The bright line that used to exist between the two agencies' mandates—one to catch domestic criminals and the other to intercept foreign agents—has been purposefully blurred since September 11. That line, originally drawn because the CIA had been caught spying on Americans, is now viewed by the Bush administration as a barrier to effective collaboration between the two agencies.[32] Bush administration officials argue that the agencies must be allowed to work together to collect secret information, though many experts agree that our intelligence system has not yet been able to analyze the information it has already collected.[33] Do we fix this broken system by simply capitulating to the executive branch's desire for more spying to collect more secret information on the American public? Is this what the Sons of Liberty had in mind?

The surveillance of political groups voicing dissent and the questioning of protestors about their activities and affiliations threaten our nation's deep historical commitment to civil disobedience, a legacy that we trace back to Martin Luther King Jr. and Henry David Thoreau. Have we decided that peaceful protest must be treated as terrorism's cousin? If so, then perhaps we have already permitted our concern about national security to overtake our most cherished democratic traditions. Such a dramatic change in our, *the People's*, values must not happen unwittingly. If we have missed the signs up until this point, then we have decisions to make and actions to undertake in order to make sure that our voice—and our choice—is heard by those who have the power to make the changes we demand.

THE FOREIGN INTELLIGENCE SURVEILLANCE ACT COURT: AMERICA'S SECRET CIVILIAN COURT

In addition to the FBI's self-imposed Levi Guidelines, Congress also responded to the advice of the Church Committee Report by offering a compromise solution to permit the executive branch to fulfill its function of preserving national security while at the same time ensuring that its activities would not run afoul of the Constitution. This solution was the establishment of the Foreign Intelligence Surveillance Court. The Foreign Intelligence Surveillance Act of 1978[34] (FISA) established a court intended to provide a judicial check on the executive branch's rampant abuse of its surveillance powers. This highly sensitive court was charged with the responsibility of reviewing the executive branch's conduct of its foreign intelligence surveillance operations—in particular, the role of foreign agents inside the United States—and providing supervision in a way that would preserve the civil liberties of those being investigated.

The Foreign Intelligence Surveillance Court is made up of eleven specially designated federal judges who are appointed by the chief justice of the United States to serve seven-year, nonrenewable terms. The court is housed in a restricted, locked, and windowless room in the Justice Department building in Washington, D.C.[35] The FISA court judges serve by rotation, and sit alone, hearing government applications for surveillance orders permitting clandestine wiretaps and physical searches. Of course, these applications are ex parte (or one-sided)—only the government is heard, not the target the government seeks to investigate. Appeals may be heard by a three-judge panel, but few such appeals have been heard because less than .01 percent of the more than sixteen thousand government surveillance applications filed have been denied.[36]

There are certain standards that the government must meet in order to obtain a FISA surveillance order. The Justice Department must show why the government believes that the proposed surveillance target is a foreign agent, why the information sought is relevant to ongoing foreign intelligence monitoring, and why less intrusive means cannot be used to gather the information. The Justice Department must also specify the manner in which the surveillance will be undertaken. It need not, however, describe the items to be seized or the place to be searched as the court decisions interpreting the Fourth Amendment warrant requirement have found to be mandatory in the general law enforcement context.[37] Furthermore, the court is not required to review the application using the traditional criminal standard whether there is probable cause to believe that the targeted individual has engaged or will engage in any criminal activity. When a FISA warrant is issued, the government is not required to provide the target with even delayed notice that his or her privacy has been invaded—even if the target is ultimately found to have been illegally targeted. In short, FISA permits the government to conduct physical searches and electronic surveillance[38] without complying with the ordinary Fourth Amendment requirements.

The surveillance process authorized by the FISA—from secret warrant application to implementation—is also very different from surveillance authorized pursuant to warrants issued in the criminal justice system. The court files no reports of its actions, with the sole exception of a single annual report to Congress in which the court lists how many surveillance applications it received during the year and how many it granted. And when a warrant does not lead to any court proceedings, there is no disclosure at all to the targets or to any other governmental body that any surveillance occurred.[39] The intent behind the use of a looser standard for FISA surveillance orders—one that is far less protective of the target's Fourth Amendment rights—was that such a standard would be appropriate if the primary purpose of the search was to intercept foreign intelligence and not to gather evidence to be used against the individual at trial.

Since FISA was enacted in 1978, Congress has made numerous changes to the law, and with each amendment, has added new surveillance tools to the executive's foreign intelligence agencies' toolbox. For example, in 1995, FISA was amended to allow the government to obtain orders—under a looser FISA standard—to engage in physical searches in addition electronic surveillance.[40] In 1998, the statute was amended again, this time to permit the installation of "pen registers" and "tap and trace" devices,[41] and allow government access to certain business records of private individuals and organizations.[42] By the time the PATRIOT Act amendments went into effect, FISA bore little resemblance to the statute Congress intended to reign in an executive branch that had engaged in the wholesale violation of Americans' First Amendment rights.

THE OPEN SECRECY OF THE PATRIOT ACT

By pushing the USA PATRIOT Act[43] through Congress in the wake of the September 11 attacks, the Bush administration achieved a long-desired goal of the Far Right: to significantly expand the executive branch's authority to conduct law enforcement in secret, with little or no judicial oversight, and with almost no public scrutiny.

Congress passed the PATRIOT Act quickly on October 26, 2001, less than six weeks after the attacks, with little committee deliberation and even less public debate.[44] The Bush administration bullied members of Congress into approving the legislation, charging that those who voted against the law would be responsible for any future terrorist attacks on the United States. The law made sweeping changes in law enforcement areas including: the interception of communications as part of both criminal investigations and domestic investigations of foreign intelligence activities; detention powers; and immigration enforcement powers.[45] In short, the executive branch's authority to conduct secret law enforcement and intelligence operations without oversight by Congress, the courts, or the public was dramatically expanded.

Section 215 of the PATRIOT Act provides the Justice Department with the authority to force anyone—including doctors, hospitals, libraries, bookstores, video stores, universities, and Internet service providers—to turn over all records on their patients, clients or customers. The Justice Department can obtain an order from the Foreign Intelligence Surveillance Court, merely by asserting that its request is related to an ongoing terrorism or foreign intelligence investigation. A showing under the Fourth Amendment to the

Constitution that the Justice Department has probable cause to believe that the person has committed or will commit a crime is no longer needed, nor is there any First Amendment prohibition against the Justice Department's request for an order based in part on a person's free speech activities. Section 215 lets the government seize entire databases at libraries, hospitals, and other institutions even when just one person is being investigated.

Section 215 not only permits the Justice Department to obtain these orders through a secret process, it also imposes a duty of secrecy on the person who must provide the records sought. This "gag" provision prohibits recipients from "disclos[ing] to any other person (other than those persons necessary to produce the tangible things under this section) that the FBI sought or obtained the tangible things under this section."[46] Another part of the Act makes it a crime for record holders to inform the public that the government has seized records.

While Bush administration officials contend that grand jury subpoenas already provided it with record-seizing power before the PATRIOT Act, they fail to acknowledge the glaring difference between grand jury subpoenas and a Section 215 order: probable cause. A grand jury subpoena is only granted when the government has shown probable cause to believe a crime has been committed and has gone to the trouble to empanel a grand jury. By contrast, no evidence of any wrongdoing whatsoever is required before Section 215 can be used. By enacting Section 215, Congress has authorized a shift that fundamentally alters our constitutional landscape; government is no longer in the business of rooting out criminal activity, it is focused on identifying those engaged in *political activity*.[47]

A powerful lobby has taken this issue on: librarians. Across the country they reacted strongly to the broad authority Section 215 provided to the Justice Department, publicly stating their vehement opposition to secret monitoring of the reading materials of library users.[48] The American Library Association (ALA) Council adopted a resolution expressly declaring that the ALA "considers sections of the USA PATRIOT Act . . . a present danger to the constitutional rights and privacy rights of library users and urges the United States Congress to . . . provide active oversight to the implementation of the

USA PATRIOT Act and other related measures . . . and . . . amend or change the sections of these laws and the guidelines that threaten or abridge the rights of inquiry and free expression. . . ."[49] In addition, the ALA posted guidelines on its Web site advising libraries to avoid creating and retaining unnecessary records.

In an attempt to determine whether the Justice Department had used Section 215 to seek information from libraries, in 2002 the chairman of the House Judiciary Committee posed a series of questions to the Justice Department. The department responded that "[t]he number of times the Government has requested or the Court has approved requests under this section since the passage of the PATRIOT Act, is *classified.* . . ."[50] More recently, responding to statements made by administration officials that law enforcement officials have not yet used their powers to demand library or bookstore records,[51] the ALA commissioned a study to examine how frequently federal, state, and local law enforcement agents demand records from libraries.[52] Because of the secrecy provisions of the PATRIOT Act, the study could not ask direct questions about whether the Act had been used to search libraries, so it asked about the frequency of law enforcement inquiries at all levels of government.[53] The study, which surveyed 5,500 public and academic libraries, determined that there were 137 formal demands for information, with at least forty-nine coming from federal officials.[54] In addition, the survey found that sixty-six libraries had received informal law enforcement requests, including twenty-four federal requests.[55] According to Emily Sheketoff, the executive director of the ALA's Washington office, the study shows that "agents are coming to libraries and they are asking for information at a level that is significant, and the findings are completely contrary to what the Justice Department has been trying to convince the public."[56]

However, the ALA's study does not give us a complete picture of the government's investigative arsenal. For, while the "library provision" of the Act has understandably alarmed people across the country, a more obscure investigative tool is used many times more frequently. Federal agents now use National Security Letters, a type of administrative subpoena, to obtain information from universities, banks, credit card companies, Internet service providers, and many other businesses. Through the use of National Security Letters, then, the government can put together a very comprehensive record of the personal life of any citizen.

Although this investigative tool has been in use since the 1970s,[57] according to the *Washington Post*, after the PATRIOT Act made it far easier for federal agents to issue them, there has been a "one hundred-fold increase" in their use.[58] Reports now indicate that the FBI is issuing thirty thousand National Security Letters every year.[59] A privacy invasion on a far grander scale, the National Security Letter (NSL) tool expanded by the PATRIOT Act provides the FBI with virtually unfettered power to demand the disclosure of personal records about innocent people. First, unlike warrants, no judicial review is required before the FBI can issue an NSL compelling a company to provide records. Second, the standard governing the FBI's use of this newly expanded power is toothless: the agency can issue an NSL so long as the agent states that the information request is "relevant" to a national security investigation. Whether the undefined showing of "relevance" has been met is determined by the executive as well. Third, while the administration argues that the Justice Department's inspector general has the power to investigate FBI misuse of this intelligence-gathering tool,[60] such oversight is only triggered by complaints from the public—people who, under this law, are prevented from knowing whether their records are being requested. Subjects are not notified of the issuance of an NSL. Finally, congressional oversight, also cited by the Bush administration as a check on abuse, is in reality minimal, and has been interpreted by the Justice Department as requiring a report only on the numbers of NSLs issued. Congressional requests for more detailed information about how subjects are selected and how the information gathered is used have been stonewalled.

In addition, three concerning facts are clear from the Justice Department's response to a November 6, 2005, *Washington Post* article, entitled "The FBI's Secret Scrutiny: In Hunt for Terrorists, Bureau Examines Records of Ordinary Americans."[61] The Justice Department has admitted that the ambiguous "relevance" standard allows the FBI to obtain confidential records of ordinary, law-abiding citizens. According to the Justice Department's letter, "some people whose records are produced in response to an NSL may not be terrorists or spies or associated with terrorists or spies," but the agency "needs to be able to check out every tip and track down every lead."[62] In addition, the Justice Department letter also makes plain that the Bush administration views its "terrorism information-sharing" mandate as permitting the FBI to share the information it collects through NSLs widely with state, local, and tribal governments, as well as private sector entities.[63] Finally, the statutory language authorizing NSLs prohibits recipients from disclosing such inquiries to "any person"; no exception is made for attorneys. In short, the NSL investigative tool is a measure coercive enough to compel the release of citizens' personal information without the real victim ever knowing about it.

Section 218 of the PATRIOT Act has caused similar consternation among civil liberties activists. This provision expands the use of the "sneak and peek" warrants that permit law enforcement authorities to conduct searches without notifying the subject of the search. The searches can involve physical entry, visual examination, taking photographs or video, copying documents, or any other kind of search that does not involve the seizure of tangible property.[64] Section 218 expands the government's "sneak and peek" power by permitting it to give the target delayed notice of the search in case notice may cause an "adverse result," which includes any action "otherwise seriously jeopardizing an investigation or unduly delaying a trial."[65] Section 218 requires only that a government official certify to the FISA court that "a significant purpose" of the surveillance is to obtain foreign intelligence information, a showing that is far more relaxed than that required for a warrant issued on a showing of probable cause of criminal activity.

The warrant and probable cause requirements have historically served as the guardians of our First Amendment interests, by preventing government from intruding on our private lives because of our interests and associations. The PATRIOT Act enables the executive branch to bypass these guardians and to take action that will most certainly "chill" protected speech. The notice requirement for warrants issued in criminal cases places a critical check on government power by forcing authorities to operate openly and providing people with the chance to protect their privacy rights by challenging the warrant.

In addition, the Fourth Amendment requires that warrants describe with particularity the place to be searched and items to be investigated. All of these boundaries are eliminated for searches authorized under Section 218; officers now have complete individual discretion over the scope of the search. There is no judicial check ensuring that your constitutional rights are honored.

The PATRIOT Act also greatly expands the electronic surveillance powers of law enforcement agencies. Fourth Amendment law requires that warrants specify the place to be searched, thus preventing random searches of the homes of innocent persons based on a warrant obtained to search the home of another: warrants are not transferable. In the context of wiretaps, this means that law enforcement agents must specify the telephone they want to tap when they seek a warrant. In 1986, Congress amended the wiretapping law that applies in criminal cases to allow for *roving wiretaps* that specify a person to be tapped rather than a particular telephone so that people cannot avoid the tap by switching telephones. This means that agents can listen in on any phone the person being targeted might use, even phones in another person's home. In 1998, Congress again amended the law, this time to narrow law enforcement's authority and require that agents establish that the target is "actually using" the line before using roving surveillance techniques.

Like many other provisions of the PATRIOT Act, Section 206 extends roving wiretap authority to "intelligence" wiretaps authorized by the Foreign Intelligence Surveillance Court. Such wiretaps are authorized secretly without a showing of probable cause and without the requirement that the agents show that the target is "actually using" the phone to be tapped. This change permits agents to allow surveillance mechanisms to remain actively in place after the target leaves that location. In short, if a person subject to a roving wiretap comes to your house, you, too, will be subject to the wiretap.

Section 216 of the Act further expands the intrusive power of law enforcement agencies. Fourth Amendment law has traditionally required court orders authorizing surveillance or searches to specify the place to be searched. If a search of another place is required, the agents must get a new warrant signed by the judge with jurisdiction over the new location. Section 216 permits a judge or magistrate in one jurisdiction (area) to issue a warrant that can be served on Internet service providers anywhere in the United States; the agents then can fill in the form with the names of the various places at which they would like the order to be served. This is the equivalent of giving agents a blank warrant. Although the PATRIOT Act has engendered many other changes that enhance executive branch powers—including a lower standard for access to Internet communications and e-mail addresses (which are difficult to separate from the content of the e-mail, thus effectively rendering both to government review)—one other provision of the Act bears discussing here. Section 203 authorizes the disclosure of foreign intelligence information collected by a federal grand jury to any federal law enforcement, intelligence, protective, immigration, national defense, or national security official. This change permits the executive branch to use the grand jury mechanism to collect information without any meaningful judicial oversight. A federal grand jury conducts its business outside the supervision of a judge, without the presence of a witness's lawyer, and under stringent rules of secrecy. Prosecutors are also bound by the rules of secrecy and cannot disclose information from the grand jury to law enforcement officials unless it is necessary to enforce federal criminal law. Expanding the list of officials who now have access to grand jury information creates the risk that the integrity of the grand jury process will be undermined and that the government will use grand juries for purely investigatory reasons in cases where no criminal prosecution is contemplated.

WHAT'S MISSING FROM THE PATRIOT ACT DISCUSSION?

The government's use of the PATRIOT Act to punish speech and impose guilt by association has not been the subject of much debate. While members of Congress and advocacy groups focus on the aspects of the Act that overtly infringe on our civil liberties, the discussion has not touched upon the use of the PATRIOT Act to deport or deny entry of foreign nationals who have supported disfavored political groups. For example, the government invoked the PATRIOT Act to revoke the visa of Tariq Ramadan, a Swiss professor who was one of the first Muslim scholars to publicly denounce the September 11 attacks. Professor Ramadan had accepted the offer of a prestigious chair at the

University of Notre Dame. The government gave no reason for revoking the visa, yet Professor Ramadan—a man who may have much to contribute toward understanding the Muslim world—is now unable to teach here. Similarly, Professor Dora Maria Tellez, a Nicaraguan citizen invited to teach at Harvard University, was denied her visa. Her "offense" was her association with the Sandinistas during the 1980s.[66]

Nor has the discussion over the PATRIOT Act included the onerous provision that authorizes the treasury secretary to freeze the assets of any organization—without evidence of wrongdoing—that it claims is "under investigation" for providing material support to groups designated as "terrorist." Although the term "terrorist" is not defined in the law, this provision has been frequently used, meaning that the Treasury Department gets to decide on its own what constitutes a "terrorist" group in each case. And if the organization challenges a freeze order in court, the government is permitted to use secret evidence of alleged wrongdoing to defend its actions. *Secret* evidence—let that concept try to find a place in your understanding of the Constitution.

THE REAUTHORIZATION DEBATE

Given that the PATRIOT Act was passed in haste with few lawmakers having had the opportunity to read it in its entirety, it would seem appropriate to ensure that deliberations over the reauthorization of certain provisions and the expansion of others are extensive and open to the public. Yet, that is precisely what the Senate Intelligence Committee decided not to do.[67] What are they hiding? Perhaps they do not want the American public—*the People*—to know that the Justice Department, pushed by the White House, had demanded even greater powers for the FBI.[68] What is the justification for such executive overreaching when the government has submitted no evidence to show that FBI agents cannot perform their duties without this expanded authority? Why is Congress not willing to hold firm and maintain its own constitutional role? Given the serious infringement of civil liberties permitted by the Act, it does not seem overly burdensome to require the executive branch to fully justify the need for such powerful and intrusive investigative tools and to regularly report on its activities to Congress and thus to *the People*. A wise Congress ought to recognize its responsibility to demand just such an accounting.

Yet, despite persistent public outcry over the privacy incursions committed under the banner of the PATRIOT Act, the House of Representatives and the Senate passed the PATRIOT Act reauthorization bill without fixing the most serious flaws in the law. On March 1, 2006, President Bush signed into law H.R. 3199, the House of Representatives conference report bill reauthorizing the PATRIOT Act, and S. 2271, a separate Senate bill containing several minor proposed changes intended to correct flaws in the conference report. Together, both bills make nearly all of the expiring provisions of the PATRIOT Act permanent. Partisan leadership refused to allow votes on the key reform amendments needed to restore the checks and balances in the three branches of government.

The reauthorized PATRIOT Act clearly still presents a significant threat to our free speech and associational rights. In both the Senate and the House, partisan leadership refused to allow votes on key amendments to reform the Act. The amendments signed into law by the president: permit the records of ordinary Americans to be secretly obtained without adequate safeguards to protect their right to privacy; allow "sneak and peek" searches to continue to be used, with new, expanded time limits allowing these searches to remain secret for months or even years when notice to the target might "seriously jeopardize" an ongoing investigation; continue the roving wiretap provision which allows courts to issue general, blank warrants for eavesdropping and searching homes and businesses without the government having to specify the name of the person or the place to be searched; places no real privacy safeguards on the sharing of confidential information gathered in criminal investigations with the CIA; and adds additional death penalties to federal crimes linked to terrorism.[69]

There are many examples of how the PATRIOT Act's chilling effect works in real life. For instance, the gag provision still operates under Section 215 of the Act, a provision that among other things permits the FBI to get an order demanding records of any sort or any other "tangible thing" from your home. Recipients of the court's order are prevented from telling anyone about the demand. Secret orders for records from libraries, bookstores, businesses, doctors' offices, financial institutions, and communications providers can still be obtained. The government need only assert "reasonable grounds" that they believe the demand is relevant to a terrorism investigation, only a slightly improved standard over that used in the original legislation.[70] Although the revised provision now permits businesses to challenge the orders, the FISA court's review remains virtually nonexistent. The review court must uphold the lower court's order unless it is "unlawful." It is not clear why a panel of FISA review court judges would find "unlawful" any order issued by a FISA judge. Also troubling is the fact that any challenge to a Section 215 order must be made before a special "petition review panel" of the FISA court in Washington, D.C., rather than another more convenient federal court, and that representative counsel must have government security clearance in order to appear to argue the case. These requirements make it exceedingly difficult for all but the wealthiest targets to challenge any order.

Again, Congress seems to have abandoned the separation of powers principle that requires the judiciary to check the unfettered exercise of executive power. But why eliminate the role of judges in ensuring constitutional compliance and the protection of citizens' privacy when the requirement of a court order for surveillance—with an extremely low threshold for issuance—will not impede a terrorism investigation?

Section 505 of the Act, the provision that authorizes the FBI to issue National Security Letters to demand records from Internet Service Providers and other businesses without court approval, also remains intact after the reauthorization process. The only significant change is that the provision now permits businesses that receive an order for records to disclose receipt to "any person to whom disclosure is necessary to comply with the order" and thus also to consult with a lawyer. A recipient of an NSL may challenge the request in federal court, and the court may set it aside if it is "unreasonable," "oppressive," or "otherwise unlawful." Gag orders may also now be challenged in federal court. However, if the government certifies that disclosure of the gag order would harm national security, interfere with an investigation or diplomatic relations, or endanger life or physical safety, the court must accept the government's assertion as "conclusive" on the matter. The certification requirement is therefore essentially meaningless. In addition, although the certification lasts only for one year, it can be renewed indefinitely. Finally, under revised Section 505, the penalties for violation of the gag order are even more punitive than before. Any employee who intentionally discloses the existence of a demand for records can go to jail for five years.

The reauthorized PATRIOT Act now includes language intended to protect libraries from being subjected to NSLs. This protection is limited, however, to only those circumstances in which libraries are functioning in their traditional lending roles. Many libraries now provide internet access to their patrons, and "electronic communication services" such as e-mail may fall within the NSL provision of the Act.

The reauthorization process did little to restrict the broad surveillance powers granted to the executive under the roving wiretap and "sneak and peek" provisions of the original law. The overbroad standard from the original Act has been preserved such that notice to the home to be searched may be delayed whenever immediate notice might "seriously jeopardize" an ongoing investigation. As many experts have commented, this standard is problematic because courts may be reluctant to second-guess the government's contention that notice will delay its investigation. The revised Act also now, incredibly, permits the government to obtain a blank or general warrant—allowing the government to eavesdrop on a telephone conversation or secretly search any home or business and, in effect, fill in the names and locations later. The judicial check on this privacy invasion, by which law enforcement officers were required to convince a court that a warrant was necessary for a particular premise, no longer exists.

Another full book could be written to discuss all of the attacks on our civil liberties launched by the reauthorized PATRIOT Act. Before concluding this brief review, however, one proposed section seems to cry out for special mention. The conference report includes new language as Section 602, which did not appear in either the House or Senate version of the bill. This new section would expand the existing authority of the Secret Service to create public "exclusion zones"—areas during events the president is attending that no unauthorized person can enter without risking federal imprisonment.[71] The original law creates a bubble surrounding the president and effectively prevents the public from speaking to (or shouting at) him. Under the new version, public exclusion zones could be imposed at any "event of national significance," a term that is not defined in the bill, *even if the president or any other person under Secret Service protection is not even expected to attend.* Under the less restrictive original version of the law, the Secret Service already routinely harassed citizens who requested entry to taxpayer-funded forums with the president across the country. For example, on March 21, 2005, two Denver students, who had obtained tickets from their Congressman, were expelled from a "town hall" forum with President Bush because their car sported an anti-war bumper sticker. Officials at the event, including one man who identified himself as a Secret Service agent, told the two students that attendance was restricted to those who shared the president's views. The students were told they would have to leave regardless of whether they had any intentions of disrupting the event. Apparently, uniformity of position is required before any person can attend a town hall meeting to hear what the president has to say about Social Security reform.

Why is Congress authorizing the expansion of the FBI's surveillance powers and the broadening of the definition of "terrorism" while at the same time permitting the erosion of the long-standing distinction between domestic law enforcement and foreign intelligence gathering? No one can seriously doubt that this recipe will create a nation of hesitant speakers, reluctant participants, and squelched speech and political action. Have we, *the People*, decided that we are willing to renounce our fundamental principles in order to strike this national security bargain? I think not.

WHO'S GUARDING YOUR FRONT DOOR NOW?: THE NSA WARRANTLESS WIRETAPPING PROGRAM

I do solemnly swear . . . that I will faithfully execute the Office of President of the United States, and will to the best of my Ability, preserve, protect and defend the Constitution of the United States.

—*Oath of Office administered in accordance with the U.S. Constitution (Article II, Section 2, Clause 3)*

On December 16, 2005, the *New York Times* revealed that within months of the September 11 attacks President Bush authorized the National Security Agency (NSA) to intercept communications from people living in the United States *without obtaining a warrant or any court order*.[72] The next day, the president admitted to the nation that he had approved the NSA's program of widespread, warrantless electronic surveillance of Americans' telephone calls and e-mails. The NSA program's objective, according to the president, was to gather intelligence on overseas terrorists' planned activities by monitoring their communications with people inside the United States.[73]

USA Today reported on June 30, 2006, that nineteen members of Congress had confirmed that the NSA had built a massive database of American's telephone records for the purpose of monitoring the telephone calling patterns of innocent Americans.[74] The newspaper was also able to confirm that AT&T and MCI participated in the spying program.[75] Politicians and citizens were outraged by the announcement, especially in light of the president's forceful statement in a 2004 speech in Buffalo, New York, assuring the audience that wiretaps require a court order and that the government only used electronic surveillance approved by a court.[76]

In 2002, the president issued a secret executive order authorizing the NSA program which—as conceded by Attorney General Alberto Gonzales— involved the interception of the "contents" of telephone, wire, and e-mail communications that occur, at least in part, in the United States.[77] The attorney general's admission undermined the administration's first effort to defend the program by claiming that it involved nothing more than "data mining" used to trace the electronic paths of phone calls and e-mails, implying the NSA did not intercept the content of any communications.[78]

The second defense offered by the administration was the now familiar claim that the president had acted within his commander-in-chief powers in the "war on terror" when he created the program to collect "signals intelligence" on the enemy abroad. According to the administration, Congress's adoption of the Authorization to Use Military Force in 2001[79] had empowered the president to use "all necessary and appropriate force" against "nations, organizations, or persons" associated with the attacks and therefore had impliedly authorized any eavesdropping activities. Neither members of Congress nor the public have found these arguments convincing.

The foundational principles of our democracy and the text of the Constitution itself undermine the Bush administration's claim to these so-called inherent war powers that enable the government to spy on American citizens. Not only was our country founded on the principles of popular sovereignty and respect for the will of *the People*, it was also grounded on the idea that these principles can survive only if government officials are made accountable to *the People*. The Declaration of Independence states this political philosophy clearly: "Governments are instituted among men deriving their just powers from the consent of the governed."[80] The very nature of secret surveillance and other clandestine government conduct renders public accountability impossible. We, *the People*, have not given our consent to such spying. Far from it; we work hard to maintain our privacy.

Equally troubling is the often repeated argument that national security requirements now demand the use of inherent, unilateral, and unfettered powers that are constitutionally housed in the office of the president.[81] As discussed in previous chapters, the language of the Constitution makes plain that although "[t]he President is the Commander in Chief of the Army and Navy of the United States,"[82] it is only Congress that has the power to make the laws, including laws regarding military affairs.[83] Article I of the Constitution makes clear that it is only Congress that has the power to declare war, to determine the resources to be provided for conducting military operations, to write the laws that govern such operations, and to decide when fundamental guarantees may be suspended.[84] We must remember here that the Bush administration's characterization of any new law, rule, or practice as "military" must be viewed with a sharply critical eye. When did we decide that the Bush administration's "war on terror" eliminated the sacred boundary between military regulations and the civil laws that govern the everyday activities of people living in this country?

What does it mean that neither President Bush nor his legal staff can locate a source of authority for the NSA spying program he started in 2002? Well, obviously one thing seems clear: the program is not authorized by any law.

The NSA domestic spying program violates our First Amendment free speech and associational rights, our Fourth Amendment privacy rights, and the separation of powers doctrine. The breadth of the government's electronic eavesdropping program means that it may sweep in anything from the most personal and intimate conversations between family members to citizen's political conversations with human rights advocates or pro-democracy activists in the Middle East. No judge determines whether probable cause justifies the surveillance, or draws any limits on it. The threat to our rights of freedom of speech and association is very great. Added to this is the "calls, details, records" program under which telecommunications companies cooperate with the NSA to provide the domestic telephone records of millions of Americans and businesses in order for intelligence analysts to examine them for hidden connections and identify terrorist plots.[85] The companies identified as participating in the program together "serve about 224 million conventional and cellular telephone customers—about four-fifths of the wired market and more than half of the wireless market."[86] The knowledge that the government is operating such an extensive domestic surveillance program has likely already greatly chilled people's desire to communicate with one another as well as their ability to work.[87]

The NSA surveillance program does not pass muster under a straightforward Fourth Amendment analysis.[88] The Supreme Court's interpretation of the contours of the Fourth Amendment has long included the notion that both tangible and intangible items—such as conversations—fall within its protections. And as technology has advanced, the Court for the most part has continued to interpret the scope of the Amendment to reach and protect communications carried by means of new technologies.[89]

The Justice Department has further conceded that the NSA surveillance program does not meet the requirements of FISA. This is because the surveillance occurs without judicial approval and without the showings that the law requires, i.e., that the subject is an agent of a foreign power, and that the surveillance does not capture the content of communications. As previously discussed, the 1978 Foreign Intelligence Surveillance Act regulates electronic surveillance in this country. The law limits warrantless domestic electronic surveillance even during a congressionally declared war; criminalizes any electronic surveillance not authorized by statute; and states FISA and the two related chapters of the criminal code governing wiretaps as the "exclusive means by which electronic surveillance . . . and the interception of domestic wire, oral, and electronic communications may be conducted."[90]

Again, the Bush administration's main defense of the NSA program is that Congress's 2001 Authorization to Use Military Force (AUMF) empowers the president to disregard the FISA statutory scheme—that it allows him to violate the law. However, there is no language in the authorization that provides the president authority for unchecked warrantless domestic wiretapping. There is no evidence that Congress, by adopting the authorization, intended to repeal FISA. In fact, Attorney General Gonzales admitted that the administration did not attempt to seek an amendment to FISA in order to permit the NSA program to go forward *because he was told that such an amendment would not pass Congress.*[91] So, because the administration thought that it could not get what it wanted from Congress, it decided to baldly violate the law to do it anyway.

The FISA law makes clear that even where Congress has declared war—a much more formal step than the 2001 AUMF—it limits warrantless wiretapping to the first fifteen days of the conflict. This very short and defined period was intended to provide Congress with sufficient time to consider whether further authorization was needed. In the end, then, the president neither sought judicial approval from the Foreign Intelligence Surveillance Court nor limited the NSA surveillance program to the required fifteen-day period, but instead acted secretly in direct contravention of the law. Even the Justice Department has not dared to argue that the law—which makes electronic surveillance, not authorized by statute a criminal offense—does not apply to the executive.[92]

HOW HAVE CONGRESS AND THE SUPREME COURT RESPONDED TO THE NSA SPYING PROGRAM?

In our democratic system, the door to Congress remains open for those who seek to change the law. This is the incremental means by which our legal system evolves. Not even the president has the power to violate or change the laws behind closed doors simply because he deems them impracticable. Calls have been made by Congressmen and civil rights groups for a full investigation into the NSA program, and bipartisan amendments to the Defense Appropriations Act for 2007 that would cut off funding for the NSA's warrantless wiretapping program.[93] These amendments seek to restore the rule of law and compel the Bush administration to use the existing law on the books—like FISA—to monitor targets of terrorism investigations.

By late July 2006, it had become clear that the administration was doing everything in its power to block any investigation into the scope of the NSA program. Senator Arlen Specter (R-PA), who chairs the Senate Judiciary Committee, had accused Vice President Dick Cheney of trying to prevent telephone company witnesses from testifying about their company's participation in the spying program.[94] As discussed in chapter 9, the Bush administration has also employed the states secrets privilege to attempt to extinguish lawsuits against AT&T and other companies, though the courts declined in July 2006 to dismiss the first case raising the issue.[95]

In a Senate Judiciary Committee hearing on "Wartime Executive Powers and the FISA Court," Senator Patrick Leahy had this to say:

> We are stuck at an impasse, lacking information or cooperation from an Administration that refuses to submit to real congressional oversight. This is, of course, nothing new from an obsessively secretive Administration that has classified historical documents for no reason, conducted energy policy and attempted to outsource port security behind closed doors, routinely blocked investigations and audits, repeatedly harassed whistleblowers, and dismissively refused to cooperate with congressional oversight for more than five years. This Administration has a paranoid aversion to openness and accountability that will not be overcome by gentle persuasion. . . . We are not here to play charades. We are here to legislate the law of the land. So any further legislation that we enact in this area should, at a minimum, include express provisions that require the President to stop

equivocating with vague, expansive and dangerous theories of inherent powers, and to accept that he is fully bound by the legislation as written. We must put an end to police state powers operating outside the law.[96]

On August 17, 2006, in the case *ACLU v. NSA*, Federal Judge Anna Diggs Taylor ruled that the Bush administration's NSA program violates American citizen's rights to free speech and privacy under the First and Fourth Amendments of the Constitution, and runs counter to the Foreign Intelligence Surveillance Act. Diggs dismissed outright the government's argument that the president "has been granted the inherent power to violate not only the laws of the Congress but the First and Fourth Amendments of the Constitution, itself."[97] The court, clearly outraged by the president's authorization of blatantly illegal activities, wrote that "[t]here are no hereditary Kings in America and no powers not created by the Constitution," so all the president's "inherent powers" must derive from the Constitution.[98]

Despite this clear ruling, Congress caved in to pressure from the Bush administration and both the Senate and the House put forth bills designed to authorize the NSA spying program. The House Bill, H.R. 5825, the Electronic Surveillance Modernization Act, was passed by the House on September 28, 2006. Although proponents of the bill portrayed it as providing judicial review of the president's NSA program and "modernizing" the Foreign Intelligence Surveillance Act, actually the bill would have *prevented* meaningful judicial review of the program and expanded to an unprecedented degree the government's power to wiretap Americans without a warrant. By defining large categories of surveillance as not being the type of "electronic surveillance" covered by FISA, the bill would have authorized the NSA to turn its vacuum cleaners on American citizens. It would have enabled the government to create a vast database of information that could be mined at will, without any judicial oversight. The bill also would have authorized warrantless surveillance for secretly renewable periods of ninety days after a terrorist attack on the United States or when the president determined that there is an "imminent threat of attack likely to cause death, serious injury, or substantial economic damage." Finally, the House bill would have established a broad swath of retroactive immunity for individuals and companies who have violated the Constitution and the FISA law and dismissed pending lawsuits against service providers.

At the time this book goes to press, the bill has not yet been approved. Congress went into recess before the House and the Senate could agree on its language. It is urgent that we, *the People*, speak out against the NSA spying program and urge our representatives to curb the Bush administration's unlawful incursions onto the rights of American citizens.

CITIZENS MUST CALL UPON CONGRESS TO PROTECT THE CONSTITUTION

We now know that the president interprets his newly fabricated "war on terror" powers as permitting him—and those under his command—not only to imprison people without charge or trial; to hide terrorism suspects in secret prisons in the U.S. and in other countries; and to send people to foreign countries for interrogation under torture or indefinite detention; but also to create an unlawful program to intercept and monitor Americans' electronic communications; a databank and analysis program to collect and store detailed telephone call records in order to mine them for hidden connections and social networks; and a program and database designed to gather the more than 12.7 million messages sent each day as international financial transactions.[99]

The president's argument with regard to these unlawful and immoral activities, as articulated to Congress in a forty-two page memorandum written by the Justice Department, is that Congress cannot restrict his inherent commander-in-chief powers to choose all of the "means and the methods of engaging the enemy." The real import of this argument should not be lost— it is a fundamental attack on the separation of powers doctrine that undergirds our democracy.

A president's power to act in a particular area is always affected by the actions taken by Congress in that area. Under our system of checks and balances, the interplay between congressional and presidential action is critical:

when Congress has either affirmed the president's power through legislation or has remained utterly silent, then the president's power is at its greatest. However, when Congress has passed a law expressly barring the type of action the president seeks to undertake, his power is at its lowest ebb. Congress has the greater constitutional power to regulate the president's conduct and it has consistently exercised this power. Historically, Congress has subjected the commander in chief to the strictures of military code and has, for instance, enacted laws prohibiting torture and ensuring access to the writ of habeas corpus for a captive to challenge their detention. Every time that this president, George W. Bush, has argued that Congress lacks the power to legislate away his "war on terror" tactics, the U.S. Supreme Court has rung the bell to remind us that: "Whatever power the United States Constitution envisions for the executive in its exchanges with other nations or with enemy organizations in times of conflict, it most assuredly envisions a role for all three branches when individual liberties are at stake."[100]

CHAPTER ELEVEN

Conclusion

WHAT VALUES HAVE WE ABANDONED BY ACQUIESING TO THE BUSH ADMINISTRATION'S PROSECUTION OF A "WAR ON TERROR"?

What can a presidential administration's penchant—or obsession really—with secrecy do to a democracy? What constitutional values have we seen buried in President Bush's "war on terror"? Secrecy not only suppresses our core First Amendment values, it also thwarts a citizenry's ability to participate in the act of governing itself. When government officials' actions are entirely veiled from public scrutiny, they cannot be held accountable. Individuals whose values are not consonant with those embedded in the Constitution have the leeway to implement policies that are antithetical to our democratic system. *The People* must have access to accurate information in order to exercise their right to discuss, evaluate, challenge, and if necessary, change government performance. Without information, the public cannot make an informed assessment of whether the government is acting within constitutional constraints or in conformity with the country's democratic goals. Knowledge of government policies enables the public to form enlightened opinions about whether particular government officials should remain in office and whether specific government practices should continue. The end result of an informed public colloquy is, at least ideally, a government both accountable and responsive to the will of *the People*.

DESTABILIZING THE CHECKS AND BALANCES

The underpinning of our constitutional democracy is that the three branches of government operate as a system of checks and balances to ensure that no branch can overtake the others and use such accumulated powers to oppress *the People* or subvert our common goals. History tells us that the chief concern behind this system was that of the inadvertent creation of an overweening executive. The Framers were haunted by the ghosts of despotic kings and the specter of authoritarianism.[1] Their concern that they might create an executive with access to totalitarian powers was present throughout the constitutional debates. It was due to these pressing concerns that the Framers awarded the power to Congress to remove the president and his cabinet members.[2]

Under the Bush administration's concept of a "unitary executive," virtually all governmental power would be housed in the office of the president. In order to accomplish this objective, the administration has attempted to forcibly drain power from Congress and the judiciary under the guise of shoring up the commander-in-chief powers to maintain national security during the global "war on terror."

The Bush administration's disregard of binding international human rights law is one major way it has manifested its idea of a "unitary executive." One of the first overarching decisions made by the president following the September 11 attacks was to unilaterally reject the laws of war and disavow the Geneva Conventions—despite the fact that the conflict in Afghanistan was an international armed conflict and therefore governed by those binding international agreements. The various changing formulations of the administration's rejection of the laws of war have not altered the fundamental fact that Taliban soldiers and affiliated government militia were denied their proper status of prisoners of war as required under the Third Geneva Convention, and that civilians (criminals, innocents, and others) were denied the rights and protections they are due under the Fourth Geneva Convention.

In this unilateral exercise of power, the Bush administration further argued that the United States is engaged in an unconventional "war on terror" in which the battlefield covers the entire world. The president declared all accused terrorists, everywhere, are "enemy combatants" who, by allegedly rejecting the rules of war, have subjected themselves to indefinite executive detention at Guantánamo or another secret detention facility; and/or to prosecution by a military commission designed to favor the government's evidence, exclude the defendant and his counsel from the key parts of the proceedings, and mete out the most severe sentences, including death.

In nearly every executive action undertaken in the name of the "war on terror," the administration has attempted to usurp the authority of Congress. The administration has attempted to shift the lawmaking functions from Congress to the president and his closest advisers and executive branch officers through the use of executive orders, presidential findings, secretly authorized programs, interim regulations, and policy directives. We have examined many of the ways these legislative mechanisms have been used by the Bush administration to great effect. From the informal orders (in violation of the Bill of Rights) to imprison immigrants without charge until they are "cleared of any connection to terrorism"; to the creation of a military commission trial system unauthorized by Congress; to the secret authorization of the NSA's program to spy on American citizens without warrants;[3] to the approval of the CIA's web of secret prisons outside of the United States where torture is permitted—the administration's unlawful actions are far too numerous to list here.

In the Bush administration's naked and avaricious power grab it has also attempted to pull down the the authority of the courts. One could safely wager that there has been no administration in American history with as an extensive record of willfully ignoring the decisions of the country's highest court. After each unsuccessful round of the legal battles over the constitutional limitations on the president's commander-in-chief power, the Bush administration has not only rededicated itself to changing the law to suit its political ends, it has also stubbornly refused to comply with the Supreme Court's rulings until it is able to accomplish those objectives. Among other offenses, the administration has blatantly flouted the Supreme Court's decision in *Rasul v. Bush* by refusing to allow the Guantánamo detainees to avail themselves of the affirmed right to judicial review of their executive detention. Indeed, so strong is the Bush administration's opposition to judicial oversight that executive branch officials routinely maneuver to avoid judges' rulings. One example, as previously discussed, is the government's transfer of Guantánamo detainees—*who had been held for more than two years after they had been found innocent*—to Albania the night before argument was scheduled in the Court of Appeals on the administration's outrageous and unconstitutional conduct.

There is simply no way to square the administration's seizure of powers under the invisible umbrella of Congress's 2001 Authorization to Use Military Force in Afghanistan with the well-established principles set down by our Supreme Court. The Court has always demanded explicit congressional authorization before permitting the executive to depart dramatically from settled constitutional law in pursuit of wartime security. While the Court has read a few congressional authorizations of force broadly when necessary, it has consistently demanded a clear statement of congressional intent whenever the executive seeks to depart from international or constitutional law in any situation outside of an immediate combat emergency. Silence is not the equivalent of congressional action. The general language of the AUMF, which speaks only of the use of "force," is nowhere near sufficient to strip the guarantee of the writ of habeas corpus from the Constitution and dissolve the Bill of Rights. And as for its absurd application in the administration's defense of the NSA surveillance program, there is simply no one left who will argue that the program does not in fact violate the Foreign Intelligence Surveillance Act.

Our Constitution, drafted with a great war fresh in mind, was not intended to exempt executive action from court oversight in times of crisis. The Supreme Court has consistently emphasized the principle that "even the war power does not remove constitutional limitations safeguarding essential liberties."[4] Individual liberties remain fully protected in wartime because "[i]t would indeed be ironic if, in the name of national defense, we would sanction the subversion of one of those liberties . . . which makes the defense of the Nation worthwhile."

THE UTTER LACK OF ACCOUNTABILITY

The Bush administration has challenged the applicability of the ICCPR, the CAT, and the Geneva Conventions to the arrest and detention of every captive in its global "war on terror." Under its interpretation, no person outside the strictest geographic boundaries of the United States can be held responsible for conduct that violates either domestic constitutional law or international humanitarian law. We have examined the well-documented result of this deeply troubling interpretation—the systematic abuse and torture of detainees held in U.S. custody in Afghanistan, Iraq, Guantánamo, and elsewhere around the world.[5]

To date, the government has refused to authorize any independent investigation of the terrible abuses visited upon "war on terror" detainees and no high-level official has ever been charged with any crime in relation to the abuse. To the contrary, a number of the officials involved in developing the very policies that led to the widespread abuse and torture have been nominated and confirmed to higher government posts. While the Bush administration likes to cite the fact that there have been twelve investigations into detainee abuse to date, these investigations have been far from adequate. Each of them has suffered from one structural deficiency or another, including narrowly circumscribed mandates, failing to investigate command officials, lack of independence from the force being investigated, and lack of subpoena power.[6]

The government continues to claim that the abuse was due simply to the actions of a few rogue soldiers, despite evidence from countless of the government's own reports showing that the systemic abuse of detainees was the direct result of policies set by high-level civilian and military leaders and their failure to uphold their legal duty to prevent torture, abuse, and mistreatment by those under their command. In one example, a memorandum from Navy Vice Admiral Jacoby states that Defense Intelligence Agency personnel in Iraq witnessed members of Special Operations Task Force 6–26 abusing detainees and then attempting to cover up the abuse.[7]

Hundreds of cases of torture and cruel, inhuman, and degrading treatment have been reported involving detainees held in U.S. custody around the world. But, to date, only about ninety detainee abuse cases—out of the more than six hundred persons implicated—have been prosecuted, mostly in the military system, resulting in relatively short sentences. The military has admitted that over one hundred detainees have died in U.S. custody in Afghanistan and Iraq since August 2002[8] and has acknowledged that thirty-four of these were likely homicides.[9] In nearly all of these cases, evidence has strongly suggested that the detainees were beaten or tortured before death.[10] Despite the government's acknowledgement that at least twenty-nine detainee deaths involved suspected abuse, only nineteen of the individuals tried have received sentences of more than one year.[11] Moreover, in those few cases in which an officer was tried and convicted of homicide, the tribunal's minor punishment could hardly have sent a more devastating message regarding our lack commitment to human rights. In one telling example, in a case involving an Army interrogator, the defendant was simply reprimanded and fined $6,000.[12]

Many thousands of "war on terror" detainees are still held in U.S. military custody around the world and remain vulnerable to these unlawful practices. We, *the People*, cannot simply sit and wait for the administration to finally decide to do the right thing. It is our responsibility as citizens to demand accountability from our government. We must call for independent investigations of all officials in the chain of command, up to the very top. There cannot be a ceiling above which authorization for torture goes unpunished and therefore condoned.

WHAT WILL BE THE LEGACY OF THE BUSH ADMINISTRATION'S UNLAWFUL SECRET POLICIES?

Given the voracious many-headed monster created by the Bush administration, any attempt to extrapolate from the current state of affairs into the future would be highly speculative. But starting with an examination of the people that President Bush and his inner circle have elevated to positions of importance within the government provides some insight into the likely direction of foreign and domestic policy. There is little doubt—given this cast of characters—that the Bush administration will continue on the lawless path that it embarked on in its first term.

In the George W. Bush's first administration, former attorney general John Ashcroft was part of a coterie of government officials who advocated positions that dispensed with the rule of law and willfully implemented unconstitutional policies. Now, in his place we have been given Alberto Gonzales, former White House counsel. Who is Alberto Gonzales? He is the man who directed White House and Justice Department attorneys to draft legal memos rewriting the definition of "torture" in order for the administration to avoid liability for engaging in unspeakable acts against detainees in U.S. custody in Afghanistan, Guantánamo, and Iraq. Gonzales was the unseen supervisor of the task force which concluded that the president is bound by neither domestic nor international laws prohibiting torture, under the theory that he has the commander-in-chief authority to take *any* action that he finds necessary to protect the nation. *Never before in the history of the United States has the position been taken that the rule of law does not apply to the president of the United States.*

We have also witnessed the elevation of Jay S. Bybee, author of the infamous "Bybee Torture Memo," to the Ninth Circuit Court of Appeals, a position with lifetime tenure. Judge Bybee was appointed and confirmed *before* the internal White House memos were released to the public in July 2004. No one in Congress who was called upon to give an opinion on Bybee's appointment was likely privy to those memos, and therefore no one could question him about his new of the definition of "torture."[13] Thus, the man who attempted to narrow the definition of torture so that almost no act the president found "necessary," perhaps even one causing death, would be outlawed, is the same man we are now supposed to trust to dispense justice with an even hand and an open heart. It might be ironic, were it not so frightening. No one can yet guess what the lasting effects will be of the lifetime appointment of such a judge to a court whose decisions are reviewable *only* by the United States Supreme Court. More fundamentally, however, we must ask whether this is the kind of person we, *the People*, want dispensing justice in this country. Does Judge Bybee recognize the democratic principles that we hold dear? Does his view of democracy square with the moral underpinnings of the Constitution, our guiding document?

White House officials like Vice President Cheney's former chief of staff, I. Lewis ("Scooter") Libby, now under indictment for obstructing justice and making false statements to a government agent and a grand jury when responding to an inquiry about the "outing" of Valerie Plame, an undercover CIA agent and the wife of diplomat Joseph Wilson, reveal the base instincts and immoral motivations underlying the administration's political strategy of retaliation against open critics.[14] The "outing" of Plame was undertaken solely to discredit Wilson's public statements refuting the Bush administration's claim that Iraq had sought to purchase enriched uranium from Niger to further its nuclear capability. Beyond their vindictiveness and deceit, administration officials' actions in the Plame affair excised the truth and smoothed the way for the push to an unlawful war.

What more need be said of Richard Cheney, now apparently slated to be remembered in history books as the "Vice President for Torture"?[15] No person could represent a more stark deviation from this country's moral center. Cheney's vehement opposition to the anti-torture amendment passed by the Senate in October 2005 by Senator John McCain (D-AZ), a veteran tortured as a POW in Vietnam, is horrifying and shameful. His lobbying efforts to exempt the CIA from the ban on torture present a picture to the world that is fundamentally at odds with our nation's values and commitment to the rule of law. The absolute ban on torture under our Constitution and under international law is acknowledged and accepted around the globe. Have we authorized this disavowal of the Geneva Convention principles intended to prevent the barbarism that took place during World War II?

And finally, how should we understand President Bush's threat to veto the defense spending bill because it contained the McCain language banning the "cruel, inhuman, or degrading" treatment of prisoners in U.S. custody? This is a president who, since 2001, has run an administration hell-bent on discarding the Geneva Conventions, disavowing other humanitarian and human rights treaties, and ignoring moral imperatives in its prosecution of the "war on terror."

It is well beyond the time to ask ourselves if these are the people that we want running our country. If our government is engaged in a debate about whether torture should be legally sanctioned, then we have already been swept backward in time to the Middle Ages. The executive branch's advocacy for torture is likely the most heinous instance in which it has taken this country out of the world community of nations and its shared consensus on legal and ethical principles. When will we demand that our government comply with the prohibitions of torture stated in the Universal Declaration of Human Rights, the Third Geneva Convention, the U.N. Convention Against Torture, all of which the United States signed and ratified and pledged to the world that it would follow?

After September 11 this country moved into an unprecedented period of operation by executive fiat. There has been an alarming executive usurpation of authority, evidenced by law enforcement actions, secret and public executive orders, and pressure on congress to enact sweeping legislation eroding civil liberties—all accompanied by nearly complete congressional acquiescence. At the same time, we are also witnessing the consequences of a series of Supreme Court decisions rendered over the last fifteen years that have systematically eroded our civil and constitutional rights. Antidiscrimination laws of all types have been undermined by the innocuous-sounding forces of "federalism" and "states' rights"—such that the power of *the People* to speak through their elected representatives has been significantly shut down in the areas of race, gender, employment, disabilities, age, and immigration status. The broad sweep of the Fourteenth Amendment's equal protection clause, once thought to be the very definition of our belief in a just society, has been so eviscerated that it now applies only to the most blatant constitutional violations. Viewed through the lens of federalism, each successive case provided an opportunity for the Supreme Court to chip away at our most fundamental constitutional rights: the right to due process of law; the right to equal protection of the laws; the right to a fair trial; the right to counsel; and the right to freedom from unlawful seizures and coerced self-incrimination. Civil rights laws that our Congress passed under its long-recognized constitutional authority have been routinely and disdainfully invalidated by a Supreme Court that has moved far beyond its role of saying what the law is, to deciding what it ought to be. With burglar stealth, the Court has stripped the citizenry of its right to enforce federal laws protecting workers, women, the disabled and the elderly, and the environment. Instead, the Court has effectively transferred those powers to a president who demonstrates shameless disregard for the will of *the People* by reversing and refusing to enforce the laws our representatives enacted.

It was this unstable foundation that paved the way for Congress's adoption of the USA PATRIOT Act and its expansion of law enforcement authority to conduct wiretaps and searches without probable cause of criminal activity. The Act provides for little to no accountability to Congress or the public. This secrecy is all the more disconcerting given that the number of FISA searches conducted annually now far exceeds the number issued on probable cause of criminal activity.[16] Here we face an expanding system of government surveillance so intrusive and unchecked that it not only eviscerates our privacy protections but also creates a climate of hypervigilance and fear such that we will start to police our own thoughts and words. "Sneak and peek" warrants have made every grassroots activist concerned about keeping such benign information as group membership lists in any accessible format. Law enforcement infiltration of organizations has made people hesitant to trust one another when planning protected activities like peace marches and rallies. And the use of federal grand juries as a tool of investigation and intimidation continues to grow. Our basic civil rights to freedom of speech and association and to protection against unreasonable searches and seizures are being unraveled at an alarming pace. Moreover, with the enlistment of the private sector to augment the government's capacity to collect and analyze data on everyone living in or passing through the United States, this pace will only increase. And truth be told, the private sector does not need much encouragement to collaborate in this endeavor, given the business opportunities presented by the government's quest for data collection and the creation of searchable databases.

The decision—by Congress and the public—to forgo discussion and debate over placing unprecedented powers in the hands of the executive branch has emboldened the executive to see no reason to submit to judicial oversight on any issue. Supreme Court decisions are disregarded with impunity, and judges are frequently challenged by the refrain of Justice Department lawyers that "judges cannot be permitted to oversee the Executive's actions in any aspect of the war on terror."

We have a new category of citizen prisoner in the United States—"enemy combatants"—who are held for years without charge, without access to counsel, and without trial, for purely investigative purposes. For three years, Jose

Padilla remained in a naval brig in South Carolina after being transferred into the custody of the Department of Defense, despite interim court victories. What balance will the courts ultimately strike between inarticulable concerns about possible future behavior and the most severe deprivation of liberty? Who knows how far the Bush administration will go if, as it appears now, given Padilla's criminal indictment in federal court, the Supreme Court is never provided the opportunity to issue a decision on these issues? Given the existing precedent in the courts, administration lawyers may still argue for indefinite detention until the end of the global "war on terror." Will we permit this terrifying executive power to be unleashed on other Americans traveling within their own country?

And who will act to reign in the Bush administration's equally lawless efforts abroad? The potential international repercussions of the administration's new wartime policies are beyond comprehension. The executive has already claimed and exercised the power to seize and kidnap any person from any country, at any time, detain him without charge or trial, and send him to Guantánamo or one of the other many secret CIA-run detention facilities around the globe.

Government lawyers, when questioned by the federal district court judge in the Guantánamo cases about the executive branch's view of this unrestrained power, stated that the administration believes that there are *no* limitations to its use around the world and that U.S. operatives in the field make the decision whether the actions of any person are a sufficient basis for seizure as a possible "enemy combatant." Every *other* person in the courtroom was horrified by the prospect that U.S. troops would enter a friendly country, abduct a citizen of that country, and hold them without charges, without process, and without hope of a trial for years in a prison inaccessible to the world. That the United States would claim a right to violate the universal norms of international and constitutional law cannot be squared with the founding principles and values imbued in our founding documents and intended to ensure that we are truly a country "of laws and not of men."[17]

In order for us to make our voices heard, we must call upon our representatives to act now. But more must be done. Those who have investigated and learned about the administration's unlawful and inhumane covert practices must educate others. We must all work to awaken the public's interest in these actions that affect our lives and those of our neighbors overseas. The capacity of our country to help those in other countries means that we cannot responsibly permit this administration to abandon the world community as it slakes its thirst for power.

James Madison wrote that "a popular government, without popular information, or the means of acquiring it, is but a prologue to a farce or a tragedy; or, perhaps both. Knowledge will forever govern ignorance: [a]nd a people who mean to be their own Governors, must arm themselves with the power which knowledge gives."[18]

The need for transparency and accountability in our government is one that permeates every aspect of our lives. However, this does not mean that we must all take up every issue in all of its various manifestations in every encounter with the government. There are many choices for action for every person who is concerned about the virus of secrecy and its ugly symptoms.

In towns and cities across the country, there are grassroots and community groups whose special missions are to ensure government accountability in many different areas, including the preservation of constitutional, civil, and human rights. If your interest is more focused on engendering greater public recognition of particular problems, your choices are numerous and can be found on bulletin boards at community colleges and in local newspaper notices. If you are concerned that too few know the truth about the government's unconstitutional and inhumane policies of torture and extraordinary rendition, then it is entirely up to you when and where you begin to take a more public stand. In this area, as in many others, you will not be alone. Many human rights groups have developed informative and accessible materials that they will provide for free or a very low cost, including documentaries, taped radio programs, written materials, posters, and draft letters to government officials. Many of these groups also have public education campaigns focused on pressuring the Bush administration to follow the rule of law, to comply with the Geneva Conventions for all military captives, and to halt practices that involve the use of torture and other abusive measures, regardless of whether they are committed by our own government or by our proxy countries. It is not difficult to join such campaigns and does not involve quitting your job or making a lifetime commitment.

With regard to some of the initiatives that are already under way, read about them, consider them carefully, and then join those you feel comfortable with. Join the call for an independent commission to investigate the use of torture by members of the armed forces and its authorization by officers and government officials up the chain of command. A broad and diverse coalition of citizens, civil leaders, and organizations requesting an independent commission modeled on the 9/11 Commission[19] would not only reinvigorate the discussion but could cause those at the top of the executive branch think twice about how Americans feel about what is done in their name. The preservation of our country's democracy depends on *the People's* access to information about how the government does its business. Without this, there can be no enlightened public debate or intelligent voting decisions. We remain blinded by the cloak of secrecy and trapped by the policies and practices that have brought this great nation low, to a position of shame and despair. But the foundation for the world's preeminent democracy remains, and there are many ready and willing to start laying the bricks to rebuild this country into the world's living example of justice, fairness, and equality.

We are *the People* referred to in the Declaration of Independence. It is time for us to remind this country's leaders of that fact.

FOR MORE INFORMATION

AMERICAN-ARAB ANTI-DISCRIMINATION COMMITTEE

4201 Connecticut Ave, NW, Suite 300
Washington, D.C. 20008
Phone: (202) 244-2990
Fax: (202) 244-3196
http://www.adc.org/
This organization works to empower Arab Americans and to combat defamation and negative stereotyping. The American-Arab Anti-Discrimination Committee also provides legal services and offers counseling on discrimination, defamation, and immigration cases.

ASIAN AMERICAN LEGAL DEFENSE AND EDUCATION FUND

99 Hudson Street, 12th floor
New York, New York 10013
Phone: (212) 966-5932
Fax: (212) 966-4303
http://www.aaldef.org/
The Asian American Legal Defense and Education Fund is a legal advocacy and educational organization focusing on economic and social justice issues in the Asian American community. Specific projects include: affirmative action, voting rights, and workplace and labor rights.

AMERICAN CIVIL LIBERTIES UNION

125 Broad Street, 18th Floor
New York, NY 10004
Phone: (212) 519-2500
http://www.aclu.org/
The ACLU works to protect the Bill of Rights as well as other constitutional guarantees and strives to extend rights to those who historically have been disenfranchised. The organization advocates for individual rights by litigating, legislating, and educating the public on a broad array of issues affecting individual freedom.

AMERICAN FRIENDS SERVICE COMMITTEE

1501 Cherry Street
Philadelphia, PA 19102Phone: (215) 241-7000
Fax: (215) 241-7275
http://www.afsc.org/
The American Friends Service Committee is associated with the Religious Society of Friends, also known as the Quakers. The organization works to understand the causes of poverty, war, and injustice and seeks to rectify the human problems associated with these social ills.

AMNESTY INTERNATIONAL-USA
5 Penn Plaza
New York, NY 10001
Phone: (212) 807-8400
Fax: (212) 627-1451
http://www.amnestyusa.org/
Amnesty International USA seeks to remedy human rights abuses committed around the globe. Domestic programs include those focusing on eradicating the death penalty, freeing prisoners of conscience, and challenging state-sponsored torture.

AMNESTY INTERNATIONAL-LONDON
Amnesty International UK
The Human Rights Action Centre
17-25 New Inn Yard
London EC2A 3EA
Phone: (020) 7033-1500
Fax: (020) 7033-1503
The London location is the central office for Amnesty International. The mission of the organization is to raise public awareness about the many human rights violations occurring across the globe.

BELLEVUE/NYU PROGRAM FOR SURVIVORS OF TORTURE
Bellevue Hospital Center
462 First Avenue C & D – 710
New York, NY 10016-9196
Phone: (212) 994-7163
Fax: (212) 994-7177
The Bellevue Center provides culturally sensitive counseling and multidisciplinary treatment for victims of torture. This group of physicians provides treatment in the areas of dermatology, gynecology, neurology, primary medical care, and psychiatric care for victims of torture. The organization has served populations in more than ninety countries.

BRENNAN CENTER FOR JUSTICE AT NYU SCHOOL OF LAW
161 Avenue of the Americas, 12th Floor
New York, NY 10013
Phone: (212) 998-6730
Fax: (212) 995-4550
http://www.brennancenter.org/
The Brennan Center advocates for the pursuit of an effective democracy. The organization seeks to provide a nonpartisan agenda of scholarship, public education, and legal action that promotes equality and protects basic liberties.

CENTER FOR NATIONAL SECURITY STUDIES
1120 19th Street, NW, 8th Floor
Washington, DC 20036
Phone: (202) 721-5650
Fax: (202) 530-0128
http://www.cnss.org/
The Center for National Security Studies monitors the operations of federal intelligence agencies such as the FBI and CIA to help prevent violations of civil liberties. The Center also works to strengthen the public's right of access to government information and to combat government secrecy.

INSTITUTE FOR DEMOCRACY STUDIES
177 East 87th Street, Suite 501
New York, NY 10128
Phone: 212-423-9237
Fax: 212-423-9352
http://www.idsonline.org/

The Institute for Democracy Studies is an education and research center that studies antidemocratic religious and political movements in the United States and around the world. The Institute's primary research involves the intersections of law and democracy, religion and democracy, and reproductive rights and democracy.

HUMAN RIGHTS FIRST

333 Seventh Avenue, 13th Floor
New York, NY 10001-5004
Phone: (212) 845 5200
Fax: (212) 845 5299
http://www.humanrightsfirst.org/
Human Rights First is an international educational and advocacy organization that seeks to advance the causes of justice, respect for the law, and human dignity around the world.

HUMAN RIGHTS WATCH

350 Fifth Avenue, 34th floor
New York, NY 10118-3299
Tel: (212) 290-4700
Fax: (212) 736-1300
http://www.hrw.org/
Human Rights Watch seeks to aid in the prevention of human rights violations by informing and educating the public, governmental officials, and international institutions. The organization undertakes activities designed to expose human rights violations, uphold political freedoms, protect against inhumane conduct during times of war, and bring human rights offenders to justice.

NAACP LEGAL DEFENSE AND EDUCATION FUND, INC.

99 Hudson Street, Suite 1600
New York, NY 10013
Phone: (212) 965-2200
http://www.naacpldf.org/
This organization is dedicated to eradicating discrimination and injustice in all of its manifestations in the United States. The Fund handles class action and other impact litigation and undertakes advocacy in all forums on behalf of the disenfranchised.

NATIONAL LAWYERS GUILD

132 Nassau Street, Suite 922
New York, NY 10038
Phone: (212) 679-5100
Fax (212) 679-2811
http://www.nlg.org/
The National Lawyers Guild seeks to unite lawyers, law students, and jailhouse lawyers across the country in a various efforts to promote and protect human rights. The organization focuses on protecting civil liberties under attack.

PEOPLE FOR THE AMERICAN WAY

2000 M Street, NW, Suite 400
Washington, DC 20036
Phone: (202) 467-4999 or (800) 326-7329eet, NW, -326-7329
http://www.pfaw.org/pfaw/general/
This organization seeks to sustain the institutions and values that support a diverse and just democratic society.

PHYSICIANS FOR HUMAN RIGHTS

2 Arrow Street, Suite 301
Cambridge, MA 02138
Phone: (617) 301-4200
Fax: (617) 301-4250
http://www.phrusa.org/

Physicians for Human Rights seeks to expose and halt the commission of human rights violations. The organization provides support for groups seeking to hold perpetrators accountable and works to educate people in the medical field about human rights issues. The organization has worked to stop disappearances and political killings and to improve sanitary conditions in prisons.

PUERTO RICAN LEGAL DEFENSE AND EDUCATION FUND

99 Hudson Street, 14th Floor
New York, NY 10013-2815
Phone: (212) 219-3360 (800) 328-2322
Fax: (212) 431-4276
http://www.prldef.org/

The Puerto Rican Legal Defense and Education Fund was established to ensure equal access to rights and benefits for the Puerto Rican community in the United States. The organization seeks to help Latinos overcome the barriers created by societal discrimination by providing the community with legal and educational resources.

INTERNATIONAL COMMITTEE OF THE RED CROSS

2100 Pennsylvania Avenue, NW, Suite 545
Washington, D.C. 20037
http://www.icrc.org/

The International Committee of the Red Cross is a nonpartisan organization that seeks to protect the lives and dignity of those involved in war. The organization defends human rights all over the world and provides direct humanitarian relief to war-stricken areas.

COUNCIL ON AMERICAN ISLAMIC RELATIONS (CAIR)

53 New Jersey Avenue, SE
Washington, DC 20003-4034
Phone: (202) 488-8787
Fax: (202) 488-0833
http://www.cair-net.org/

CAIR seeks to protect religious and human rights, and strives to ensure that the Muslim voice is heard in society American society. The organization works to establish an on-going dialogue in order to promote a mutual understanding between Muslims and non-Muslims.

Acknowledgments

First, and above all, I would like to thank Craig Acorn, an extraordinary writer and editor as well as a noted civil rights lawyer, who gave many, many hours of his time for this book.

I would also like to express my deep gratitude to my friends, colleagues, and mentors at the Center for Constitutional Rights who have worked on many of the issues described in this book and remain, as always, at the forefront of the fight for human dignity. It has been a privilege and an honor for me to work alongside some of this country's greatest human rights lawyers and activists like Nancy Chang, David Cole, Ron Daniels, Michael Deutsch, Bill Goodman, Jules Lobel, and Michael Ratner, and all of the folks at the Center both past and present. It has been their courage and vision that has kept the fight alive during a very dark time. Thank you also to all of my colleagues at the many human rights organizations, law schools, universities, and law firms that have helped me so much with my own work at the Center over the years.

Finally, this book also would not have happened without the unwavering encouragement of Greg Ruggiero, Meg Lemke, and the staff at Seven Stories Press. Their commitment to publishing the truth is a great inspiration.

Notes

INTRODUCTION

1. In September 2002, President George W. Bush released his "National Security Strategy of the United States," officially detailing the doctrine of preemptive strikes. The policy position borrowed heavily from the PNAC's white paper, "Rebuilding America's Defenses." Farrell, 3.
2. In 1997, the Project for the New American Century (PNAC) was founded, with Donald Rumsfeld, Dick Cheney, and Paul Wolfowitz among the list of supporters. In 1998, this organization urged President Bill Clinton to remove Saddam Hussein from power and, in 2000, published a paper outlining core U.S. military missions intended to entail "multiple, simultaneous major theater wars." Maureen Farrell, "The Nature of the Threat," (hereafter "Farrell") *Buzzflash.com*, Feb. 25. 2004, http://www.buzzflash.com/farrell/04/02/far04005.html. *See also* http://www.newamericancentury.org for more information on this group.
3. The full name of the USA PATRIOT Act is the "Uniting and Strengthening America by Providing Appropriate Tools Required to Intercept and Obstruct Terrorism Act of 2001." It is often referred to in this publication simply as the Act.
4. Editorial, "Patriot Act Redux" and "In the Dark," *New York Times*, June 1, 2005. Farrell at 3.
5. In addition, Lynn Cheney's group, the American Council of Trustees, "issued a list of 117 anti-American statements, including Rev. Jesse Jackson's observation that the U.S. 'build bridges and relationships, not simply bombs and walls.'" Farrell, 3.
6. *See* http://judiciary.senate.gov.
7. *Hamdi v. Rumsfeld*, 542 U.S. 507, 535 (2004) (emphasis supplied).
8. *See* http://www.newamericancentury.org.
9. Maureen Farrell, "The Nature of the Threat," *BuzzFlash.com*, Feb. 25, 2004, http://www.buzzflash.com/farrell/04/02/far04005.html.
10. Gary Schmitt, "Power & Duty: U.S. Action is Crucial to Maintaining World Order," *Los Angeles Times*, Mar. 23, 2003, http://www.newamericancentury.org/global-032303.htm.
11. *Id.* at 2.
12. There are many scholars and politicians around the world who contend that President George W. Bush's decision to attack Iraq without the express authorization of the United Nations violates the U.N. Charter and Article VI of the United States Constitution, but that issue will not be taken on here. For in-depth treatment of that issue, *see, e.g.,* Jennie Green et al., *Against War with Iraq: An Antiwar Primer*, (New York: Seven Stories Press, 2002).

CHAPTER ONE

1. Dana Priest, "CIA Holds Terror Suspects in Secret Prisons," *Washington Post*, Nov. 2, 2005; Eric Schmitt and Douglas Jehl, "Army Says CIA Hid More Iraqis Than It Claimed," *New York Times*, Sept. 10, 2004; Eric Schmitt and Douglas Jehl, "CIA Hid More Prisoners Than It Has Disclosed, Generals Say," *New York Times*, Sept. 9, 2004; Dana Priest and Josh White, "Detainee Reportedly Was Lost in System," *Washington Post*, June 17, 2004, A19; Jamie McIntyre, "Pentagon: Iraqi Held Secretly At CIA Request," *CNN* Washington Bureau, June 17, 2004; Eric Schmitt and Thom Shanker, "Prison Abuse: Rumsfeld Issued An Order to Hide Detainee In Iraq," *New York Times*, June 17, 2004; Tim Golden, "In U.S. Report, Brutal Details of 2 Afghan Inmates' Deaths," *New York Times*, May 20, 2005.

CHAPTER TWO

1. Under the Illegal Immigration Reform and Immigrant Responsibility Act of 1996, immigration inspectors at the borders were given the authority to order the immediate deportation of people who arrive in the United States without proper identification and travel documents. The law requires the detention of asylum seekers during the expedited removal process; they are entitled to release on parole only if they can show or establish (i) a credible fear of persecution; (ii) their identity; (iii) that they have family in the United States or other community ties; and (iv) that they pose no danger to the community and are not otherwise barred from seeking asylum.

2. For a full examination of the changes in the country's immigration laws relating to asylum, *see* Human Rights First Report, "In Liberty's Shadow: U.S. Detention of Asylum Seekers in the Era of Homeland Security," Human Rights First, 2004.

3. 50 U.S.C. §§ 1811, 1809, 18 U.S.C. § 2511(2)(f).

4. While the U.S. Immigration and Naturalization Service (INS) has sometimes in the past sought to remove noncitizens for these violations, it generally has *not detained* them during their removal proceedings. As of September 2003, INS changed its name to U.S. Citizenship and Immigration Services (USCIS).

5. In order to hold grand jury witnesses, federal prosecutors must demonstrate the witness's value to a specific case and show that he or she may otherwise be unavailable to the court if released. The law says that people may be held for a "reasonable period of time." Plainly, this language was not intended to mean that people could be held for indefinite detentions. This is clear from the purpose of the material witness law, which was intended to allow the government to hold people so that it could get them before a grand jury, and from the Constitution itself, which mandates that hearings to evaluate detentions take place expeditiously after arrest (in cases assessing criminal detention, the courts have set the deadline at forty-eight hours; in cases of mental hygiene detention, the courts have set the deadline at seventy-two hours).

6. Challenges to the Bush administration's use of the material witness statute in this way resulted in a decision holding that the material witness statute was applicable to pretrial investigations and that the government could lawfully detain a witness, notwithstanding the witness's willingness to have her or his testimony preserved, provided that the grounds for detention were subject to judicial review. *See United States v. Awadallah*, 349 F.3d 42 (2d Cir. 2003).

7. All facts are derived from interviews with Mr. Turkmen and are included the complaint filed in *Turkmen v. Ashcroft*, No. 02-CV-2307 (JG), a class action lawsuit seeking punitive damages on behalf of Mr. Turkmen and others who were detained by the INS after September 11.

8. *See, e.g.,* Amnesty International Report, "USA: U.S. detentions in Afghanistan: an aide-memoire for continued action," Amnesty International, June 7, 2005.

9. The Freedom of Information Act was passed in 1966 and amended in 1974. Its primary purpose is to provide for disclosure of records kept by agencies of the U.S. federal government. *See Department of the Interior v. Klamath Water Users Protective Association,* 532 U.S. 1, 8 (2001).

10. The request queried whether the detentions were based on immigration charges, criminal charges, material witness needs, possible terrorism charges, or other grounds.

11. The FOIA request was made on October 29, 2001.

12. *See Center for National Security Studies v. U.S. Department of Justice,* 215 F. Supp. 2d 94, 103 (D.D.C. 2002).

13. *See* Government's Reply Brief in *Center for National Security Studies* Case at 9.

14. *See Statement of White House Press Secretary Ari Fleischer,* Apr. 2, 2002, http://www.whitehouse.gov/news/releases/2002/04/20020403-2.html; *Secretary of Defense Donald Rumsfeld, Press Briefing,* Apr. 3, 2002, http://defenselink.mil/news/Apr2002/t04032002_t0403sd .html; *Remarks of President George W. Bush at Connecticut Republican Committee Luncheon,* Apr. 9, 2002, http://www.whitehouse.gov/news/releases/2002/04/20020409-8.html; Judith Miller and David Johnston, "FBI Chief Says Al Qaeda Aide's Arrest Will Help Prevent Attacks by Terrorists," *New York Times,* Apr. 4, 2002, A14.

15. *See* Richard Cohen, "Ashcroft's Attitude Problem," *Washington Post,* June 10, 2003, A21.

16. *See Linn v. Department of Justice,* 1995 U.S. Dist. LEXIS 9302, at 8 (D.D.C. June 6, 1995).

17. *See Center for National Security Studies v. U.S. Department of Justice,* 215 F. Supp. 2d 94, 103 (D.D.C. 2002).

18. *See Center for National Security Studies v. U.S. Department of Justice,* 331 F.3d 918, 926-32 (D.C. Cir. 2003). The Court of Appeals of the District of Columbia accepted the government's explanation that national security concerns governed the issue and that the Freedom of Information Act's exemption permitting agencies to withhold information when release might "interfere with enforcement proceedings" permitted the Justice Department to take such action.

19. *Center for National Security Studies v. U.S. Department of Justice,* 331 F.3d 918, 926-32 (D.C. Cir. 2003).

20. *Id.,* 331 F.3d at 926-32.

21. *Id.,* 331 F.3d at 926-32.

22. In fact, in a statement made by the government in January 2002, only 718 people are being held on immigration violations.

23. *See* Amnesty International Report, "Amnesty International's Concerns Regarding Post September 11 Detentions in the USA," Amnesty International, Mar. 2002.

24. OIG Report at 113.

25. OIG Report at 114.

26. OIG Report at 115.

27. Researchers from Amnesty International were told by immigration officials that attorneys could not be notified before the transfer of any detainees because of security reasons. *See* Amnesty International Report, "Amnesty International's Concerns Regarding Post September 11 Detentions in the USA," Mar. 2002, 22.

28. *See* Amnesty International Report, "Amnesty International's Concerns Regarding Post September 11 Detentions in the USA," Mar. 2002, 7.

29. *See* Michael Creppy, Chief Immigration Judge, "Memorandum to All Immigration Judges," Sept. 21, 2001, on file with the author.

30. *See Detroit Free Press v. Ashcroft,* 303 F.3d 681 (6th Cir. 2002), *reh'g en banc denied,* (Jan. 22, 2003).

31. *See Detroit Free Press v. Ashcroft,* 303 F.3d 681, 683 (6th Cir. 2002).

32. *See North Jersey Media Group v. Ashcroft,* 205 F. Supp. 2d 288 (D.N.J. 2002).

33. *See North Jersey Media Group v. Ashcroft,* 308 F.3d 198 (3d Cir. 2002), *cert. denied,* 123 S. Ct. 2215 (2003).

34. *See North Jersey Media Group v. Ashcroft,* 308 F.3d 198 (3d Cir. 2002), *cert. denied,* 123 S. Ct. 2215 (2003); "Supreme Court Allows Secrecy to Stand in Deportation Cases," *New York Times,* June 29, 2002; Editorial, "Closing the Door to Public Scrutiny," *New York Times,* June 29, 2002, A14.

35. 8 C.F.R. § 287.3 (2003).

36. *See Reno v. Flores,* 507 U.S. 292, 295 (1993).

37. *See* 8 C.F.R. § 1236.1(d)(1) (2004).

38. *See, e.g., Barbour v. District Director,* 491 F.2d 573 (5th Cir. 1974).

39. *See* allegations in *Turkmen v. Ashcroft,* No. 02-CV-2307 (JG), pending in the United States District Court in the Eastern District of New York. *See also* OIG Report at 14-37.

40. See Tova Wang, "The Devil's in the Details: Overlooked Highlights of the Justice Department's Report on 9/11 Detainees," The Century Foundation, 2005.

41. *See* Robert Scheer, "With Powers Like These, Can Repression Be Far Behind?," *The Nation,* Oct. 31, 2001.

42. *See* allegations in *Turkmen v. Ashcroft,* No. 02-CV-2307 (JG), pending in the United States District Court in the Eastern District of New York. *See* Paul Chavez, "Four Iranian Brothers Released After Long Detention in Los Angeles," Associated Press, Mar. 17, 2005.

43. *See Zadvydas v. Davis,* 533 U.S. 678, 690 (2001).

44. *See* David Cole, "We've Aimed and Missed Before," *Washington Post,* June 6, 2003.

45. *See* OIG Report; "Amnesty International's Concerns Regarding Post September 11 Detentions in the USA," Amnesty International, Mar. 2002, 14.

46. OIG Report at 18.

47. *See Henry v. United States,* 361 U.S. 98, 102 (1959); *Weyant v. Okst,* 101 F.3d 845, 852 (2d Cir. 1996).

48. *See Gerstein v. Pugh,* 420 U.S. 103, 120 n.21 (1975).

49. *See County of Riverside v. McLaughlin,* 500 U.S. 44, 55 (1991).

50. *See Adams v. United States,* 399 F.2d 574, 577 (D.C. Cir. 1968), *cert. denied,* 393 U.S. 1067 (1969).

51. *See McLaughlin,* 500 U.S. at 56.

52. *See Willis v. City of Chicago,* 999 F.2d 284, 288-89 (7th Cir. 1993) (recognizing that the two reasons for prosecutorial delay are certainly analogous), *cert. denied,* 510 U.S. 1071 (1994).

53. *See Turkmen v. Ashcroft,* No. 02-CV-2307 (JG). The lawsuit charges that the plaintiffs were detained despite having received and accepted deportation orders, and that they were subjected to severe conditions during their detainment, including beatings, verbal abuse, solitary confinement, and denial of the right to religious practice. The suit seeks punitive damages and a declaratory judgment that the detention of these individuals is unconstitutional and violates customary international law. The defendants in the case include then United States Attorney General John Ashcroft, who had ultimate responsibility for the implementation and enforcement of the immigration laws and who the lawsuit claims condoned and/or ratified "unreasonable and excessively harsh condition under which plaintiffs and other class action members have been detained." Other defendants named in the suit include Robert S. Mueller III, Federal Bureau of Investigations Director; Dennis Hasty, Metropolitan Detention Center warden; and unnamed MDC correctional officers.

54. Mr. Saffi is currently living with his wife and two daughters in France.

55. OIG Report at 69, 70.

56. OIG Report at 27-31. Although the Immigration and Nationality Act authorizes detention, even for what are seen as noncriminal immigration violations, such as tourist visa overstays, before September 11, the immigration system had evolved over many years such that few individuals were detained during immigration proceedings; they were either not detained at all or were given the opportunity to seek release on bond or on personal recognizance. This decades-old system changed without notice overnight.

57. OIG Report at 112-14.

58. OIG Report at 105.

59. OIG Report at 15-17.

60. OIG Report at 17.

61. OIG Report at 16.

62. OIG Report at 16.

63. OIG Report at 70.

64. OIG Report at 71.

65. OIG Report at 70.

66. OIG Report at 196.

67. *See* Dr. Stuart Grassian, "Out of Mind, Out of Sight: Report on Confinement of Mentally Ill Prisoners in Ireland," *Disability World,* Mar.–Apr. 2001.

68. OIG Report at 115-18.

69. OIG Report at 42.

70. OIG Report at 136.

71. Apr. 24, 1963, TIAS 6820, 21 U.S.T. 77.

72. *See* Office of the Inspector General of the U.S. Department of Justice, "Supplemental Report on September 11 Detainees' Allegations of Abuse at the Metropolitan Detention Center in Brooklyn, New York," December 2003 (Supp. OIG Report).

73. Supp. OIG Report at 8-20.

74. Supp. OIG Report at 3, 34.

75. Supp. OIG Report at 8-23; BOP P.S. 5566.05.

76. *See generally,* Office of the Inspector General of the U.S. Department of Justice, "The September 11 Detainees: A Review of the Treatment of Aliens Held on Immigration Charges in Connection with the Investigation of the September 11 Attacks," June 2, 2003; Office of the Inspector General of the U.S. Department of Justice, Supp. OIG Report.

77. *See* Supplemental Declaration of James S. Reynolds, paragraphs 3-5, filed February 5, 2002 in *Center for National Security Studies v. U.S. Department of Justice.*

78. Owais Tohid, "Pakistanis Tell of U.S. Prison Horror," *BBC News,* June 30, 2002; Susan Sachs, "U.S. Deports Most of Those Arrested in Sweeps After 9/11," *New York Times,* July 11, 2002; Steve Fainaru, "U.S. Deported 131 Pakistanis In Secret Airlift," *Washington Post,* July 19, 2002; Wayne Parry, "Palestinian Detainees Deported to Gaza," Associated Press, Dec. 20, 2002

79. Steve Fainaru, "U.S. Deported 131 Pakistanis In Secret Airlift," *Washington Post,* July 19, 2002.

80. *Id.*

81. Susan Sachs, "U.S. Deports Most of Those Arrested in Sweeps After 9/11," *New York Times,* July 11, 2002.

82. Brendan Lyons, "Sudden Deportation Shatters Family," *Albany Times Union,* July 21, 2002.

83. *Id.*

84. *Id.*

85. *See* Amnesty International Report, "Amnesty International's Concerns Regarding Post September 11 Detentions in the USA," Amnesty International, Mar. 2002, 26–27.

86. The United States has acceded to the 1967 Protocol to the 1951 U.N. Convention relating to the Status of Refugees and has enacted additional legislation implementing its obligations under the Convention Against Torture.

87. Barbara Comstock, Director of Public Affairs, "Statement Regarding the IG's Report on 9/11 Detainees," (June 2, 2003), http://www.usdoj.gov/opa/pr/2003/June/03_opa_324.htm.

88. *See* Richard Cohen, "Ashcroft's Attitude Problem," *Washington Post*, June 10, 2003, A21.

89. *See* Fox Butterfield, "A Police Force Rebuffs FBI on Querying Mideast Men," *New York Times*, Nov. 21, 2001, B7.

90. Mark Bixler, "Judge Prevents Man's Deportation; Address Lapse Said Not To Be Sufficient Cause," *Atlanta Journal Constitution*, Aug. 6, 2002, A1.

91. Eric Schmitt, "U.S. Will Seek to Fingerprint U.S. Visa Holders," *New York Times*, June 5, 2002, A1.

92. *See* U.S. Department of Justice Announcement, "Attorney General Ashcroft Announces Implementation Of The First Phase Of The National Security Entry-Exit Registration System," U.S. Department of Justice (Aug. 12, 2002), http://www.usdoj.gov/opa/pr/2002/August/02_ag_466.htm.

93. *Id.* The announcement also stated: "Under the NSEERS program, the fingerprints of a small percentage of entering foreign visitors will be matched against a database of known criminals and a database of known terrorists. These visitors will be selected according to intelligence criteria reflecting patterns of terrorist organizations' activities. . . . In addition to requiring the fingerprinting of higher-risk visiting aliens at the port of entry, the NSEERS program will require the same individuals to periodically confirm where they are living and what they are doing in the United States, as well as to confirm their exit from the country.

94. *Id.*

95. Federal Register, Final Rule dated Aug. 12, 2002; 8 CFR 264.

96. Asian American Legal Defense and Education Fund (AALDEF), "Special Registration: Discrimination and Xenophobia as Government Policy at 1," AALDEF (2004), http://www.aaldef.org/images/01-04_registration.pdf.

97. Immigration Policy Center, "Targets of Suspicion: The Impact of Post-9/11 Policies on Muslims, Arabs and South Asians in the United States," *Immigration Policy IN FOCUS*, 3, issue 2 (May 2004): 7, http://www.ailf.org/ipc/ipf051704.pdf.

98. *See* U.S. Department of Justice Announcement, "Special Call-in Procedures for Certain Non-Immigrants, Call-in Group 1, Federal Register Notice," http://international.tamu.edu/iss/regulations/CALL_IN_1.pdf.

99. Stephen F. Rhode, "The USA Unpatriotic Act and Homeland Insecurities: The Assault on the Right of Privacy and How the People Can Restore Our Constitutional Democracy," *Journal of California Politics & Policy* (June 2003): 85.

100. *Id.*

101. Andrew F. Tully, "U.S.: Washington Shifts Immigration Policy Criticized by Arab, Muslim Advocates," GlobalSecurity.org, 2003.

102. Stephen F. Rhode, "The USA Unpatriotic Act and Homeland Insecurities: The Assault on the Right of Privacy and How the People Can Restore Our Constitutional Democracy," *Journal of California Politics & Policy* (June 2003): 85.

103. *See* American-Arab Anti-Discrimination Committee, "Examples of the Impact of Post-9/11 Policies," (2003), on file with the author.

104. *See Wong Wing v. United States*, 163 U.S. 228 (1896) (holding that because noncitizens within the U.S. are protected by the Fifth and Sixth Amendments to the Constitution, they cannot be punished

without a trial and conviction); *Plyler v. Doe*, 457 U.S. 202, 210 (1982) ("[e]ven those unlawfully present in the U.S. are "persons" guaranteed Fifth and Fourteenth Amendment due process rights."); *Mathews v. Diaz*, 426 U.S. 67, 77 (1976) ("[E]ven one whose presence in this country is unlawful, involuntary, or transitory is entitled to . . . constitutional protection."). *See* Gerald L. Neuman, *Strangers to the Constitution: Immigrants, Borders, and Fundamental Law* (Princeton, N.J.: Princeton University Press, 1996), 1–15.

105. *See Miller v. Johnson*, 515 U.S. 900, 904 (1995).

106. *See* Naftali Bendavid, "Bush OK's Terror Tribunals; U.S. Seeks 5,000 Foreign Nationals for Questioning in Investigation," *Chicago Tribune*, Nov. 14, 2001, 1.

107. *See* David Cole, "Enemy Aliens," 54 *Stan. L. Rev.* 953, 975 (May 2002); Natsu Taylor Saito, "Will Force Trump Legality After September 11? American Jurisprudence Confronts the Rule of Law," 17 *Geo. Immigr. L.J.* 1, 18 (Fall 2002).

108. Warren Hoge, "A Nation Challenged: The Convert; Shoe-Bomb Suspect Fell In With Extremists," *New York Times*, Dec. 27, 2001, B6.

109. U.N. Charter, art. 1, P3.

110. International Convention on the Elimination of All Forms of Racial Discrimination, entered into force, Jan. 4, 1969, 660 U.N.T.S. 195.

111. Racial discrimination is defined in the convention as "any distinction, exclusion, restriction or preference based on race, colour, descent, or national or ethnic origin which has the purpose or effect of nullifying or impairing the recognition, enjoyment or exercise, on an equal footing, of human rights and fundamental freedoms in the political, economic, social, cultural or any other field of public life. *Id.* at art. 1, P1.

112. *Id.* at arts. 2, 4, 7.

113. Universal Declaration of Human Rights, art. 2.

114. Universal Declaration of Human Rights, art. 7.

115. International Convenant on Civil and Political Rights, adopted Dec. 16, 1966, Annex to G.A. Res. 2200, 21st Sess., Supp. No. 16, at 52, U.N. Doc. A/6316 (1966) (entered into force Mar. 23, 1976).

116. *See* Natsu Taylor Saito, "Will Force Trump Legality After September 11? American Jurisprudence Confronts the Rule of Law," 17 *Geo. Immigr. L.J.* 1, 44-45 (Fall 2002).

117. *See Hirabayashi v. United States*, 320 U.S. 81 (1943); *Yasui v. United States*, 320 U.S. 115 (1943); *Korematsu v. United States*, 323 U.S. 214 (1944).

118. *See* C. Harvey Gardner, *Pawns in a Triangle of Hate: The Peruvian Japanese and the United States* (Seattle: University of Washington Press, 1981); Higashide Seiichi, *Adios to Tears: Memoirs of a Japanese Peruvian Internee in U.S. Concentration Camps* (Seattle: University of Washington Press, 1994).

119. *See* Natsu Taylor Saito, "Justice Held Hostage: U.S. Disregard for International Law in the World War II Internment of Japanese Peruvians—A Case Study," 19 *British Columbia Third World Law Journal* 275, 290-315 (1998).

120. *See* Natsu Taylor Saito, "Will Force Trump Legality After September 11? American Jurisprudence Confronts the Rule of Law," 17 *Geo. Immigr. L.J.* 1, 18 (Fall 2002).

121. *See* David Cole, "Enemy Aliens," 54 *Stan. L. Rev.* 953 (2002), for a detailed critique of this troubling trade-off.

122. *Yick Wo v. Hopkins*, 118 U.S. 356, 359 (1886).

123. *Zadvydas v. Davis*, 533 U.S. 678, 693 (2001).

124. *See Almeida-Sanchez v. United States*, 413 U.S. 266 (1973); *see also Wong Wing v. United States*, 163 U.S. 228 (1896) (holding that noncitizens charged with crimes are protected by the Fifth, Sixth, and Fourteenth Amendments); *Nishimura Ekiu v. United States*, 142 U.S. 651, 660 (1892) (noting that foreign nationals incarcerated in the U.S. have a constitutional right to habeas corpus).

125. *See* David Cole, "Rounding Up the Usual Suspects: Human Rights In The Wake of 9/11: Are Foreign Nationals Entitled to the Same Constitutional Rights As Citizens?" 25 *San Diego Justice Journal* 367, 368 (Spring, 2003).

126. *Id.*

127. *Yamataya v. Fisher*, 189 U.S. 86 (1903) (The Japanese Immigrant Case); *Chae Chan Ping v. United States*, 130 U.S. 581 (1889) (The Chinese Exclusion Case).

128. *Porterfield v. Webb*, 263 U.S. 225 (1923) (upholding Washington's alien land law); *Terrace v. Thompson*, 263 U.S. 197 (1923) (upholding California's alien land law). To date, these laws have not been held unconstitutional. Brant T. Lee, *A Racial Trust: The Japanese YWCA and the Alien Land Law*, 7 *Asian Pac. Am. L.J.* 1, 28 (2001).

129. *See Galvan v. Press*, 347 U.S. 522 (1954).

130. *See Foley v. Connelie*, 435 U.S. 291 (1978) (permitting states to require citizenship when hiring state troopers); *Ambach v. Norwick*, 441 U.S. 68 (1979) (permitting states to require citizenship in hiring public school teachers).

131. *See* Louis Henkin, "Rights: American and Human," 79 *Columbia L. Rev.* 406, 408-09 (1979).

132. Madison's Report on the Virginia Resolutions (1800), reprinted in 4 *The Debates in the Several State Conventions on the Adoption of the Federal Constitution* 556 (J. Elliot ed., 2d ed. 1836).

133. *See* Neuman, *Strangers to the Constitution: Immigrants, Borders, and Fundamental Law* at 52-63.

134. Universal Declaration of Human Rights, G. A. Res. 217A (III), U.N. GAOR, 3d. Sess., Supp. No. 13, at 71, U.N. Doc. A/810 (1948).

135. Universal Declaration of Human Rights, pmbl., art. 7-11, 19, 20(1), G. A. Res. 217A (III), U.N. GAOR, 3d. Sess., Supp. No. 13, at 71, U.N. Doc. A/810 (1948).

136. *See* David Weissbrodt, *Prevention of Discrimination and Protection of Indigenous Peoples and Minorities: The Rights of Noncitizens*, at 30, U.N. Doc. E/CN.4/Sub.2/2001/20 (2001).

137. *See, e.g.,* the International Covenant on Civil and Political Rights, Human Rights Committee commentary, General Comment 15, *The Position of Aliens Under the Covenant*, Human Rights Committee, U.N. Doc. HRI/GEN/1/Rev.1, at 18 (1994), 27th Sess. 1986, at para. 7.

138. *See* David Cole, "Rounding Up the Usual Suspects: Human Rights In The Wake of 9/11: Are Foreign Nationals Entitled to the Same Constitutional Rights As Citizens?" 25 *San Diego Justice Journal* 367, 370 (Spring, 2003) (discussing the extension of fundamental rights guarantees to noncitizens by Sweden, Canada, Italy, Germany, and Great Britain).

139. *Dred Scott v. Sanford*, 60 U.S. 393 (1856).

140. Civil Rights Act of 1866, Ch. 31, 1, 14 Stat. 27.

141. *See* David Cole, "Rounding Up the Usual Suspects: Human Rights In The Wake of 9/11: Are Foreign Nationals Entitled to the Same Constitutional Rights As Citizens?" 25 *San Diego Justice Journal* 367, 370 (Spring, 2003).

142. *See* Government's Reply Brief in *Center for Security Studies* Case at 9.

CHAPTER THREE

1. The November 13 Presidential Order can be found in the Federal Register at 66 Fed. Reg. 57831 (2001). Estimates indicate that the order applies to more than 20 million noncitizens currently living in the United States, the vast majority of whom are legal residents.

2. The "enemy combatant" category, as discussed *infra*, includes people seized by the United States in other parts of the world far from any zone of military hostilities and with no connection to the war in Afghanistan.

3. *See* International Committee of the Red Cross, *International Humanitarian Law*, available online at http://www.icrc.org/Web/Eng/siteeng).nsf/html/ihl (last visited May 17, 2005) (defining international humanitarian law).

4. Each of the four Conventions prescribes rules defining the proper treatment of one category of "protect persons" – the sick and wounded on land; the sick, wounded, and shipwrecked at sea; prisoners of war; and civilians. The central idea of the Conventions is to ensure compliance with a minimum standard for the treatment of persons subject to the authority of the enemy.

5. The four Geneva Conventions, for example, have been ratified by 192 nations, including the United States. U.S. Dept. of State, Treaties in Force 398-99 (1994) (referring to Convention for the Amelioration of the Condition of the Wounded and Sick in Armed Forces in the Field, Aug. 12, 1949, 6 U.S.T. 3114, 75 U.N.T.S. 31; Convention for the Amelioration of the Condition of Wounded, Sick and Shipwrecked Members of Armed Forces at Sea, Aug. 12, 1949, 6 U.S.T. 3217, 75 U.N.T.S. 85; Convention Relative to the Treatment of Prisoners of War, Aug. 12, 1949, 6 U.S.T. 3316, 75 U.N.T.S. 135; Convention Relative to the Protection of Civilian Persons in Time of War, Aug. 12, 1949, 6 U.S.T. 3516, 75 U.N.T.S. 287). For a comprehensive overview of the history and current status of the laws of war, *see* Howard S. Levie, *Terrorism in War: The Law of War Crimes* (1993).

6. International Committee of the Red Cross, Commentary to Geneva (J. Pictet, ed., 1960), at 23.

7. Geneva Convention Relative to the Treatment of Prisoners of War, Aug. 12, 1949, arts. 13-32, 82-88, 99-108, 119-119, 75 U.N.T.S. 135, 6 U.S.T. 3316.

8. *See* Third Geneva Convention, art. 5.

9. *See* Third Geneva Convention, arts. 8-11, 13, 15, 17, 18, 19, 99-108, 102.

10. Fourth Geneva Convention, arts. 4, 5, 71-76 & 126.

11. International humanitarian law is a branch of public international law that seeks to circumscribe the boundaries of armed conflicts and reduce the suffering that they cause in the world. This branch of international law is based on the notion that the methods and means of warfare are subject to ethical and legal limitations and that the victims of armed conflict are entitled to humanitarian care and protection. International humanitarian law constitutes one of the two branches of the laws of armed conflict and is termed the *jus in bello* (the law in war). The other branch is known as the *jus ad bellum* (the law to war).

12. *Ex parte Quirin*, 317 U.S. 1 (1942).

13. *Ex parte Quirin*, 317 U.S. at 27-36.

14. The Supreme Court has used the term "enemy combatant" in only two cases since *Ex parte Quirin*, and in both cases, the Court used the term synonymously with the term enemy belligerent. *See In re Yamashita*, 327 U.S. 1, 11 (1946); *Madsen v. Kinsella*, 343 U.S. 341 (1952).

15. *Ex parte Quirin*, 317 U.S. at 31.

16. *See* Regulations Respecting the Laws and Customs of War on Land, Art. 1, annex to Convention (No. IV) Respecting the Laws and Customs of War on Land, Oct. 18, 1907, 36 Stat. 2277, 1 Bevans 631; Geneva Convention III, Art. 4; Protocol Additional to the Geneva Conventions of 12 August 1949, and Relating to the Protection of Victims of International Armed Conflicts, opened for signature Dec. 12, 1977, Arts. 43, 44, 1125 U.N.T.S. 3.

17. The internal secret procedure for determining who may be designated an "enemy combatant" plainly does not comport with any notion of due process, whether that notion is anchored in our domestic jurisprudence or in the law of war. At a minimum, the drafters of Article 5 made clear that the competent tribunal requirement ensures that "decisions which might have the gravest consequences

[would] not be left to a single person." Jean de Preux et al., *Geneva Convention Relative to the Treatment of Prisoners of War: Commentary 77* (1960).

18. Government's Supreme Court Brief in *Rumsfeld, Secretary of Defense v. Padilla*, No. 03-1027 at 9.

19. U.S. Const., art. I, § 8, cl. 1.

20. U.S. Const., art. I, § 8, cl. 12, 13.

21. U.S. Const., art. I, § 8, cl. 14.

22. U.S. Const., art. I, § 8, cl. 10.

23. U.S. Const., art. I, § 8, cl. 11.

24. U.S. Const., art. I, §§ 8, 9.

25. U.S. Const., art. II, §§ 2, 3.

26. U.S. Const., art. III.

27. *See* Presidential Declaration of June 9, 2002, filed in Civil Action No. 02-CV-0445 (MBM). On November 20, 2005, Padilla was ordered released from detention by the secretary of defense and transferred to the control of the U.S. attorney general for the purpose of criminal proceedings against him. *See* Associated Press, "U.S. Indicts Padilla After 3 Years in Pentagon Custody," Nov. 22, 2005.

28. Mobbs Declaration, dated September 30, 2002, filed in Civil Action No. 02-CV-0445 (MBM).

29. *Id.*

30. *Id.*

31. Padilla cannot be tried before a military commission because he is a citizen and therefore is exempt from prosecution under the president's November 13, 2001, Military Order.

32. Jacoby Declaration, dated January 9, 2003, submitted in Civil Action No. 02-CV-0445 (MBM).

33. *Id.*

34. These conditions are permitted only for those who commit serious crimes while they are already incarcerated.

35. *Padilla v. Rumsfeld*, 243 F. Supp. 2d 42, 49 (S.D.N.Y. 2003) (quoting Jacoby Decl.).

36. The Jacoby Declaration implies that seven months of incarceration (the length of Padilla's detention at the time the Jacoby Declaration was submitted) is not a sufficient amount of time to convince Padilla of the hopelessness of his situation.

37. The executive has not claimed (and could not) that Chicago's O'Hare International Airport was a battlefield when Padilla was deplaning from a commercial flight. Nor has it claimed (nor could it) that the Bureau of Prisons facility where Padilla was held as a material witness—and from which he was taken as a declared "enemy combatant"—was a battlefield.

38. Vanessa Blum, "Government Implicates Padilla As Terror Conspirator," *Legal Times*, Sept. 17, 2004.

39. *See* Associated Press, "U.S. Indicts Padilla After 3 Years in Pentagon Custody," Nov. 22, 2005.

40. These are the facts as they have been alleged in the habeas corpus petition—the procedural petition demanding that jailers justify in court their detention of a person—filed on Hamdi's behalf by his father and his attorneys.

41. Government's Supreme Court Brief in *Hamdi et al. v. Rumsfeld, Secretary of Defense, et al.*, No. 03-6696, at 5.

42. *Id.* at 4.

43. *Id.* at 6-7.

44. Reports of interviews of Hamdi were deemed exculpatory by United States District Judge Ellis in *United States v. John Phillip Walker Lindh*, Crim. No. 02-37-A (E.D. Va., Alexandria Division, 2001) on the issue of whether Lindh was an "enemy combatant." These interview reports are nonclassified and were turned over to counsel for Lindh in that case, who have said that it is not unreasonable to infer that Hamdi's statements are exculpatory to him as well on the "enemy combatant" issue.

45. 67 Fed. Reg. 35596 (May 20, 2002).

46. The district court observed that "[t]he declaration is silent as to what level of 'affiliation' is necessary to warrant enemy combatant status."

47. The government places great emphasis on the fact that Hamdi was armed in reaching its conclusion that there is sufficient evidence to establish that he was an "enemy combatant." However, because carrying a weapon in Afghanistan is commonplace, it does not support an inference that one is a combatant. People in Afghanistan even take weapons to weddings and fire celebratory shots in the air. *See* Eric Schmitt, "U.S. Describes Ground Fire From Afghan Wedding," *New York Times*, July 4, 2002, A6. The *Washington Post* described this as "the traditional, exuberant spraying of rifle fire in the air." Pamela Constable, "Before Attack, We Never Heard the Sound of the Planes," *Washington Post*, July 4, 2002, A16.

48. Joint appendix, submitted in *Hamdi et al. v. Rumsfeld, Secretary of Defense, et al.*, No. 03-6696, at 148-150.

49. *Id.*

50. Although the Mobbs Declaration is silent on this point, the government suggests that Taliban detainees are "unlawful combatants" based on a presidential determination to that effect. The government, however, argued to the Supreme Court that it need not address the issue of whether Hamdi is an unlawful combatant. As noted above, under the Third Geneva Convention, 6 U.S.T. 3316, 75 U.N.T.S. 135, and current U.S. military regulations, such determinations must be made on an individual basis by a competent tribunal.

51. *See Padilla v. Rumsfeld*, 243 F. Supp. 2d 42, 49 (S.D.N.Y. 2003) (quoting Jacoby Decl.).

52. Department of Defense News Briefing, 2002 WL 2206773, at 11 (June 12, 2002).

53. Attorney General John Ashcroft, Testimony before the House Committee on the Judiciary, Sept. 24, 2001, http://www.usdoj.gov/ag/testimony/2001/agcrisisremarks9+uscore+24.htm; Attorney General John Ashcroft, Testimony before the Senate Committee on the Judiciary, Sept. 25, 2001, http://www.usdoj.gov/ag/testimony/2001/0925AttorneyGeneralJohnAshcroftTestimonyBeforethe-SenateCommitteeontheJudiciary.htm.

54. The Bush administration's "war on terror" has spawned a new vocabulary which has created considerable confusion among members of both the public and the military. Thus, while Executive Order 13224, signed on September 23, 2001, permits the Secretary of State to designate certain persons and organizations that he believes pose a "significant risk of committing acts of terrorism" and to block all property and assets of such individuals or entities when they come within the control of the U.S., it does *not* state what criteria are used to determine who may pose a risk to our national security, foreign policy, or economy. No mention is made in the Executive Order of the "enemy combatant" category. Executive Order 13224 of September 23, 2001, http://www.state.gov/s/ct/rls/fs/2002/16181.htm (last visited May 23, 2006).

On March 23, 2005, the U.S. military released a proposed joint military policy intended to formalize the category of "enemy combatant" as including detainees who are not entitled to the protections of the Geneva Conventions. This draft document, entitled "Joint Doctrine for Detainee Operations: Joint Publication 3-63" (JP 3-63), was purportedly intended to set forth "authoritative guidance" that would take precedence over any conflicting armed service publication. While there are many egregious problems with JP 3-63, one thing is clear: this guidance document was not issued until nearly—if not all—of the detainees had already been declared "enemy combatants" and held for more than three years in Guantánamo.

55. *Ex parte Quirin*, 317 U.S. 1 (1942).

56. The AUMF specifically authorized President Bush to use force against "Nations, organizations, or persons . . . that] *planned, authorized, committed or aided the terrorist attacks on September 11, 2001*, or [that] harbored such organizations or persons in order to prevent any future acts of international

terrorism against the United States by such nations, organizations, or persons. Nations, organizations, or persons . . . [that] *planned, authorized, committed or aided the terrorist attacks on September 11, 2001,* or [that] harbored such organizations or persons in order to prevent any future acts of international terrorism against the United States by such nations, organizations, or persons." AUMF, Pub. L. 107-40, 115 Stat. 224 (Sept. 18, 2001).

57. *Ex parte Quirin,* 317 U.S. at 20-21.

58. *Id.* at 20-21, 46.

59. *Id.* at 29.

60. The fact that the *Quirin* court determined that a military tribunal may, in certain cases, provide constitutionally adequate process for unlawful combatants charged with violations of the law of war, does not mean that military tribunals are necessarily appropriate for all those properly determined to be unlawful combatants. As the Supreme Court acknowledged in *Quirin:* "[T]here are some acts regarded . . . as offenses against the law of war which would *not* be triable by military tribunal here, either because they are not recognized by our courts as violations of the law of war or because they are of that class of offenses constitutionally triable only by a jury." 317 U.S. at 29 (emphasis added).

61. The government claimed the petitioners "must be denied access to the courts, both because they are enemy aliens or have entered our territory as enemy belligerents, and because the President's Proclamation undertakes in terms to deny such access to the class of persons defined by the Proclamation." *Quirin,* 317 U.S. at 24-25. The Court emphatically rejected the government's construction: "[N]either the Proclamation nor the fact that they are enemy aliens forecloses consideration by the courts of petitioners' contentions that the Constitution and laws of the United States constitutionally enacted forbid their trial by military commission." *Id.* at 24-25.

62. *Id.*

63. The *Quirin* saboteurs acknowledged that they were Nazi agents who had surreptitiously crossed enemy lines in military uniform with weapons, then hidden their uniforms and weapons. They defended themselves on the ground that, despite these preparations, they did not, in fact, intend to carry out the acts of sabotage for which they were prepared. Their defense was not credited. *Ex parte Quirin,* 317 U.S. at 20-21.

64. *Cramer v. United States,* 325 U.S. 1 (1945); *United States v. Haupt,* 136 F.2d 661 (7th Cir. 1943); Louis Fisher, *Nazi Saboteurs on Trial,* 80-83 (University of Kansas Press, 2003).

65. *See, e.g., Youngstown Sheet & Tube Co. v. Sawyer,* 343 U.S. 579 (1952); *Ex parte Endo,* 323 U.S. 283 (1944); *Raymond v. Thomas,* 91 U.S. 712 (1875); *Ex parte Milligan,* 71 U.S. (4 Wall.) 2 (1866); *Ex parte Merryman,* 17 F. Cas. 144 (C.C.D. Md. 1861).

66. *Quirin,* 317 U.S. at 27-28.

67. *Filartiga v. Pena-Irala,* 630 F.2d 876, 880 (2d Cir. 1980).

68. Today, 193 nation-states, including the United States, have ratified the Geneva Conventions.

69. International Committee of the Red Cross (ICRC), Commentary: Geneva Convention (IV) Relative to the Protection of Civilian Persons in Time of War, 51 (Geneva: 1958) (emphasis in original).

70. *Prosecutor v. Delalic et al.* Judgment, ICTY, IT-96-21, p. 271 (Nov. 16, 1998).

71. *Rumsfeld v. Padilla,* 542 U.S. 426 (2004).

72. *Id.*

73. *Padilla v. Hanft,* 389 F. Supp. 2d 678 (D.S.C. 2005).

74. *Padilla v. Hanft,* 423 F.3d 386 (4th Cir. 2005).

75. *Hamdi v. Rumsfeld,* 542 U.S. 507 (2004).

76. Of particular note was the alliance of Justice Stevens, one of the Supreme Court's most liberal justices, with Justice Scalia, one of the Court's most conservative justices. The two together argued in their dissent that the liberty interest protected by due process does not permit the creation of special

regimes to address circumstances like those of Hamdi. In their view, the Court should have ordered that Hamdi be indicted and tried by a criminal court in the normal fashion or released. Justice Thomas, on the other end of this continuum, stated in his dissent that the president as commander in chief must have absolute power over the pursuit of military objectives once Congress has authorized that action, and that no court may review the president's decisions in that regard.

77. S.J. Res. 23, Pub. L. No. 107-40, 115 Stat. 224 (2001).

78. *See* the Non-Detention Act, 18 U.S.C. § 4001(a). Justices Souter and Ginsburg concluded that Hamdi's detention was barred by the Non-Detention Act but concurred in the result of the plurality opinion to provide a basis for a majority decision.

79. *Hamdi v. Rumsfeld*, 542 U.S. 507 (2004).

80. *Id.*

81. *Id.*

82. *Id.*

83. *Id.*

84. *Id.*

85. Ronald Dworkin, "What the Court Really Said," *New York Review of Books*, 51, no. 13 (Aug. 12, 2004).

86. Adam Liptak, "Still Searching for a Strategy Four Years After Sept. 11 Attacks," *New York Times*, Nov. 23, 2005.

87. *Id.*

88. *See* President George W. Bush, "President's November 20, 2005 Memorandum for the Secretary of Defense," (Nov. 20, 2005), on file with the author.

89. Matt Welch, "Dirty Bummer: Why the White House Should Make Its Case Against Jose Padilla, but Won't," *Hawaii Reporter* Nov. 23, 2005.

90. *Id.*

91. *See* Associated Press, "U.S. Indicts Padilla After 3 Years In Pentagon Custody," *Associated Press*, (Nov. 22, 2005).

92. Order denying motion to transfer petitioner, Dec. 21, 2005, *Padilla v. Hanft*, No. 05-6396 (4th Cir. filed Dec. 21, 2005).

93. *Hanft v. Padilla*, 126 S. Ct. 978 (Roberts, Circuit Judge 2006).

94. *See* Editorial, "Government Blinks in 'Dirty Bomber' Case," *Miami Herald* Nov. 25, 2005.

95. *See Osborn v. Bank of the United States*, 22 U.S. (9 Wheat.) 738, 827 (1924) ("[A naturalized citizen] becomes a member of the society, possessing all the rights of a native citizen, and standing, in the view of the Constitution, on the footing of a native. The Constitution does not authorize Congress to enlarge or abridge those rights."); *Agosto v. INS*, 436 U.S. 748, 753 (1978).

96. Under Mr. Lindh's plea agreement, in exchange for Mr. Lindh's ongoing cooperation with government investigations, the government expressly agrees to "[forgo] any right it has to treat [Mr. Lindh] as an unlawful enemy combatant." Plea Agreement, *United States v. Lindh*, (E.D. Va. 2002) (No. 02-37-A), p. 21.

97. The Bush administration has to date been unwilling or unable to explain how it decides whether someone is an "enemy combatant" and can be held without charge, or a criminal subject to federal law. According to a report in the *New York Law Journal*, "Walking a Thin Line," published on November 22, 2002: "When asked how an enemy combatant designation is made, the White House referred the question to the Justice Department. The Justice Department referred the question to the White House. The White House did not return subsequent phone inquiries." http://www.nylawyer.com/news/02/11/112202h.html.

98. *See* Jess Bravin, "More Terror Suspects May Sit In Limbo," *Wall Street Journal*, Aug. 8, 2002, A4; Jonathan Turley, "Camps for Citizens: Ashcroft's Hellish Vision," *Los Angeles Times*, Aug. 14, 2002; Anita Ramasastry, "Do Hamdi and Padilla Need Company? Why Attorney General Ashcroft's Plan To Create Internment Camps For Supposed Citizen Combatants Is Shocking and Wrong," *Findlaw Commentary*, Aug. 21, 2002.

99. Anita Ramasastry, "Do Hamdi and Padilla Need Company? Why Attorney General Ashcroft's Plan To Create Internment Camps For Supposed Citizen Combatants Is Shocking and Wrong," *Findlaw Commentary*, Aug. 21, 2002.

100. *Hamdi v. Rumsfeld*, 542 U.S. 507 (2004) (emphasis added).

101. Additional Protocol I, art. 43(2).

102. *Id.*, art. 51(3) ("Civilians shall enjoy the protection afforded by this Section, unless and for such time as they take a direct part in hostilities.").

103. *See* ICRC Commentary on the Additional Protocols 619 (C. Pilloud et al., eds., 1987) (noting that there is "a clear distinction between direct participation in hostilities and participation in the war effort," for large portions of the civilian population may indirectly support the war effort and should not by virtue of that become targets).

104. *See* Fourth Geneva Convention, arts. 42, 43, 78; Additional Protocol I, art. 75(4).

105. *See* Declaration of Michael Mobbs, Special Advisor to the Undersecretary of Defense for Policy at 1, *Padilla v. Bush* (Aug. 27, 2002).

106. *See* Jennifer Elsea, "Presidential Authority to Detain Enemy Combatants," 33 *Presidential Studies Quarterly*, 568 (Sept. 2003).

107. *See Ex parte Milligan*, 71 U.S. (4 Wall.) 2, 15, 21, 131 (1866).

108. *See United States ex rel. Wessels v. McDonald*, 256 F. 754 (E.D.N.Y. 1920).

109. *See United States v. Fricke*, 259 F. 673 (S.D.N.Y. 1919); *United States v. Robinson*, 259 F. 685 (S.D.N.Y. 1919).

110. *See Hamdi v. Rumsfeld*, 542 U.S. 507 (2004).

111. The legislative history from the time of the passage of the act makes clear that Congress was concerned about the possibility that a president might seek to exercise exactly the type of detention power that President Bush has exercised in the "war on terror." The central purpose of § 4001(a) was to ensure that a declaration of war—or a simple authorization of the use of military force—would not be deemed to provide the president with the authority to detain American citizens without charge or trial, as many tens of thousands of Japanese American citizens had been detained under President Roosevelt's 1942 Executive Order. Congressman Railsback, who introduced the provision now codified at 18 U.S.C. § 4001(a), explained that express purpose of the provision was "to try to do something about what occurred in 1942 through President Roosevelt's Executive Order." 117 *Cong. Rec.* 24, 31550 (1971).

112. *See* Daniel J. Meador, *Habeas Corpus and Magna Carta: Dualism of Power and Liberty* 24 (1966).

113. The Federalist No. 84 (Hamilton).

114. U.S. Const. art. I, § 9, cl. 2; *Ex parte Bollman, 8 U.S. (4 Cranch) 75, 101 (1807); Ex parte Merryman, 17 F. Cas. 144, 148-49 (C.C.D. Md. 1861).*

115. U.S. Const. art. I, § 9, cl. 2; *see* 2 Joseph Story, Commentaries on the Constitution of the United States § 1342 (5th ed. 1891).

116. *See Kennedy v. Mendoza-Martinez*, 372 U.S. 144, 160 (1963).

117. *See Youngstown Sheet & Tube Co. v. Sawyer*, 343 U.S. 579, 649-50 (1952) (Jackson, J., concurring).

118. *Youngstown Sheet & Tube Co. v. Sawyer*, 343 U.S. 579, 587-88 (1952).

119. U.S. Const. art. I.

120. U.S. Const. art. II, § 3.

121. *Field v. Clark*, 143 U.S. 649, 692 (1892).
122. *New York Times Co. v. United States*, 403 U.S. 713, 742-43 (1971).
123. AUMF, Pub. L.107-40, 115 Stat, 224 (Sept. 18, 2001).
124. *Id.* (emphasis added).
125. *See Hamdi*, 542 U.S. 507, 124 S. Ct. at 2640, 2641-42 ("[T]he AUMF authorizes the President to use 'all necessary and appropriate force' against 'nations, organizations, or persons' *associated with the September 11, 2001, terrorist attacks.*") (Emphasis added).
126. U.S. Const., art. II, cl. 2.
127. *Ex parte Quirin*, 317 U.S. at 28.
128. *Loving v. United States*, 517 U.S. 748, 758 (1996) ("The lawmaking function belongs to Congress . . . and may not be conveyed to another branch or entity.").
129. *See, e.g., United States v. Curtis-Wright Export Corp.*, 299 U.S. 304, 315 (1936) ("That there are differences between [external and internal affairs], and that these differences are fundamental, may not be doubted."); *Youngstown Sheet & Tube Co. v. Sawyer*, 343 U.S. 579, 645-46 (1952) (Jackson, J., concurring) ("I should indulge the widest latitude of interpretation to sustain [the president's] exclusive function to command the instruments of national force, at least when turned against the outside world for the security of our society. But, when it is turned inward . . . it should have no such indulgence."). *See also* Hon. Juan R. Torruella, "On the Slippery Slope of Afghanistan: Military Commissions and the Exercise of Presidential Power," 4 *U. Pa. J. Const. L.* 648, 655 (2002).
130. *Youngstown*, 343 U.S. at 642 (Jackson, J., concurring).
131. *Youngstown*, 343 U.S. at 644 (Jackson, J., concurring).
132. The Declaration of Independence, http://www.archives.gov/national_archives_experience/declaration_transcript.html (last visited June 22, 2005).
133. *Dow v. Johnson*, 100 U.S. 158, 169 (1879).
134. *See Little v. Barreme*, 6 U.S. 170 (1804) (Court found that the president's military order exceeded the limited war powers that Congress had delegated him and was therefore unlawful).

CHAPTER FOUR

1. Ted Conover, "In the Land of Guantánamo," *New York Times*, June 29, 2003.
2. *See* Amnesty Interntational, "Memorandum for Amnesty International to the United States Government on the rights of people in custody in Afghanistan and Guantánamo Bay," Apr. 24, 2002, http://web.amnesty.org/ai.nsf/recent/AMR510532002; Human Rights Watch, "U.S.: Growing Problem of Guantánamo Detainees," May 30, 2002, www.hrw.org/; American Red Cross, "ICRC Visits Afghan Detainees," Jan. 18, 2002, http://www.redcross.org/news/in/intlaw/020118detainees.html.
3. Christopher Cooper, "Detention Plan in Guantánamo, Prisoners Languish in a Sea of Red Tape," Wall Street Journal, Jan. 26, 2005.
4. *Id.*
5. Carol Rosenberg, "Guantánamo Bay: Stadium Lights to Boost Security," Miami Herald, Jan. 10, 2006. In fact, the activists marched in Santiago Province miles away from the facility.
6. Christopher Cooper, "Detention Plan in Guantánamo, Prisoners Languish in a Sea of Red Tape," Wall Street Journal, Jan. 26, 2005.
7. Christopher Cooper, "Detention Plan in Guantánamo, Prisoners Languish in a Sea of Red Tape," Wall Street Journal, Jan. 26, 2005 (quoting Brigadier General Jay Hood, then Guantánamo's commander).

8. *See* Mark Huband, "US Officer Predicts Guantánamo Releases, Financial Times," Oct. 4, 2004, http://news.ft.com/cms/s/192851d2-163b-11d9-b835-00000e2511c8.html; John Mintz, "Most at Guantánamo to Be Freed or Sent Home, Officer Says," Washington Post, Oct. 6, 2004, A16.

9. *See* Tim Golden and Don Van Natta, Jr., "U.S. Said to Overstate Value of Guantánamo Detainees," N.Y. Times, Jun. 21, 2004 (stating that "[o]fficials of the Department of Defense now acknowledge that the military's initial screening of the prisoners for possible shipment to Guantánamo was flawed"); *id.* (citing 2002 report by a "senior CIA analyst" concluding that "a substantial number of the detainees appeared to be either low-level militants . . . or simply innocents in the wrong place at the wrong time"); "Frontline: Son of Al Qaeda," PBS Television Broadcast, Apr. 11, 2004, http://www.pbs.org/wgbh/pages/frontline/shows/khadr/interviews/khadr.html (quoting CIA operative who had spent a year undercover at Guantánamo as estimating that "only like 10 percent of the people that are really dangerous, that should be there and the rest are people that don't have anything to do with it, don't even, don't even understand what they're doing here").

The administration's assertion that the Guantánamo detentions enable the military to gather vital intelligence has now been seriously questioned by senior military officials, including Steve Rodriguez, the Head of Interrogations at Guantánamo. *See* 'Peter Jennings Reporting: Guantánamo," (ABC television broadcast, June 25, 2004) (quoting Mr. Rodriguez as stating that only "20, 30, 40, maybe even 50 [of the Guantánamo detainees] are providing critical information today"); *id.* (quoting Lt. Col. Anthony Christino as stating that there is a continuing intelligence value . . . for [s]omewhere around a few dozen, a score at the most" of the Guantánamo detainees). *See* http://abcnews.go.com/2020/2020_Guantánamo_040625_1.html.

10. Samara Kalk Derby, "How Expert Gets Detainees to Talk," The Capital Times & Wisconsin State Journal, Aug. 16, 2004, 1A.

11. Human Rights Watch, "The Road to Abu Ghraib," June 5, 2004; "Suspect at Guantánamo Attempts Suicide," Associated Press, Aug. 26, 2003.

12. *See* e.g., "Tales of Despair From Guantánamo," New York Times, June 17, 2003.

13. "U.S. Admits Gitmo Numbers Puzzle," Reuters via the New York Post, Aug. 12, 2003.

14. The British and Australian governments have confirmed some of the detainees who are incarcerated on the base.

15. *Rasul v. Bush*, 542 U.S. 466 (2004).

16. Bob Herbert, "Stories from the Inside," New York Times, Feb. 7, 2005.

17. *Id.*

18. Geneva Convention III Relative to the Treatment of Prisoners of War, art. 5, Aug. 12, 1949, 6 U.S.T. 3316, U.N.T.S. 135.

19. Arlie Hochschild, "Arrested Development," New York Times, June 29, 2005.

20. *Id.*

21. *Id.*

22. *Id.*

23. *See* Human Rights Watch Report, "The New Iraq? Torture and Ill-Treatment of Detainees In Iraqi Custody," Jan. 2005, http://www.hrw.org/reports/2005/iraq0105/index.htm.

24. Ted Conover, "In the Land of Guantánamo," New York Times, June 29, 2003.

25. *Id.* The United States signed the CRC on February 16, 1995, but it has never sent the treaty to the Senate for ratification.

26. The Optional Protocol to the CRC extends its protections to all children under the age of eighteen. *See also* United Nations Rules for the Protection of Juveniles Deprived of their Liberty, U.N. GA Res. 45/113 (14 December 1990) at p. 11(a) ("A juvenile is every person under the age of 18."), http://www.ohchr.org/english/law/res45_113.htm; African Charter On the Rights and Welfare of

the Child, art. 2 (*entered into force* Nov. 29, 1999) ("[A] child means every human being below the age of 18 years.").

27. Lois Whitman, Human Rights Watch letter to Defense Secretary Donald Rumsfeld, Human Rights Watch Apr. 24, 2003, avail. at http://www.hrw.org.

28. *Id.*

29. In addition, international law has recognized the need for stronger protections for children involved in armed conflict. On December 23, 2002, the United States became a party to the Optional Protocol to the Convention on the Rights of the Child on the involvement of children in armed conflict. Under Article 7 of the Protocol, the United States must also assist in the demobilization, rehabilitation, and social reintegration of children who have been recruited or used in armed conflict.

30. *O.K., et al. v. Bush*, 377 F. Supp. 2d 102 (D.D.C. 2005) (denying detainee's motion for a preliminary injunction to stop the government from subjecting him to torture or interrogation); *O.K., et al. v. Bush*, 344 F. Supp. 2d 44 (D.D.C. 2004) (denying detainee's motion to compel the government to allow an independent medical evaluation and to produce medical records).

31. Carol Rosenberg, "Pentagon Moving Ahead with Tribunal for Canadian Teenager," *Knight Ridder News Service*, Dec. 1, 2005.

32. *Roper v. Simmons*, 543 U.S. 551 (2005).

33. The ICCPR was signed by the United States on October 5, 1977, and ratified on June 8, 1992.

34. The Republic of The Gambia is a republic located in West Africa, surrounded by Senegal on three sides and the Atlantic Ocean. The Gambia was colonized by Britain and gained its independence on February 18, 1965. The Gambia is a member of the British Commonwealth of Nations. The Gambia's most recent elections were deemed free and fair by international observers. Extradition from The Gambia to the United States is controlled by the Extradition Treaty between the United States and the United Kingdom signed on December 22, 1931. The Gambia and the United States are at peace.

35. Telegrams were sent by MI5, the British Intelligence Service, to the CIA informing them that Mr. Al-Rawi knew a leading Islamist, Abu Qatada. According to Mr. Al-Rawi, however, he had been enlisted by MI5 to assist them with "the non-violent arrest of Abu Qatada, and British agents had even thanked him for doing so." Council of Europe, Parliamentary Assembly, Committee on Legal Affairs and Human Rights, "Alleged Secret Detentions and Unlawful Inter-state Transfers Involving Council of Europe Member States," ¶ 168, June 7, 2006, Draft Report - Part II (Mr. Dick Marty, Special Rapporteur).

36. Council of Europe, Parliamentary Assembly, Committee on Legal Affairs and Human Rights, "Alleged Secret Detentions and Unlawful Inter-state Transfers Involving Council of Europe Member States," ¶¶ 165-167, June 7, 2006, Draft Report - Part II (Mr. Dick Marty, Special Rapporteur). According to the Special Rapporteur, the telegrams were made public on March 27, 2006, after a public hearing in the Queens Bench Division of the High Court in London, before Lord Justice Latham and Mr. Justice Tugendhat.

37. Amnesty International, "Partners in Crime: Europe's Role in US Renditions," Aug. 1, 2006, 42-43.

38. Council of Europe, Parliamentary Assembly, Committee on Legal Affairs and Human Rights, "Alleged Secret Detentions and Unlawful Inter-state Transfers Involving Council of Europe Member States," ¶ 167, June 7, 2006, Draft Report - Part II (Mr. Dick Marty, Special Rapporteur).

39. First Amended Habeas Petition ¶¶ 1-19, *El-Banna v. Bush*, No. 1:04-CV-01144 (D.D.C. filed July 8, 2004).

40. Amnesty International, "Partners in Crime: Europe's Role in US Renditions," Aug. 1, 2006, 42-43.

41. *Id.*, 43.

42. First Amended Habeas Petition ¶ 19, *El-Banna v. Bush*, No. 1:04-CV-01144 (D.D.C. filed July 8, 2004).

43. *See* Affidavit of Solicitor Gareth Peirce filed in *El-Banna v. Bush*, Exhibit B (Mar. 9, 2004), p. 5. *See* Amnesty International, Human Rights Forgotten in U.S.A.'s 'War on Terrorism,'" Amnesty International, Mar. 2003.

44. Council of Europe, Parliamentary Assembly, Committee on Legal Affairs and Human Rights, "Alleged Secret Detentions and Unlawful Inter-state Transfers Involving Council of Europe Member States," ¶ 173, June 7, 2006, Draft Report - Part II (Mr. Dick Marty, Special Rapporteur).

45. *Id.*, Pierce Affidavit at p. 23.

46. Council of Europe, Parliamentary Assembly, Committee on Legal Affairs and Human Rights, "Alleged Secret Detentions and Unlawful Inter-state Transfers Involving Council of Europe Member States," ¶ 173 and n.155, June 7, 2006, Draft Report - Part II (Mr. Dick Marty, Special Rapporteur).

47. *See generally, Boudellaa v. Bosnia and Herzegovina*, Nos. CH/02/8679; CH/02/8689; CH/02/8690; CH/02/8691, H.R. Chamber for Bosnia and Herzegovina (Oct. 11, 2002).

48. *See* Boumedienne Petition for A Writ of Habeas Corpus, Civil Action No. 04-1166 (RL).

49. Decision and Order of the Supreme Court of the Federation of Bosnia-Herzegovina, No. Ki-1001/01 (Sarajevo, Jan. 17, 2002).

50. *See* H.R. Chamber Decision at pp. 53-55.

51. *See* J. David Yeager, "The Human Rights Chamber for Bosnia and Herzegovina: A Case Study in Transnational Justice," 14 Int'l Legal Persp. 44, 51 (2004).

52. *See id.*

53. Michelle Faul, "Guantánamo Prisoners Say Arabs, Muslims Sold by Pakistanis to Americans," Associated Press, June 9, 2005.

54. *Id.*

55. Ann Woolner, "Top Court Tells Bush He Isn't Above the Law, Again," Bloomberg.com (June 30, 2006).

56. *Id.*

57. Michelle Faul, "Guantánamo Prisoners Say Arabs, Muslims Sold by Pakistanis to Americans," Associated Press, June 9, 2005.

58. *Id.*

59. *Id.*

60. Saul Hudson, "Zarkawi Bounty May Go Unpaid But Rewards Aid Fight," Reuters, June 9, 2006.

61. Katharine Q. Seelye, "A Nation Challenged: Captives; An Uneasy Routine at Cuba Prison Camp," *New York Times*, Mar. 16, 2002 (quoting Deputy Commander at Guantánamo). In fact, it seems likely that many of the people thought to be "victims of circumstance" are those who were turned in to the Northern Alliance or U.S. forces under the "bounty program" established by the government. Under the government's program, amounts ranging from $5,000 to $35,000 were paid for each alleged Al Qaeda follower turned over to the U.S. authorities in Afghanistan. *See* National Public Radio Report, "Hamdi to Go Free in Detainee Compromise," Sept. 23, 2004.

62. Charles Savage, "For Detainees At Guantánamo, Daily Benefits—and Uncertainty," *Miami Herald*, Aug. 24, 2003.

63. Ted Conover, "In the Land of Guantánamo," *New York Times*, June 29, 2003.

64. *Id.*

65. In 2003, the Center for Constitutional Rights, the American Civil Liberties Union, Physicians for Human Rights, Veterans for Common Sense, and Veterans for Peace filed a FOIA request seeking documents from the Central Intelligence Agency, Department of Justice, the Department of State, the Department of Defense and the Federal Bureau of Investigation, concerning treatment of detainees in U.S. custody in Afghanistan, Guantánamo Bay, Cuba, and Iraq. The vast majority of documents were released only following protracted and ongoing litigation and court orders directing government

agencies to produce documents. Stipulation and Order, *American Civil Liberties Union Foundation v. Dep't of Defense*, No. 04-cv-4151 (S.D.N.Y. Aug. 17, 2004), *available at* http://www.aclu.org/torturefoia/legaldocuments/eeOrderforResponsivedocs.pdf.

66. *See* Eric Saar & Viveca Novak, Inside The Wire: A Military Intelligence Soldier's Eyewitness Account Of Life At Guantánamo (2005); James Yee & Aimee Molloy, For God And Country: Faith And Patriotism Under Fire (2005).

67. Robert K. Goldman, *Trivializing Torture: The Office of Legal Counsel's 2002 Opinion Letter and International Law Against Torture*, Human Rights Brief, at 3.

68. Shafiq Rasul and Asif Iqbal, Open letter to the U.S. Senate Armed Services Committee, May 13, 2004.

69. Guantánamo Bay Detainee Statements: Jum'ah Mohammed AbdulLatif Al Dossari, Isa Ali Abdulla Al Murbati, Abdullah Al Noaimi and Adel Kamel Abdulla Haji 5 (May 2005). Joshua Colangelo-Bryan, of the law firm Dorsey & Whitney, telephone interview with author, June 8, 2005.

70. Guantánamo Bay Detainee Statements, Jum'ah Mohammed AbdulLatif Al Dossari, Isa Ali Abdulla Al Murbati, Abdullah Al Noaimi and Adel Kamel Abdulla Haji 5 (May 2005). Joshua Colangelo-Bryan, of the law firm Dorsey & Whitney, telephone interview with author, June 8, 2005.

71. *Id.*

72. Shafiq Rasul, Asif Iqbal, Rhuhel Ahmed, "Composite Statement: Detention in Afghanistan and Guantánamo Bay" (July 23, 2004), avail. at http://www.ccr-ny.org/v2/reports/docs/Gitmo-compositestatementFINAL23july04.pdf

73. Center for Constitutional Rights, "*Summary of FBI Interview of Detainee at Guantánamo Bay*" (Detainees #3913-14), Oct. 12, 2002 (date of record), www.aclu.org/torturefoia/released/052505.

74. "Hunger Strikers Force-fed at Camp X-Ray," Assoc. Press, Apr. 1, 2002; "Watching Over the World's Most Infamous Prisoners," Newhouse News Service, Mar. 22, 2002 ("The protests began Feb. 27, a day after an Army guard removed a turban from the head of a detainee who said he was praying. . . . At the peak 194 detainees refused meals, but the number has been getting smaller."); *see also* Jim Garamone, "Tensions Ease at Guantánamo Holding Facility," Am. Forces Press Serv., Mar. 1, 2002, *available at* www.defenselink.mil/news/Mar2002/n03012002_200203012.html.

75. Sgt. 1st Class Kathleen T. Rhem, "Some Al Qaeda, Taliban Detainees Refuse Food," Am. Forces Press Serv., Feb 28, 2002, *available at* www.defenselink.mil/news/Feb2002/n02282002_200202284.html.

76. "U.S. Stops Tracking Food Refusals at Guantánamo," CNN, Mar. 14, 2002.

77. *Id.*

78. "Two 'Hard Core' Detainees Accept First Meal In Two Weeks, Breaking Longstanding Hunger Strike," Assoc. Press, Mar. 13, 2002.

79. "Lone Detainee in Guantánamo Continues Hunger Strike," Assoc. Press, May 10, 2002.

80. *Summary of FBI Interview of Detainee at Guantánamo*, (Detainees #3913), Oct. 12, 2002 (date ofrecord), *available at* www.aclu.org/torturefoia/released/052505; *Summary of FBI Interview of Detainee at Guantánamo*, (Detainees #3939), Nov. 28, 2002 (date of record), *available at* www.aclu.org/torturefoia/released/052505; *Summary of FBI Interview of Detainee at Guantánamo*, (Detainees #3943), Dec. 2, 2002 (date of record), *available at* www.aclu.org/torturefoia/released/052505.

81. Audiolink available at http://roberts.senate.gov/press_releases.html (July 11, 2005).

82. Daniel Conney, "Two Men Claim Hunger Strike at Guantánamo," Assoc. Press, Jul. 21, 2005.

83. Statement made to Mr. Deghayes habeas counsel, Clive Stafford Smith, on record with the author.

84. Jonathan Hafetz of the Brennan Law Center, telephone interview by author, May 15, 2006.

85. *Id.*

86. Stevenson Jacobs, "U.S. Denies Guantánamo Bay Prison Abuse," Assoc. Press, Sept. 2, 2005.

87. *Id.*
88. *Id.*
89. Declaration of Julia Tarver, Esq., *Majid Abdulla Al Joudi, et al. v. George W. Bush*, et al., 05-civ-0301 (GK) (Oct. 2005), on file with the author.
90. *Id.*
91. Tim Golden, "Tough U.S. Steps in Hunger Strike at Camp in Cuba," *New York Times*, Feb. 9, 2006.
92. Eric Schmitt and Tim Golden, "Force-Feeding at Guantánamo Is Now Acknowledged," *New York Times*, Feb. 22, 2006.
93. *Id.*
94. Carlotta Gall and Neil A. Lewis, "Threats and Responses: Captives—Tales of Despair from Guantánamo," *New York Times* June 17, 2003, A1.
95. "Suspect at Guantánamo Attempts Suicide," Associated Press, Aug. 26, 2003.
96. Katherine Q. Seelye, "Guantánamo Bay Faces Sentence of Life as Permanent U.S. Prison," *New York Times*, Sept. 16, 2002 (quoting prison hospital director Capt. Albert Shimkus).
97. Paisley Dodds, "23 at Guantánamo Attempted Suicide in 2003," Associated Press, Jan. 24, 2005.
98. *Id.*
99. "Terror Suspects at Guantánamo Attempted Mass Hanging and Strangling Protest in 2005, U.S. Military Reports," Associated Press, Jan. 25, 2005; "Detainees Sought Suicide En Masse; Guantánamo Jail Attempts Revealed," *Chicago Tribune*, Jan. 25, 2005, at 1.
100. *Id.*
101. *Id.*
102. . Josh White, "U.S.: 3 Guantánamo Inmates Commit Suicide," *Washington Post* (June 10, 2006).
103. Carol Rosenberg, "Saudi Suicide Victims Identified; Navy Imam Arrives at Guantánamo," Miami Herald (June 11, 2006).
104. BBC Today Programme, "Interview with Mark Denbeaux," (June 12, 2006).
105. Michael Gordon, "Guantánamo Guards Tighten Security to Prevent More Deaths," Knight Ridder Newspapers (June 12, 2006).
106. Terry Henry, Senior Trial Attorney, U.S. Department of Justice (representing the government), telephone interview with author, June 12, 2006.
107. Carol Rosenberg, "Saudi Suicide Victims Identified; Navy Imam Arrives at Guantánamo," Miami Herald (June 11, 2006).
108. Peter Graff, "U.S. Rows Back from Guantánamo Suicide Comments," Reuters (June 12, 2006).
109. Manuel Roig-Franzia, "Risk That Detainees Will Harm Themselves Is Heightened By Conditions At Prison, Say Psychologists," *Washington Post* (Mar. 2, 2003).
110. Manuel Roig-Franzia, "Risk That Detainees Will Harm Themselves Is Heightened By Conditions At Prison, Say Psychologists," *Washington Post* (Mar. 2, 2003).
111. *See* Geneva Convention Relative to the Treatment of Prisoners of War, art. 3, ¶ 1, August 12, 1949, 75 U.N.T.S. 135 (Third Convention), and Geneva Convention Relative to the Protection of Civilian Persons in Time of War art. 3, ¶ 1, August 12, 1949, 75 U.N.T.S. 287 (Fourth Convention).
112. *See* Third ConventionI, art. 130, and Fourth Convention, art. 147.
113. International Covenant on Civil and Political Rights, G.A. Res. 2200A (XXI), Art. 4, 21 U.N. GAOR, 21st Sess., Supp. No. 16, at 52, U.N. Doc. A/6316 (1966) (entered into force Jan. 3, 1976), *available at* http://www.ohchr.org/english/law/pdf/iccpr.pdf.
114. *General Comment No. 20, supra* note 20, ¶ 3.
115. Convention against Torture and Other Cruel, Inhuman, or Degrading Treatment or Punishment art. 2, ¶ 2, GA Res. 39/46, (Dec. 10 1984), *reprinted in* 23 ILM 1027 (1984), *as modified,* 24 ILM 535 (1985).

116. ICCPR art. 4.

117. U.N. Human Rights Committee, *GeneralComment 29 (States of Emergency, Article 4) in Compilation of General Comments and General Recommendations* Adopted By Human Rights Treaty Bodies, 13, U.N. Doc. CCPR/C/21/Rev.1/Add.11 (Aug. 31, 2001), http://www.hri.ca/fortherecord2001/documentation/tbodies/ccpr-c-21-rev1-add11.htm; U.N. Human Rights Committee, *General Comment 20 (Article 7)*, http://www.unhchr.ch/tbs/doc.nsf/0/ca12c3a4ea8d6c53c1256d500056e56f/$FILE/G0441302.pdf.

118. Article 3 states "no one shall be subjected to torture or to inhuman, or degrading treatment or punishment."

119. In *Chahal v United Kingdom* (1996) 23 EHRR 413, the European Court stated "Article 3 enshrines one of the most fundamental values of democratic society. The Court is well aware of the immense difficulties faced by States in modern times in protecting their communities from terrorist violence. However, even in these circumstances, the Convention prohibits in absolute terms torture or inhuman, or degrading treatment or punishment, irrespective of the victim's conduct. Unlike most of the substantive clauses of the Convention . . . Article 3 makes no provision for exceptions and no derogation from it is permissible under Article 15 even in the event of a public emergency threatening the life of the nation."

120. Goldman, *supra* note 46, at 3.

121. *Rochin v. California*, 342 U.S. 165, 172-173 (1952) (finding the illegal break-in of the petitioner's homeby government agents, the struggle to force open petitioner's mouth, and the forcible extraction of his stomach's contents to retrieve pills "shock[ed] the conscience" and violated Rochin's due process rights).

122. *Trop v. Dulles*, 356 U.S. 86, 101 (1958).

123. *See, e.g., City of Revere v. Massachusetts Gen. Hosp.*, 463 U.S. 239, 244 (1983); *County of Sacramento v. Lewis*, 523 U.S. 833, 849-50 (1998) (affirming that due process rights of pretrial detainees are "at least as great as the Eighth Amendment protections available to a convicted prisoner").

124. *See, e.g., Hope v. Pelzer*, 536 U.S. 730, 738 (2002) (finding "gratuitous infliction of 'wanton and unnecessary'" pain when officers made inmate take his shirt off, attached him to a hitching post in the sun for seven hours, given no bathroom break, given water only once or twice and at least one guard taunted Hope for being thirsty); *Estelle v. Gamble*, 429 U.S. 97 (1976) (failure to provide essential medical treatment constitutes cruel and unusual punishment); *see also Simpson v. Socialist People's Libyan Arab Jamahriya*, 326 F.3d 230, 234 (D.C. Cir. 2003) (to assess whether an act is cruel or degrading treatment a court must look at the victims' suffering which depends upon the totality of circumstances. "[T]orture is a label 'usually reserved for extreme, deliberate and unusually cruel practices, for example . . . tying up or hanging in positions that cause extreme pain'").

125. The five experts included the chairperson of the Working Group on Arbitrary Detention four Special Rapporteurs on torture, the independence of lawyers and judges, the right to health, and the right to religious freedom.

126. U.N. Commission on Human Rights, "Situation of the Detainees at Guantánamo Bay," U.N. Doc. E/CN.4/2006/120 (Feb. 15, 2006), http://news.bbc.co.uk/1/shared/bsp/hi/pdfs/16_02_06_un_Guantánamo.pdf.

127. U.N. Commission on Human Rights, "Situation of the Detainees at Guantánamo Bay," ¶87, U.N. Doc. E/CN.4/2006/120 (Feb. 15, 2006).

128. U.N. Commission on Human Rights, "Situation of the Detainees at Guantánamo Bay," ¶87, U.N. Doc. E/CN.4/2006/120 (Feb. 15, 2006); U.N. CAT Report at ¶22; *see also* ¶36.

129. *See* U.N. Committee against Torture, "Conclusions and Recommendations of the Committee against Torture: United States," (May 19, 2006), http://www.ohchr.org/english/bodies/cat/docs/AdvanceVersions/CAT.C.USA.CO.2.pdf. The U.N. Committee against Torture is the body created

to oversee country compliance with the Convention Against Torture and Other Cruel, Inhuman, or Degrading Treatment or Punishment.

130. See U.N. Committee against Torture, "Conclusions and Recommendations of the Committee against Torture: United States," (May 19, 2006), http://www.ohchr.org/english/bodies/cat/docs/AdvanceVersions/CAT.C.USA.CO.2.pdf.

131. "EU Parliamentarians Call for Tribunal to Replace Guantánamo," Deutsche Well (June 15, 2006).

132. Reuters, "Geneva Convention Doesn't Cover Detainees," Jan. 11, 2002.

133. The Geneva Conventions consist of four international law instruments: the Geneva Convention for the Amelioration of the Condition of the Wounded and Sick in Armed Forces in the Field, Aug. 12, 1949, 6 U.S.T. 3114, 75 U.N.T.S. 31; the Geneva Convention for the Amelioration of the Condition of the Wounded, Sick and Shipwrecked Members of Armed Forces at Sea, Aug. 12, 1949, 6 U.S.T. 3217, 75 U.N.T.S. 85; the Geneva Convention Relative to the Treatment of Prisoners of War, Aug. 12, 1949, 6 U.S.T. 3316, 75 U.N.T.S. 135; and the Geneva Convention Relative to the Protection of Civilian Persons in Time of War, Aug. 12, 1949, 6 U.S.T. 3516, 75 U.N.T.S. 287. Article 2, common to all four Geneva Conventions, provides that "the present Convention shall apply to all cases of declared war or of any other armed conflict which may arise between two or more of the High Contracting parties, even if the state of war is not recognized by one of them."

134. U.S. Const. art. VI.

135. The supremacy clause declares the following: "This Constitution, and the Laws of the United States which shall be made in Pursuance thereof; and all Treaties made, or which shall be made, under the Authority of the United States, shall be the supreme Law of the Land; and the Judges in every State shall be bound thereby, any Thing in the Constitution or Laws of any State to the Contrary notwithstanding." (U.S. Const. art VI., cl. 2).

136. U.S. Const. art. III, § 2, cl. 1 (emphasis added).

137. See Army Regulation 190-8, Enemy Prisoners of War, Retained Personnel, Civilian Internees and Other Detainees § 1-5(a)(2) (1997), http://www.apd.army.mil/pdffiles/r190_8.pdf. Army Regulation 190-8 states that: "In accordance with Article 5, [Third Geneva Convention], if any doubt arises as to whether a person, having committed a belligerent act and been taken into custody by U.S. Armed Forces, belongs to any of the categories enumerated in Article 4, [Third Geneva Convention], such persons shall enjoy the protection of the present Convention until such time as their status has been determined by a competent tribunal." (AR 109-8 § 1-6(a) (1997)).

138. U.S. Const. art. VI, cl. 2.

139. Third Geneva Convention, art. 13, 75 U.N.T.S. at 146.

140. Id.

141. Id.

142. Id., art. 17, 75 U.N.T.S. at 150.

143. See id., art 21, 75 U.N.T.S. at 152-54; art. 22, 75 U.N.T.S. at 154.

144. See Army Regulation 109-8.

145. See AR 109-8 §§ 1-6(c), (e).

146. Department of Defense, Conduct of the Persian Gulf War: Final Report to Congress, Appendix L at 577 (1992), http://www.ndu.edu/library/epubs/cpgw.pdf.

147. George H. Aldrich, The Taliban, Al Qaeda, and the Determination of Illegal Combatants, 96 Am. J. Int'l L. 891, 898 (2002).

148. See Jim Garamone, DefenseLink News (US Military), American Forces Press Service, Feb. 7, 2002.

149. Alberto R. Gonzales, White House Counsel, "Memorandum from Alberto R. Gonzales to the President," Jan. 25, 2002, copy on file with the author.

150. On January 22, 2002, Jay Bybee, Assistant Attorney General working in the Office of Legal Counsel, wrote a memorandum to Alberto Gonzalez, Counsel to the president, and William J. Haynes III, General Counsel of the Defense Department. This memo concluded that "customary international law does not bind the president or the U.S. Armed Forces in their decisions concerning the detention and conditions of al-Qaeda and Taliban prisoners." Jay S. Bybee , "Memorandum to Alberto Gonzales, Counsel to the President and William J. Haynes, General Counsel, Department of Defense, *Re: Application of treaties and laws to al Qaeda and Taliban detainees*," (Jan. 22, 2002) at 37, http://www.gwu.edu/~nsarchiv/NSAEBB/NSAEBB127/02.01.22.pdf.

151. *Id.*

152. The War Crimes Act, 18 U.S.C. § 2241, authorizes punishment for the commission of a war crime, including torture and humiliating or degrading treatment, by or against a U.S. national, including members of the armed forces.

153. *Id.*

154. *Id.*

155. Colin Powell, Secretary of State, "Memorandum from Secretary of State Colin Powell to Counsel to the President and Assistant to the President for National Security Affairs," Department of State, Jan. 26, 2002. The Powell Memo noted that disavowing the Conventions, among other things, would: (a) "undermine the protections of the laws of war for our troops, both in this specific conflict and in general"; (b) have a "high cost in terms of negative international reaction, with immediate adverse consequences for our conduct of foreign policy"; (c) "undermine public support among critical allies making military cooperation more difficult to sustain"; (d) "provoke some individual foreign prosecutors to investigate and prosecute our officials and troops"; (e) "make us more vulnerable to domestic and international legal challenge and deprive us of important legal options"; (f) "be challenged in international fora"; and (g) "deprive[] us of a winning argument to oppose habeas corpus actions in U.S. courts." Powell Memo at 1-3.

156. *See* John Ashcroft, U.S. Attorney General, "Letter to President George W. Bush," Feb. 1, 2002, copy on file with the author.

157. President George W. Bush, "Memorandum from President George W. Bush to the Vice President, et al., Re: Humane Treatment of al Qaeda and Taliban Detainees," (Feb. 7, 2002) at 2, http://www.gwu.edu/~nsarchiv/NSAEBB/NSAEBB127/02.02.07.pdf.

158. President George W. Bush, "The Humane Treatment of Al Qaeda and Taliban Detainees," White House Memorandum, Feb. 7, 2002.

159. Written responses from Timothy Flanigan to questions submitted by U.S. Senator Richard Durbin following Flanigan's confirmation hearing to become U.S. Deputy Attorney General, (July 26, 2005), 2, http://balkin.blogspot.com/flanigan.durbin.pdf.

160. *See* Reuters, "Geneva Convention Doesn't Cover Detainees," Jan. 11, 2002.

161. Secretary Rumsfeld stated that the government would "for the most part, treat them in a manner that is reasonably consistent with the Geneva Conventions, to the extent they are appropriate." Reuters, "Geneva Convention Doesn't Cover Detainees," Jan. 11, 2002.

162. *See* Patrick F. Philbin and John C. Yoo, "Memorandum for William J. Haynes, II, General Counsel for the Department of Defense, Possible Habeas Jurisdiction over Aliens Held in Guantánamo Bay, Cuba," Dec. 28, 2001, http://www.msnbc.msn.com/id/5022681/site/newsweek.

163. *Id.* at 8.

164. Dana Priest and R. Jeffrey Smith, "Memo Offered Justification for Use of Torture," *Washington Post*, June 8, 2004.

165. Jay S. Bybee, Office of Legal Counsel, Justice Department, "Memorandum for Alberto R. Gonzales, Counsel to the President," (Aug. 1, 2002), http://news.findlaw.com/wp/docs/doj/bybee80102mem.pdf.

166. *Id.* at 1.
167. *Id.*
168. *Id.* at 3.
169. *Id.* at 4.
170. *Id.* at 8.
171. *Id.* at 22.
172. *See id.* at 39-41.
173. *Id.* at 41.
174. *Id.* at 42.
175. *Id.* at 44-45.
176. Convention Against Torture, art. 16.
177. *Id.*
178. The Geneva Conventions also incorporate this principle. The Third Geneva Convention protects even unlawful combatants who do not qualify as prisoners of war from "humiliating and degrading treatment" and "mutilation, cruel treatment and torture." Art. 3, 1.
179. *See* Daniel Levin, Acting Assistant Attorney General, "Memorandum to James B. Comey, Deputy Attorney General," Dec. 30, 2004, copy on file with the author.
180. U.S. Department of Defense, "Working Group Report on Detainee Interrogations in the Global War on Terrorism: Assessment of Legal, Historical, Policy and Operational Considerations," at 2 (Apr. 4, 2003).
181. *Id.*
182. Department of Defense, "Working Group Report," at 358-59.
183. Donald Rumsfeld, "Memorandum from Donald Rumsfeld, Secretary of Defense to Commander, US Southern Command, Re: Counter-Resistance Techniques in the War on Terrorism," (Apr. 16, 2003), at 1-4, http://www.washingtonpost.com/wp-srv/nation/documents/041603rumsfeld.pdf.
184. Department of Defense, "Working Group Report," at 354, 358-59.
185. Donald Rumsfeld, "Memorandum from Donald Rumsfeld, Secretary of Defense to Commander, US Southern Command, Re: Counter-Resistance Techniques in the War on Terrorism," (Apr. 16, 2003), at 1-4, http://www.washingtonpost.com/wp-srv/nation/documents/041603rumsfeld.pdf.
186. ACLU, "Enduring Abuse: Torture and Cruel Treatment by the United States at Home and Abroad," (April 2006), 23, Annex B1-3; *see also* Josh White, "Soldiers' 'Wish Lists' of Detainee Tactics Cited," *Washington Post*, Apr. 19, 2005.
187. James R. Schlesinger, et al., "Final Report of the Independent Panel to Review DoD Detention Operations," (Aug. 2004), 14, http://www.defenselink.mil/news/Aug2004/d20040824finalreport.pdf.
188. Eric Lichtblau, "Gonzales Says Humane-Policy Order Doesn't Bind CIA," N.Y. Times, Jan. 19, 2005.
189. *John B. Bellinger III Delivers Opening Remarks at the U.N. Committee Against Torture*, May 5, 2006, eMediaMillworks Political Transcripts (published May 10, 2006), *available in* Westlaw, allnewsplus database. *See also* Committee Against Torture, *Summary Record of the 703d Meeting, Consideration of Reports Submitted by State Parties under Article 19 of the Convention, Second periodic report of the United States of America,* ¶¶ 38-40, at 8, CAT/C/SR.703, May 12, 2006, http://daccessdds.un.org/UNDOC/GEN/G06/418/46/G0641846.pdf?OpenElement.
190. *See* William Pfaff, "The Truth About Torture," *American Conservative*, Feb. 14, 2005.
191. *See* http://action.aclu.org/torturefoia for FBI documents detailing conflict with Defense Department personnel on proper interrogation techniques.
192. *See* William Pfaff, The Truth About Torture, *American Conservative*, Feb. 14, 2005.
193. 28 U.S.C. § 2241.
194. 28 U.S.C. § 2241 (c) (3).

195. *Rasul v. Bush,* 542 U.S. 466 (2004).
196. *Rasul v. Bush,* 542 U.S. 466 (2004);
197. Agreement for the Lease to the United States of Lands in Cuba for Coaling and Naval Stations, 23 Feb. 1903, art. III, T.S. No. 418. The terms "exclusive jurisdiction and control" and "ultimate sovereignty" are not defined in the lease.
198. *See The History of Guantánamo Bay: An Online Edition,* http://www.nsgtmo.navy.mil/history.htm.
199. Gerald L. Neuman, *Surveying Law and Borders: Anomalous Zones,* 48 STAN. L. REV. 1197, 1198 (1996).
200. *See, e.g., United States v. Lee,* 906 F.2d 117 (4th Cir. 1990) (criminal case involving Jamaican national); *United States v. Rogers,* 388 F. Supp. 298, 301 (E.D. Va. 1975) (criminal case involving U.S. citizen working at Guantánamo).
201. *Rasul v. Bush,* 542 U.S. 466 (2004).
202. 28 U.S.C. § 2241.
203. *Rasul v. Bush,* 542 U.S. 466 (2004).
204. 28 U.S.C. § 1350.
205. *Rasul v. Bush,* 542 U.S. 466 (2004).
206. *Rasul v. Bush,* 542 U.S. 466, 124 S. Ct. 2686, 2696 (2004).
207. *Id.*
208. *Id.* at 2698 n.15.
209. *Id.* at 2693.
210. *See, e.g., Ex parte Quirin,* 317 U.S. 1, 19-20 (1942) (German saboteurs given right to present facts in aid of their habeas petition through counsel); *Yamashita v. Styer,* 327 U.S. 1, 5 (1946) (Japanese general accused of supervising war crimes in the Philippines given right to present facts through counsel); *see also Ludecke v. Watkins,* 335 U.S. 160, 173 (1948); *Ex parte Milligan,* 71 U.S. 2, 5-6, 107 (1866); *Colepaugh v. Looney,* 235 F.2d 429, 431 (10th Cir. 1956).
211. *Ex parte Hull,* 312 U.S. 546, 549 (1941); see *Johnson v. Avery,* 393 U.S. 483, 485 (1969); *Wolff v. McDonnell,* 418 U.S. 539, 579 (1974).
212. *In re Guantánamo Detainee Cases,* 355 F. Supp. 2d 443 (D.D. C. 2005).
213. *In re Guantánamo Detainee Cases,* 355 F. Supp. 2d. 443 (D.D. C. 2005).
214. *See* Memorandum from Paul Wolfowitz, Deputy Sec'y of Defense, to the Sec'y of the Navy, Order Establishing Combatant Status Review Tribunal (July 7, 2004), http://www.defenselink.mil/news/Jul2004/d20040707review.pdf.
215. The U.S. government appears to recognize, correctly, that the constitutional validity of the procedures should be judged by the standard articulated by the U.S. Supreme Court plurality decision in *Hamdi v. Rumsfeld,* 124 S. Ct. 2633 (2004). In *Hamdi,* a plurality of the Court declared that "enemy combatants" must be given a "fair opportunity to rebut the government's factual assertions before a neutral decision maker." 124 S. Ct. at 2648; *see also, e.g., Concrete Pipe & Prods. v. Constr. Laborers Pension Trust,* 508 U.S. 602, 617 (1993) ("[D]ue process requires a 'neutral and detached judge in the first instance.'") (quoting *Ward v. Monroeville,* 409 U.S. 57, 61-62 (1972)). The Court in *Hamdi* also recognized that the petitioner in that case had been accorded "unmonitored" access to his counsel and "unquestionably has the right to access to counsel in connection with the proceedings on remand." 124 S. Ct. at 2652. The CSRT procedures do not remotely satisfy the standards articulated in *Hamdi* because they do not provide a "neutral decision maker," do not give the petitioners a "fair opportunity" to rebut the government's allegations, and do not involve representation by counsel.
216. CSRT Order, ¶ a (emphasis added).
217. CSRT Order, ¶ e.

218. *Cf. Gibson v. Berryhill*, 411 U.S. 564, 577 (1973) (where a state board "was incompetent by reason of bias to adjudicate the issues before it . . . [the district court] need not defer to the Board"); *Cinderella Career & Finishing Schools, Inc. v. FTC*, 425 F.2d 583, 591 (D.C. Cir. 1970) (administrative hearings "must be attended, not only with every element of fairness but with the very appearance of complete fairness" and as a result "[t]he test for disqualification . . . is whether a disinterested observer may conclude that the agency has in some measure adjudged the facts as well as the law in advance of hearing it").

219. *See* U.N. H.R. Committee *General Comment No. 20: Replaces General Comment No. 7 concerning prohibition of torture and cruel treatment or punishment (Art. 7)* (March 10, 1992), ¶ 12 (hereinafter *General Comment No. 20*) (to discourage violations of Article 7's prohibition of torture and cruel, inhuman, or degrading treatment, "the law must prohibit the use or admissibility in judicial proceedings of statements obtained through torture or other prohibited treatment").

220. Mark Denbeaux, "No-Hearing Hearings, CSRT: The Modern Habeas Corpus?" Seton Hall University, Nov. 2006, http://law.shu.edu/news/final_no_hearing_hearings_report.pdf .

221. Mark Denbeaux, "No-Hearing Hearings, CSRT: The Modern Habeas Corpus?" Seton Hall University, Nov. 2006, http://law.shu.edu/news/final_no_hearing_hearings_report.pdf .

222. CSRT Order, ¶ (g)(8).

223. Mark Denbeaux, "No-Hearing Hearings, CSRT: The Modern Habeas Corpus?" Seton Hall University, Nov. 2006, http://law.shu.edu/news/final_no_hearing_hearings_report.pdf .

224. CSRT Order, ¶ (g)(12).

225. 124 S. Ct. at 2696.

226. Indeed, in at least one instance, the government has neglected to provide a detainee with a letter from counsel advising him not to participate in the CSRT hearing.

227. 124 S. Ct. at 2639.

228. CSRT Order, ¶ (a).

229. Stevenson Jacobs, *Guantánamo: Prisoner Says Taliban Forced Him to Cook*, Associated Press (Aug. 12, 2004).

230. *See* Kathleen T. Rhem, *Reporters Offered Look Inside Combatant Status Review Tribunals*, American Forces Press Service (Aug. 29, 2004).

231. John Riley, "The 'Gulag Of Our Times'; In Warning To U.S., Amnesty International Says Guantánamo Abuses May Lead To Leaders' Prosecutions," NEWSDAY (May 26, 2006), at A4. *See also* Dep't of Defense "Order Re: Administrative Review Procedures for Enemy Combatants in the Control of the Department of Defense at Guantánamo Bay Naval Base, Cuba," (May 11, 2004), ¶3(A)(iii)(a)(3), http://www.defenselink.mil/news/May2004/d20040518gtmoreview.pdf.

232. "Dep't of Defense Designated Civilian Official Administrative Review of the Detention of Enemy Combatants at U.S. Naval Base Guantánamo, Cuba. Memorandum Subject: Implementation of Administrative Review Procedures for Enemy Combatants Detained at U.S. Naval Base Guantánamo Bay, Cuba," (Sept. 14, 2004), http://www.defenselink.mil/news/Sep2004/d20040914adminreview.pdf. *See also* Press Release, "U.S. Dep't of Defense, GTMO Detainees (Mar. 28, 2006), http://www.defenselink.mil/home/dodupdate/documents/20060328a.html; "Memorandum from Gordon England, Sec'y of the Navy to Sec'y of State, et al., *Re: Implementation of Combatant Status Review Tribunal Procedures for Enemy Combatants Detained at Guantánamo Bay Naval Base, Cuba,"* (July 29, 2004), http://www.defenselink.mil/news/Jul2004/d20040730comb.pdf; *In re Guantánamo Detainee Cases*, 355 F.Supp.2d at 450 (The opinion summarizes the tribunals by writing "[t]he detainees do not have a right to counsel in the proceedings, although each is assigned a military officer who serves as a 'Personal Representative' to assist the detainee in understanding the process and

presenting his case. Formal rules of evidence do not apply, and there is a presumption in favor of the government's conclusion that a detainee is in fact an 'enemy combatant.'").

233. *See generally* http://www.defenselink.mil/news/Combatant_Tribunals.html.

234. U.S. Defense Department, "Detainee Transfer Announced," July 20, 2005, http://www.defenselink.mil/cgi-bin/dlprint.cgi?http://www.defenselink.mil/releases/2005/nr20050720-4122.html.

235. Memorandum Opinion of Federal Judge Gladys Kessler, *Al-Joudi v. Bush*, Civ. No. 05-301 (Apr. 4, 2005), 3.

236. *Id.* at 4.

237. Memorandum Opinion of Federal Judge Gladys Kessler, *Al-Joudi v. Bush*, Civ. No. 05-301 (Apr. 4, 2005), 4.

238. *Id.* at 9.

239. *Id.* at 9; *see* U.S. State Department, "Country Reports on Human Rights," 2004, http://www.state.gov/g/drl/rls/hrrpt/2004.

240. *See, e.g.,* Nancy Gibbs with Viveca Novak, *Inside "The Wire"; Security breaches. Suicidal detainees. A legal challenge heading to the Supreme Court. Welcome to Guantánamo,* Time Magazine, December 8, 2003, at 40. ("U.S. officials concluded that some detainees were there because they had been kidnapped by Afghan warlords and sold for the bounty the U.S. was offering for al-Qaeda and Taliban fighters. 'Many would not have been detained under the normal rules of engagement,' the source concedes").

241. Amnesty International has reported that for Mr. al-Qadasi's transfer to Guantánamo "[h]is head was shaved, he was blindfolded, made to wear ear muffs and a mouth mask, handcuffed, shackled, loaded on to a plane and flown out to Guantánamo. [...] He told Amnesty International that the flight to Guantánamo lasted around 24 hours." Amnesty International, "Torture and Secret Detention: Testimony of the 'Disappeared' in the War on Terror," 2005, at 12-13, http://web.amnesty.org/library/index/engamr511082005.

242. *See generally* Department of State, "Country Reports on Human Rights Practices, 2004: Yemen," at § 1(c) (Noting many reports of government security forces using torture on detainees and that "[t]he [Yemeni] Government acknowledged publicly that torture occurred"), http://www.state.gov/g/drl/rls/hrrpt/2004/41736.htm. The State Department's report continues, "[p]rison conditions [in Yemen] were poor and did not meet internationally recognized standards, and the Government permitted limited visits by independent human rights observers. The Government allowed limited access to detention facilities by parliamentarians and some nongovernmental organizations (NGOs). Prisons were extremely overcrowded, sanitary conditions were poor, and food and health care were inadequate to nonexistent. Prison authorities often exacted bribes from prisoners to obtain privileges, or refused to release prisoners who completed their sentences until family members paid a bribe. In some cases, authorities arrested without charge and held refugees, persons with mental disabilities, and illegal immigrants in prisons with common criminals." *Id.* at § 1(c).

243. Department of State, "Country Reports on Human Rights Practices, 2004: Yemen," http://www.state.gov/g/drl/rls/hrrpt/2004/41736.htm.

244. Human Rights Watch, "Report on Yemen," 2005, http://www.hrw.org/wr2k/Mena-11.htm.

245. Dana Priest, "Long-Term Plan Sought for Terror Suspects," *Washington Post*, Jan. 2, 2005.

246. *See* Reuters, "Lugar Condemns Plan to Jail Detainees for Life," Jan. 3, 2005.

247. *See* "Guantánamo Takes on the Look of Permanency," Associated Press, Jan. 9, 2005; Jonathan Steele. "A Global Gulag to Hide the War on Terror's Dirty Secrets," *The Guardian*, Jan. 15, 2005.

248. Reuters, "Haliburton to Build New $30 Million Guantánamo Jail," June 16, 2005.

249. Carol Rosenberg, "New Guantánamo Prison Funds Sought," *Miami Herald*, Feb. 18, 2005.

250. *See* Brief for the Commonwealth Lawyers Association submitted as amicus curiae and Brief of Legal Historians submitted as amici curiae filed in *Rasul v. Bush.*

251. 2 S.C.R. 587, pp. 25, 44, 46, 48.

252. *See* the discussion of *R. v. Cook* in the Brief of Omar Ahmed Khadr as *amicus curiae* submitted in *Rasul v. Bush.*

253. *R. v. Sec'y of State for Foreign and Commonwealth Affairs,* [2002] EWCA (Civ) 1598, at p. 66.

254. Lord Johan Steyn, Address to the British Institute of International and Comparative Law for the Twenty-Seventh F.A. Mann Lecture, (Nov. 25, 2003), http://www.nimj.org.

255. *See* M. Cherif Bassiouni, "Human Rights in The Context of Criminal Justice: Identifying International Procedural Protections And Equivalent Protections in National Constitutions," 3 Duke J. Comp. & Int'l L. 235, 261 n. 177 (1993 (listing 119 national constitutions that protect the right to be free from arbitrary arrest and detention).

256. Universal Declaration of Human Rights, art. 9, G.A. Res. 217A (III), U.N. Doc. A/810 at 71, 73 (1948). Though the Universal Declaration is not a treaty, the United States recognizes that Article 9 embodies a rule of customary international law. Richard B. Lillich & Hurst Hannum, International Human Rights: Problems of Law, Policy, and Practice 136 (3rd ed. 1995).

257. International Covenant on Civil and Political Rights, G.A. Res. 2200A (XXI), 21 U.N. GAOR Supp. No. 16, at 15, U.N. Doc. A/6316 (1966), 999 U.N.T.S. 171 [ICCPR]. The relevant provisions of the ICCPR, which the United States ratified in 1992, are unambiguous: Article 9(1): Everyone has the right to liberty and security of the person. No one shall be subjected to arbitrary arrest or detention. No one shall be deprived of his liberty except on such grounds and in according with such procedure as are established by law. . . . Article 9(4): Anyone who is deprived of his liberty by arrest or detention shall be entitled to take proceedings before a court, in other that that court may decide without delay on the lawfulness of his detention and order his release if the detention is not lawful. ICCPR, art. 9(1), 9(4); *Senate Resolution of Ratification of International Covenant on Civil and Political Rights,* 138 Cong. Rec. S4781, •S4784, 102nd Cong. (1992) (ratified Apr. 2, 1992. Of the 151 states, including the United States, that have ratified the ICCPR, none has made a relevant reservation to these provisions. *See* United Nations Treaty Collection, http://www.unhchr.ch/ html/menu3/b/ treaty4_asp.htm.

258. American Declaration of the Rights and Duties of Man, art. XXV, O.A.S.T.S. 11, adopted by the Ninth International Conference of American States (1948), *reprinted in* Basic Documents Pertaining to Human Rights in the Inter-American System, OEA/Ser.L.V/II.82 doc.6 rev.1 at 17 (1992).

259. Unlike the U.S. Supreme Court, the International Court of Justice is expressly charged to render advisory opinions at the request of an authorized body. *See* Statute of the International Court of Justice, arts. 65-68, http://www.icj-cij.org/icjwww/ibasicdocuments/ibasictext/ibasicstatute.htm. *See also Legality of the Threat or Use of Nuclear Weapons,* 1996 I.C.J. 226, 240 (Advisory Opinion of July 8), *reprinted in* 35 I.L.M. 809, 820.

260. *See* Human Rights Committee, Gen. Cmt. 8, art. 9 (16th, 1982), Compilation of General Comments and General Recommendations Adopted by Human Rights Treaty Bodies, U.N. Doc. HRI\GEN\1\Rev.1 at 8 (1994) at p. 1; Human Rights Committee, General Comment 29, States of Emergency (Article 4), U.N. Doc. CCPR/C/21/Rev.1/Add.11 (2001) at p. 16.

261. *See also Aksoy v. Turkey,* 23 E.H.R.R 553 (1996) (though Turkey had lawfully declared a national emergency, it could not hold a suspected terrorist for fourteen days without judicial intervention); *Chahal v. United Kingdom,* 23 E.H.R.R 413, p. 131 (1997) (concern for national security, though legitimate, "does not mean . . . that the national authorities can be free from effective control by the domestic courts whenever they choose to assert that national security and terrorism are involved"). *See also Ocalan v. Turkey,* Eur. Ct. H. R., [2003] ECHR 46221/99, 12 MARCH 2003, PARS. 45, 66-

76 (2003)(prompt judicial review required of detention of alleged terrorist accused of responsibility for more than 4,000 deaths).

262. *See* International Committee of the Red Cross, "States Party to the Geneva Conventions and their Additional Protocols," http://www.icrc.org/Web/Eng/siteeng0.nsf/htmlall/party_gc#a7 (May 20, 2003). The requirements of the Geneva Conventions are discussed in detail by several amici. *See* Brief of Former American Prisoners of War as *amicus curiae*; Brief of Retired Military Officials as amicus curiae.

263. Geneva Convention IV Relative to the Protection of Civilians in Time of War, Aug. 12, 1949, 6 U.S.T. 3516, 75 U.N.T.S. 287.

264. Commentary on Geneva Convention IV of Aug. 12, 1949, 51 (Jean S. Pictet, ed., 1958).

265. Decision on Request for Precautionary Measures (Detainees at Guantánamo Bay, Cuba), Inter-Am. C.H.R. (Mar. 12, 2002), *reprinted in* 41 I.L.M. 532, 533 (2002). The United States has also rejected the view of the United Nations High Commissioner for Human Rights, the United Nations Working Group on Arbitrary Detention, the United Nations Special Rapporteur on the independence of judges and lawyers, the European Parliament, the Parliamentary Assembly of the Council of Europe, the Parliamentary Assembly of the Organization for Security and Co-operation in Europe, and the International Committee of the Red Cross (ICRC), all of which disagree with the government's position on Guantánamo. *See* Statement of High Commissioner for Human Rights on Detention of Taliban and Al Qaida Prisoners at U.S. Base in Guantánamo Bay, Cuba, 16 Jan. 2002; Report on the Working Group on Arbitrary Detention, U.N. GAOR, Hum. Rts. Comm., 59th Sess., U.N. Doc. E/CN.4/2003/8 at 19-21, Dec. 16, 2002; Statement of Special Rapporteur on the independence of judges and lawyers, Dato' Param Cumaraswamy, http://www.unhchr.ch/huricane/huricane.nsf/0/0C5F3E732DBFC069C1256CE8002D76C0?opendocument (March 12, 2003); European Parliament Resolution on the European Union's Rights, Priorities and Recommendations for the 59th Session of the U.N. Commission on Human Rights in Geneva: http//europa.eu.int/abc/doc/off/bull/en/200301/p102001.htm, (Mar. 17–Apr. 25, 2003); Rights of Persons Held in the Custody of the United States in Afghanistan and Guantánamo Bay, Parliamentary Assembly Resolution No. 1340 (2003) (adopted June 26, 2003), http://assembly.coe.int/ Documents/Adopted Texts; Organization for Security and Co-operation in Europe Parliamentary Assembly Rotterdam Declaration and Resolutions Adopted during the 12th Annual Session (Rotterdam, July 5-9, 2003), http://www.osce.org/documents/pa/2003/07/495_en.pdf; International Committee of the Red Cross, "Overview of the ICRC's Work for Internees," (Nov. 6, 2003), http://www.icrc.org/Web/Eng/siteeng0.nsf/iwpList454/951C74F20D2A2148C1256D8D002CA8DC.

266. *See* U.N. Committee against Torture, "Conclusions and Recommendations of the Committee against Torture: United States," (May 19, 2006), http://www.ohchr.org/english/bodies/cat/docs/AdvanceVersions/CAT.C.USA.CO.2.pdf.; U.N. Commission on Human Rights, "Situation of the Detainees at Guantánamo Bay," ¶87, U.N. Doc. E/CN.4/2006/120 (Feb. 15, 2006).

267. Amy Goodman, Archbishop Desmond Tutu on Guantánamo, President Bush and the Invasion of Iraq," DemocracyNow (Oct. 5, 2004), http://www.democracynow.org/article.pl?sid+04/10/05/1411259.

268. Cassandra Vinograd, "Guantánamo Detentions Disgraceful," Assoc. Press (July 30, 2005).

269. BBC News, "Williams Attacks Guantánamo Camp," BBC News Online (Mar. 5, 2006), http://news.bbc.co.uk/1/hi/uk/4775446.stm.

270. *Id.*

CHAPTER FIVE

1. 66 F.R. 57833 (Nov. 16, 2001).
2. Order, § 2(a).
3. Order at §§ 4(b) and (c).
4. Order at §§ 4(8) and 7(b)(2).
5. Leigh Sales, "Leaked Emails Claim Guantánamo Trials Rigged," ABC (AU) News Online, Jan. 8, 2005.
6. *Id.*
7. *Id.*
8. *Id.*
9. *Id.*
10. *Hamdan v. Rumsfeld,* 344 F. Supp. 2d 152, 173-74 (D.D.C. 2004).
11. *Id.*
12. *Id.*
13. *Hamdan v. Rumsfeld,* 415 F.3d 33 (D.C. Cir. 2005).
14. *Id.*
15. 2005 U.S. LEXIS 8222 – Chief Justice Roberts, who was on the panel that decided the case in the Court of Appeals, took no part in consideration of the petition for certiorari, and recused himself from consideration of the case before the Supreme Court.
16. Detainee Treatment Act, Pub. L. No. 109-148, 119 Stat. 2739 (2005).
17. Detainee Treatment Act, § 1005(e).
18. *See* Brief for Respondent United States in Opposition to Petitioner's Emergency Motion for Injunction Against Further Torture of Mohammed Bawazir at 14-20, *Al Adahi v. Bush,* No. 05-0280 (D.D.C. filed Feb. 7, 2005).
19. Paul Wolfowitz, Deputy Secretary of Defense, "Memorandum For the Secretary of the Navy: Order Establishing Combatant Status Review Tribunal," July 7, 2004, at 1, http://www.defenselink.mil/news/Jul2004/d20040707review.pdf.
20. Paul Wolfowitz, Deputy Secretary of Defense, "Implementation of the Combatant Status Tribunal Review Procedures, " July 29, 2004, http:///www.defenselink.mil/news/Jul2004/d20040729review.pdf.
21. The phrase is Latin for "you [should] have the body".
22. A *writ* of habeas corpus is a court order addressed to a prison official ordering the official to bring the detainee to the court so that the court can determined whether or not that person is imprisoned lawfully and whether or not he should be released from custody.
23. *See* President's Statement on the Department of Defense, Emergency Supplemental Appropriations to Address Hurricanes in the Gulf of Mexico, and Pandemic Influenza Act, 2006, 41 Weekly Comp. Pres. Doc. 1920 (Dec. 30, 2005),http://frwebgate.access.gpo.gov/cgi-bin/getdoc.cgi?dbname+2005_presidential_documents&docid=pd30de05_txt-6.pdf.
24. *See* Brief for Respondent United States' Motion to Dismiss for Lack of Jurisdiction, at 1-2, *Hamdan v. Rumsfeld,* No. 05-185 (S. Ct. filed Aug. 8, 2005), http://www.usdoj.gov/osg/briefs/2005/3mer/2mer/2005-0184.resp.pdf.
25. *Hamdan v. Rumsfeld,* 126 S. Ct. 2749 (2006).
26. *Hamdan v. Rumsfeld,* 126 S. Ct. 2749, 2798 (2006).
27. Section 836(a) of the UCMJ.
28. *Hamdan v. Rumsfeld,* 126 S. Ct. 2749, 2798 (2006).
29. *Hamdan v. Rumsfeld,* 126 S. Ct. 2749, 2798 (2006).

30. Jonathan Weisman and Michael Abramowitz, "White House Shifts Tack on Tribunals: Bush to Propose Only Minor Changes," *Washington Post* (July 20, 2006).
31. Military Commissions Act of 2006, Pub. L. No. 109-366, 120 Stat. 2600 (2006).
32. President George W. Bush, "Press Release of June 9, 2006," (stating that "we would like to end the Guantánamo [operations] . . . I believe [the detainees] ought to be tried in courts here in the United States."), http://www.whitehouse.gov/news/releases/2006/06/20060609-2.html; President George W. Bush, "Press Release of June 14, 2006," (stating that "I'd like to close Guantánamo . . . There are some who need to be tried in U.S. courts . . . there out to be a way forward in a court of law."), http://www.whitehouse.gov/news/releases/2006/06/20060614.html.
33. Attorney General Alberto Gonzales, "Statement before the Armed Services Committee, United States Senate, Concerning Legislation in Response to *Hamdan v. Rumsfeld*," Aug. 2, 2006.
34. President George W. Bush, "Press Conference Statement of July 7, 2006,"), http://www.whitehouse.gov/news/releases/2006/06/20060707-1.html.
35. 152 Cong. Rec. S10262 (daily ed. Sept. 27, 2006), S10403.
36. MCA, Section 948a (1)(i).
37. MCA, Section 948a (1)(ii).
38. *See* David G. Savage, "Law's Reach Extends to Jails in U.S.," L.A. Times, Oct. 18, 2006.
39. *See* John Warner, John McCain, Lindsay Graham, "Looking Past the Tortured Distortions," *Wall Street Journal*, Oct. 2, 2006.
40. *See* Section 1(E) of the Military Order.
41. "Common crimes" is a legal term referring to criminal offenses that are neither war crimes nor political offenses. *See* Joan Fitzpatrick, "The Constitutional and International Invalidity of Military Commissions under the November 13, 2001 'Military Order', " on file with the author.
42. Furthermore, as the American Civil Liberties Union has correctly pointed out, the Military Order could easily be extended to include United States citizens who were tried before military commissions during World War II. *See* Timothy Edgar, "ACLU Memorandum: President Bush's Order Establishing Military Trials In Terrorism Cases" (Nov. 29, 2001), on file with the author. In the case of *Ex parte Quirn*, 317 U.S. 1 (1942), the Supreme Court held that one of the saboteurs' status as an American citizen did not exempt him from trial before the military commission because he "had violated the law of war by committing offenses constitutionally triable by military tribunal." *Id.* at 44.
43. *Wong Wing v. United States*, 163 U.S. 228 (1896)
44. *Zadvydas v. Davis*, 121 S. Ct. 2491, 2500 (2001).
45. *Id.*
46. MCA, Section 950v (b)(28).
47. Human Rights First Briefing Paper, "Trials Under Military Order" (June 2004).
48. *See Lanzetta v. New Jersey*, 306 U.S. 451 (1939). The Court recently reaffirmed the vitality of this principle in the criminal context in *Posters 'N' Things, Ltd. v. United States*, 511 U.S. 513, 524 (1997). The due process concerns embodied in the vagueness test are twofold; the doctrine is intended to ensure that (1) citizens are given fair notice of what is prohibited so that they may conform their behavior to the dictates of the law, *see Papachristou v. City of Jacksonville*, 405 U.S. 156, 162 (1972), and (2) the discretion of law enforcement officials is limited by explicit legislative standards so as to preclude arbitrary, capricious, and discriminatory enforcement. *See Grayned v. City of Rockford*, 408 U.S. 104, 108–109 (1972); *Coates v. City of Cincinnati*, 402 U.S. 611, 614 (1971).
49. *See* Elizabeth Holtzman, "Bush Seeks Immunity for Violating the War Crimes Act," *Chicago Sun Times*, September 23, 2006, http://www.suntimes.com/output/otherviews/cst-edt-ref23b.html.
50. Bradley S. Klapper, "U.S. Anti-Terror Law Concerns Red Cross," Associated Press, Oct. 19, 2006.

51. *See* Interim Rule on *Monitoring of Communications With Attorneys To Deter Acts of Terrorism*, 28 C.F.R. Parts 500 and 501 [BOP-1116; AG Order No. 2529-2001], RIN 11200-ABO8, issued by the United States Department of Justice on October 30, 2001 (Interim Rule). The Interim Rule permits the attorney general, without a prior court order, to authorize the monitoring of all communications between a person in federal custody and that person's lawyer whenever the attorney general has "reasonable suspicion" to believe that a person "may use communications with attorneys or their agents to further or facilitate acts of terrorism." 28 C.F.R. § 501.3(d). The Interim Rule is applicable to all persons in federal custody, citizens and noncitizens alike. "Terrorism" is not defined in the rule, and the notice provision of the rule states that "all communications between the inmate and attorneys may be monitored, to the extent determined to be reasonably necessary for the purpose of *deterring future acts of violence or terrorism*." 28 C.F.R. § 501.3(d)(2)(i). (Emphasis supplied.)

52. *See, e.g.,* "Memorandum on Government Monitoring of Attorney-Client Communications submitted by lawyers and legal scholars to Attorney General John Ashcroft and Patrick J. Leahy, Chairman of the Senate Committee on the Judiciary" (Dec. 4, 2001), on file with the author.

53. *See,* e.g., Reuters, "Ashcroft Defends Actions to Congress" (Dec. 6, 2001) (quoting Ashcroft as stating that "[i]f you fit this definition of a terrorist, fear the United States because you will lose your liberties"); Statement of Secretary of Defense Donald H. Rumsfeld and Deputy Secretary of Defense Paul Wolfowitz to the Senate Armed Services Committee (hereafter referred to as the Rumsfeld Statement) (Dec. 12, 2001), http://www.defenselink.mil/speeches/2001/s20011212.socdef.html.

54. U.S. Const. art. II, § 2.

55. Pub. L. 107–40 (Sept. 18, 2001).

56. 10 U.S.C. §§ 821, 836.

57. 317 U.S. 1 (1942).

58. *See* Rumsfeld Statement to the Senate Armed Services Committee.

59. These statutes were repealed in 1956 when Congress adopted the current Uniform Code of Military Justice. 10 U.S.C. §§ 1553, 1554 (repealed by Pub. L. 84-1028 (1956)).

60. International humanitarian law or "the laws of war" are designed to protect the life, health, and safety of civilians and other noncombatants (such as soldiers who are wounded or captured) and to delineate boundaries and rules regarding the methods and means by which governments may pursue a war.

61. The U.S. Department of Defense defines the law of war as follows: "3.1. Law of War. That part of international law that regulates the conduct of armed hostilities. It is often called the law of armed conflict. The law of war encompasses all international law for the conduct of hostilities binding on the United States or its individual citizens, including treaties and international agreements to which the United States is a party, and applicable customary law."

62. The Geneva Convention, Common Article 2 provides that "the present Convention shall apply to all cases of declared war or of any other armed conflict which may arise between two or more of the High Contracting Parties, even if the state of war is not recognized by one of them."

63. Part I, Art. 1(1), Protocol Additional to the Geneva Conventions of 12 August 1949, and Relating to the Protection of Victims of Non-International Armed Conflicts (Protocol II), opened for signature December 12, 1977, 1125 U.N.T.S. 609.

64. Al Qaeda does not have the same control over territory as the Taliban, and it is unlikely that it has a disciplinary system in place through which it could enforce the rules of the law of war.

65. *See,* e.g., William Carlsen, "A Cautionary Tale From Another War," *San Francisco Chronicle,* Nov. 30, 2001.

66. *See* 10 U.S.C. § 802 (listing people that are subject to the Uniform Code of Military Justice).

67. 71 U.S. 2, 210 (1866). *See* Kathleen Clark, "President Bush's Order on Military Trials of Nonciti-zens: Beyond His Constitutional or Statutory Authority," Testimony presented to the U.S. Senate Judiciary Committee Hearing on DOJ Oversight: Preserving Our Freedoms While Defending Against Terrorism, at 2–3 (Nov. 28, 2001).
68. 71 U.S. at 210.
69. 71 U.S. at 209.
70. As discussed below, any use of military commissions may be unlawful under international law even for trying violations of the laws of war.
71. Geneva Convention for the Amelioration of the Condition of the Wounded Sick in the Field, August 12, 1949 (Geneva I); Geneva Convention for the Amelioration of the Condition of the Wounded, Sick, and Shipwrecked Members of the Armed Forces at Sea, August 12, 1949 (Geneva II); Geneva Convention Relative to the Treatment of Prisoners of War, August 12, 1949 (Geneva III); Geneva Convention Relative to the Protection of Civilian Persons in Time of War, August 12, 1949 (Geneva IV); Protocol Additional to the Geneva Conventions of 12 August 1949 and Relating to the Protec-tion of Victims of International Armed Conflicts, June 8, 1977 (Protocol I); Protocol Additional to the Geneva Conventions of 12 August 1949 and Relating to the Protection of Victims of Non-Inter-national Armed Conflict, June 8, 1977 (Protocol II). The United States has ratified all four of the Geneva Conventions but neither of the protocols.
72. Since 1949, international law has recognized that armed conflict can arise within the territory of a sin-gle nation. Traditionally, intrastate conflicts, or civil wars, were considered purely matters for the states to handle by themselves, and no international law applied. However, with the adoption of Arti-cle 3 common to the four Geneva Conventions, this view was modified.
73. *See* 3rd Restatement on Foreign Relations (1987); Montevideo Convention of 1933.
74. *See generally* the Geneva Conventions; Uniform Code of Military Justice.
75. Indeed, the Pentagon's *Judge Advocate General Handbook* contains the same admonition: "when doubt exists" about a prisoner's status, "tribunals must be convened" to make a determination.
76. Amnesty International has reported that thousands of prisoners in Afghanistan are at risk from hunger, dysentery, pneumonia, and hepatitis, and that the overcrowded prison camps are suffering from severe shortages of food, medical supplies, and adequate shelter against the harsh conditions of winter. The conditions there, as well as those in Camp X-Ray, paint a terrible picture of America's descent into inhumane law enforcement measures.
77. During the Vietnam War, the United States sought revisions in the Geneva Protocols specifically to ensure that any persons captured in war are protected by the treaties, whether they were civilians, military personnel, militia, or fell into none of these categories.
78. In ratifying this covenant, the United States undertook an obligation to respect and uphold the inter-national human rights guaranteed by the covenant, not only for its own citizens, but for "all individuals within its territory and subject to its jurisdiction . . . without distinction of any kind, such as race, colour, sex language, religion, political or other opinion, national or social origin, property, birth or other status." ICCPR, Article 2.
79. Article 4 of the ICCPR provides that a country may derogate from the covenant's obligations when: (i) there is a "time of public emergency which threatens the life of the nation," (ii) the existence of such a state of affairs is "officially proclaimed," (iii) the derogation is limited to "the extent strictly required by the exigencies of the situation," (iv) the measures taken are not "inconsistent with their other obligations under international law," and (v) the measures taken do not "involve discrimination solely on the ground of race, colour, sex, language, religion, or social origin."

80. If the president or the secretary of defense were to adopt a code of offenses to be tried by military commission and then apply these laws retroactively, the United States would then be in the position of having violated the non-derogable right to be free from ex post facto laws.

81. ICCPR, Article 4(3).

82. *See,* e.g., Reuters, "UN Rights Head Backs Afghan Probe, Criticizes U.S.," Dec. 7, 2001 (reporting the concerns of U.N. Human Rights Chief Mary Robinson about the lack of safeguards built into the Military Order); Reuters, "U.S. Heads for Civil Liberties Showdown," Nov. 30, 2001 (reporting that several foreign governments, including Spain, "have come out strongly against the use of military tribunals").

83. Statement of Vice President Cheney as reported in "Bush Defends Investigation Tactics," Associated Press, Nov. 30, 2001.

84. *See,* e.g., Peter A. Schey, *Marching the War on Terrorism Towards Injustice: Military Tribunals and Constitutional Tunnels,* Publication of the Center for Human Rights and Constitutional Law, (Nov. 30, 2001), on file with the author.

85. *See,* e.g., Omnibus Diplomatic Security and Antiterrorism Act of 1986, 18 U.S.C. § 2331 (providing federal courts with extraterritorial jurisdiction over terrorist acts committed abroad against U.S. nationals); Antiterrorism and Effective Death Penalty Act of 1996, 18 U.S.C. § 2332b (creating a new federal offense penalizing acts of terrorism that transcend national boundaries).

86. *See,* e.g., 18 U.S.C. § 3521. The government has also employed special procedures to safeguard the identity of jurors, and the Bail Reform Act authorizes courts to detain a defendant pending trial.

CHAPTER SIX

1. Dana Priest and Barton Gellman, "U.S. Decries Abuse But Defends Interrogations," *Washington Post,* Dec. 26, 2002.

2. *Ker v. Illinois,* 119 U.S. 436 (1886); *Frisbie v. Collins,* 342 U.S. 519 (1952). The continued viability of the *Ker-Frisbie* doctrine, which ostensibly permits "regular" rendition, was recently affirmed by the Supreme Court in the case *Sosa v. Alvarez Machain,* 504 U.S. 655 (1992).

3. Two Presidential Decision Directives, PDD 39 and PDD 62, issued by President Clinton in the aftermath of the Oklahoma City bombings seem to have provided the foundation for the practice.

4. Douglas Jehl and David Johnston, "Rule Change Lets CIA Freely Send Suspects Abroad to Jails," *New York Times* Mar. 6, 2005.

5. 9/11 Commission Interim Report, "Formulation and Conduct of U.S. Counterterrorism Policy: Hearing before the National Commission on Terrorist Attacks Upon the United States," Mar. 23, 2004, http://www.9/11commission.gov/archive/hearing8/9/11Commission_Hearing_2004-03-23.pdf.

6. Press Release, U.S. Dep't of State, "Rice Says United States Does Not Torture Terrorists," Dec. 5, 2005, http://usinfo.state.gov/eur/Archive/2005/Dec/05-471726.html (includes transcript of Sec'y Rice's remarks upon her departure for Europe on December 5, 2005: "Renditions take terrorists out of action, and save lives. . . . Such renditions are permissible under international law.").

7. National Commission on Terrorist Attacks upon the United States, "Intelligence Policy, Staff Statement No. 7, at 2, http://www.9-11commission.gov/staff_statements/staff_statement_7.pdf. Counterterrorism Policy: Hearing Before the National Commission on Terrorist Attacks Upon the United States, at 19, Mar. 24, 2004 (statement of George Tenet, former Director of CIA), http://www.9-11commission.gov/hearings/hearing8/tenet_statement.pdf.

8. *See* Association of the Bar of the City of New York & Center for Human Rights and Global Justice, *Torture By Proxy: International and Domestic Law Applicable to "Extraordinary Renditions*, at 41-42 (New York: ABCNY & NYU School of Law, 2004).

9. *Id.* at 42.

10. R. Jeffrey Smith, "Gonzales Defends Transfer of Detainees," *Washington Post*, Mar. 8, 2005. *See also* Human Rights Watch, "Still at Risk: Diplomatic Assurances No Safeguard Against Torture," April 2005, http://hrw.org/reports/2005/eca0405.

11. United States Department of State, Second Periodic Report to the Committee against Torture, U.N. Doc. CAT/C/48/Add.4 (June 2005), § II ¶30.

12. Dana Priest and Barton Gellman, "U.S. Decries Abuse But Defends Interrogations," *Washington Post*, Dec. 26, 2002 (quoting senior United States official as stating that after an individual is rendered, the CIA is "still very much in control" and that it often "feed[s] questions to their investigators").

13. Dana Priest, "Covert CIA Program Withstands New Furor: Anti-terror Effort Continues to Grow," *Washington Post*, Dec. 30, 2005.

14. *Id.*

15. *Id.*

16. *Id.*

17. Dana Priest, "Covert CIA Program Withstands New Furor: Anti-terror Effort Continues to Grow," *Washington Post*, Dec. 30, 2005 (quoting one of the congressional and intelligence officials who were briefed on the covert presidential order).

18. *Id.*

19. *Id.*

20. *Id.*

21. Wikipedia, The Free Encyclopedia, "Unitary executive theory," Aug. 11, 2006, http://en.wikipedia.org/w/index.php?title=Unitary_executive_theory&oldid=69018898.

22. Calabresi & Rhodes, "The Structural Constitution: Unitary Executive, Plural Judiciary," Harv. L. Rev. 105: 1566 (1992).

23. Wikipedia, The Free Encyclopedia, "Unitary executive theory," Aug. 11, 2006, http://en.wikipedia.org/w/index.php?title=Unitary_executive_theory&oldid=69018898.

24. Ralph Ketchum, ed. The Anti-Federalist Papers and the Constitutional Convention Debates (Signet Classic, 1986), p. 67 ("MR. [James] WILSON entered into a contrast of the principal points of the two plans [i.e. the Virginia Plan and the New Jersey Plan]… These were… A single Executive Magistrate is at the head of the one – a plurality is held out in the other.")

25. *See*, e.g., Jeffrey Goldberg, "Breaking Ranks: What turned Brent Scowcroft against the Bush Administration," *New Yorker*, Oct. 31, 2005.

26. According to a 2005 article in the *New Yorker*, the "rendition" process was originally "a program aimed at a small, discrete set of suspects—people against whom there were outstanding foreign arrest warrants," but after September 11 came to include a "wide and ill-defined population that the administration terms 'illegal enemy combatants.'" Jane Mayer, "Outsourcing Torture," *The New Yorker*, Feb. 14, 2005, http://www.newyorker.com/fact/content/?050214fa_fact6, p. 7.

27. *See*, e.g., Megan K. Stack & Bob Drogin, "Detainee Says U.S. Handed Him Over for Torture," *L.A. Times*, Jan. 13, 2005, A1 ("News accounts, congressional testimony and independent investigations suggests [sic] that [the CIA] has covertly delivered at least 18 terrorism suspects since 1998 to Egypt, Syria, Jordan and other Middle Eastern nations where, according to State Department reports, torture has been widely used on prisoners.").

28. Dana Priest, "CIA Holds Terror Suspects in Secret Prisons," *Washington Post*, Nov. 2, 2005.

29. David Morgan, "U.S. Has Sent 60-70 Terror Suspects to Egypt – PM," Reuters, May 15, 2005.

30. U.S. Department of State Country Reports on Human Rights Practices 2003: Egypt, http://www.state.gov/g/drl/rls/hrrpt/2003/27926.html.

31. Dana Priest and Barton Gellman, "U.S. Decries Abuse But Defends Interrogations," *Washington Post*, Dec. 26, 2002.

32. Dana Priest and Dan Eggen, "Terror Suspect Alleges Torture: Detainee Says U.S. Sent Him to Egypt Before Guantánamo," *Washington Post*, Jan. 6, 2005. (quoting habeas petition filed in *Habib v. Bush*).

33. *Id.*

34. *See* Council of Europe, Parliamentary Assembly, Committee on Legal Affairs and Human Rights, "Alleged Secret Detentions and Unlawful Inter-state Transfers Involving Council of Europe Member States," June 7, 2006, Draft Report - Part II (Mr. Dick Marty, Special Rapporteur).

35. Amnesty International, "Partners in Crime: Europe's Role in U.S. Renditions," p. 16, June 14, 2006, http://web.amnesty.org/library/index/engeur010082006.

36. *See, e.g.,* U.S. Department of Defense, News Release: Detainee Releases Announced," Feb. 9, 2006, http://www.defenselink.mil/releases/2006/nr20060209-12461.html.

37. Data collected by the author from oral interviews with habeas counsel for the Guantánamo detainees.

38. Human Rights Watch, "U.S.: Don't Send Detainees Back to China," Nov. 26, 2003, http://www.hrw.org/press/2003/11/us112603.html.

39. J. White and R. Wright, "U.S. Holding Talks On Return Of Detainees," *Washington Post*, Aug. 9 2005.

40. *See* U.S. Department of Defense, Office of the Assistant Secretary of Defense (Public Affairs), News Release, "Detainee Transfer Announced," Aug. 22, 2005 (announcing that one detainee was released to Yemen, and one was released to Tajikistan), http://www.defenselink.mil/Utility/PrintItem .aspx?print=http://www.defenselink.mil/releases/2005/nr20050822-4501.html.

41. U.S. Department of State Country Reports on Human Rights Practices 2003 (see full cite at 30).

42. *See* U.S. Department of Defense, Office of the Assistant Secretary of Defense (Public Affairs), News Release, "Detainee Transfer Announced," May 5, 2006, http://www.defenselink.mil/releases/ 2006/nr20060505-12980.html.

43. Makfax, "China and Russia Request Extradition of Five Persons from Albania," Ind. News Agency, May 25, 2006.

44. J. White and R. Wright, "Afghanistan Agrees To Accept Detainees; U.S. Negotiating Guantánamo Transfers," *Washington Post*, August 5, 2005.

45. Associated Press, "Prison in Afghanistan Being 'Refurbished' for Guantánamo Detainees," Jan. 24, 2006.

46. *Id.*

47. Amnesty International, "Torture and Secret Detention: Testimony of the 'Disappeared' in the War on Terror," AMR 51/108/2005, http://web.amnesty.org/library/index/engamr511082005.

48. Dana Priest, "Long-Term Plan Sought For Terror Suspects," *Washington Post*, Jan. 2, 2005, A1.

49. U.S. Department of State Country Reports on Human Rights Practices 2004: Syria, avail. at www.state.gov/g/drl/rls/hrrpt/2004/41732.htm.

50. U.S. Department of State Country Reports on Human Rights Practices 2004: Syria, avail. at www.state.gov/g/drl/rls/hrrpt/2004/41732.htm.

51. Sixty Minutes II Television News Report, *His Year in Hell* (2004), on file with the author.

52. A Parliamentary Public Inquiry in Canada is a process much like that involved when a special prosecutor is appointed to investigate allegations of wrongdoing in the U.S. federal government.

53. The Royal Canadian Mounted Police is the Canadian analog to the FBI.

54. DeNeen L. Brown and Dana Priest, "Deported Terror Suspect Details Torture in Syria," *Washington Post*, Nov. 5, 2003, A1.

55. Douglas Jehl and David Johnston, "Rule Change Lets CIA Freely Send Suspects Abroad to Jails," *New York Times*, Mar. 6, 2005.

56. In a November 7, 2003, speech, President Bush stated that Syria had created "a legacy of torture, oppression, misery and ruin." Dana Priest, *Washington Post*, Nov. 20, 2003, A24.

57. See *Sibel Edmonds v. United States Department of Justice*, 02 CV 01448 (RBW), now No. 04-5286 on appeal.

58. *Id.*

59. Complaint ¶ 2, *El-Masri v. George Tenet*, No. 1:05cv1417 (D.D.C. filed Dec. 6, 2005), http://www.aclu.org/images/extraordinaryrendition/asset_upload_file829_22211.pdf. German Chancellor Angela Merkel told a joint news conference in Berlin with Secretary of State Condoleezza Rice that the United States had acknowledged it made a mistake in the case of Khaled el-Masri. U.S. administration officials later said the U.S. government did not admit to a "mistake" regarding El-Masri and that the U.S. had informed Germany about El-Masri's detention and release. Saul Hudson and Mark Trevelyan, "U.S.Germany Differ on CIA Abduction Case," REUTERS, Dec. 6, 2005. 60. Amnesty International, "Partners in Crime: Europe's Role in US Renditions," Aug. 1, 2006, 28.

61. Craig Whitlock, "Europeans Investigate CIA Role in Abductions, Suspects Possibly Taken To Nations That Torture," *Washington Post*, Mar. 13, 2005.

62. Institute for War and Peace Reporting, "Investigation: Macedonia Implicated in 'Abduction' Case," BCR (Balkan Crisis Report) No.538, Jan. 21, 2005, http://www.iwpr.net/?=bcr&s=f&o=242469&apc_state=henibcr2005.

63. Complaint ¶¶ 1-20, *El-Masri v. George Tenet*, No. 1:05cv1417 (D.D.C. filed Dec. 6, 2005), http://www.aclu.org/images/extraordinaryrendition/asset_upload_file829_22211.pdf.

64. Amnesty International, "Partners in Crime: Europe's Role in US Renditions," Aug. 1, 2006, 27.

65. *Id.*

66. Complaint ¶¶ 1-20, *El-Masri v. George Tenet*.

67. Amnesty International, "Partners in Crime: Europe's Role in US Renditions," Aug. 1, 2006, 28.

68. Dana Priest and Dan Eggen, "Terror Suspect Alleges Torture: Detainee Says U.S. Sent Him to Egypt Before Guantánamo," *Washington Post*, Jan. 6, 2005. (quoting habeas petition filed in *Habib v. Bush*).

69. Complaint ¶¶ 54, *El-Masri v. George Tenet*, No. 1:05cv1417 (D.D.C. filed Dec. 6, 2005), http://www.aclu.org/images/extraordinaryrendition/asset_upload_file829_22211.pdf.

70. Complaint ¶¶ 1-20, *El-Masri v. George Tenet*.

71. *Id.*

72. Craig Whitlock, "Europeans Investigate CIA Role in Abductions, Suspects Possibly Taken To Nations That Torture," *Washington Post*, Mar. 13, 2005.

73. *Id.*

74. *El-Masri v. Tenet*, 2006 WL 1391390, *8 (E.D. Va. May 12, 2006) (Ellis, J.).

75. ACLU press release, "Day in Court Denied for Victim of CIA Kidnapping and Rendition, Khaled El-Masri," May 19, 2006.

76. Press Release, U.S. Dep't of State, "Rice Says United States Does Not Torture Terrorists," Dec. 5, 2005, http://usinfo.state.gov/eur/Archive/2005/Dec/05-471726.html (includes transcript of Sec'y Rice's remarks upon her departure for Europe on December 5, 2005: "Renditions take terrorists out of action, and save lives. . . . Such renditions are permissible under international law.").

77. R. Jeffrey Smith, "Gonzales Defends Transfer of Detainees," *Washington Post*, Mar. 8, 2005.

78. See United Nations High Commissioner for Refugees, "UNHCR Note on Diplomatic Assurances and International Refugee Protection," ¶ 16 and note 25, Aug. 2006, http://www.unhcr.org.

79. U.S. Reservations and Understandings Upon Ratification of the Convention against Torture and Other Cruel, Inhuman, or Degrading Treatment or Punishment, http://www.ohchr.org/english/countries/ratification/9.htm.

80. Eric Lichtblau, "Gonzales Says Humane-Policy Order Doesn't Bind C.I.A.," N.Y. Times, Jan. 19, 2005.

81. U.S. Reservations and Understandings Upon Ratification of the Convention against Torture and Other Cruel, Inhuman, or Degrading Treatment or Punishment, http://www.ohchr.org/english/countries/ratification/9.htm.

82. Department of Defense, "Working Group Report on Detainee Interrogations in the Global War on Terrorism: Assessment of Legal, Historical, Policy and Operational Considerations," Apr. 4, 2003, reprinted in THE TORTURE PAPERS; THE ROAD TO ABU GHRAIB, at 289 (Karen J. Greenberg and Joshua L. Dratel, ed., Cambridge Univ. Press, 2005).

83. John C. Yoo, Deputy Assistant Attorney General, Office of Legal Counsel, Letter to Alberto Gonzales, Counsel to the President, Aug. 1, 2002, reprinted in THE TORTURE PAPERS: THE ROAD TO ABU GHRAIB, at 220.

84. Jay S. Bybee, "Memorandum from Jay S. Bybee, Assistant Attorney General, Office of Legal Counsel to Alberto Gonzales, Counsel to the President, Re: Standards of Conduct for Interrogation Under 18 U.S.C. §§ 23440-23440A," Aug. 1, 2002, http://news.findlaw.com/wp/docs/doj/bybee80102mem.pdf.

85. Daniel Levin, Acting Deputy Assistant Attorney General, Office of Legal Counsel, "Memorandum to James Comey, Deputy Attorney General, Re. Legal Standards Applicable Under 18 U.S.C. § 2340-2340A," Dec. 30, 2004, http://www.usdoj.gov/olc/dagmemo.pdf.

86. From: Responses from Alberto R. Gonzales (then Nominee for Attorney General) to the written questions ofSenator Dianne Feinstein (Jan. 2005), *excerpt available at* http://web.amnesty.org/library/Index/ENGAMR510832005?open&of=ENG-IRQ. See also: Eric Lichtblau, "Gonzales Says Humane-Policy Order Doesn't Bind C.I.A.," N.Y. Times, Jan. 19, 2005.

87. U.N. Committee Against Torture, "Conclusions and Recommendations of the Committee Against Torture: United States of America," ¶ 15, May 2006, http://www.un.org/

88. U.N. Committee Against Torture, "Conclusions and Recommendations of the Committee Against Torture: United States of America," ¶ 20, May 2006, http://www.un.org/

89. Special Rapporteur of the U.N. Commission on Human Rights on torture and other cruel, inhuman, or degrading treatment or punishment, "Report submitted pursuant to General Assembly resolution 58/164," at ¶ 37, Sept. 1 2004, U.N. document A/59/324.

90. The U.S. government has consistently refused to provide information on how diplomatic assurances are negotiated and secured.

CHAPTER SEVEN

1. Major General Antonio Taguba, "Article 15-6 Investigation of the 800th Military Police Brigade." (an investigative report, on alleged abuses at U.S. military prisons in Abu Ghraib and Camp Bucca, Iraq), ¶ 33 (emphasis added).

2. Dana Priest and Scott Higham, "At Guantánamo , a Prison Within a Prison," *Washington Post*, Dec. 17, 2004.

3. David Johnston and Scott Shane, "CIA Fires Senior Officer Over Leaks," *New York Times*, Apr. 22, 2006.

4. *See* Dana Priest, "CIA Holds Terror Suspects in Secret Prisons," *Washington Post*, Nov. 2, 2005.

5. *See* Dana Priest, "CIA Holds Terror Suspects in Secret Prisons," *Washington Post*, Nov. 2, 2005.

6. Dana Priest, "CIA Holds Terror Suspects in Secret Prisons," *Washington Post*, Nov. 2, 2005.

7. Jay S. Bybee, Office of Legal Counsel, Justice Department, "Memorandum for Alberto R. Gonzales, Counsel to the President," Aug. 1, 2002, http://news.findlaw.com/wp/docs/doj/bybee90102mem.pdf.

8. Josh White, "Rumsfeld Authorized Secret Detention of Prisoner," *Washington Post*, June 18, 2004, A22.

9. Amnesty International, "The Threat of A Bad Example—Undermining International Standards as 'War on Terror' Detentions Continue," AI Index: AMR 51/114/2003, Aug. 2003.

10. Human Rights First, "Ending Secret Detention," June 18, 2004. *See also* Human Rights Watch, "Enduring Freedom: Abuses by U.S. Forces in Afghanistan," (Mar. 2004), http://www.hrw.org/reports/2004/afghanistan0304/.

11. Amnesty International, "Human Dignity Denied," 101-02.

12. Dana Priest and Scott Higham, "At Guantánamo, A Prison Within a Prison," *Washington Post*, Dec. 17, 2004, A1; David Johnston and Neil Lewis, "Officials Describe Secret CIA Center at Guantánamo Bay," *New York Times*, Dec. 18, 2004. Apparently, the Secret CIA Center was closed in 2004. See Dana Priest, "CIA Held Terror Suspect in Secret Prisons," *Washington Post*, (Nov. 2, 2005).

13. Lieutenant General Anthony R. Jones and Major General George Far, "AR 15-6 Investigation of Intelligence Activities at Abu Ghraib," 4.

14. Lieutenant General Anthony R. Jones and Major General George Fay, "AR 15-6 Investigation of Intelligence Activities at Abu Ghraib," 44-45.

15. Human Rights First, "Behind the Wire," Mar. 2005, 5.

16. *See* "Final Report of the Independent Panel To Review DOD Detention Operations," 87, Aug, 2004; "Rumsfeld Ordered Prisoner Hidden," CBS NEWS, June 17, 2004, http://www.cbsnews.com/stories/2004/06/17/iraq/main624411.shtml.

17. Human Rights First, "Behind the Wire," Mar. 2005, 5; Amnesty International, "USA: Guantánamo and Beyond," May 13, 2005, 4.

18. Douglas Jehl and Neil A. Lewis, "U.S. Said to Hold More Foreigners in Iraq Fighting," *New York Times*, Jan. 8, 2005, A1.

19. Douglas Jehl, "U.S. Sees No Basis to Prosecute Iranian Opposition 'Terror' Group Being Held in Iraq," N. Y. Times, July 27, 2004.

20. Dana Priest, "Memo Lets CIA Take Detainees Out of Iraq Practice Called Serious Breach of Geneva Conventions, " *Washington Post*, Oct. 25, 2004

21. Eric Schmitt and Thom Shanker, "Prison Abuse: Rumsfeld Issued An Order to Hide Detainee In Iraq," *New York Times*, June 17, 2004.

22. *Id.*

23. Josh White, "Rumsfeld Authorized Secret Detention of Prisoner," *Washington Post*, June 18, 2004, A22.

24. Major General Antonio Taguba, "Article 15-6 Investigation of the 800th Military Police Brigade."

25. Major General Antonio Taguba, Article 15-6 Investigation of the 800th Military Police Brigade, at p. 33.

26. Eric Schmitt and Douglas Jehl, "Army Says CIA Hid More Iraqis Than It Claimed," *New York Times*, Sept. 10, 2004.

27. Senate Armed Services Committee, "Investigation of the 205th Military Intelligence Brigade at Abu Ghraib Prison, Iraq: Before the Senate Armed Services Comm., 108th Cong., Sept 9, 2004 (statement of General Paul Kern).

28. *Id.;* Eric Schmitt and Douglas Jehl, "Army Says CIA Hid More Iraqis Than It Claimed," *New York Times*, Sept. 10, 2004.

29. *See* Human Rights Watch, "The United States' Disappeared: The CIA's Long-term 'Ghost Detainees'," (Oct. 2004), 8; John McWethy, ABC News: Nightline, May 13, 2004.

30. *See* Department of the Army, The Inspector General, "Detainee Operations Inspection," July 21, 2004, 46, 56-58.

31. Human Rights First Report, "Behind the Wire: An Update to Ending Secret Detentions," Mar. 2005; Amnesty International, "USA: Guantánamo and Beyond," May 13, 2005, 3-5; ICRC, International Committee of the Red Cross, "ICRC Operational Update," Mar. 29, 2005; U.S. Department of Defense, "Department of Defense Briefing on Detention Operations and Interrogation Techniques," Mar. 10, 2005.

32. Dana Priest, "CIA Avoids Scrutiny of Detainee Treatment," *Washington Post,* Mar. 3, 2005, A1; Amnesty International, "USA: Guantánamo and Beyond," May 13, 2005, 142; Human Rights First, "Behind the Wire," Mar. 2005, 2.

33. Human Rights First, "Behind the Wire," Mar. 2005, 2.

34. *See respectively,* Department of the Army, Inspector General, "Detainee Operations Inspection," Appendix C, July 21, 2004; Carlotta Gall, "Afghan Man's Death at U.S. Outpost is Investigated," N.Y. Times, July 5, 2004; Larry Neumeister, "Army Destroyed Mock Execution Pictures," Assoc. Press, Feb. 18, 2005, http://abcnews.go.com/Politics/wireStory?id=511104; Dana Priest and Joe Stephens, "Secret World of U.S. Interrogation: Long History of Tactics in Overseas Prisons is Coming to Light," *Washington Post,* May 11, 2004; John Daniszewski, "Afghans Report Abuse in Jails," L.A. Times, May 23, 2004; Human Rights Watch, "Behind the Wire," March 2005 (Interview with released Afghan detainee-1 in Kabul, Afghanistan (Aug. 16, 2004); Interview with detainee 1]; Interview with released Afghan detainee-2 in Kabul, Afghanistan (Aug. 18, 2004); Interview with released Afghan detainee-3 in Kabul, Afghanistan (Aug. 18, 2004).

35. Department of the Army, The Inspector General, "Detainee Operations Inspection," July 21, 2004, 30.

36. Human Rights First, "Behind the Wire," Mar. 2005, 2.

37. Human Rights First, "Behind the Wire," Mar. 2005, 3; Amnesty International, "USA: Guantánamo and Beyond," May 13, 2005, 4.

38. President George W. Bush, "Memorandum to Vice President Richard Cheney," Feb. 7, 2002, http://www.washingtonpost.com/wp-srv/nation/documents/dojinterrogationmemo20020801.pdf.

39. *See* "Final Report of the Independent Panel to Review DoD Operations," Aug. 2004, 81.

40. International Committee of the Red Cross, "United States: ICRC President Urges Progress on Detention-Related Issues," Press Release, Mar. 4, 2004, http://www.icrc.org/Web/Eng/siteeng0.nsf/iwpList74/774F1B35A7E20CC9C1256E1D007741C1.

41. "Rights Groups Raise Concerns over Secret U.S.-Run Prisons in Afghanistan," Agence France-Presse, June 19, 2004.

42. Human Rights First, "Behind the Wire," Mar. 2005, 11; Carlotta Gall and Mark Lander, "A Nation Challenged: The Captives," *New York Times,* Jan. 5, 2002, at A5; Roy Gutman, Christopher Dickey and Sami Yousafzai, "Guantanamo Justice?," *Newsweek,* July 8, 2003, http://www.cageprisoners.com/pr_articles.php?aid=41 (accessed Jan. 20, 2005);

43. Human Rights First, "Behind the Wire," Mar. 2005, 11;Yossi Melman, "CIA Holding Al-Qaida Suspects in Secret Jordanian Lockup," Haaretz, Oct. 13, 2004, http://www.informationclearinghouse.info/article7066.htm (accessed Jan. 19, 2005); David Kaplan and Ilana Ozernoy, "Al Qaeda's Desert Inn," *U.S. News and World Report,* June 2, 2003, at 22-3.

44. Human Rights First, "Behind the Wire," Mar. 2005, 11; Gadi Dechter, "Britain: No U.S. Interrogations on Our Soil," UPI, May 19, 2004, *available at* LEXIS, News Library; Hansard Parliamentary Debates, Jan. 8, 2003, Col. 1020, http://www.parliament.the-stationeryoffice.co.uk/

pa/ld199900/ldhansrd/pdvn/lds03/text/30108-04.htm. (accessed Jan. 21, 2005); Hansard Parliamentary Debates, March 3, 2003, Col. 603, http://www.publications.parliament.uk/pa/cm200203/cmhansrd/vo030303/debtext/30303-11.htm#30303-11_spnew0 (accessed Jan. 21, 2005); Dana Priest and Barton Gellman, "U.S. Decries Abuse but Defends Interrogations: 'Stress and Duress' Tactics Used on Terrorism Suspects Held in Secret Overseas Facilities," *Washington Post*, Dec. 26, 2002, A1; Mark Seddon, "Is There Another Guantanamo Bay on British Soil," Independent (London), Dec. 13, 2003, at 21; Dana Priest, "Long-Term Plan Sought For Terror Suspects," *Washington Post*, Jan. 2, 2005, A1; Dana Priest and Scott Higham, "At Guantanamo, a Prison Within a Prison," *Washington Post*, Dec. 17, 2004, at A1.

45. See Expeditionary Strike Force One, U.S. Naval Special Operations Command Office of Public Affairs, "ESG 1 Strikes From the Sea," Jan. 5, 2004 (reporting coalition force .takedowns. of vessels carrying drugs, including one with 15 individuals with possible links to Al Qaeda, and reporting ten of the individuals from . . . two takedowns have been transferred to a secure, undisclosed location for further questioning by U.S. officials.), http://www.navsoc.navy.mil/esg1/pdf/dhowtakedown.pdf (accessed Jan. 20, 2005); Grant Holloway, *Australia to Question al Qaeda Fighter*, CNN.COM, Dec. 19, 2001, *available at* http://www.cnn.com/2001/WORLD/asiapcf/auspac/12/19/aust.talban-dit20.12/ (accessed Jan. 20, 2005); "Australian Taliban Fighter Handed Over to U.S. Military Forces in Afghanistan," ASSOC. PRESS, Dec. 17, 2001, http://multimedia.belointeractive.com/attack/military/1217australia.html (accessed Jan. 20, 2005).

46. Human Rights First, "Behind the Wire," Mar. 2005, 10 (referring to U.S. Army Criminal Investigation Command Report received in response to FOIA request).

47. Yossi Melman, "CIA Holding Al-Qaida Suspects in Secret Jordanian Lockup," Haaretz, Oct. 13, 2004, http://www.informationclearinghouse.info/article7066.htm.

48. David Kaplan and Ilana Ozernoy, "Al Qaeda's Desert Inn," U.S. News and World Report, 22-23, June 2, 2003.

49. ACLU, "Enduring Abuse: Torture and Cruel Treatment by the United States at Home and Abroad," Apr. 2006, Annex B70-71 (Sworn Statement of Counterintelligence Agent of June 4, 2004).

50. Major General George R. Fay, "AR 15-6 Investigation of the Abu Ghraib Detention Facility and the 205th Military Intelligence Brigade," 53-54, 2004.

51. Dana Priest, "CIA Avoids Scrutiny of Detainee Treatment," *Washington Post*, Dec. 30, 2005.

52. *Id.*

53. Associated Press, "Prisoner Deaths in U.S. Custody," Mar. 16, 2005; *see also* Human Rights First, "Command Responsibility: Detainee Deaths in U.S. Custody in Iraq and Afghanistan," § 1 (Feb. 2006), http://www.humanrightsfirst.info/pdf/06221-etn-hrf-dic-rep-web.pdf.

54. U.S. Army, Criminal Investigation Division, "Army Criminal Investigators Outline 27 Confirmed or Suspected Detainee Homicides for Operation Iraqi Freedom, Operation Enduring Freedom," Mar. 25, 2005, http://www.cid.army.mil/Documents/OIF-OEF%20Homicides.pdf.

55. ACLU, "Enduring Abuse: Torture and Cruel Treatment by the United States at Home and Abroad," Apr. 2006, 70 (Sworn Statement of Counterintelligence Agent of June 4, 2004).

56. *Id.*

57. Editorial, "The CIA's Prisoners," *Washington Post*, July 15, 2004, A20. On Thursday, June 17, 2004, a four-count indictment was handed up in North Carolina, against David Passaro, a former Army Ranger hired by the CIA to conduct interrogations, for the June 21, 2003, killing of Abd al-Wali.

58. Eric Schmitt and Douglas Jehl, "CIA Hid More Prisoners Than It has Disclosed, Generals Say," *New York Times*, Sept. 9, 2004.

59. *See* Council of Europe, Parliamentary Assembly, Committee on Legal Affairs and Human Rights, "Alleged Secret Detentions and Unlawful Inter-state Transfers Involving Council of Europe Member States," January 2006, Information Memorandum II (Mr. Dick Marty, Special Rapporteur).

60. Eric Schmitt and Douglas Jehl, "CIA Hid More Prisoners Than It has Disclosed, Generals Say," *New York Times*, Sept. 9, 2004.

61. Organization of American States, "Inter-American Convention on Forced Disappearance of Persons," 2003, Preamble, p. 3.

62. U.N. General Assembly, *Question of Enforced or Involuntary Disappearances* (New York: United Nations, 1994), A/RES/49/193.

63. Special Rapporteur on Torture, "Statement of the Special Rapporteur of the Commission on Human Rights on Torture," 59th Session of the General Assembly, Oct. 27, 2004, http://www.unhchr.ch/huricane.nsf/view01/E82937EB87109CCAC125709E002 (last visited on December 5, 2004).

64. Department of Defense, "Directive No. 2310.1, Department of Defense Program for Enemy Prisoners of War and Other Detainees," §§ 4.2.3, 4.2.4, Aug. 18, 1994, http://www.dtic.mil/whs/directives/corres/text/d23101p.txt. The Secretary is also required to report to the Defense Secretary, the Chairman of the Joint Chiefs of Staff, other U.S. Government Agencies, and the ICRC on compliance with the Geneva Conventions. *Id.* at § 4.2.5.

65. Department of Defense, "Directive No. 2310.1, Department of Defense Program for Enemy Prisoners of War and Other Detainees," §§ 4.2.3, 4.2.4, Aug. 18, 1994, http://www.dtic.mil/whs/directives/corres/text/d23101p.txt.

66. Department of Defense, Directive No. 2310.1, at § 4.2.4.

67. Army Reg. 190-8, Enemy Prisoners of War, Retained Personnel, Civilian Internees and Other Detainees, § 1-7(b) (1997).

68. *See* Maj. Gen. Antonio Taguba, "AR 15-6, Investigation of the 800th Military Police Brigade," Feb. 2004, http://www.humanrightsfirst.org/us_law/800th_MP_Brigade_MASTER14_Mar_04-dc.pdf.

69. "Final Report of The Independent Panel To Review DOD Detention Operations," 29, Aug. 2004.

70. Ronald W. Reagan National Defense Authorization Act, Pub. L. No. 108-375, § 1092, 118 Stat. 2069-70 (2004).

71. *Id.* at § 1093(c), 118 Stat. 2070-71.

72. Human Rights First, "Behind the Wire," Mar. 2005, 7.

CHAPTER EIGHT

1. *See* Rep. Henry A. Waxman, Committee on Government Reform—Special Investigations Division, "Secrecy in the Bush administration" (Sept. 14, 2004) (comprehensive analysis of the Bush administration's actions with regard to the nation's open government laws).

2. *See,* e.g., Reporters Committee for Freedom of the Press, "Homefront Confidential: How the War on Terrorism Affects Access to Information and the Public's Right to Know" (4th ed., Sept. 2003); *U.S. News and World Report*, "Keeping Secrets: The Bush administration Is Doing the Public's Business out of the Public's Eye," Dec. 22, 2003; Center for American Progress and OMB Watch, "Special Interest Takeover: The Bush administration and the Dismantling of Public Safeguards," 87-99 May 2004. *See also* Stephen Pizzo, "Hiding the Truth? President Bush's Need-to-Know Democracy," Oct. 29, 2003, http://www.misleader.org/pdf/specialreport2_secrecy.pdf.

3. 5 U.S.C. §552.

4. *See John Doe Agency v. John Doe Corp.*, 493 U.S. 146, 151 (1989).

5. *See* Committee on Government Reform, U.S. House of Representatives, "A Citizen's Guide on Using the Freedom of Information Act and the Privacy Act of 1974 to Request Government Records" (2003) (H. Rept. 108-172).

6. *Department of Air Force v. Rose*, 425 U.S. 352, 361 (1976).

7. 5 U.S.C. § 552(a)(3)(A) (stating requirement of agency disclosure).

8. *Id.*

9. The nine exemptions are the following: (1) classified materials; (2) matters related solely to the internal personnel rules and practices of an agency; (3) matters specifically exempted in other statutes; (4) trade secrets and confidential business information; (5) internal agency documents that would be exempt from discovery in litigation (e.g., attorney-client privileged documents); (6) personnel and medical files; (7) certain information compiled for law enforcement purposes; (8) records regarding supervision of financial institutions; and (9) geological and geophysical information concerning wells.

10. *See, e.g.,* "Government Openness at Issue as Bush Holds onto Records," *New York Times,* Jan. 3, 2003; "Under Bush, Expanding Secrecy," *Washington Post,* Dec. 23, 2003; "Supreme Court to Hear Cheney Secrecy Case," *Los Angeles Times,* Dec. 16, 2003.

11. *See* Rep. Henry A. Waxman, Committee on Government Reform—Special Investigations Division, "Secrecy in the Bush administration," 3 (Sept. 14, 2004).

12. *See* Rep. Henry A. Waxman, Committee on Government Reform—Special Investigations Division, "Secrecy in the Bush administration," 4 (Sept. 14, 2004) (quoting Professor Philip Melanson, University of Massachusetts, and Professor Jane Kirtley, University of Minnesota).

13. Janet Reno, Attorney General, "Memorandum for Heads of Departments and Agencies, Subject: The Freedom of Information Act," Oct. 4, 1993.

14. John Ashcroft, Attorney General, "Memorandum for Heads of Departments and Agencies, Subject: The Freedom of Information Act," Oct. 12, 2001.

15. Andrew H. Card Jr., Assistant to the President and Chief of Staff, "Memorandum for the Heads of Executive Departments and Agencies; Subject: Action to Safeguard Information Regarding Weapons of Mass Destruction and Other Sensitive Documents Related to Homeland Security," Mar. 19, 2002.

16. *Id.*

17. *Id.*

18. *See* Rep. Henry A. Waxman, Committee on Government Reform—Special Investigations Division, "Secrecy in the Bush administration," 7 (Sept. 14, 2004).

19. Andrew H. Card Jr., Assistant to the President and Chief of Staff, "Memorandum for the Heads of Executive Departments and Agencies; Subject: Action to Safeguard Information Regarding Weapons of Mass Destruction and Other Sensitive Documents Related to Homeland Security," Mar. 19, 2002.

20. *See* Letter from Sandy Ford, FOIA/Privacy Act Officer, Defense Threat Reduction Agency, to Steven Aftergood, Federation of American Scientists (Dec. 12, 2003) (on file with Representative Henry Waxman).

21. *See* Letter from Steven Aftergood, Federation of American Scientists to Maj. Gen. Trudy H. Clark, Deputy Director, Defense Threat Reduction Agency (Dec. 12, 2003) (on file with Representative Henry Waxman).

22. "Censored Study on Bioterror Doubts U.S. Preparedness," *New York Times,* Mar. 29, 2004.

23. *See* Rep. Henry A. Waxman, Committee on Government Reform—Special Investigations Division, "Secrecy in the Bush administration," 24 (Sept. 14, 2004).

24. *Id.*

25. *Id.* at 25.

26. 42 U.S.C. § 5195c(e).

27. *See* Mark Tapscott, Director, Heritage Foundation's Center for Media and Public Policy, "Too Many Secrets," *Washington Post,* Nov. 20, 2002.

28. 5 U.S.C. § 552(a)(4)(A)(ii).

29. *Id.*

30. 5 U.S.C. § 552(a)(4)(A)(iii).

31. *See*, e.g., "Federal Charge of $25,280 to Fulfill Records Request Angers Activist," *Los Angeles Times,* Jan. 8, 2004; "DOE Charges Watchdog for Lab Data," *Albuquerque Journal,* Dec. 20, 2002.

32. *See* Rep. Henry A. Waxman, Committee on Government Reform—Special Investigations Division, "Secrecy in the Bush administration" 17-18 (Sept. 14, 2004).

33. *Electronic Privacy Information Center v. Dept. of Defense,* 241 F. Supp. 2d 5, 9, 12 (D.D.C. 2003).

34. *See* Rep. Henry A. Waxman, Committee on Government Reform—Special Investigations Division, "Secrecy in the Bush administration," 19 (Sept. 14, 2004).

35. *Id.*

36. Executive Order No. 13292, 68 Fed. Reg. 15315 (Mar. 25, 2003).

37. Executive Order No. 12958, 60 Fed. Reg. 19825 (Apr. 17, 1995).

38. Executive Order No. 12958 at § 1.2(b).

39. *Id.*

40. *Public Citizen,* "Analysis of Executive Order 13292: Changes in Classification Policy Imposed by the Bush administration Executive Order," Public Citizen, (2003).

41. Executive Order No. 12958, 60 Fed. Reg. 19825 (Apr. 17, 1995) at § 1.3(c).

42. Executive Order No. 13292, 68 Fed. Reg. 15315 (Mar. 25, 2003) at § 1.5(b).

43. Executive Order No. 13292, 68 Fed. Reg. 15315 (Mar. 25, 2003) at § 3.3(a).

44. Executive Order No. 13292, 68 Fed. Reg. 15315 (Mar. 25, 2003) at § 5.3.

45. 66 Fed. Reg. 64347 (Dec. 10, 2001); 67 Fed. Reg. 31109 (May 6, 2002); 67 Fed. Reg. 61465 (Sept. 26, 2002).

46. Executive Order No. 12958 at § 1.8(c).

47. Executive Order No. 13292 at § 1.7(c).

48. 49 U.S.C. § 40119(b)(1).

49. Transportation Security Administration, "Protection of Sensitive Security Information," 69 Fed. Reg. 28066 (May 18, 2004) (interim final rule).

50. *Id.*

51. National Archives and Records Administration, Information Security Oversight Office, "Report to the President 2003," 5 (Mar. 31, 2004).

52. National Archives and Records Administration, Information Security Oversight Office, "Report to the President 2002," 27 (June 30, 2003).

53. *See* Rep. Henry A. Waxman, Committee on Government Reform—Special Investigations Division, "Secrecy in the Bush administration," 43 (Sept. 14, 2004).

54. Eileen Sullivan, "Too Much Secrecy: Overclassification Hampers Cooperation," The Freedom of Information Center, Federal Times Online, Sept. 13, 2004.

55. "Half of All Secrets Improperly Classified, Official Says," *Secrecy News,* Aug. 25, 2004; "Too Much Secrecy," *Washington Post,* Aug. 28, 2004.

56. Department of Defense, News Transcript: Defense Department Operational Update Briefing (May 4, 2004) (http://www.fas.org/sgp/news/2004/05/dod050404.html).

57. Rep. Henry A. Waxman, Committee on Government Reform—Special Investigations Division, "Secrecy in the Bush administration," 43 (Sept. 14, 2004) (quoting J. William Leonard, Director, Information Security and Oversight Office, The Importance of Basics (June 15, 2004) (remarks before the National Classification Management Society's Annual Training Seminar).

58. *United States Department of Justice v. Reporters Committee for Freedom of the Press*, 489 U.S. 749 (1989).

59. *Id.*, 489 U.S. at 772. Justices Blackmun and Brennan noted in their concurrence that such a categorical exemption would prevent disclosure of a rap sheet that discloses a congressional candidate's conviction of tax fraud five years before his or her campaign began.

60. *See* Electronic Freedom of Information Act Amendments of 1996.

61. *United States Department of State v. Ray*, 502 U.S. 164 (1991).

62. *Id.*, 502 U.S. at 167-68.

63. *Id.*, 502 U.S. at 176-78.

64. *National Archives and Records Administration v. Favish*, 124 S. Ct. 1570 (2004).

65. *Favish*, 124 S. Ct. at 1575.

66. *Favish*, 124 S. Ct. at 1580.

67. *See* OpenTheGovernment.org, "Dead Weight in the Balance," *The News Media & The Law*, Spring 2004, vol. 28, no. 2.

68. *See* OpenTheGoverment.org, "Secrecy Report Card: Quantitative Indicators of Secrecy in the Federal Government (Aug. 26, 2004), http://www.openthegovernment.org.

69. *See* OpenTheGovernment.org, Press Release (Aug. 26, 2004), http://www.openthegovernment.org.

70. *Id.*

71. *See McGrain v. Daughtery*, 273 U.S. 135, 174 (1927).

72. *See* Congressional Research Service, "CRS Report for Congress: Congressional Oversight" (Jan. 21, 2001) (97-936 GOV).

73. 31 U.S.C. § 712.

74. *See* Rep. Henry A. Waxman, Committee on Government Reform—Special Investigations Division, "Secrecy in the Bush administration," at 70 (Sept. 14, 2004) (citing Letter from David S. Addington, Counsel to the Vice President, to Anthony Gamboa, General Counsel, General Accountability Office (June 7, 2001)).

75. *See* Letter from Reps. John D. Dingell and Henry A. Waxman to Comptroller General David M. Walker (Apr. 19, 2001), http://www.democrats.reform.house.gov/Documents/20040831095928-35054.pdf.

76. *See* Rep. Henry A. Waxman, Committee on Government Reform – Special Investigations Division, "Secrecy in the Bush administration," 70 (Sept. 14, 2004) (citing Letter from Vice President Richard B. Cheney to the House of Representatives (Aug. 2, 2001), http://www.democrats.reform.house.gov/Documents/20040830233716-42929.pdf.

77. *See* Congressional Research Service, *Walker v. Cheney: District Court Decision and Related Statutory and Constitutional Issues*, 5-6 (Mar. 8, 2004).

78. *See* Congressional Research Service, *Walker v. Cheney: District Court Decision and Related Statutory and Constitutional Issues*, 6-7 (Mar. 8, 2004).

79. 5 U.S.C. § 2954.

80. *See Waxman v. Evans*, 2002 U.S. Dist. LEXIS 25975 (C.D. Cal. 2002), vacated as moot, 52 Fed. Appx. 84 (9th Cir. 2002), as amended by *Waxman v. Evans*, No. 02-55825 (9th Cir. Jan. 9, 2003) (order clarifying that the judgment of the district court was not reversed).

81. *See* Rep. Henry A. Waxman, Committee on Government Reform—Special Investigations Division, "Secrecy in the Bush administration," 75 (Sept. 14, 2004).

82. *See* Rep. Henry A. Waxman, Committee on Government Reform—Special Investigations Division, "Secrecy in the Bush administration," 75 (Sept. 14, 2004) (Letter from Rep. Henry A. Waxman, et al. to President George W. Bush (June 3, 2004)).

83. *See* Rep. Henry A. Waxman, Committee on Government Reform – Special Investigations Division, "Secrecy in the Bush administration," 77 (Sept. 14, 2004).

84. Title VI of the Intelligence Authorization Act for Fiscal Year 2003 (P.L. 107-306).

85. "9/11 Commission Says U.S. Agencies Slow Its Inquiry," *New York Times*, July 9, 2003.

86. *See*, e.g., "White House vs. 9/11 Panel: Resistance, Resolution," *Washington Post*, Mar. 9, 2004; "GOP Officials Press Rice to Testify on 9/11," *Baltimore Sun*, Mar. 29, 2004.

CHAPTER NINE

1. Rebecca Carr, "FOIA Overhaul Stalled," Cox News Service, Aug. 4, 2006. Leahy's remarks are on Congress's inability to overcome political maneuvering stalling the passage of overhaul legislation that gives the public access to federal government records.

2. The petitioners in the case included Reporters Committee for Freedom of the Press, *Washington Post*, *New York Times*, Gannett, Knight Ridder, ABC, CNN, and others.

3. Dan Christensen, "Still A Secret," *Miami Daily Business Review*, Feb. 24, 2004.

4. *Id.*

5. *Id.*

6. *Id.*

7. Reporters Committee for Freedom of the Press, "Discovering Secret Docket" (2003), http://www.rcfp.org/secretjustice/secretdockets/pg1.html.

8. *Id.*

10. *See* The Reporters Committee for Freedom of the Press, *Pleading the First*, vol. 28, no.2 (Spring 2004).

11. *Id.; ABC, Inc. v. Stewart,* 360 F.3d 90 (2d Cir. 2004).

12. *Ellsberg v. Mitchell,* 709 F.2d 51, 56 (D.C. Cir. 1983).

13. *In re Under Seal,* 945 F.3d 1285, 1287 n.2 (4th Cir. 1991).

14. *In re United States,* 872 F.2d 472, 476 (D.C. Cir. 1989).

15. *Fitzgerald v. Penthouse Internat'l, Ltd.,* 776 F.2d 1236, 1242 (4thCir. 1985).

16. *Ellsberg v. Mitchell,* 709 F.2d 51, 58 (D.C. Cir. 1983).

17. *Reynolds v. United States,* 345 U.S. 1, 11 (1953).

18. *Id.*

19. Courts have generally considered and ruled on the state secrets privilege in response to particular discovery requests, and not in support of a motion to dismiss an entire action prior to any discovery. *See, e.g., DTM Research L.L.C. v. A.T. & T. Corp.,* 245 F.3d 327, 330 (4th Cir. 2001); *Bowles v. United States,* 950 F.2d 154, 156 (4th Cir. 1991) (privilege invoked in response to plaintiffs' discovery requests); *In re Under Seal,* 945 F.2d at 1287 (privilege invoked after many depositions and other discovery had already occurred); *Fitzgerald,* 776 F.2d at 1238 (privilege invoked after discovery and on eve of trial); *Heine v. Raus,* 399 F.2d 785, 787 (4th Cir. 1968) (privilege invoked during discovery).

20. *In re Grand Jury Subpoena Dated August 9, 2000,* 218 F. Supp. 2d 544, 560 (S.D.N.Y. 2002).

21. *Ellsberg,* 709 F.2d at 57

22. *In re Under Seal,* 945 F.2d at 1289-90 (summary judgment granted only after plaintiff could not show genuine issue of material fact with nonprivileged evidence); *Ellsberg,* 709 F. 2d at 64 n.55 (remanding where district court had dismissed case on basis of privilege but "did not even consider whether the plaintiffs were capable of making out a prima facie case without the privileged information."); *Molerio v. Federal Bureau of Investigation,* 749 F.2d 822, 826 (D.C. Cir. 1984) (terminating

suit only after evaluating plaintiffs' nonprivileged evidence); *Clift v. United States*, 597 F.2d 826, 830 (2d Cir. 1979) (remanding for further proceedings where plaintiff has "not conceded that without the requested documents he would be unable to proceed, however difficult it might be to do so."); *Bareford v. General Dynamics Corp.*, 973 F.2d 1138, 1141 (5th Cir. 1992), *vacated in part on denial of reargument* (Oct. 14, 1992) (holding that plaintiff's case could go forward "without the privileged information and would be dismissed only if the remaining information were insufficient to make out a prima facie case").

23. 399 F.2d at 791.

24. *See Halpern*, 258 F.2d at 41; *see also Tenet*, 125 S. Ct. at 1237 (noting "the more frequent use of *in camera* judicial proceedings").

25. Mark Follman, "The Bush Code Of Secrecy: How The White House Is Covering Up CIA Abductions, Brutal Interrogations And Spying On Americans," Salon.com News, June 23, 2006.

26. *Id.*

27. *Id.*

28. Sec'y of State Condoleeza Rice, Remarks Upon Her Departure for Europe at the Andrews Air Force Base (Dec. 5, 2005), *available at* http://usinfo.state.gov/eur/Archive/2005/Dec/05-471726.html (Rice also said, "Renditions take terrorists out of action, and save lives. . . . Such renditions are permissible under international law").

29. Opinion, *El-Masri v. George Tenet*, No. 1:05cv1417 (D.D.C. May 12, 2006), *available at* http://jurist.law.pitt.edu/elmasriorder.pdf.

30. Mark Follman, "The Bush Code Of Secrecy: How The White House Is Covering Up CIA Abductions, Brutal Interrogations And Spying On Americans," Salon.com News, June 23, 2006.

31. Judge Declines to Dismiss Privacy Suit Against AT&T, *The New York Times*, July 21, 2006.

32. Mark Follman, "The Bush Code Of Secrecy: How The White House Is Covering Up CIA Abductions, Brutal Interrogations And Spying On Americans," Salon.com News, June 23, 2006.

33. *Id.*

34. *See Gannett Co. v. DePasquale*, 443 U.S. 368 (1979).

35. S. 817.

CHAPTER TEN

1. Recently, the FISA court considered some modest rule changes and for the first time made its rules public and subject to comment. Among other things, the proposed new rules would require the government to submit documents explaining new surveillance equipment and techniques and would require government lawyers to correct misstatements and misrepresentations it makes on a continuous basis. New rules would also permit nongovernment lawyers to appear before the court, but only if they had special security clearance.

2. Lisa Myers, et al., "Is the Pentagon Spying on Americans?" MSNBC.com, Dec. 14, 2005.

3. Walter Pincus, "Pentagon's Intelligence Authority Widens," *Washington Post*, Dec. 19, 2005.

4. See, e.g., Walter Pincus, "Unverified Reports of Terror Threats Linger," *Washington Post*, Jan. 31, 2006; Michael Isikoff, "The Other Big Brother," Newsweek, Jan. 30, 2006; "Bad Targeting," *Washington Post*, Jan. 30, 2006 (editorial); Frances Grandy Taylor, "The Pacifist Threat: Disclosure of Recent Government Surveillance of Quaker Activities Doesn't Surprise Members, " Hartford Courant, Jan. 16, 2006.

5. Walter Pincus, "Pentago Will Review Database on U.S. Citizens," Wash.Post, Dec. 15, 2005.

6. *See* ACLU Complaint, *American Friends Service Committee, et al. v. United States Department of Defense*, E.D. Pa., June 14, 2006.

7. *See* ACLU Complaint, *American Friends Service Committee, et al. v. United States Department of Defense*, E.D. Pa., June 14, 2006, 6 (based on information gleaned from Freedom of Information Act requests).

8. *See* ACLU Complaint, *American Friends Service Committee, et al. v. United States Department of Defense*, E.D. Pa., June 14, 2006, 10 (based on information gleaned from Freedom of Information Act requests).

9. *See* Will Dunham, "Pentagon Admits to More Spying on Peace Activists," Reuters, April 5, 2006; ACLU Press Release, "ACLU Sues Pentagon for Documents on Peace Groups," June 14, 2006, on file with the author.

10. *See* S. Rep. 95-604, at 11 (1977).

11. *See* 2 Senate Select Comm. to Study Governmental Operations with Respect to Intelligence Activities and the Rights of Americans, *Final Report*, S. Rep. 94-755 (1976).

12. *See Halkin v. Helms*, 690 F.2d 977 (D.C. Cir. 1982).

13. *See* 2 Senate Select Committee Report at 2.

14. *See* Adam Liptak, "Changing the Standard," *New York Times*, May 31, 2002.

15. *See* David Johnston and Don Van Natta, "Ashcroft Seeking to Free FBI to Spy on Groups," *New York Times*, Nov. 30, 2001.

16. *See* David Johnston and Don Van Natta, "Ashcroft Seeking to Free FBI to Spy on Groups," *New York Times*, Nov. 30, 2001.

17. *See* Neil A. Lewis and David Johnston, "Mueller Plans to Turn Focus Toward Terror," *New York Times*, May 29, 2002.

18. *See* Adam Liptak, "Changing the Standard," *New York Times*, May 31, 2002; David Johnston and Don Van Natta, "Ashcroft Seeking to Free FBI to Spy on Groups," *New York Times*, Nov. 30, 2001.

19. *See*, e.g., Adam Liptak, "Changing the Standard," *New York Times*, May 31, 2002.

20. *See*, e.g., Elizabeth Barclay, "Protestors Face Intimidation by Police," *Seattle Post Intelligencer*, Nov. 28, 2003.

21. Eric Lichtblau, "FBI Scrutinizes Antiwar Rallies," *New York Times*, Nov. 23, 2003.

22. *Id.*

23. *Id.*

24. *Id.*

25. *Id.*

26. *See* Michelle Goldberg, "Outlawing Dissent," *Salon.com*, Feb. 11, 2004, http://www.salon.com/news/feature/2004/02/11/cointelpro/index_np.html.

27. *See* Michelle Goldberg, "A Thousand J. Edgar Hoovers," *Salon.com*, Feb. 12, 2004, http://www.salon.com/news/feature/2004/02/12/cointelpro/index_np.html.

28. *See* Alexander Panetta and Jim Bronskill, "Legal Concerns Delay Canadian Version of U.S.-style Terror List for Air Passengers," *The Canadian Press*, Oct. 31, 2004.

29. *Id.*

30. *See* Michelle Goldberg, "Outlawing Dissent," Salon.com, Feb. 11, 2004, http://www.salon.com/news/feature/2004/02/11/cointelpro/index_np.html.

31. *Id.*

32. *See* Tim Weiner, "The CIA's Domestic Reach," *New York Times*, Jan. 20, 2002.

33. *Id.*

34. 50 U.S.C. § 1804.

35. *See* Nola K. Breglio, "Leaving FISA Behind: The Need to Return to Warrantless Foreign Intelligence Surveillance," 113 *Yale L. J.* 179, 187 (Oct. 2003).

36. *Id.* at 188.

37. *See Dalia v. United States*, 441 U.S. 238, 255 (1979) (delineating Fourth Amendment warrant requirements).

38. The statute was amended more than once to provide the government with access to new tools in the FISA context. For example, in 1995, FISA was amended to permit orders for physical searches in addition to electronic surveillance, and in 1998, it was amended to allow the government to use "pen registers" and "tap and trace" devices. *See* 50 U.S.C. §§ 1821-29; 1841-46.

39. Jeremy D. Mayer, "9/11 and the Secret FISA Court: From Watchdog to Lapdog?" 34 *Case W. Res. J. Int'l L.* 249, 250 (Fall 2002).

40. *See* 50 U.S.C. §§ 1821-29.

41. *See* 50 U.S.C. §§ 1841-46.

42. *See* 50 U.S.C. §§ 1861-62.

43. Pub. L. 107-56, 115 Stat. 272 (2001).

44. *See* Rep. Henry A. Waxman, Committee on Government Reform – Special Investigations Division, "Secrecy in the Bush administration," 57 (Sept. 14, 2004), http://democrats.reform.house.gov/features/secrecy_report/pdf/pdf_secrecy_report.pdf.

45. *See* Congressional Research Service, "The USA PATRIOT Act: A Legal Analysis" (Apr. 15, 2002) (RL31377), http://fas.org/irp/crs/RL31377.pdf.

46. 50 U.S.C. § 1861(d).

47. *See* David Cole, "The Missing Patriot Debate," *The Nation*, May 30, 2005.

48. Congressional Research Service, "Libraries and the PATRIOT Act," 1 (Feb. 26, 2003) (RS21441).

49. American Library Association, "Resolution on the USA PATRIOT Act and Related Measures That Infringe on the Rights of Library Users" (Jan. 29, 2003), http://www.ala.org.

50. Congressional Research Service, "Libraries and the PATRIOT Act," 1 (Feb. 26, 2003) (RS21441) (quoting Letter from Assistant Attorney General Daniel J. Bryant to House Judiciary Committee Chairman F. James Sensenbrenner, Jr. (Aug. 26, 2002)) (emphasis added).

51. *See* Eric Lichtblau, *Libraries Say Yes, Officials Do Quiz Them About Users, New York Times* (June 20, 2005).

52. *Id.*

53. *Id.*

54. *Id.*

55. *Id.*

56. *Id.*

57. Richard B. Schmitt, "Was the Focus of the Patriot Act Debate a Dodge?" *The Nation*, Dec. 11, 2005.

58. *Id.*

59. *Id.*

60. *See* William E. Moschella, Assistant Attorney General, "Letter to the Honorable F. James Sensenbrenner, Jr., Chairman, Committee on the Judiciary," U.S. Department of Justice, Office of Legislative Affairs (Nov. 23, 2005), on file with the author.

61. Barton Gellman, "The FBI's Secret Scrutiny: In Hunt for Terrorists, Bureau Examines Records of Ordinary Americans," *Washington Post*, Nov. 6, 2005, A1.

62. *See* William E. Moschella, Assistant Attorney General, "Letter to the Honorable F. James Sensenbrenner, Jr., Chairman, Committee on the Judiciary," U.S. Department of Justice, Office of Legislative Affairs (Nov. 23, 2005), 2, on file with the author.

63. *See* William E. Moschella, Assistant Attorney General, "Letter to the Honorable F. James Sensenbrenner, Jr., Chairman, Committee on the Judiciary," U.S. Department of Justice, Office of Legislative Affairs (Nov. 23, 2005), 3, on file with the author,

64. *See* Congressional Research Service, "The USA PATRIOT Act: A Legal Analysis" (Apr. 15, 2002) (RL31377).

65. 18 U.S.C. § 2705(a)(2).

66. Duncan Campbell, "U.S. bars Nicaragua heroine as 'terrorist,'" *UK Guardian*, Mar. 4, 2005.

67. Editorial, "Patriot Act Redux, and in the Dark," *New York Times*, June 1, 2005.

68. *See*, e.g., Eric Lichtblau and Carl Hulse, "Lawmakers Agree to Renew Patriot Act," *New York Times*, (July 14, 2005); Editorial, "Patriot Second Act," *Washington Post*, (June 13, 2005); Editorial, "No Backtracking," *Baltimore Sun*, May 31, 2005.

69. USA Patriot Improvement and Reauthorization Act, Title II, 120 Stat. at 230-32.

70. Under the original PATRIOT Act, the FBI had only to assert that the records were "sought" for an authorized investigation.

71. 18 U.S.C. § 1752 currently provides criminal penalties for entrance into "any posted, cordoned off, or otherwise restricted area of a building or grounds where the President or other person protected by the Secret Service is or will be temporarily visiting. . . ."

72. James Risen and Eric Lichtblau, "Bush Lets US Spy on Callers Without Courts," *N.Y. Times*, Dec. 16, 2005, at 1, 22.

73. Jennifer Loven, "Bush Reveals Rationale Behind Surveillance in Candid Remarks to Fellow Republicans," *Associated Press*, Feb. 11, 2006.

74. Susan Page, "Lawmakers: NSA Database Incomplete," *USA Today*, June 30, 2006; *see also* Maura Reynolds, " Cheney Defends Domestic Spying," *L.A. Times*, Dec. 21, 2005.

75. Susan Page, "Lawmakers: NSA Database Incomplete," *USA Today*, June 30, 2006.

76. Maura Reynolds, "Cheney Defends Domestic Spying," *L. A. Times*, Dec. 21, 2005.

77. Attorney General Alberto Gonzales, "Press Briefing," Dec. 19, 2005, http://www.whitehouse.gov/news/releases/2005/12/print/20051219-1.html.

78. Laurence Tribe, "Letter to the Honorable John Conyers, Jr.," (Jan. 6, 2006), on file with the author.

79. Authorization for the Use of Military Force against Al Qaeda, Pub.L. No, 107-40, 115 Stat. 224 §2 (a) (2001).

80. Vikram Amar and Alan Brownstein, "Why the President's Defense of Executive Power to Wiretap Without Warrants Can't Succeed in the Strict Constructionist Court He Wants," *Findlaw*, Feb. 17, 2006.

81. Liz Halloran, "Everyone's Spinning the Spying," *U.S. News and World Report*, Feb. 13, 2006.

82. U.S. Const., art. II.

83. U.S. Const., art. I.

84. *Id.*

85. Barton Gellman & Arshad Mohammed, "Data on Phone Calls Monitored," *Wash. Post,* May 12, 2006, AO1.

86. *Id.*

87. *See* Complaint, *ACLU v. NSA*, No. 06-10204 (E.D. Mich., filed Jan. 17, 2006).

88. *See Smith v. Maryland*, 442 U.S. 735 (1979).

89. *See, e.g., Katz v. United States*, 389 U.S. 347, 353 (1967) (holding for the first time that the protections of the Fourth Amendment extend to the electronic surveillance of oral communications done without physical intrusion.).

90. According to Law Professor David Cole, in addition to the 1182 suspected terrorists that Attorney General John Ashcroft admitted the government had seized and detained, the government eventually

admitted to arresting another 3900 people, nearly all foreign nationals, as part of its antiterrorism initiatives here in the United States. *See* David Cole, Enemy Aliens: Double Standards and Constitutional Freedoms in the War on Terrorism, 24-25 (2003).

91. Press Briefing by Attorney General Alberto Gonzales and General Michael Hayden, Principal Deputy Director for National Intelligence, Dec. 19, 2005, http://www.whitehouse.gov/news/releases/2005/12/20051219-1.html.

92. 18 U.S.C. § 1809.

93. An initial attempt to begin an inquiry made by the New Jersey Attorney General was blocked by the Bush administration's invocation of the "state's secret privilege" – an evidentiary privilege used in litigation when a party claims that he cannot release a document that may cause a risk to national security if released to the public.

94. Editorial, "Secret NSA Program Needs More Oversight: Proposed Deal Stops Short of Genuine Compromise," *Miami Herald,* July 21, 2006.

95. Judge Declines to Dismiss Privacy Suit Against AT&T, *The New York Times,* July 21, 2006.

96. Senator Patrick Leahy, "Statement of Senator Patrick Leahy, Hearing on NSA III: Wartime Executive Powers and the FISA Court," Mar. 28, 2006, http://judiciary.senate.gov/member_statement.cfm?id=1825&wit_id=2629.

97. *ACLU v. NSA,* Case No. 06-CV-10204 (Aug. 17, 2006) (Hon. Anna Diggs Taylor).

98. *Id.*

99. Jonathan Turley, "'Big Brother' Bush and Connecting the Dots," *L.A. Times,* June 24, 2006.

100. *Hamdi v. Rumsfeld,* 542 U.S. 507 (2004).

CHAPTER ELEVEN

1. See, e.g., Raoul Berger, Impeachment: The Constitutional Problems, at 4 (Cambridge, Mass., 2d ed. 1974).

2. Id. at 5.

3. See ACLU v. NSA, 06-CV-10204 (ADT) (Aug. 17, 2006). See also Eric Lichtblau and Scott Shane, "The Basis for Spying in the US is Doubted," N.Y. Times, Jan. 7, 2006.

4. Home Bldg. & Loan Ass'n v. Blaisdell, 290 U.S. 398, 426 (1934); see also Ex parte Milligan, 71 U.S. 2, 121 (1866) ("No doctrine, involving more pernicious consequences, was ever invented by the wit of man than that any of [the Constitution's] provisions can be suspended during any of the great exigencies of government. Such a doctrine leads directly to anarchy or despotism.").

5. See Human Rights Watch Reports, "Getting Away with Torture: Command Responsibility for the U.S. Abuse of Detainees," April 2005, vol. 17, no. 1(G); "Still at Risk: Diplomatic Assurances no Safeguard against Torture," April 2005, vol. 17, no. 3(D); "The Road to Abu Ghraib," June 2004; "Empty Promises: Diplomatic Assurances No Safeguard Against Torture," April 2004, vol.16 no.4 (D); "Enduring Freedom:" Abuses by U.S. Forces in Afghanistan," March 2004, vol. 16, no. 3(C).

6. See Human Rights First, "Getting to Ground Truth 2," Sept. 2004, at 2-3, 16, 20, http://www.humanrightsfirst.org/us_law/PDF/detainees/Getting_to_Ground_Truth_090804.pdf.

7. L.E. Jacoby, Vice Admiral, U.S. Navy, "Memorandum to Under Sec'y of Defense for Intelligence," June 25, 2004, http://www.aclu.org/projects/foiasearch/pdf/DODDIA000154.pdf.

8. Using information provided by the U.S. military and documents obtained by the American Civil Liberties Union, The Associated Press compiled a partial list of 108 people who have died while in

U.S. custody in Iraq and Afghanistan. See: http://www.sfgate.com/cgi-bin/article.cgi?f=/n/a/2005/03/16/national/w113007S95.DTL.

9. Hina Shamsi, "Command's Responsibility: Detainee Deaths in U.S. Custody in Iraq and Afghanistan," Human Rights First Report, Feb. 2006, 1.

10. See U.S. Diplomatic Mission to the United Nations in Geneva, "U.S. Delegation Oral Responses to CAT Committee Questions, May 5, 2006, http://geneva.usmission.gov/Press2006/CAT-MAY5-SPOKEN.pdf.

11. See U.S. Diplomatic Mission to the United Nations in Geneva, "U.S. Delegation Oral Responses to CAT Committee Questions, May 5, 2006, at 6, http://geneva.usmission.gov/Press2006/CAT-MAY5-SPOKEN.pdf.

12. "Iraq General's Killer Reprimanded," BBC World Service, Jan. 24, 2006.

13. Jay S. Bybee, Office of Legal Counsel, Justice Department, "Memorandum for Alberto R. Gonzales, Counsel to the President" (Aug. 1, 2002), http://news.findlaw.com/wp/docs/doj/bybee80102mem.pdf.

14. Elizabeth de la Vega, "Scooter Libby's Doomed Defense," *The Nation*, Nov. 18, 2005, http://www.thenation.com/doc/20051205/delavega.

15. Editorial, "Vice President for Torture," *Washington Post*, Oct. 26, 2005, A18.

16. Judiciary on the USA PATRIOT Act" (May 25, 2005), http://judiciary.senate,gov/print_testimony.cfm.?id+1493&wit_id+4257.

17. Marbury v. Madison, 5 U.S. 137, 1 Cranch 137(1803).

18. James Madison, 9 *The Writings of James Madison* 103 (G. Hunt ed. 1910) (Letter to W. T. Barry, August 4, 1822).

19. For example, the independent commission could be bipartisan, congressionally funded, led by commissioners with pertinent backgrounds and unimpeachable credentials, and empowered with the authority to subpoena documents and compel testimony.

Index

BARBARA OLSHANSKY is the Leah Kaplan Distinguished Professor in Human Rights at Stanford University. Previously, she was deputy legal director for the Center for Constitutional Rights (CCR) and director counsel of the Guantánamo Global Justice Initiative there. She was one of the lead attorneys who brought the landmark U.S. Supreme Court case that resulted in a decision allowing the nearly 600 detainees held at the Guantánamo Bay Naval Base in Cuba to challenge their unlawful indefinite detentions. She's the coauthor most recently of *The Case for Impeachment: The Legal Argument for Removing George W. Bush from Office* (St. Martins, 2006), among other titles, and author of *Secret Trials and Executions: Military Tribunals and the Threat to Democracy* (Open Media Series/Seven Stories Press, 2002).

Before joining CCR, Olshansky was a senior attorney with the Environmental Defense Fund and prior to that practiced union-side labor and plaintiffs' employment discrimination law at the law firm of Vladeck, Waldman, Elias & Engelhard, P.C. Upon graduation from law school, Barbara clerked for the Honorable Rose Bird, Chief Justice of the California Supreme Court. Barbara received her J.D. from Stanford University and her two undergraduate degrees, *summa cum laude*, from the University of Rochester.